THIS IS PERFORMANCE ART

MEL BRIMFIELD

black dog publishing
london uk

THIS IS PERFORMANCE ART

CONTENTS

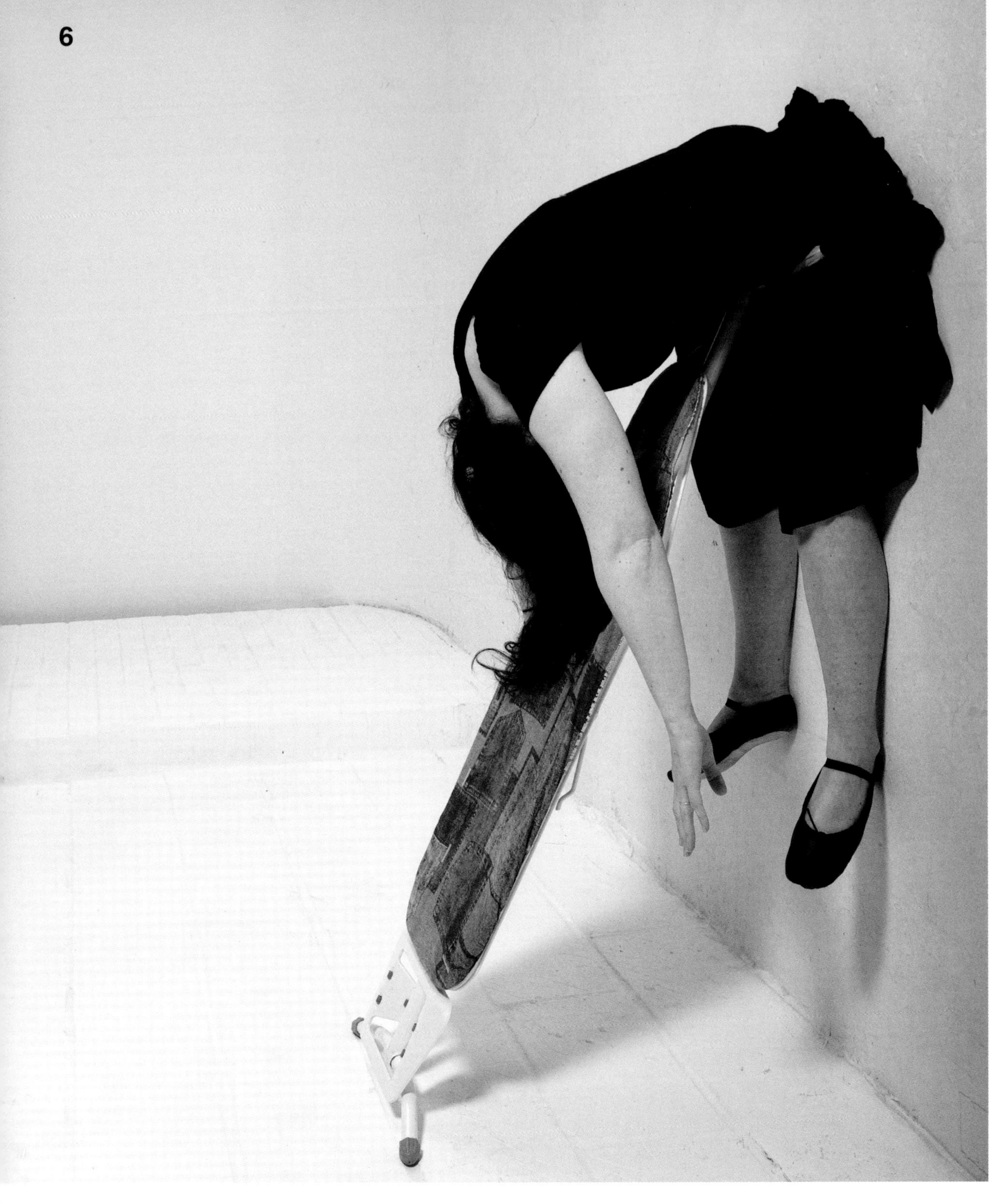

FOREWORD

Matt Fenton

> In his autobiography, *Miracles of Life*, the author JG Ballard recalls that the computer-generated poems he published in the literary magazine *Ambit* in the 1960s were considered by the publication's editor, Martin Bax, to be as good as the real thing. Ballard goes further: "they were the real thing".

I cannot recall when I first saw Mel Brimfield's *On Board*, the image on the front of this book, or in what context. Certainly well before seeing it in a formal exhibition setting, at Yorkshire Sculpture Park, in April 2011. Perhaps it was as a printed reproduction in a magazine, received as a digital image in an e-flyer, a thumbnail glimpsed on a website. More uncomfortably, but closer to the hall of mirrors we find at the heart of Brimfield's work, maybe it was in pre-publication publicity for this book, well before I was asked to contribute. At the time (when, exactly?) I did not question its authenticity or intent, though the dark humour was apparent. I also have no idea whether Charles Ray's *Plank Piece*, from which Brimfield's image closely derives, echoed unconsciously or not until I saw the photograph again of that 1973 work. I wonder then, from the outset, how many people will see the image on the cover, read the book's title, or fire something like it into a search engine and, missing the echo of *This Is Spinal Tap*, buy it unaware of Brimfield's mischievous intent. At what point might they realise they are on a slightly different trajectory through the history of performance art than the one they were expecting? And at what point might they start to get the joke and enjoy the ride? In any case, the paths that Brimfield's work will lead them on are likely to be richer and closer to the point than looking at the few perpetually reproduced documents of performance art history, photographs that have problematically come to stand in for, or even become, the work they purport to document. The journey is likely to be closer to the dangerous beauty and dark humour in much of the work, from Vito Acconci to Franko B, that can get bleached out in fixed historical accounts.

The image in question is a carefully-staged performative act from the life of fake female performance artist Alex Owens, no doubt to be briefly and tartly dismissed by the (also fake) art critic Sir Francis Spalding in his voluminous memoirs. A woman is pinned against a wall by a sharply-angled ironing board, her hair falling down across the board, obscuring her face. The performer's weight passes through the domestic object effectively mounting herself on the wall (I think of Bedwyr Williams firing himself at gallery walls to see if he would stick). It performs Brimfield's function well: it is both funny and slightly disturbing; it has a pun for a title; it implies a readable gender politics, and indeed for a knowing audience is a playful re-gendering of Ray's original; above all, and this is where it gets the purported period aesthetic just right and we get a hint of Brimfield's wider practice—it looks like you could try it at home. The photograph itself is implacable, but a very useful entry point to Brimfield's work, not entirely clear without the context of her

Mel Brimfield, produced in association with Edward Moore and Joanna Neary, *On Board*, 2010, Colour photograph, 27.6 x 41.3 in. / 105 x 70 cm. Image courtesy the artist and Ceri Hand Gallery.

wider practice that the piece is indeed ironic. "Are we allowed to laugh?" we might ask, as a lot of people might have asked, through much of the true history of performance art.

To play Brimfield's game a while longer, are we to assume that the photograph is a document of a fleeting moment in a wider performance work, or rather, as the white walls and floor suggest, a gallery-based durational performance that lasted many hours? Did the public (other artists, students and curators, let's say it like it is) explore this and other actions located around the gallery and, let us imagine, its surrounding corridors, offices, foyer and toilets? The image is somehow entirely tongue-in-cheek and completely serious; it is simultaneously a sly insertion into the opaque history of performance art, an affectionate homage and cheeky spoof on a field of action-based performance-making, and a carefully constructed document of an event that never was.

And yet was. As with much of her more performative work, the act was staged, performed and documented with the help of another artist, on this occasion the comedian Joanna Neary. The resulting archival object, that photograph, might give rise in future to a new action by Brimfield herself, her collaborator, or, more intriguingly, by a young artist on seeing the image but with no idea of Brimfield's intent. The most exciting possibility is the least knowing. To get closer to something like a truth, the creation of the document proposes itself as a making strategy in its own right, a viable response by a critically aware artist to a history of performance art accessible, for the most part, through poor photographs and unreliable anecdotes; a history that sits uncomfortably but persistently in the margins of the official accounts of the culture: of theatre, sculpture, orchestral music, opera and ballet. As Brimfield has more than hinted, her documentation-based work is indeed consciously intended as a performance methodology that folds back into live, cross-disciplinary events that are themselves documented by the means of the day, over which she has perhaps more limited control. (How much will future artists and scholars pore through Flickr images, watch grainy YouTube clips?). It is therefore a devising process in reverse, a collaborative art practice that starts with the documentation and works backwards to the event.

> I have tried for years to piece together the fragments of it, and to reconstruct the thing, but it's just not possible to work out what it was. An extraordinary statement you might think, from one who was actually there, in the audience. But there you have it. You would be hard pressed to find two people with the same accounts.
> Sir Francis Spalding, *Art-Breaker: Confessions of a Critic*
> (Episode 53, Part 7)

Importantly then, Brimfield's is a practice that produces new events, new and unexpected performative layers, new mythologies. Pseudo-histories blur with real ones, and slip across timescales and disciplinary boundaries. Real

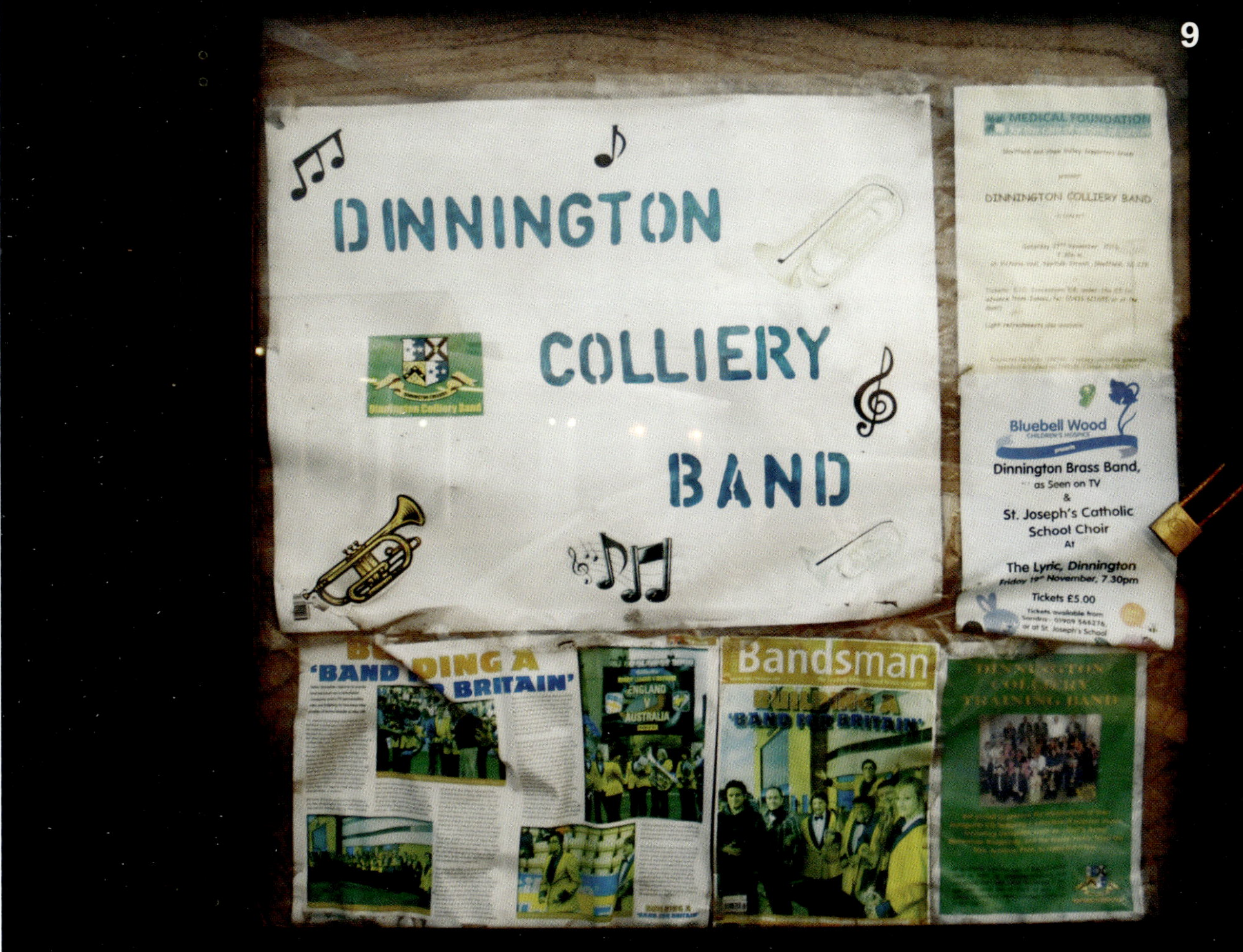

Dinnington Colliery Band notice board.

characters, artists and commentators, as well as a mash-up of high cultural, avant-garde and trash references, fill both her posters and Spalding's criticism, yet all are sprinkled with non-sequiturs, inconsistencies and chronological impossibilities. Fictional characters on the other hand take on more life than was originally intended, enter other artists' material, get taken up into other people's acts, become fact. Larger-scale, live events propose themselves and are staged: the sculptural work *Intergender Wrestling Championship Belt* from Brimfield's 2008 exhibition Waiter, waiter there's a sculpture in my soup becomes in 2011 a live wrestling event featuring performance artists, comedian Simon Munnery, the Dinnington Colliery Band and Helen Lederer. Again the event is a response to, and an opening up of performance art history: this time the deeply discomforting series of man-on-woman wrestling bouts instigated by Andy Kaufman. Looking at the documentation of Brimfield's event, you cannot help wonder whether those witnessing are friends of the artist, stooges invited to 'play' an audience. Performers and audience seem to be (re)enacting, in quite self-conscious ways, carefully co-curated versions of themselves. Is this not uncomfortably close to the reality of many live events, whatever their provenance or intent, from the TV studio audience to the live art happening, be the event spoof, gently knowing or earnestly 'for real'?

In his recent DIY residency in Lancaster and Morecambe, supported by the Live Art Development Agency, artist Manuel Vason led a series of photographic encounters with a group of performance makers. Vason, a name with which future researchers of live art might become very familiar, has spoken of the process of generating performances and installations through the act of conceiving, collaboratively, the photographic document of an event, and, echoing Ballard, of the photographs as performances in their own right, the real thing. The residency led to a photographic series created amongst the derelict spaces of Morecambe's Winter Gardens, itself a site with a rich history of performance from Laurel and Hardy to Ken Dodd. Its creaking stage holds the memory of Laurence Olivier playing Archie Rice in the 1960 film of Osborne's *The Entertainer*, filmed on location in Morecambe, and marking the moment when music hall corpsed into variety, before blurring into Saturday night game-show TV. The audience moved to the front-room, and the Winter Gardens closed in 1977. During the residency, Vason and the participating artists conceived a number of possible scenarios for performative images that were never made. The descriptions of these performances haunt those that made it onto film, and the texts describing them were exhibited in Lancaster alongside the Winter Garden images. Crazy, impossible images of artists being buried alive, becoming landscape.

In their performed series of letters read to camera, *Somewhere Near Variety*, artist Tim Etchells and writer Adrian Heathfield speak of childhoods in which "the TV was always on". They speak of a shared sense that in Eric Morecambe and Tommy Cooper they were experiencing the beginnings of a fascination with the points at which performances fray and unravel. Sketches that become more like durational performances, impossible tasks, ever-repeating glitches. Acts where the scenery wobbles, the stagehands come on before cue, the grins freeze; and failure, always failure to quite deliver the punch-line, the gag to pay off, the trick to reach its impressive climax. If a rabbit is to be pulled from a hat, by the time it happens it is probably dead. Brimfield too is richly immersed in a popular British cultural history; one that takes in *Opportunity Knocks*, *The Generation Game*, *It's a Knockout* and *Give Us A Clue*, and beyond to where it all gets messy and irony impossible, Legs and Co dancing to The Sex Pistols on *Top of the Pops*. That she sees this history as running parallel, or rather as part of the experimental avant-garde, is somehow very timely. Future histories might call her bluff on this, but for the most part the British prefer their conceptual performance art funny, working class and on TV, rather than serious, highfalutin and in an art gallery. The semi-naked men on plinths and boxing in the first series of *The Smell of Reeves and Mortimer* gently mocks Gilbert & George's experiments in live sculpture, but also admits, inclusively, that we all recognise the image and, like Brimfield, the absolute closeness of Gilbert & George to Morecambe & Wise. Brimfield's much closer homage to Gilbert & George

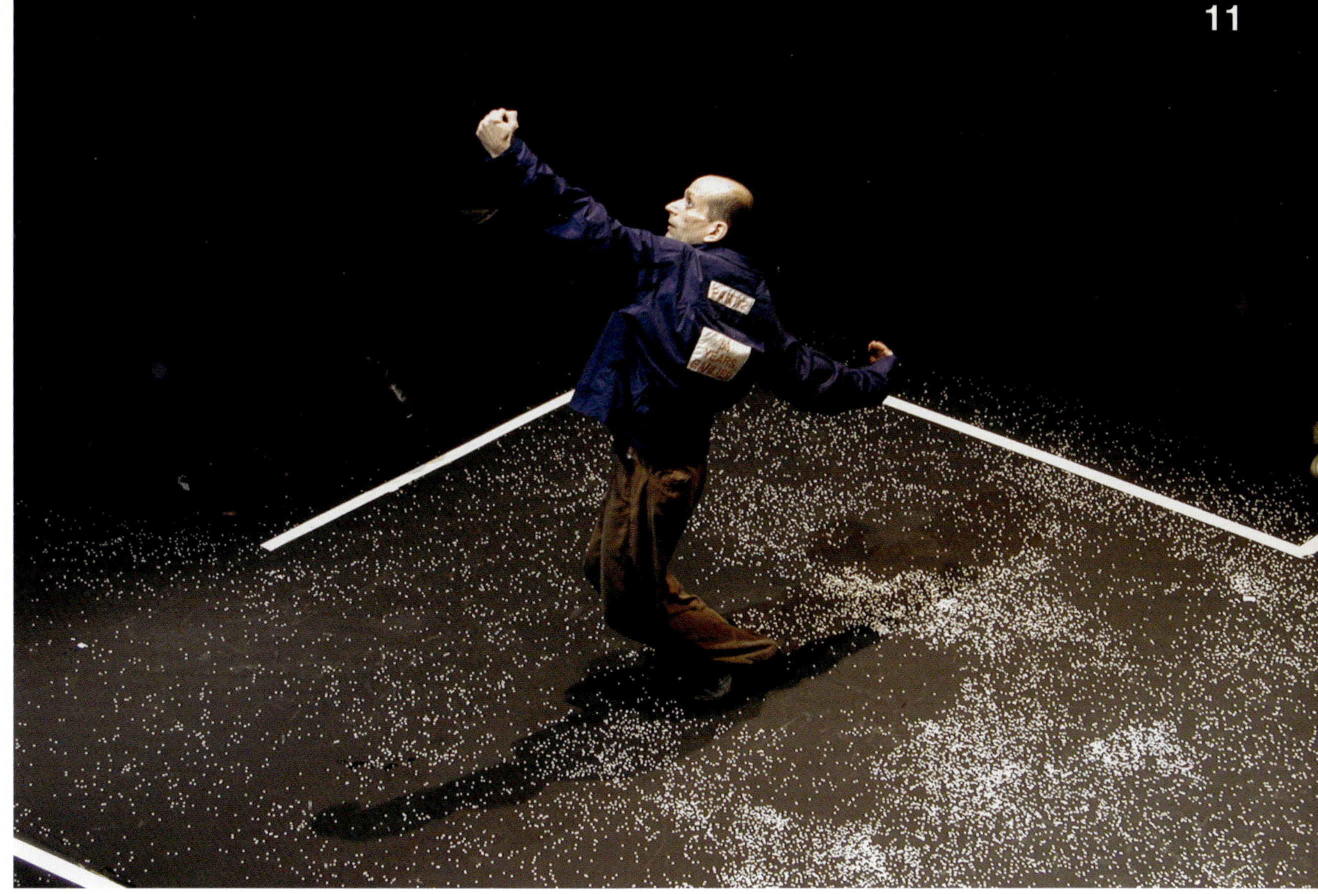

Matthew Ghoulish, *It's an Earthquake in My Heart*, 2001. Photo: Rebecca M Groves, Mousonturm, Frankfurt, Germany.

is made with dance artists Pete Shenton and Tom Roden of New Art Club, whose own breakthrough show, *This is Modern*—Spinal Tap again—was a spoof on contemporary dance that functioned simultaneously as affectionate send-up, demystifying strategy, and choreographic device.

Goat Island performance company member Matthew Goulish admits to the loss of a borrowed video-tape containing rare documentary footage of Pina Bausch's *Die Fensterputzer*. Goulish had spent several months trying to perfect from the video a short movement sequence by dancer Dominique Mercy, a performer of such singular virtuosity that Goulish could not hope to emulate him. Through repetition, Goulish speaks of imagining his body becoming both himself and Mercy, as if through this fusion his own movement might take on the other's embodied impulses. The sequence becomes an important motif in Goat Island's performance work *It's an Earthquake in My Heart*.

There is then a complex web of relationships set up by Brimfield's work: between herself and her many collaborators, with a personal sense of cultural history, and with the artists whose work she recreates. In a mirroring of Paul Auster and Sophie Calle's strange skirting of reality and fiction, blurring the edges of the author/character/artist, Brimfield has recently started to engage directly with artist Bruce McLean, whose work is shadowed in many of Brimfield's pieces. Going as far as inventing a fictitious work for McLean based on her admittedly partial understanding of his performance/sculptural practice, Brimfield has invited him to restage this work as if part of his canon. A closed loop of uncertainty. A response to archive and their shared interest in variety. The outcome will inevitably be a weird, multiple and slippery thing—part document of a collaboration, a fictional moment of back-catalogue, a mirroring of Bruce's own interests in performative restaging through pose band Nice Style, and a creative trashing of the notion of archive as something fixed and knowable.

In a final disturbance of history, the production values throughout Brimfield's work are consistently high. Her choice of virtuosic performers to recreate her actions is careful in the extreme, and the undeniable structural and compositional quality of the photographs almost gives the lie to their origins as documentation. At what point then does simulation enter the space of art? Or the more satisfying position of being both simulation and simulation becoming art? And when does an opening up of such possibility itself become closed again into documentation and, worse, canonisation? It is such canonisation, in the end, that Brimfield so beautifully critiques and lampoons, and then jemmies open as a site for play and possibility. As Brimfield herself remarks: "What do the faulty mechanics of archival, museological and curatorial approaches to assimilating live art omit, forget, exclude and lose?" For whom does canonisation serve? Not the work, nor the artists (at least not when they need the money), certainly not the public. Ultimately, it serves institutions: curators, publishers and academics. And it is Francis Spalding who is made most vividly manifest by Brimfield's practice, Brimfield herself always ducking out of sight behind a plinth or a staging flat. It is the male critic alone who is given hours of (almost) prime-time airtime to speak, who contextualises, who ascribes value. At what point, therefore, in writing about Brimfield does one find oneself becoming Spalding? In the end, in all Brimfield's work, I am painfully aware that as curators, critics and academics, the final joke is rightly, and very profoundly, on us.

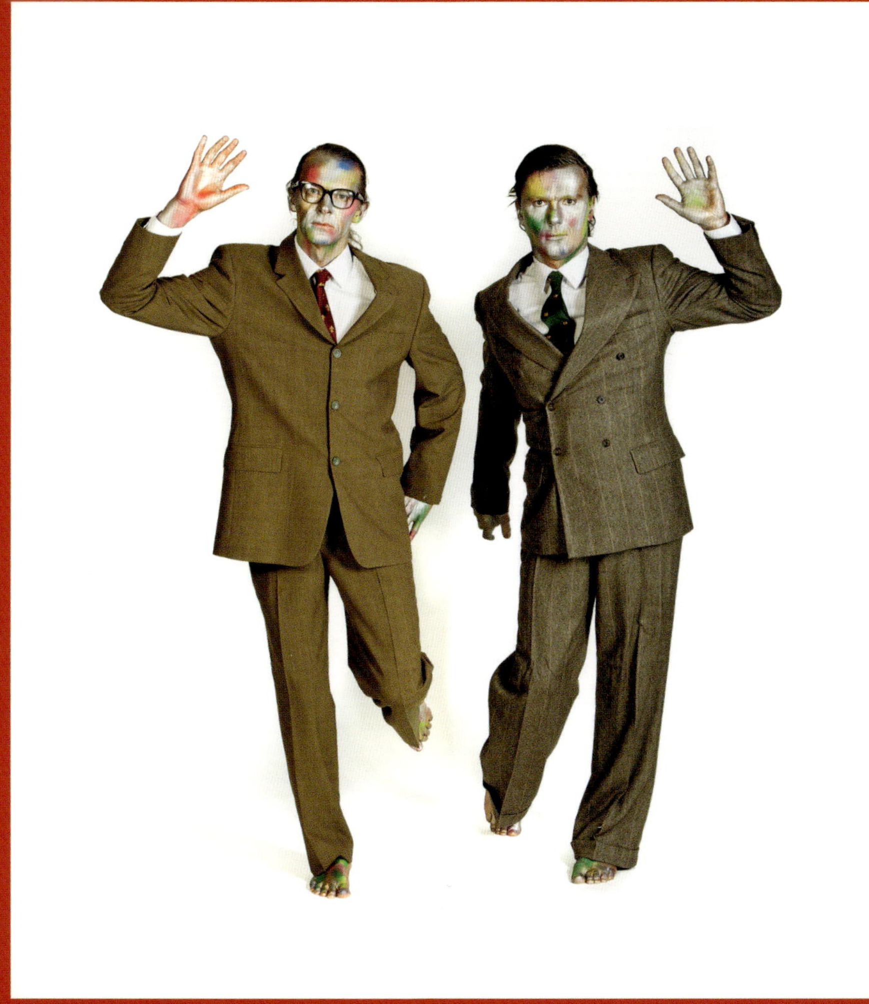

New Art Club (Tom Roden and Pete Shenton) as Gilbert & George and Morecambe & Wise, preparation for the *Breakfast Sculpture* performance at Yorkshire Sculpture Park, 2011.

GENITAL PANIC

Renowned polymath and art critic Sir Francis Spalding is widely celebrated for his unconventional approach to cultural analysis. Amongst dozens of seminal texts too numerous to mention, his ground-breaking bestseller *Here's Looking at Euclid—Geometry and the Films of Humphrey Bogart* is notable for being included in this year's Pulitzer long list. His role in the complicated litigation surrounding the publication of the libelous *Genital Panic* programme is well-documented—the following transcript appeared in much of the media coverage at the time:

My client was appointed the task of sub-editing the programme notes for the *Genital Panic* revue, with particular emphasis on the Foreword and introduction supplied by Peter Stringfellow and Kenneth Williams respectively. With characteristic diligence, he took the task seriously, deciding that the provision of footnotes would be useful in elucidating the many specific cultural references contained within the text for a broad international audience. He submitted a more or less final version of his annotated manuscript to the Windmill's publicity department before departing to deliver the keynote address for a three-day academic symposium at the Baldock Hinxworth Travelodge.

On reviewing the text in his suite, he placed a telephone call to his personal secretary outlining a number of corrections to be made to the proofs, including instructions that footnote number three should be deleted on the grounds that it was overly 'fussy'. My client stressed the importance of renumbering all of the footnotes accordingly.

The secretary's sworn testimony is as follows: "I reviewed the main body of the text first, reading it carefully for printing errors and overall sense. I attended to Sir Francis' minor amendments, and then returned to the separate sheet of footnotes. I looked at the first change, appearing at the end of Peter Stringfellow's Foreword. The sentence read 'It will come as no small surprise to many of you that the lovely Yoko is also celebrated as a popular gardening columnist for erstwhile women's magazine *The Lady*.' After the word 'Lady' came a small superscript '3', directing the reader to a simple explanatory footnote on the separate sheet, which read 'England's oldest women's weekly magazine, founded by Thomas Gibson Bowles, the maternal grandfather of the Mitford sisters. He also founded the English magazine *Vanity Fair*.' This was the footnote to be deleted—I couldn't see why at such a late stage, but went ahead with the alteration as directed. I crossed out the little '3' in the text, leaving a clear mark for the printer in the margin, and set about changing all the numbers which followed it: '4' became '3', '5' became '4' and so on. I left the footnotes themselves untouched at this stage.

I had just changed the final '12' to '11', when I was interrupted by a flurry of phone calls from the media asking for Sir Francis' comments on the breaking news of Valerie Solanas' guilty plea for the attempted assassination of Anne Widdecombe. The remainder of the afternoon was spent making complicated travel arrangements for sequential appearances on *Richard and Judy*, *Newsnight* and *The Day Today* programme. On her own initiative, in an effort to clear the backlog of administration, my assistant posted the proofs back to the Windmill publicity department, with the footnotes uncorrected, and not re-numbered."

This, then, is the catalogue of human error that led to the publication of the *Genital Panic* programme and its 'libelous' content. My client's attention to detail initiated a regrettable chain of events that are clearly mitigated by the extraordinary circumstances of the assassination attempt and the extended media circus that was to follow—certainly Sir Francis cannot be allowed to bear the weight of responsibility.

The court agreed, and dismissed the case. The Windmill Theatre were ordered to pay all legal costs, with Peggy Googleheim agreeing out-of-court settlements with Anne Widdecombe, Germaine Greer and Edwina Currie, the details of which were not disclosed.

OVERLEAF

Mel Brimfield, *Genital Panic*, 2009, Gouache and collaged ink on paper on mount board, 23.2 x 33.1 in. / 59 x 84 cm. Image courtesy the artist and Ceri Hand Gallery. Private collection.

Mel Brimfield, *Genital Panic Souvenir Programme*, 2009, Gouache, enamel, Indian ink and collage on prepared aluminium panel, 7.87 x 10 in. / 20 x 26 cm. Image courtesy the artist and Ceri Hand Gallery.

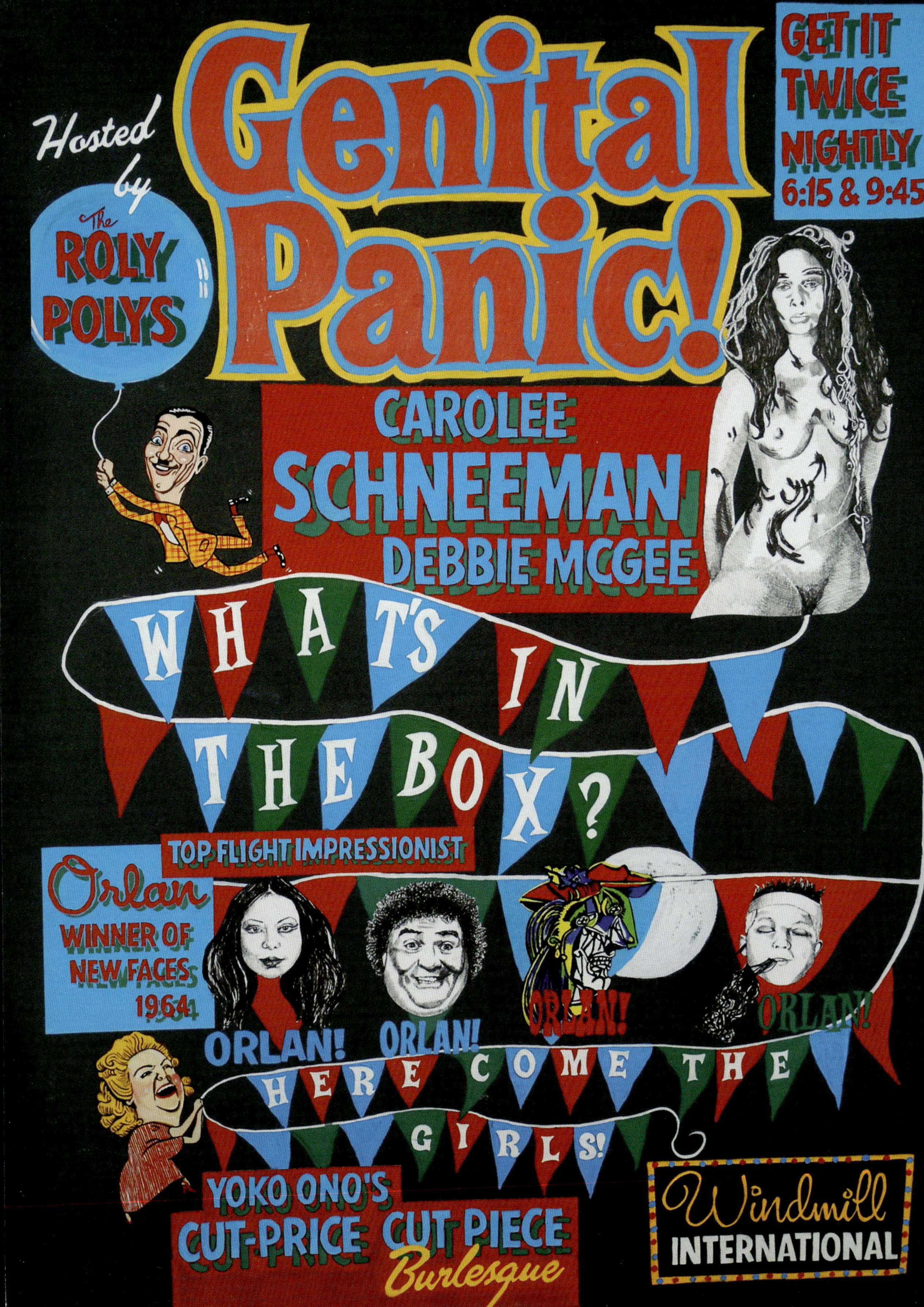

Hosted by
The ROLY POLYS
Genital Panic!
GET IT TWICE NIGHTLY 6:15 & 9:45
CAROLEE SCHNEEMAN
DEBBIE MCGEE
WHAT'S IN THE BOX?
TOP FLIGHT IMPRESSIONIST
Orlan
WINNER OF NEW FACES 1964
ORLAN!
ORLAN!
ORLAN!
ORLAN!
HERE COME THE GIRLS!
YOKO ONO'S CUT-PRICE CUT PIECE
Burlesque
Windmill INTERNATIONAL

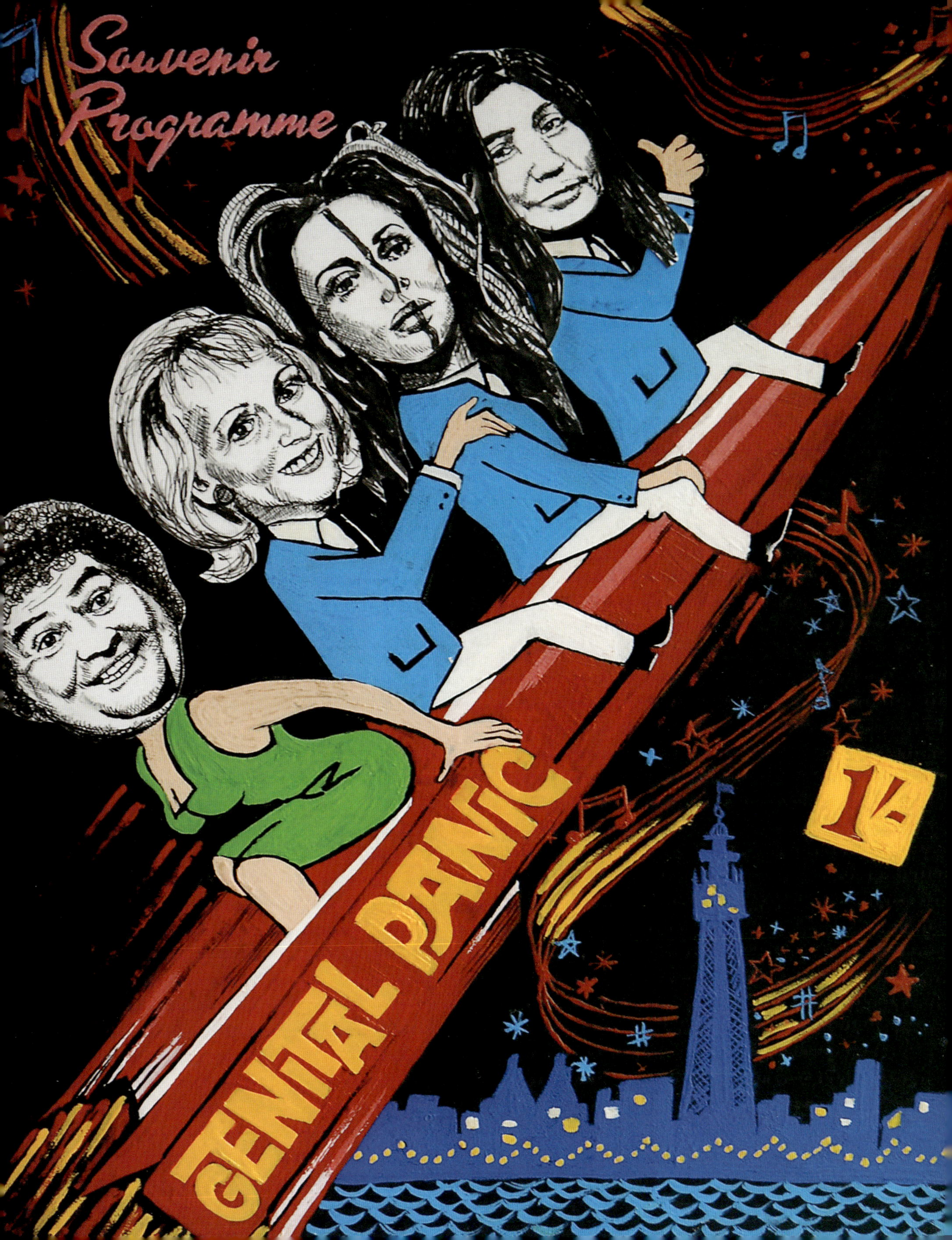
Souvenir
Programme
GENITAL PANIC
1/-

Which comes first?
The show – or fabulous
Lyons Maid ice cream?

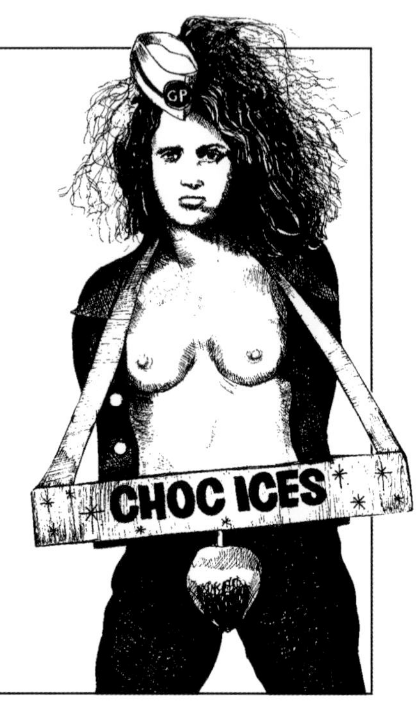

Relax and enjoy them both. They go so well together. In fact, there's nothing like refreshing Lyons Maid ice cream to add to the fun. Enjoy it often – in all its exciting varieties. Have fun with Lyons Maid.

Lyons Maid

ONE AND NINE = WELCH'S BiG 8

- ★ Toffee Assortment
- ★ Fruit Drops
- ★ Clear Mints
- ★ Spearmint Chews
- ★ Sherbet Lemons
- ★ Fruit Bon Bons
- ★ Assorted Chocolate Eclairs
- ★ Chocolate Limes

WELCH'S 1/9D
TOFFEE ASSORTMENT
MINIMUM WEIGHT 7½ OZ. INCLUDING IMMEDIATE WRAPPINGS
MADE BY WELCH & SONS LTD. TYNEMOUTH, ENGLAND

the choice at 1/9

Attractive Packets : Quality Flavours : Generous Value

enjoy the show and enjoy the delicious taste of Welch's sweets **WELCH'S** Makers of the biggest selection of packeted sweets in the country

WELCH & SONS LTD., TYNEMOUTH, NORTHUMBERLAND.

FOR THE 1965 SUMMER SEASON

PEGGY GOOGLEHEIM AND THE WINDMILL THEATRE in association with PETER STRINGFELLOW present

DEBBIE MCGEE AND CAROLEE SCHNEEMAN

Present

WHAT'S IN THE BOX?

As seen on TV

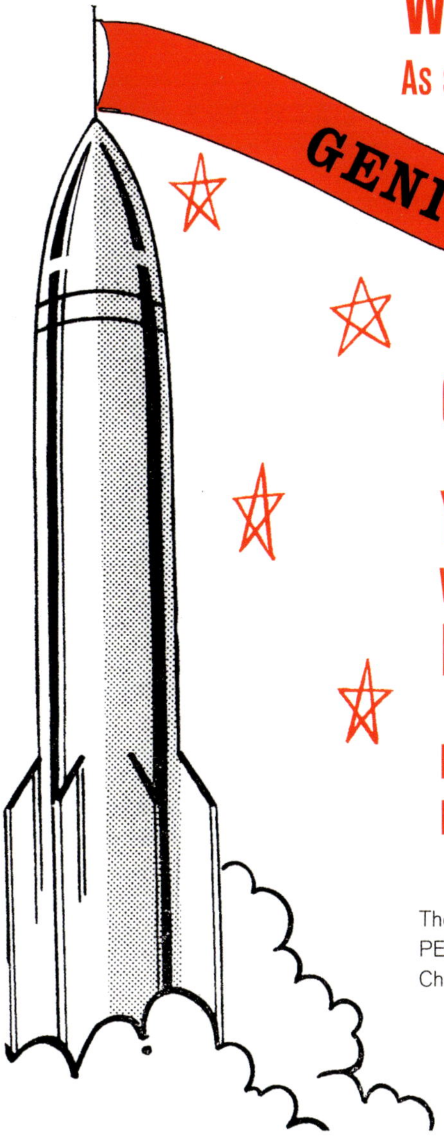

GENITAL PANIC

ORLAN

YOKO ONO

WITH SPECIAL GUEST STAR

BARBARA STREISAND

HOSTED BY THE ROLY POLYS

NICE STYLE – THE WORLD'S FIRST POSE BAND

The Show devised and produced by
PEGGY GOOGLEHEIM & VIVIAN VAN DAMM
Choreography by Two Left Feet

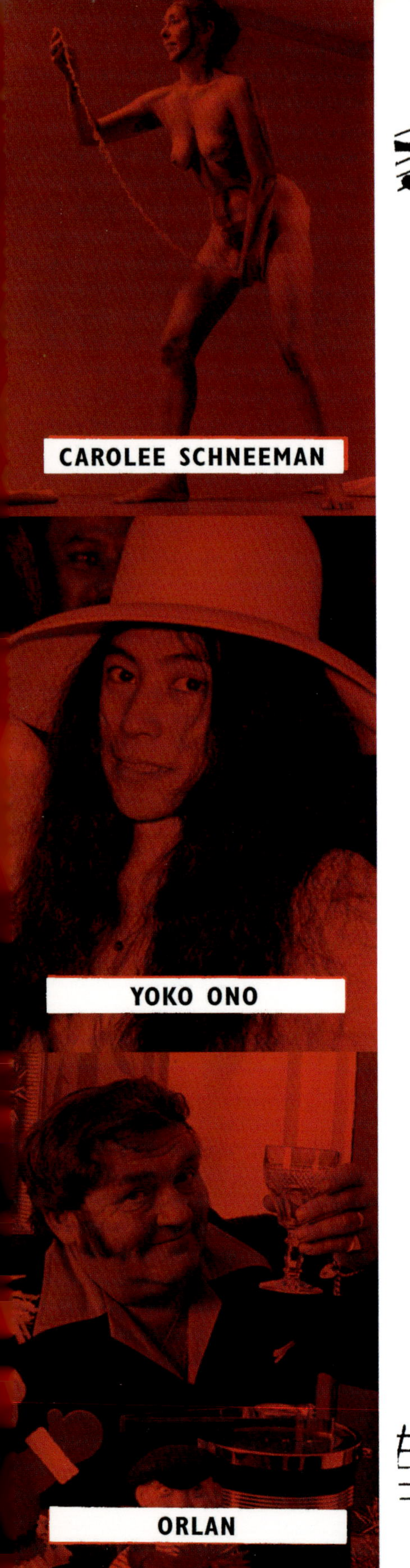

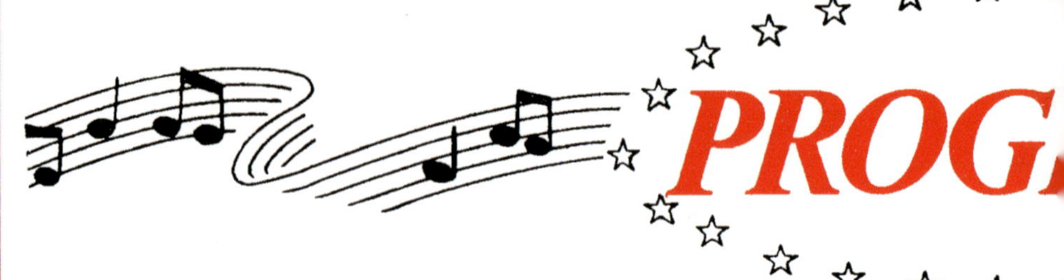

OVERTURE

Wally Stott and his Big Band

★ ★ ★

"ROLL OUT THE BARREL"

with The Roly Polys

With introductions to our special guest star

BARBARA STREISAND

and

"1965 Rear of the Year"

YOKO ONO

"Medley of disco hits including triple platinum chart-topper Enough is Enough"

★ ★ ★

Woman of a Thousand Faces

ORLAN

Winner of New Faces 1964

"SHAKE, RATTLE AND ROLL"

with The Roly Polys

★ ★ ★

NICE STYLE

The World's First Pose Band

Nude Tableaux Vivant – If They Move, It's Rude!

"MERMAIDS"

Devised, produced and directed by BRUCE MCLEAN

Presented as originally seen at the Tropicana Hotel, Las Vegas

★ ★ ★

INTERVAL

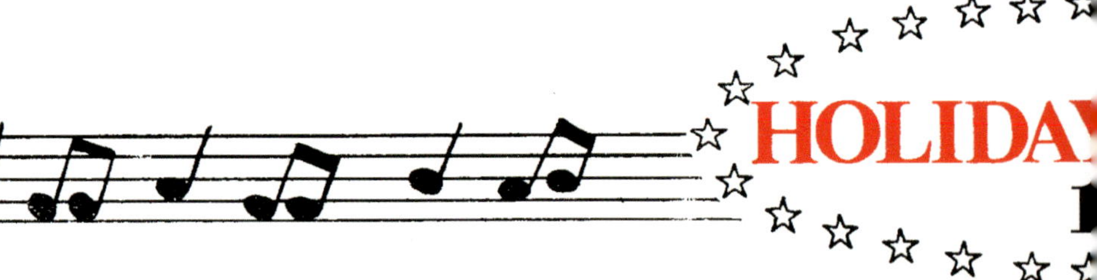

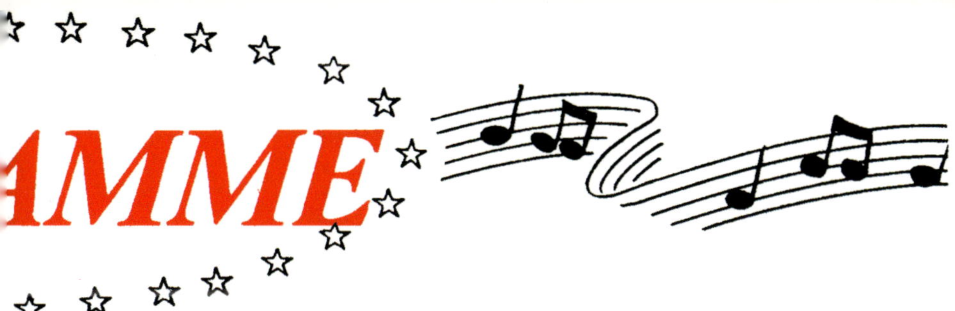

"ROLL OVER, BEETHOVEN"
with The Roly Polys

★ ★ ★

YOKO ONO
With Wally Stott and his Big Band

AWARD-WINNING BURLESQUE EXTRAVAGANZA
"CUT-PIECE"

★ ★ ★

Stars of T.V. and Radio
DEBBIE MCGEE AND CAROLEE SCHNEEMAN
present
"WHAT'S IN THE BOX?"

★ ★ ★

FINALE

"WE'LL MEAT AGAIN"
PERFORMED BY THE COMPANY
with Les Dawson at the Theatre Organ

★ ★ ★

The Show Produced by
PEGGY GOOGLEHEIM IN ASSOCIATION WITH
PETER STRINGFELLOW
Orchestrations by Wally Stott

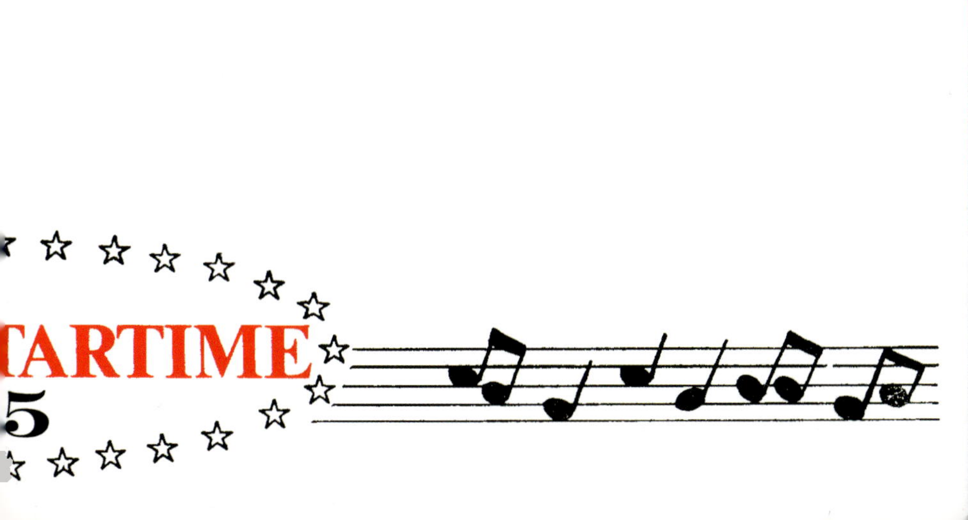

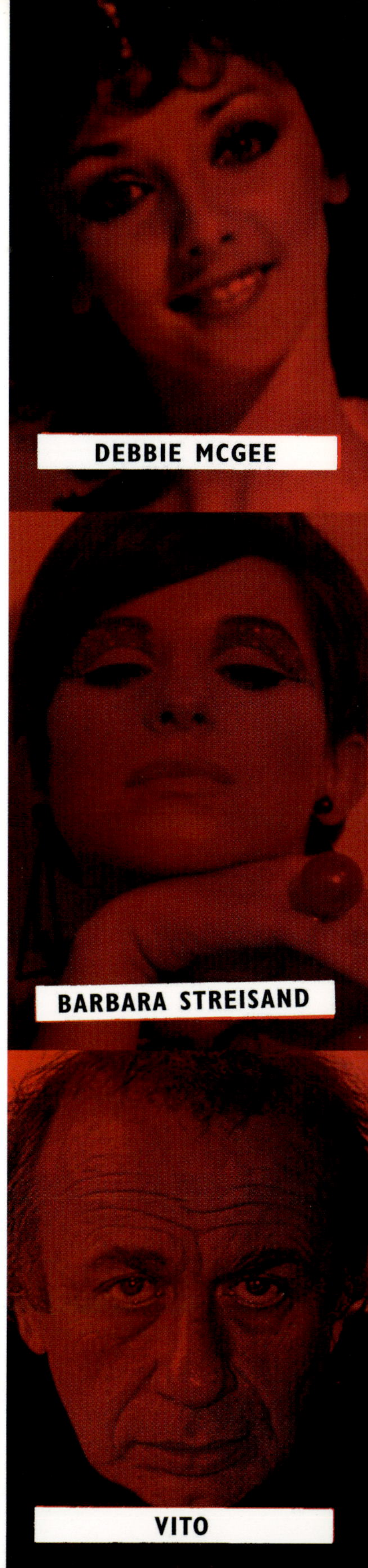

GENITAL PANIC – KENNETH WILLIAMS REMEMBERS

Peggy Googleheim's 20-year creative partnership with theatre impresario Vivian Van Damm is, of course, the stuff of legend. The brightest stars in the showbiz firmament have all trod the Windmill boards at one time or another. One can only speculate as to the importance future generations will place on the cultural legacy of the theatre, but the spectacular success of Genital Panic is richly deserved. It is a cabaret without a bit of padding anywhere – the wit is wonderfully economical and the rhythms brilliantly contrived. It has, however, been a production plagued by misunderstanding from its inception.

As I settle into another solitary meal (a rather dear individual turbot soufflé, actually – I do rather rely these days on the copy of Delia Smith's *One Is Fun*[4] that I pulled from the Women's Institute Summer Fete Bran Tub in June), I reflect that the artistic trailblazers among us are perhaps too often condemned to tread a lonely path. Certainly the hateful hoo-hah surrounding Genital Panic's opening night was enough to test the metal of the most committed iconoclast. There were furious street protests lead by the Christian Voice organization; in fact, they followed the tour around the country, singing hymns, carrying placards, handing out leaflets and, at press conferences, threatening to bring a civil action against Peggy and Vivian on the grounds of criminal obscenity. Such a nuisance, so horribly stressful for everyone, and really not helped by the fact that in the same week the papers were full of the publication of that rather sordid little book on masturbatory technique by *Deep Throat* 'actress' Linda Lovelace[5].

Censorship and standards in public life became something of a cause célèbre for a while, with every tabloid of the muckier type running salacious editorials feigning moral outrage. Of course, it was just a pretext for publishing lurid accounts of the supposed filth at the Windmill, but it was a point of discussion across the board, actually, even becoming the subject of Parliamentary questions at the height of the 'scandal'. In a transparently self-serving attack on the decline of public decency, MP for Maidstone and the Weald, Anne Widdecombe[6], gained some crucial political points and massive media coverage for the Conservatives, subsequently beating off stiff competition to appear in a party political broadcast advocating Christian family values. It was all so mealy mouthed, and her remarks concerning 'homosexuals and deviants of all kinds' left me speechless. So, while I abhor violence in any form, I can certainly share in the sense of thwarted fury that was to inspire Valerie Solanas[7] to take such drastic action.

The media has picked the story clean, of course, so I will outline only the baldest of details here. After the second of Anne Widdecombe's poisonous attacks on Genital Panic

4. A popular feminist essay on patriarchal culture advocating male gendercide, the creation of an all-female society and the New World Order.

5. Notably the book of choice for Tory MP Edwina Currie on Radio 4's popular programme *Desert Island Discs*. She insisted 'My favourites, for the record, are Toad in the Hole and the splendid Pig in a Blanket. The joys of a straightforward sausage sandwich cannot be underestimated, though.'

6. As the star of one of the first pornographic films to feature a plot, character development and relatively high production values, she enjoyed something of a cult following. Despite earning mainstream attention, the film was the subject of an obscenity trial in the 1970s.

7. Her ardent religious views are widely publicised. Along with John Gummer, she changed denomination from Church of England to the Roman Catholic Church following the decision that women could become priests.

A WORD FROM OUR SPONSOR, PETER STRINGFELLOW...

Peter Stringfellow XX

Welcome! It is with great pleasure that I introduce you to a show on its last legs – the last legs of a multi-award winning international tour, that is! And if I may say so, we've got some of the shapeliest pins in showbiz on this red-hot, all-girl bill, high-kicking right back on to the stage where it all started – the Windmill Theatre! It falls to me to introduce you to the ladies. It's a dirty job, but someone's got to do it, eh?

I first saw headliners Carolee Schneeman and Debbie McGee paired up for the Double Action cabaret[1] at this very venue. With a madcap duo like that on stage there was, as you can imagine, scarcely a dull moment! I think I'm right in saying that it was the very first time that their legendary *What's In The Box?* performance saw the light of day[2]. An absolute knockout, and not a dry seat in the house, I can assure you. Utterly hilarious and devastating all at once, and the standing ovation when Carolee 'gave up' the Flags of Nations bunting was deafening. I was a-hooting and a-hollering along with the best of 'em. It's a classic, so get ready to be amazed!

Also joining the line-up is sexy French impressionist Orlan. Hands off, lads – she's taken! I was there on the edge of my seat with the rest of the nation for the nail-biting season finale of ITV talent show *New Faces* last year, when she won our hearts and our votes, triumphing over Showaddywaddy, Marti Caine and future husband Mike Yarwood to scoop the crown! She comes to us tonight live, and in persons, with a medley of her greatest hits!

And what a year it's been for the final act, Yoko Ono. It's been a thrill a minute, from her sensational show-stopping performance of triple-platinum selling single *Don't Worry, Kyoko, Mummy's Only Looking for Her Hand In The Snow*, at last month's Royal Variety Performance with Herb Alpert and the Plastic Ono Band, to the hotly anticipated release of her book *Burlesque and the Art of the Tease*. It will come as no small surprise to many of you that the lovely Yoko is also celebrated as a popular gardening columnist for erstwhile women's magazine *The Lady* (I'm a subscriber!), and as Rear of The Year at an awards ceremony presided over by a jury of independent judges (I was one of them!). She performs her signature *Cut Piece* routine tonight. Here's hoping you brought your scissors!

The evening will be hosted by the evergreen Roly Polys in association with Marxist dance quarterly *Two Left Feet*, which tonight celebrate the release of its 'Fat Feminist' issue. Copies are available in the foyer with a substantial reduction for ticket holders, along with a special edition of *The SCUM manifesto*[3], produced to celebrate the end of the Genital Panic Tour. Strap yourself in for the ride of your life, and see you in the bar afterwards. Mine's a Slippery Nipple!

1. Ongoing Windmill cabaret, credited with bringing together some of the most influential double acts in performance history, including Barbara Streisand and Joseph Beuys; Art & Language, and Russ Abbott and Elvis Costello, to name but a few.

2. Proto-feminist magic act later made popular as gameshow format co-hosted by Schneeman, McGee and Des O'Connor. Contestants were famously invited to 'Open the Box or Take the Money' at the climax. The show was a primetime hit in over 70 countries.

3. England's oldest women's weekly magazine, founded by Thomas Gibson Bowles, the maternal grandfather of the Mitford sisters. He also founded the English magazine *Vanity Fair*.

in Parliament, I had arranged to meet my good friend Barbara Windsor[8] for lunch (Biagi's in Upper Berkeley Street, as it goes – they do a marvellous Brown Windsor). Even as we perused the (very reasonably priced) bill of fare and chatted inconsequentially of this and that, Solanas was lying in wait among the ragbag of liberal protestors picketing the exit. As Widdecombe approached the gaggle of pressmen congregated at the bottom of the steps, Solanas calmly pulled a revolver from her coat pocket and shot her.

Of course, it was an unsuccessful assassination attempt, and Solanas immediately gave herself up, pleaded guilty and received a three-year sentence. Widdecombe refused to press charges, remarking that she 'would not participate in turning a dangerous psychopath into a martyr', preferring that 'the NHS should provide rehabilitation under Section 12 of the 1953 Mental Health act '. I recall that public debate around the case continued ceaselessly for months, with the Windmill benefiting from a sell-out season, despite continued daily demonstrations outside the theatre. Leading feminist commentator Germaine Greer[9] made the obvious point that the cabaret's success was assured from the very moment Widdecombe singled it out for criticism. Ironically, the production of Solanas's first play *Up Your Ass*, about a man-hating prostitute and panhandler[10] staged at the Royal Court just three months after the attack, had, in fact, also been made commercially viable by the storm of Christian protest.

I would like to take this opportunity to congratulate Peggy Googleheim and Vivian Van Damm on their unflinching commitment to theatre. They have endured and continue to stage the best groundbreaking performance work against virtually insurmountable odds. I wish them the best of luck and look forward to the premiere screening next month at the Windmill of my latest feature film, *Carry On up The Khyber*[11]. I'll be in the bar with Peter after the show, and would much prefer a large gin and tonic with ice and a twist of lemon!

8. Outspoken radical feminist writer; author of a self-published manifesto for the Society for Cutting Up Men (or S.C.U.M.)

9. She is best known for her portrayal of a 'good-time girl' in nine *Carry On* films. Her most famous scene is in *Carry On Camping* when, during a strenuous routine of outdoor aerobic exercise, her bikini top flies off. Regarded by many as something of a national treasure, she now appears as Peggy Mitchell in BBC soap opera *EastEnders*.

10. Greer's profile has increased significantly since her appointment as a regular commentator on BBC arts review programme *The Late Show*. She has made numerous appearances at literary festivals around the UK.

11. Self-appointed moral crusader Mary Whitehouse pursued a private prosecution against the production, which featured a scene of simulated anal rape, invoking section 13 of the Sexual Offences Act, 1956, and describing the offence as 'procuring an act of gross indecency'.

12. *Carry On Up the Khyber* is the 16th *Carry On* film, released in 1968 and starring Sid James as Sir Sidney Ruff-Diamond and Kenneth Williams as Randy Lal, the Khasi of Kalabar

COMING SOON FOR OUR CHRISTMAS SEASON...

CINDERELLA

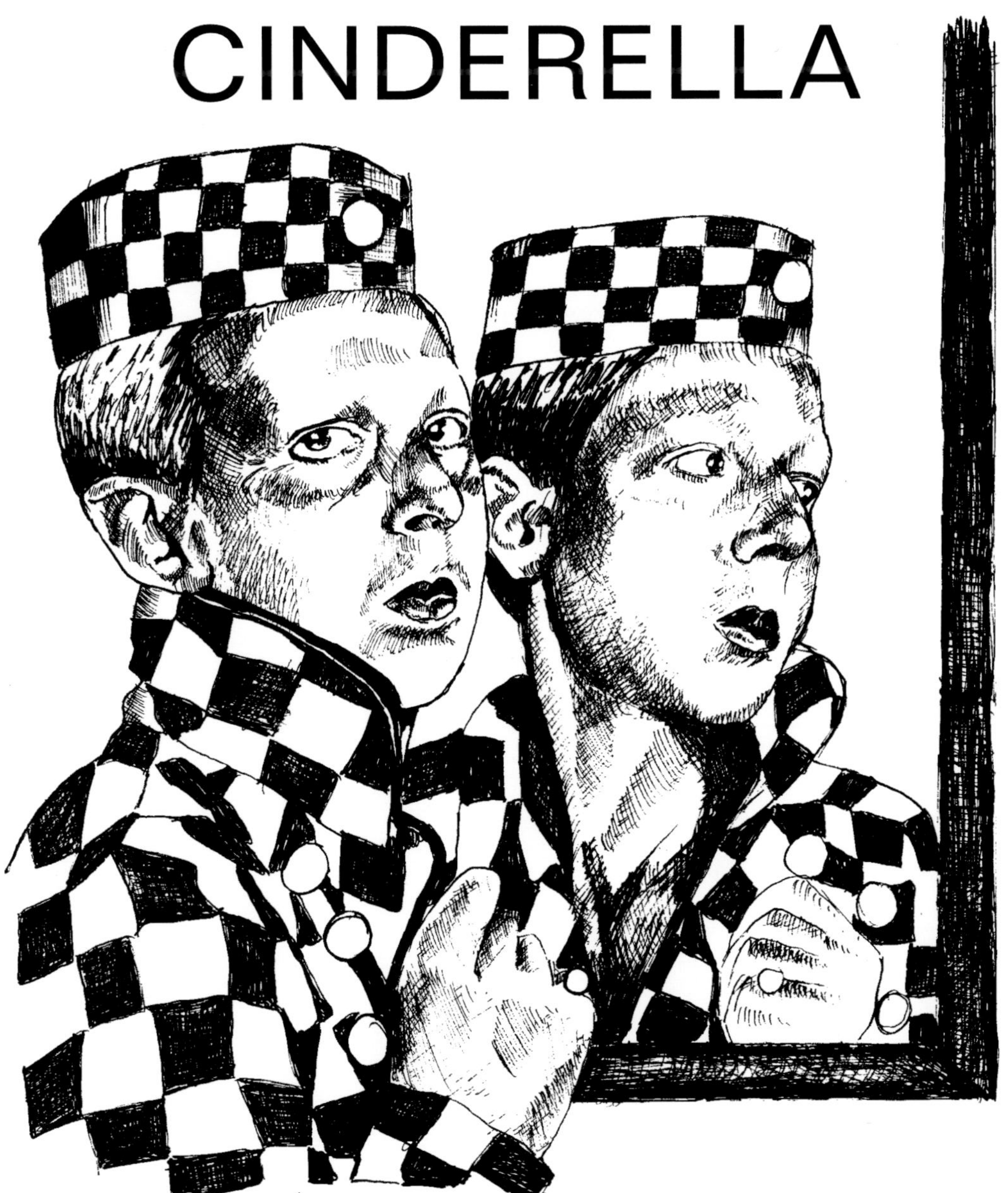

STARRING CLAUDE CAHUN AS BUTTONS

5th December – 18th January

BOOK NOW!

THE GENERATION GAME

PERFORMANCE, SCULPTURE AND THE COMEDIC IMAGINATION OF MEL BRIMFIELD

Jon Wood

"Art is the only serious thing in the world. And the artist is the only person who is never serious." [1]

"Nice to see you, to see you nice." [2]

Bill Woodrow hovers between 'Slapstick' and 'Ventriloquism', Orlan between 'Aerobics and Body/Sculpture' and 'Burlesque', and Bruce McLean, neighbouring Robert Longo, hangs under 'Tableaux Vivants' and above 'Nice Style: The World's First Pose Band' and the dance troupe 'Hot Gossip'.

It's a funny old world, isn't it? And just in case we might have lost sight of this, Mel Brimfield is determined to make sure that we don't. As the recent exhibition, This is Performance Art staged at the Yorkshire Sculpture Park, once again demonstrates, Brimfield has both an acute eye and ear for the absurdity of art—and sculpture and performance in particular—and a heightened sensitivity for the potentialities of those comedic strands of popular culture, such as variety acts, stand-up routines, sitcoms, game shows, and other TV and theatre entertainments that we love but are reluctant to take seriously.[3] In Brimfield's mind both these worlds of art and entertainment are highly interrelated. Both are seen to be part of the same zeitgeist and extended cultural moment and to share similar strategies, images, tropes and modes of operation. Through this, both are to be compared and contrasted; the qualities of one informing and qualifying the other. Brimfield's is a curious and complex project in which much is articulated simultaneously, as the spaces between practices and traditions are at once charged and closed in subtle ways. Affinities, correspondences and parallels between acts and protagonists, between narratives and objects, are revealed at the same time as the pretensions of one are punctured and deflated in the company of the other.

Brimfield is in a fascinating and unusual position to juggle these worlds and to explore the connections between them. Born in 1976, she trained as an artist, firstly at Bath School of Art and Design (where she studied sculpture) and then at Chelsea School of Art. Having worked after college with Bob and Roberta Smith as a studio assistant, her technical skill at painted letter writing and her knowledge of art, 'performance art' and its histories of the last 50 years sit alongside an excellent knowledge both of British comedy of the last half century and of the comedy circuit today. Recently she has explored these concerns as a curator in recordings, books and exhibitions. In 2003 she curated Radio Radio in which artists and comedians were invited to do their own versions of well-known radio programmes. In 2007, she curated Our Comic Book, where her own fascination with fictionalised artist-celebrity love stories was given an early airing, in this instance through "Barbara 'n Joe", aka Barbara Streisand and

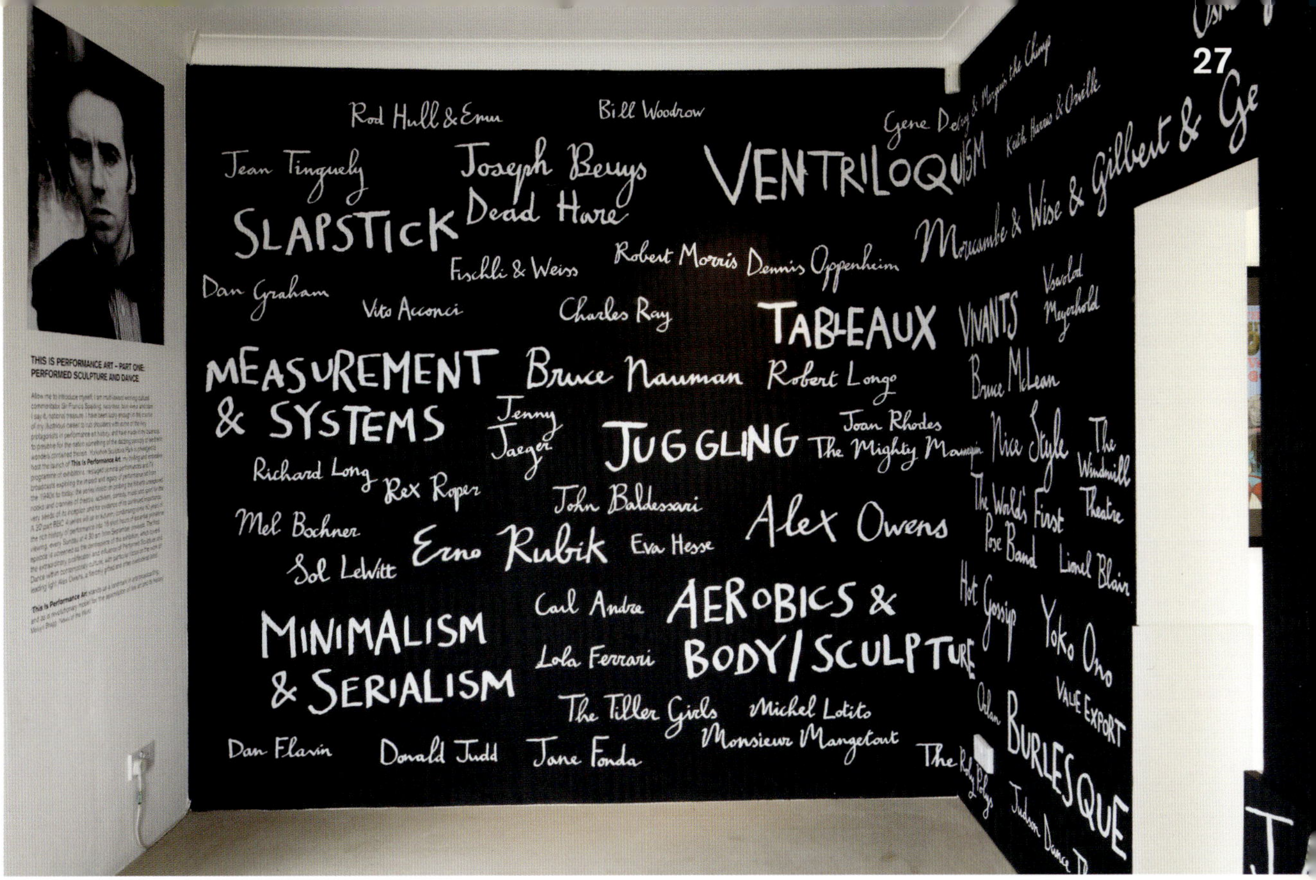

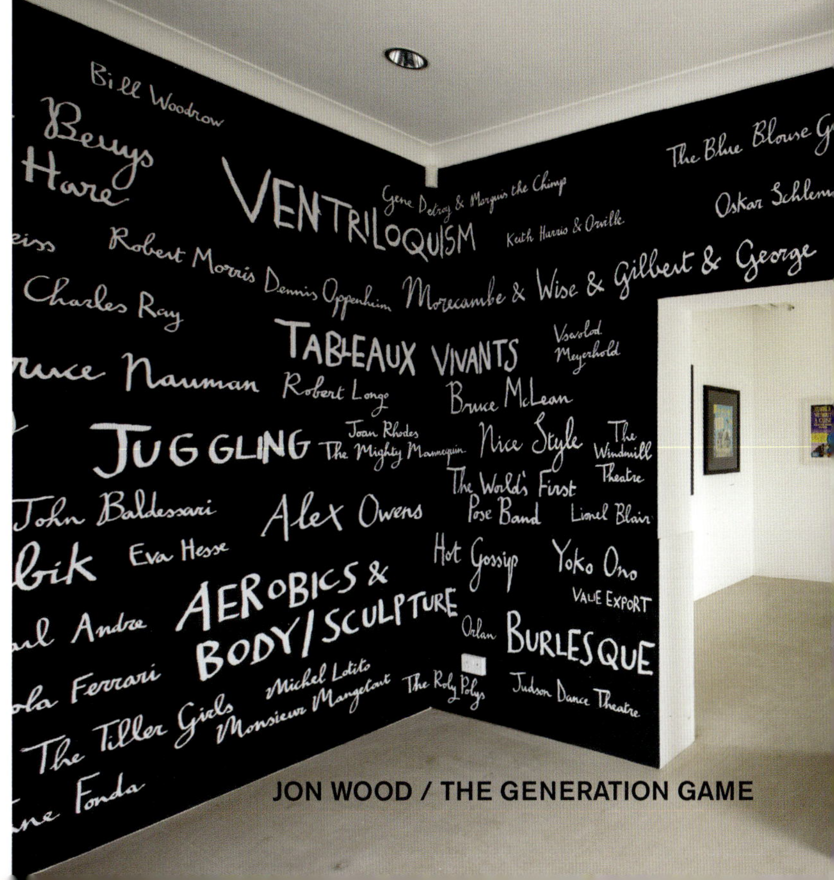

Two installation shots of Room 1. Mel Brimfield, *This is Performance Art* (installation views), Yorkshire Sculpture Park. Images courtesy the artist and Yorkshire Sculpture Park. Photo: Jonty Wilde.

Joseph Beuys. And in 2008 she curated The Golden Record: Sounds of Earth, in which she reprised Carl Sagan's 1977 record for NASA's space mission. Brimfield brought together artists and comedians, about 130 in all, to remake Sagan's record 30 years later. Brimfield herself had recently turned 30 at the time, so there was a personal, generational poetry to the project and, as with much of Brimfield's work, the clock is temporarily turned back to reflect, in the here and now, upon earlier ideas, events and phenomena. The mood of her appropriations is complex: a combination of satirical critique and humourous fondness, tinged at times with a knowing nostalgia.

Unlike many artists who make comic art, Brimfield straddles both camps, you might say, and as well as being primarily a visual artist, making posters, drawings, photographs, props, performances and films, she is also a writer. This diversity of media is indicative not only of the huge variety of material available on her subject, but perhaps also of her sensibility and her personal approach towards her subject. As Gary Stevens has written, "there is a manic and relentless pursuit that can never resolve itself into a finished piece.... Always striving, trying, impossibly, to keep the balls in the air." [4]

One of the ways Brimfield steadies, orders and gives structure to her subject, in *This is Performance Art* and elsewhere, is through beautifully written and measured narratives. Although her authorial voice (and sense of humour) is to be heard throughout her writings, she doesn't present her texts under her own name. Instead she opts for a kind of ventriloquism, putting her ideas mischievously in the mouths of other commentators, some fictional, others real. For the *This is Performance Art* project, her main narrator is Sir Francis Spalding (played by Tony Green). This character is a satirical and hybrid one: based on a combination of a stereotypical, traditional art historian and a jobbing theatre critic, with a self-regarding pomposity that might be associated with both. Note the Sir Anthony Blunt-ish knighthood. The plausibility of this character—and 'plausibility' is an ambition across this extended project—is further enhanced by the fact that Frances (not Francis) Spalding is also the name of an actual art historian. Brimfield here has adopted and co-opted her name, changing the spelling and gender, to create her new actor-commentator. 'Spalding' thus allows Brimfield to direct the narrative from the shadows whilst also compressing the two worlds of art and comedy into the same persona. He also allows viewers to view and read the work through the illusionistic critical distance that such an intermediary construct enables, temporarily suspending their awareness that Brimfield is, of course, always in charge. Spalding begins:

> Allow me to introduce myself, I am multi-award winning cultural commentator Sir Francis Spalding, *raconteur, bon viveur* and, dare I say it, national treasure. I have been lucky enough in the course of my illustrious career to rub shoulders with some of the key protagonists in performance art history, and have made it my business to preserve for the nation something of the dazzling panoply of aesthetic wonders contained therein.[5]

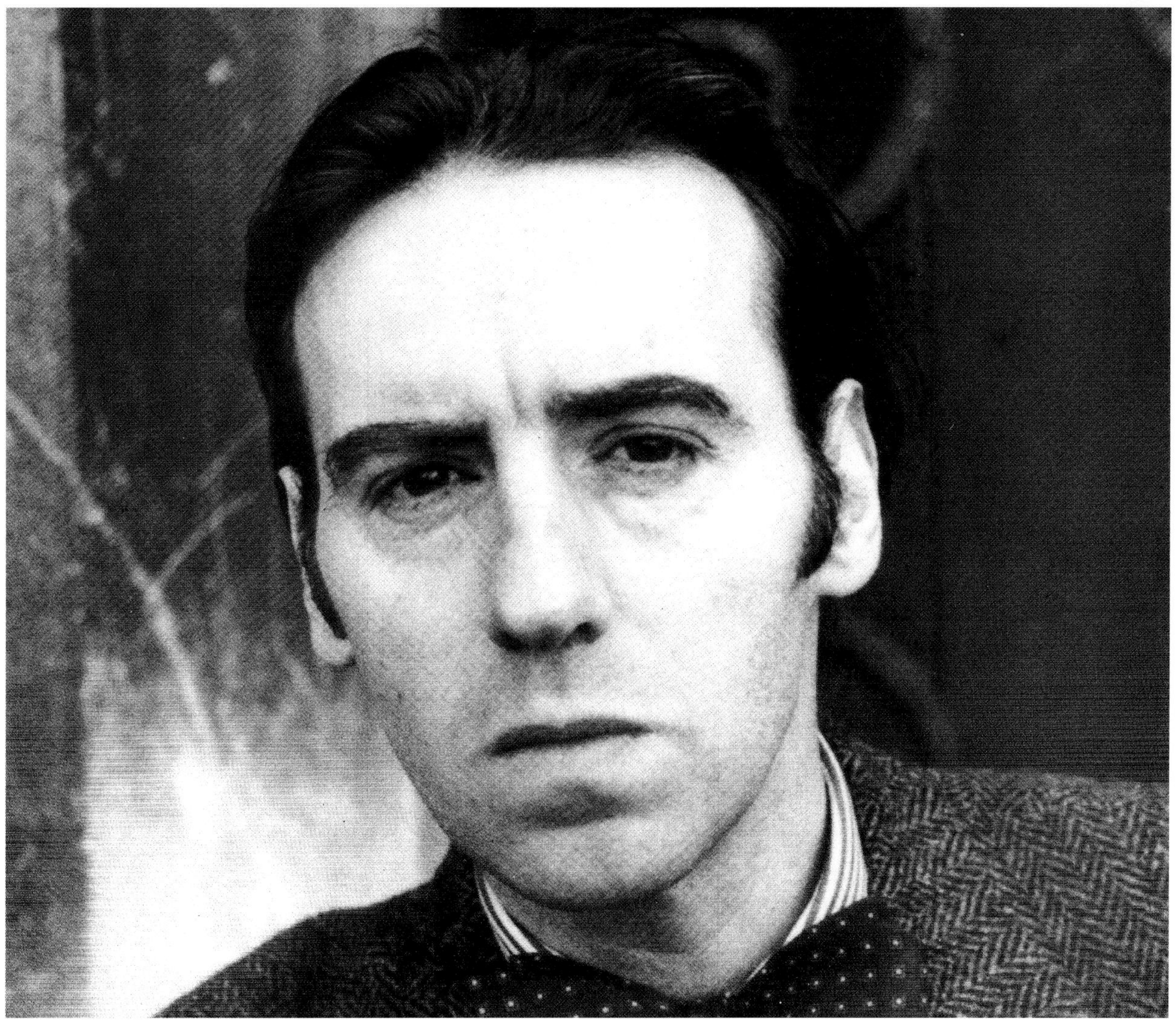

Sir Francis Spalding, photographer unknown, 2010.

For the 'landmark television series' manifestation of *This is Performance Art*, Spalding draws upon a number of co-commentators to support his observations, amongst them: "tabloid hack and celebrity gossip columnist Rosalind Krauss" and "influential and often controversial showbiz historian Clement Greenberg".[6] Moreover, the 'performance art' historian Rose Lee Goldberg, now a journalist for the *Daily Mail*, is quoted as saying about Brimfield's own project: "Where Minimalism meets Disco—not a dry seat in the house!" What 'performed sculpture artiste' could wish for better praise! Art and art criticism are sent up for being trivial and the spoken voices, often uncomfortably self-indulgent, emphasise this. Brimfield's witty folding of one career into another, is also applied to the other characters in her spoof history, through text, image or both. Thus we find Joseph Beuys as a ventriloquist, Morecambe & Wise as Gilbert & George, Bruce McLean as Burt Reynolds (and then Nick Kamen in the 1980s Levi advertisement), Judson Dance Theater as the Kids from Fame, Kevin Bacon as Bruce Nauman, and so on, with all kinds of other games of darts and d'arts.... Their works appear in significant journals of the day, such as the "influential Marxist dance quarterly *Two Left Feet*", whilst Michael Fried's "infamous Art and Objecthood" essay finds itself published in *Private Eye*.

Sometimes she creates real-time imaginary possibilities, at other times witty anachronisms. Time gets wonderfully stretched and twisted in Brimfield's work, as the 1960s, 1970s and 1980s, all share the same zone of retro-exchange, roughly 15 years or so either side of her mid-1970s birthdate. *Top of the Pops*, Keith Harris and Orville, *The Krankies*, Twister, Hula Hoops, *Grease*, *Flashdance*, The Kids from Fame, *Animal Magic*, Bob Carolgees, *Take Hart* all appear.... In keeping with this, her posters, advertising spoof exhibitions and events, only list the date and the month, leaving us to imagine the year. These decades witnessed the mainstream shift in photography and film from black and white to colour, and the bold palette of her posters, coupled with their hand-made typographies and styles, put her graphic work in an eternal dated/date-less present, outmoded and *à la mode* simultaneously. Spalding also narrates a date-less documentary, despite the evocation of a linear, chronological narrative.

Interestingly, unlike the other critics and artists she mentions, the main protagonist in *This is Performance Art*, namely Alex Owens (played by Joanna Neary), is an invented character. Brimfield's performance artist is described by Spalding as "something of an unlikely art-world heavyweight, a long-legged, doe-eyed *ingénue*, innocent of the brute machismo of the late 60s art scene".[7] With a career that includes works that appropriate those of Charles Ray (*On Board*), Martha Rosler (*The Semiotics of the Kitchen*), and in turn Bobby Baker, Brimfield has Owens lead her avant-garde dance troupe, which metamorphoses from the 'Roly Polys' to 'Hot Gossip'. Its success enables Owens to take her place in art history with her *Cubular Belles* performance ("co-commissioned by BBC Two and the Tate as part of the influential *Out of The Box* programme of live dance broadcasts referencing minimalist sculpture") and her subsequent 'Body/Sculpture' exercise plan "that was to establish her reputation as both an exercise guru and an interstellar art superstar".[8] The idea of a career is important to Brimfield's storylines across the *This is Performance Art* project. Through it we find the satirical blending of stereotypical career trajectories in which female celebrities have ended up making fitness videos. Brimfield kills Owens off whilst jogging, and shortly before the publication of her final book *The Complete Book of Running*.

It is difficult not to find seriousness in the absurd comedy of this and the tragic-comic conclusion of *This is Performance Art* focuses the mind on the kind of statement Brimfield might be making here through this fictionalised artist's biography. Owens is not, of course, Brimfield's imaginary self-portrait, but there is a power and urgency in her portrayal that suggests Brimfield is emotionally and intellectually very close to the broader meaning

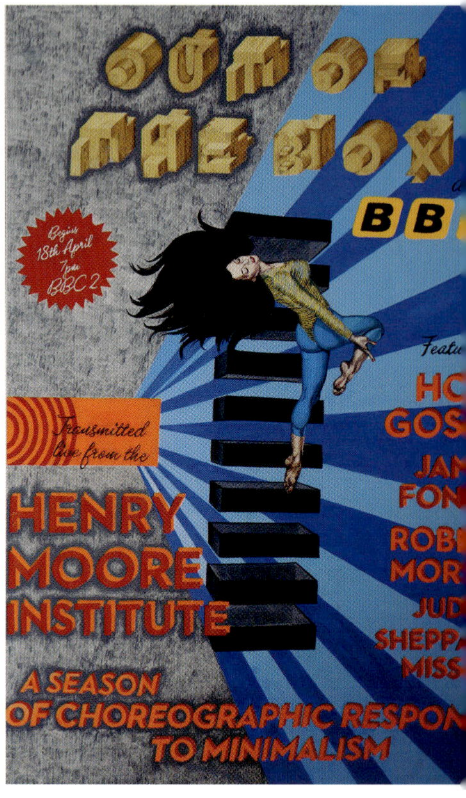

ABOVE

Mel Brimfield, *Out of the Box*, 2011, Gouache on board, 32.7 x 21.3 in. / 83 x 54 cm. Image courtesy the artist and Ceri Hand Gallery.

OPPOSITE

Mel Brimfield, *The Monsters of Rock vs. Hot Gossip*, 2011, Gouache on board, 31.5 x 21.3 in. / 80 x 54 cm. Image courtesy the artist and Ceri Hand Gallery.

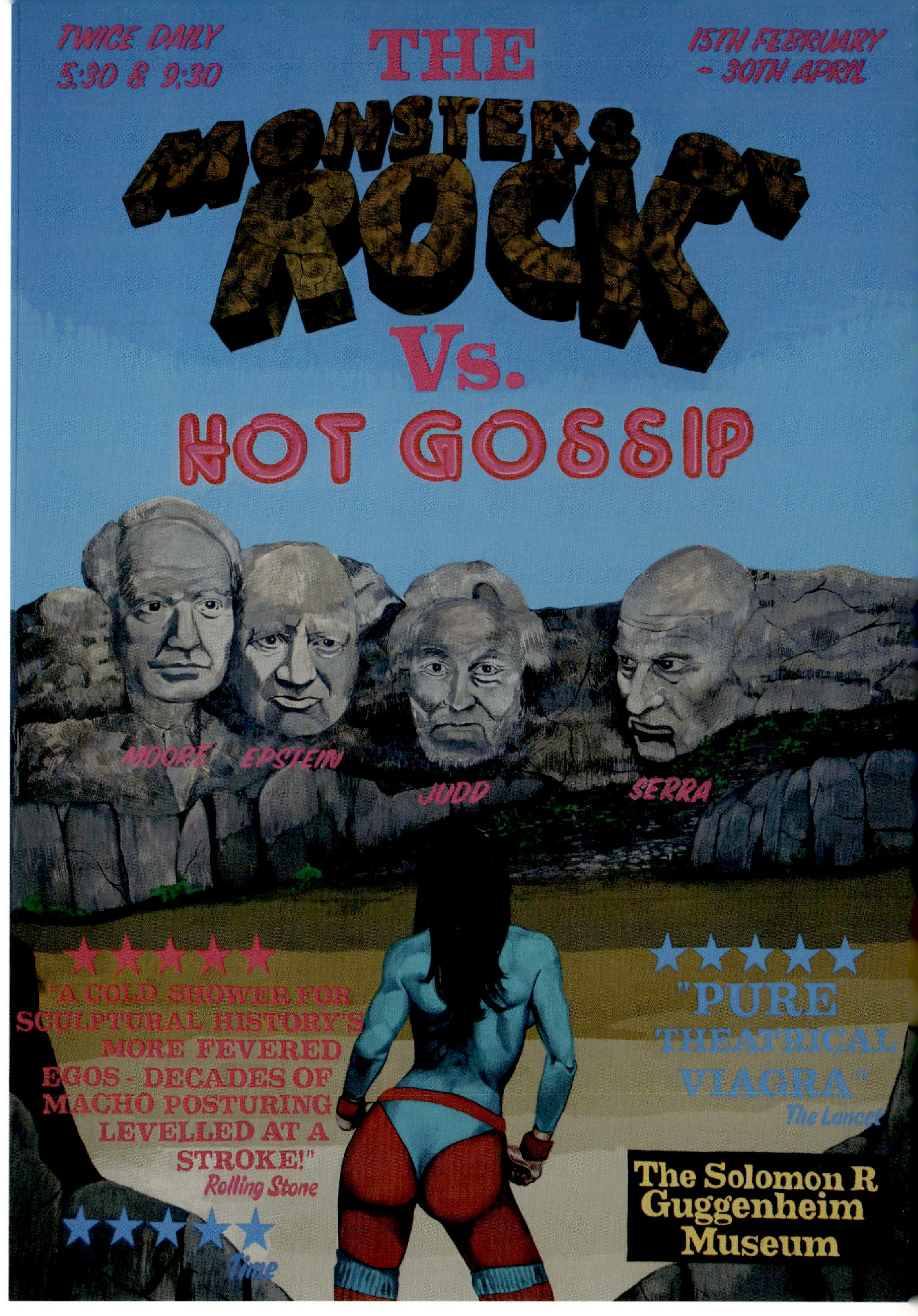
TWICE DAILY
5:30 & 9:30
THE
15TH FEBRUARY
- 30TH APRIL
MONSTERS OF ROCK
Vs.
HOT GOSSIP
MOORE
EPSTEIN
JUDD
SERRA
★★★★★
"A COLD SHOWER FOR SCULPTURAL HISTORY'S MORE FEVERED EGOS - DECADES OF MACHO POSTURING LEVELLED AT A STROKE!"
Rolling Stone
★★★★★
"PURE THEATRICAL VIAGRA"
The Lancet
★★★★★
Time
The Solomon R Guggenheim Museum

and relevance of this character's predicaments. While Brimfield is uneasy about her work being seen as being purposefully about the role of women in art or 'feminist' in outlook, *This is Performance Art* is clearly on one level about ridiculing the notion of the heroic male artist and the idea of the sculptor, in particular. In her *Monsters of Rock* poster, Jacob Epstein, Henry Moore, Donald Judd and Richard Serra are sent up as the massive sculptor presidents of Mount Rushmore. Despite the British coordinates of her comedic imagination, Brimfield's satire reaches across the Atlantic too (slightly changing its bearings on the way), and Serra, as well as Moore, come in for particularly extensive attention, though in quite different ways. Serra is cast, in posters such as her one for the spoof Leo Castelli exhibition Richard Serra: Heavy Metal, Hard Rock, as a ripped body builder, as tough, heavy and hard as the material with which he works.[9] Moore, on the other hand, is satirised for his misguided Pygmalion-like imaginings in her *Love Lives of the Artists* poster. Moore is again the object of satirical attention in Brimfield's *Barbara Hepworth* monologue, staged at the ICA in May 2011 in Bob and Roberta Smith's Women Should Be In Charge programme. Brimfield's Hepworth states:

> Inevitably, people will insist on asking me about the nature of my relationship with that endearing old duffer Henry Moore, almost before they step over the threshold of my studio to look at my fucking work. Dear, dear bumbling Henry. I always thought that he was something of an unlikely so-called genius behind closed doors, I must say—he was hampered throughout his life by poor motor skills and an almost complete inability to hold a mallet or chisel in his ham-fisted grip, but he didn't let it hold him back; such marvellous spirit despite his obvious shortcomings. He was the son of a mining engineer, and indeed his working class roots were only too audible in his speech—at points the guttural cadence of his thick Northern brogue rendered his speech impenetrable to the general ear. Elocution lessons certainly helped, but much of what he said remains a lovely mystery to us all.[10]

Hepworth then ends mercilessly: "Perhaps in many ways it is as well for him—he wasn't the brightest, but then, there are times when a low wattage bulb is just what you need."[11]

Alongside such satires and caricatures, Brimfield's project (as her Hepworth monologue highlights) is also about re-imagining the period from a point of view in which women and the predicament of female artists are in the foreground. What makes Brimfield's project so intriguing is that alongside this, her creative, quasi-art historical revisionism is played out with a nice blend of homage and critique for those heroes and villains, cowboys and Indians, cops and robbers, who are part of her story. Brimfield is involved in "debunking the debunkers", as Gary Stevens has said, but in doing so she also highlights their achievements.[12] Brimfield is not naive to these, nor is she unaware that she is herself tapping into critical positions and possibilities, initially created by artists who emerged using both performance and sculpture in the 1960s and 1970s, such as Bruce McLean, Gilbert & George, Keith Arnatt and many others.

Sculpture, in particular, was the subject of radical critical reassessment in these decades. Brimfield is all too aware of this, as she is of the fact that any consideration of the relationship between sculpture and comedy has to acknowledge sculpture's own comic, satirised and caricatured status. This is perhaps one of the reasons she keeps coming back to it in her work, apart from the fact that she studied it as a student. For sculpture has regularly been the butt of jokes—with comics, cartoonists and satirists sending it up relentlessly over the years, poking fun at all of its pretensions and vulnerabilities, including its weight problem, its material bulk, obduracy, awkwardness and clumsiness, its muteness, its misplaced aspiration for permanence, its wedding cake plinths, its pompous and extravagant monuments, its commemorative ambitions, its dodgy political validations and its often out of touch relation with the world of which it is a part.

We might also think about all those cartoons that respond to pygmalionism and sculpture's mythic ability to transform clay and marble into 'living and breathing' flesh and bone. This trope has been one of the popular in such derisions, and the eroticism of pygmalionism—as of nude figurative sculpture generally—has often been a feature of this, as all those smutty seaside postcards remind us. And although sculpture has changed radically over the last 50 years, it is striking how persistent this cardboard cut-image of sculpture—as monolithic and as statuary, as figurative and realistic—has been.

Sculpture, from a comedic point of view, is thus always and automatically 'performed sculpture' from the outset outside the shared and overlapping histories of these two subjects. From the sculptor's point of view, comedy, from a sculpture point of view, has played (and continues to play) an important role in enabling artists to reflect critically on the idea of sculpture and develop new works. In this way, sculpture carries on because of, as much as in spite of, this burgeoning comedic interest—assisting in its persistence—and, in this way, comedy is a highly generative impulse in modern and contemporary sculpture, in Britain in particular.

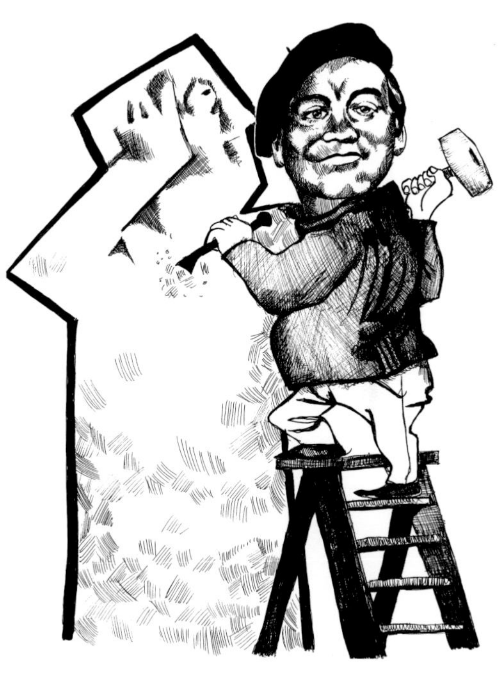

Tony Hancock in *The Rebel*.

Such ideas and the critiques which accompanied them were not only circulating in the art worlds of the 1960s, but also in the world of British comedy. In Robert Day's 1961 film, *The Rebel*, for example, Tony Hancock exchanges bowler hat and umbrella for beret, paintbrush and chisel. And leaving behind his commuter job in the city, he starts a career as a sculptor in his digs, under the disapproving eye of his landlady Mrs Crevatte. The moment she discovers Hancock with his huge sculptural masterpiece, *Aphrodite at the Watering Hole*, is occasioned by some wonderful exchanges: "How did you get it up here?" Mrs Crevatte asks furiously.

Hancock's speedy reply accounts for every block of this multipartite sculpture, whilst also satirising the tendency of modern sculptors (such as Gaudier-Brzeska, Modigliani and others) to use salvaged materials for their work. He says: "I brought it up the stairs, bit by bit. She is 15 bits of stone, all

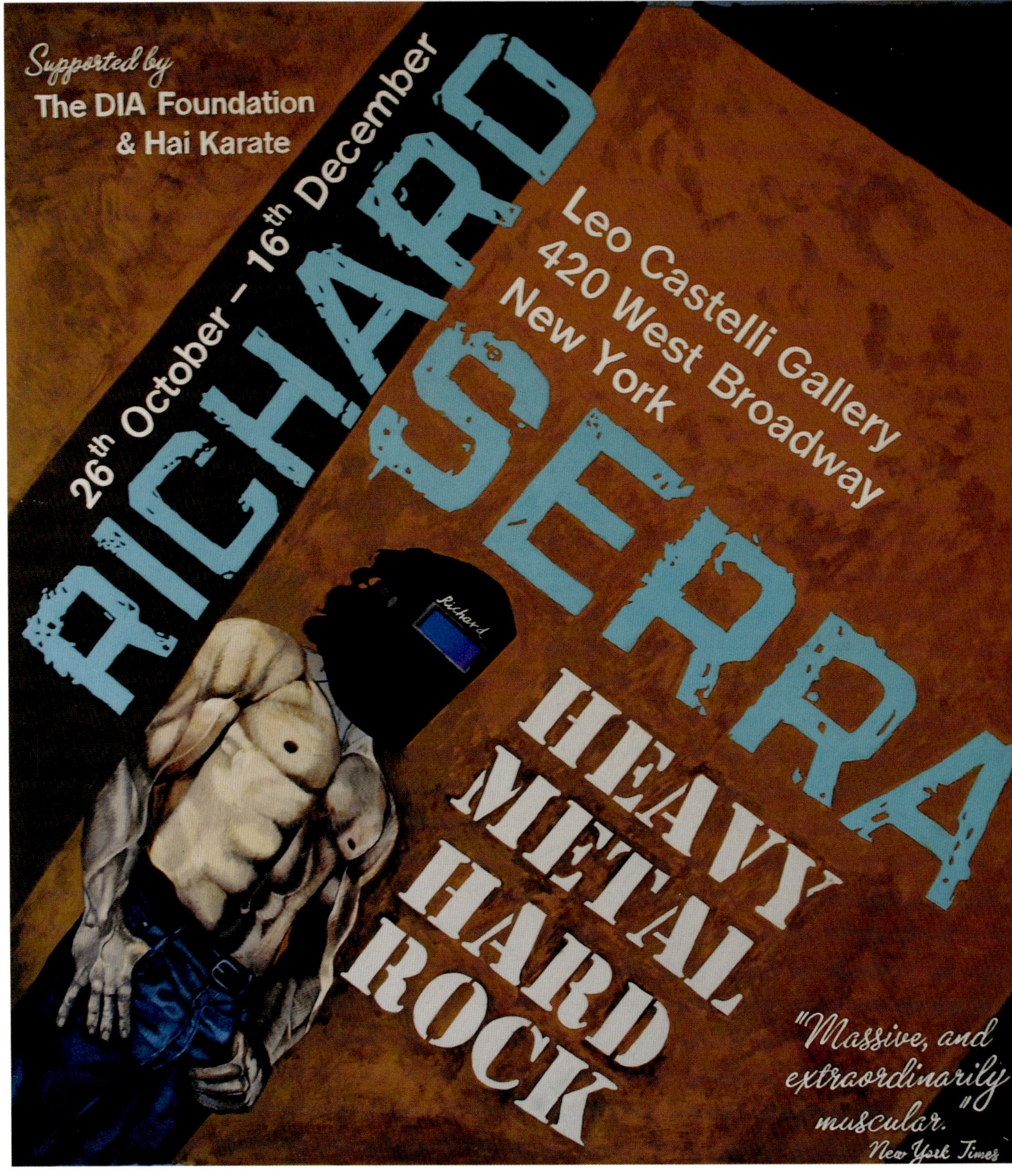

Mel Brimfield, *Heavy Metal Hard Rock*, 2011, Gouache on board, 37.8 x 35 in. / 96 x 89 cm.
Image courtesy the artist and Ceri Hand Gallery.

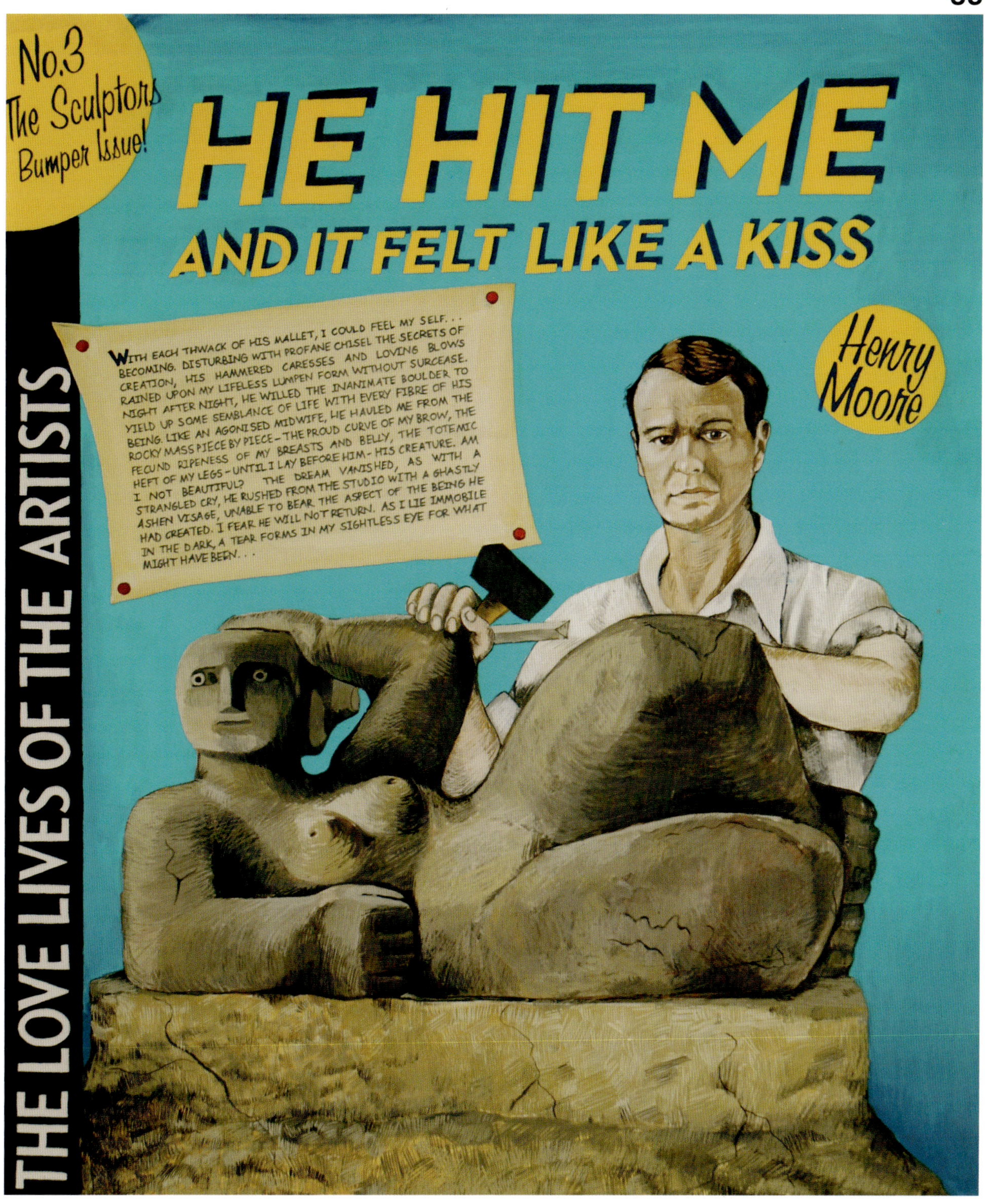

Mel Brimfield, *He Hit Me… And It Felt Like A Kiss*, 2010, Gouache on paper, 33.5 x 29.1 in. / 85 x 74 cm.
Image courtesy the artist and Ceri Hand Gallery.

held up with iron bars, which I got from the breaker's yard. The head is the foundation stone from the 'Dog and Duck' up the road. Her left leg is a bit of the old war memorial and the rest of it is made up of six chunks of the town hall, two bits of railway bridge and a lump of the public library." She replies: "It's disgusting." And later, with a line that neatly blends the artistic with the comedic, Hancock says: "I'm not of the realist school, I'm an impressionist." "Well, it don't impress me!" Mrs Crevatte replies, and so it goes on.... And *Aphrodite at the Water Hole*, Hancock's masterpiece, is made three times during the film, because each time he makes it, it falls through the floor.

Brimfield has a particular fondness for *The Rebel*, which was also, in turn, one of the films that Bruce McLean used to encourage his first year students at the Slade School of Art to watch as they began their studies. It is tempting to try and see the young McLean in Hancock's character, as well as read the more general lesson, advocated by the older McLean before his younger students, about the dangers of the art world.

McLean himself occupies a fascinating and crucial place in *This is Performance Art*. Spalding introduces him as follows:

> One man can lay more of a claim than most to toppling the unwieldy macho edifice from its dusty plinth. I refer of course to Bruce McLean. His path to global stardom proves what the human spirit can accomplish when relentless drive and determination converge with dreams. His long and arduous journey from two-bit pub stripper collecting tips in a bucket to becoming one of the world's most accomplished and innovative artists is an inspiration to all who face overwhelming obstacles and challenges along the road to success.[13]

The 'dusty plinth' problem was the subject around which ideas about sculpture gravitated for McLean's generation of St Martin's students in the 1960s. "Does a sculpture need a plinth?" and "Why not put it on the floor?" were the questions posed by the work of Anthony Caro and other 'New Generation' sculptors against Moore's plinth-supported work. These questions were passed on to the students of St Martin's School of Art at the time. McLean's response was "where actually is the floor?", reminding them that since the St Martin's sculpture department was on the ninth floor, they were already actually on and in a plinth, albeit of a large scale architectural kind, even though they were being taught there to place sculpture on the 'floor'. His point, a simple one, was that the floor was not the ground, and McLean pursued this line of enquiry with his *Fallen Warrior*, 1969, in which he acted out Moore's *Falling Warrior* throwing himself down on a small plinth, placed at sea level on a Thames embankment in Barnes in 1969. McLean took his anti-plinths teachers to task in ways that both put another nail in the plinth's coffin and opened doors for its reappearance.

Interestingly, Brimfield's first reference to Bruce McLean was a response to one of his works of which she had only known the title—the

Waiter, waiter, there's a sculpture in my soup—Performance Art and Comedy from Gutai to the Present, 2008, exhibition invite. Design by Uniform.

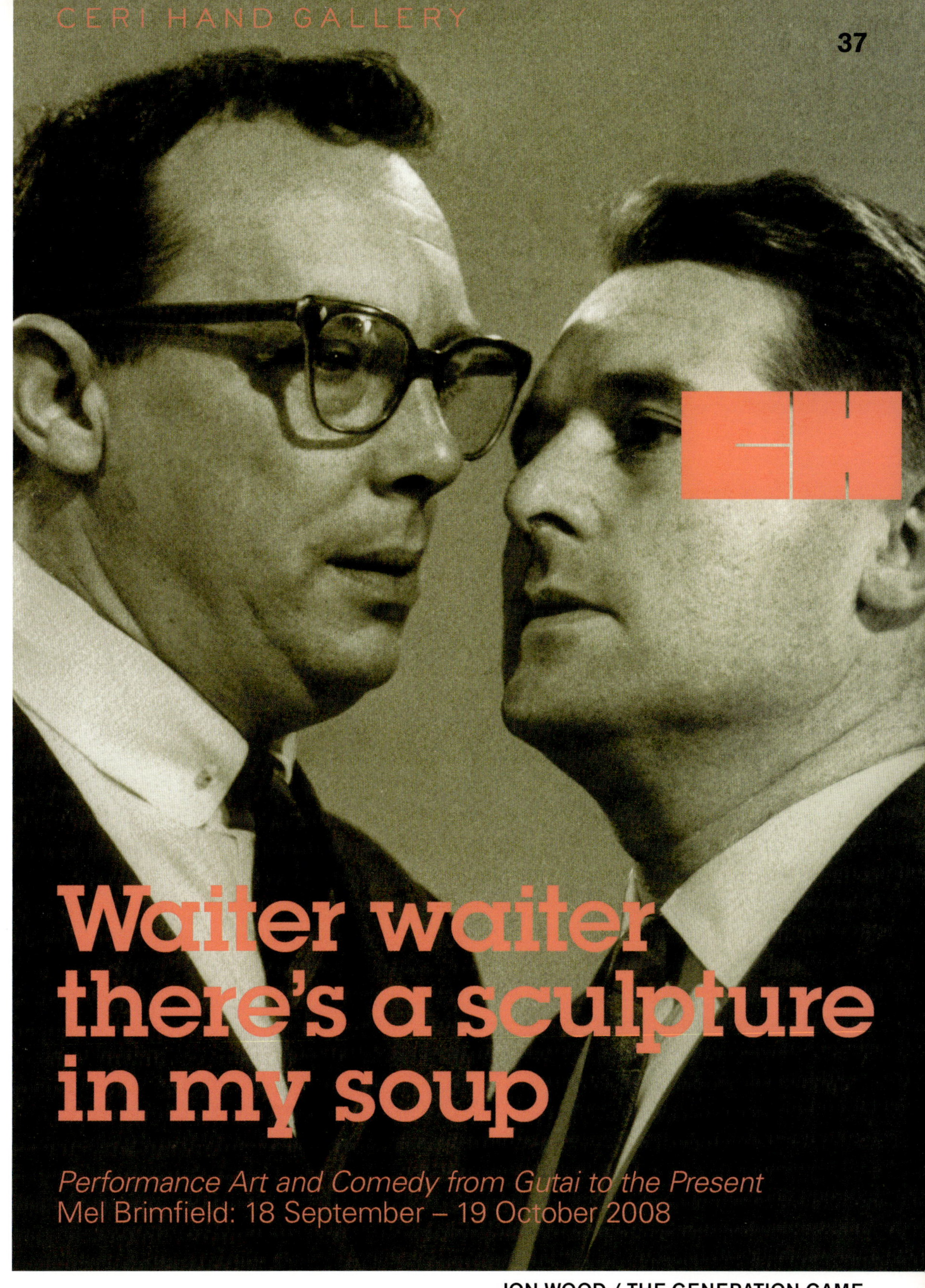
CERI HAND GALLERY
CH
Waiter waiter there's a sculpture in my soup
Performance Art and Comedy from Gutai to the Present
Mel Brimfield: 18 September – 19 October 2008

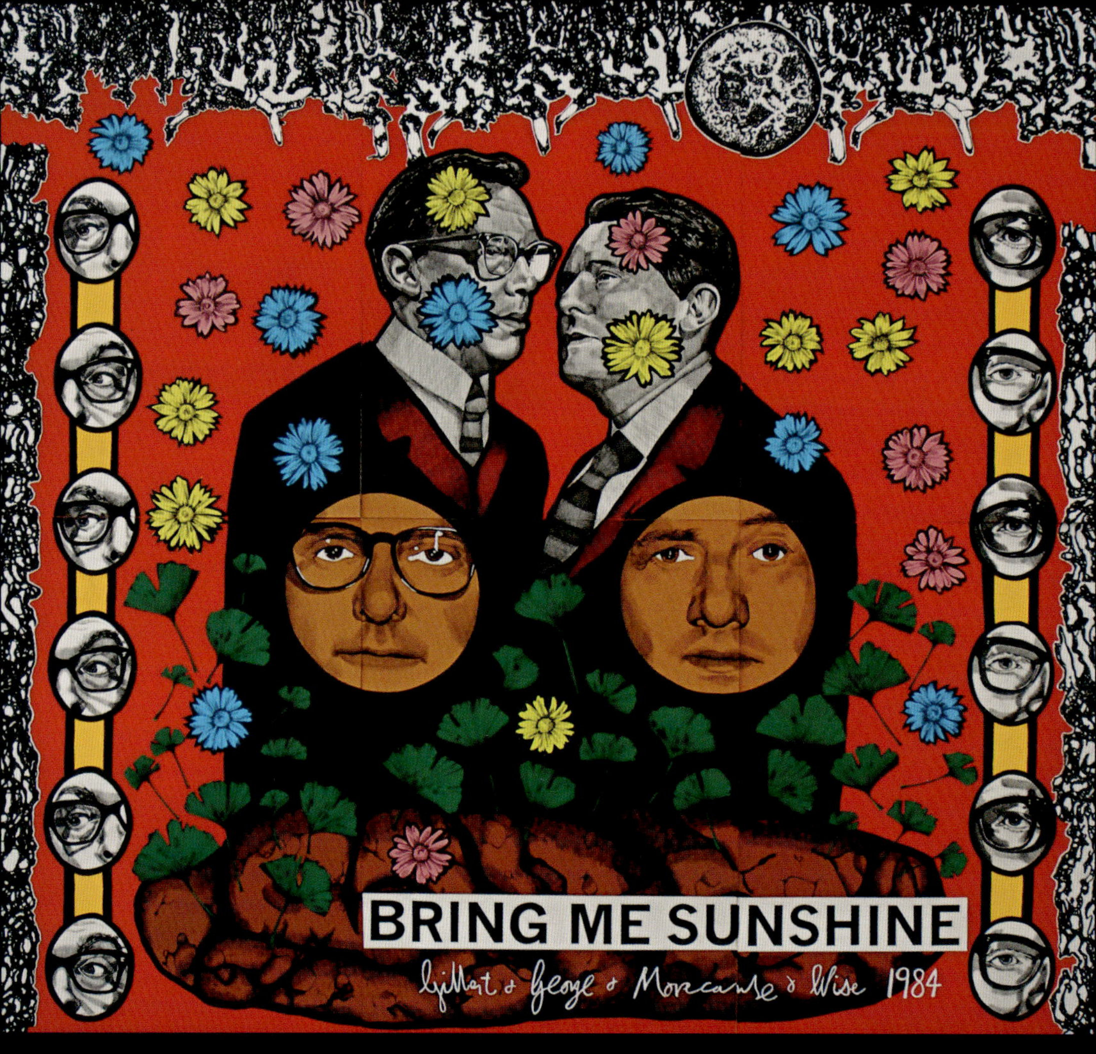
BRING ME SUNSHINE
Gilbert & George & Morecambe & Wise 1984

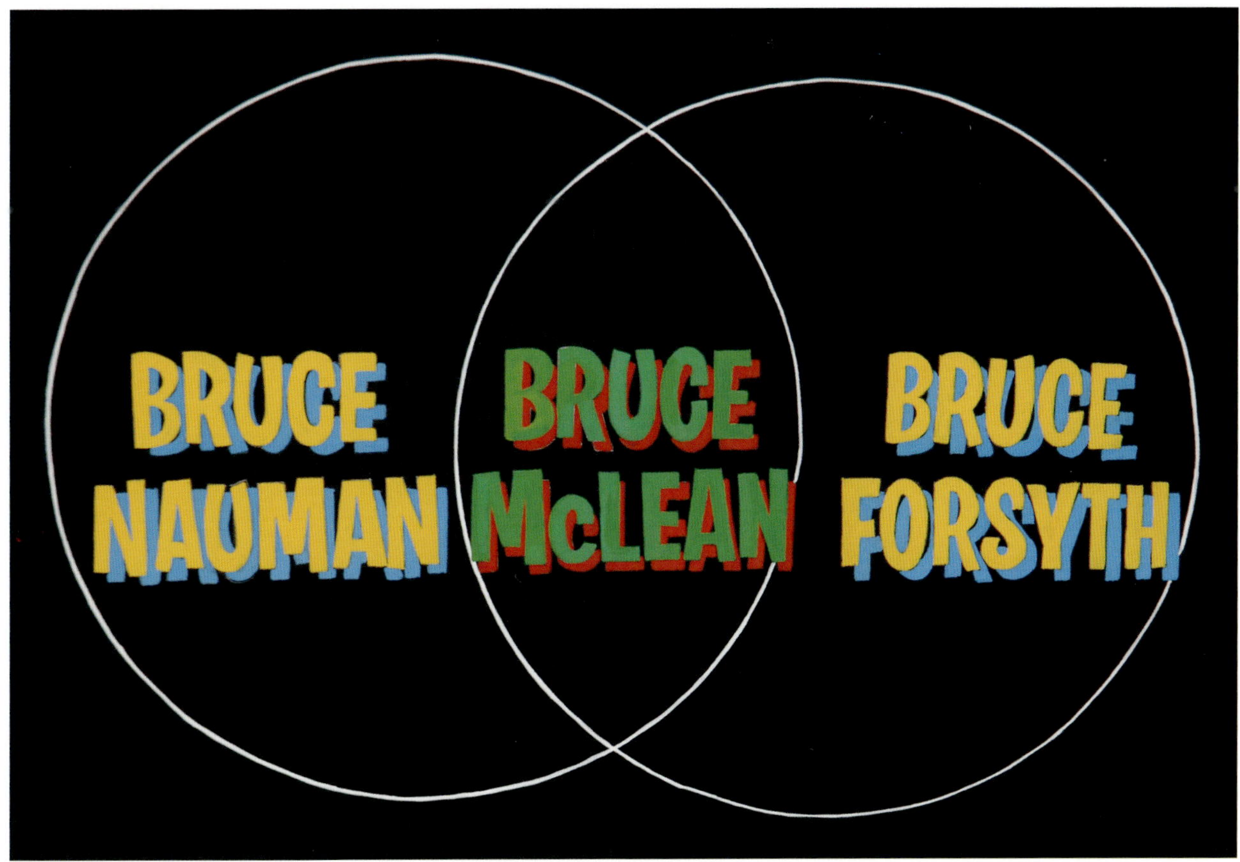

OPPOSITE

Mel Brimfield, *Bring Me Sunshine*, 2008, Gouache and Indian ink on paper and board, 70.5 x 66.1 in / 179 x 168 cm. Image courtesy the artist and Ceri Hand Gallery.

ABOVE

Mel Brimfield, *Venn Diagram*, Gouache on board, 12.9 x 16.9 in. / 32 x 43 cm. Image courtesy the artist and Ceri Hand Gallery. Private collection.

original work, a film of 1970, now being lost. Waiter, waiter, there's a sculpture in my soup, the title of her exhibition at the Ceri Hand Gallery in Liverpool and at the Pump House Gallery in Battersea, used McLean's text, but not his image or his visual art work. Instead, in the exhibition preview card and in her poster for the exhibition, she used photographs of Morecambe & Wise, and Ken Dodd and Vito Acconci, respectively.

In a way this comes as no surprise, as across Brimfield's work we find an ongoing fascination with double acts and with real and imaginary male partnering. Her friend(s) Bob and Roberta Smith share(s) not dissimilar interests and Gilbert & George, who themselves drew inspiration from the music hall duo Flanagan and Allen for their *Underneath the Arches* text and *Singing Sculpture* performance, play a key role across her work. In Brimfield's *Double Action*, 2008, they share the bill with Cannon and Ball, Barbara and Jo, Morecambe & Wise, Les Tennis and Dennis Elbow, Carolee Schneemann and Debbie McGee and The Nice Style Pose Band. This imaginary nightly revue, staged at the London Palladium, is compered by Bruce Forsyth. Forsyth himself for many years on *The Generation Game*, of course, sang the praises of double acts, with the ditty: "Life is the name of the game, and I wanna play the game with you. Life can be terribly tame, if you don't play the game with two."[14]

What better compere than Bruce for *Double Action*? Roles and identities are even further blurred and blended the same year in her large *Bring Me Sunshine*, 2008, poster/painting, in which Brimfield creates a double-double-act, interestingly 'signed' at the bottom by all four performers—Gilbert & George and Morecambe & Wise—and dated 1984.

Her fascination with such double acts reminds us that on a broader level her whole art research project itself is poised somewhat on a double-act structure: on a straight man (sculpture), funny man (comedy) pivot. It was a line that McLean's own work has walked and Brimfield's recent Venn diagram, showing the overlapping worlds of Bruce Forsyth/Bruce McLean/Bruce Nauman, is one that McLean (flanked by the other two Bruces) is likely to smile at. McLean himself has joked about this world of contemporaneous 'Bruces', playfully adding 'Bruce Lee' and 'Bruce Lacey' into the mix too.[15]

Indeed such is Brimfield's interest in and sensitivity to McLean's work that on occasion her spoof readings of his work come close to his original and sometimes forgotten artistic intentions. Her reading of McLean's *Pose Work for Plinths*, 1971, is a notable example of this.

This work, staged at Situation in London, has frequently been read as being a joke about Moore's reclining figures and their various postures and compositions. The art critic Richard Cork at the time, for example, wrote: "Straddled uncomfortably across three uneven plinths, McLean here exploits his natural talent for clowning to guy the lumbering weight of a Moore bronze."[16] Though it carried such possibilities and whilst McLean was relaxed at the time about such interpretations, he has recently talked about them again as being a series of body exercises (akin, in his words, to Gormley's later figurative sculptures) in which the body is bent and shaped by its surrounding architecture, in this case a group of standard art gallery plinths.[17] In this way, Brimfield's *BODY/ROCK*, 2010, performance, in which Italian Olympic gymnast Alice Capitani performs a series of postures and poses, is close in spirit, if a hyperbolised version of it, to McLean's original situation work.

Such correspondences point, finally, to the Venn diagram of concerns that Brimfield's revivified concept of Performance Art History contains. For as well as being 'Performance Art' on the creative terms of her own practice, her project also presents a kind of 'performed art history' and, through this, it tentatively proposes a new kind of visual history of sculpture and performance in which the formal and physical correspondences between things are given primary and privileged attention, before the written word and in advance of more official, textual histories

Those interested in studying the art of the last 50 years have a lot to learn from such an approach. Putting books down and having a good look and a think can never be a bad idea. And the humour and comedy of her approach is acute and timely in an age of heightened attention to and institutional valorisation of artistic research.

Bruce McLean's *Pose Work for Plinths* was, whatever else might have been said about it, on one basic level (and for him personally) about

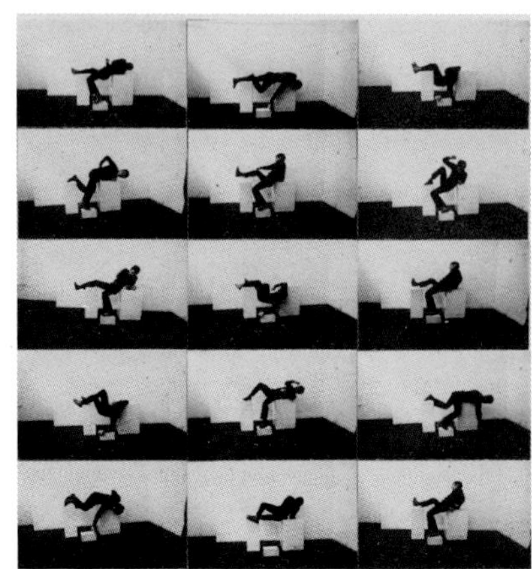

Bruce McLean, *Pose Work for Plinths 3*, 1971, Photographs on board, 29.5 x 26.9 in. / 75 x 68.2 cm. Image courtesy the artist and Richard Saltoun, London.

the challenging movements of the body in restricted space; Gilbert & George and Morecambe & Wise were popular and cultural neighbours, and performed sculpture, whether you foreground Keith Harris and Orville or some other, more historical ventriloquist act, does have a great deal in common with ventriloquism and its handling of figurative and spatial dynamics, both in deeply playful and deeply serious ways.[18] It's a funny old world and sometimes, as Brimfield's work continually reminds us, life (to use that worn-to-a-shine cliché) is stranger than fiction.

---

1. Wilde, Oscar, "A Few Maxims for the Instruction of the Over-Educated", *Saturday Review*, 17 November 1894. Aphorism used by the artist Bruce McLean in 2007, in his designs for Dalry School in Scotland.
2. Forsyth, Bruce, *The Generation Game*, 1980s. Opening catchprase.
3. *This is Performance Art*, Yorkshire Sculpture Park, Spring 2011.
4. Stevens, Gary, "Ta Da!", in Mel Brimfield, Camden Arts Centre/April–June 2010. File Note # 54.
5. Introductory wall text, *This is Performance Art*, Yorkshire Sculpture Park, Spring 2011.
6. *This is Performance Art*, script.
7. *This is Performance Art*, script.
8. *This is Performance Art*, script.
9. Anecdote from Mel and Ceri re art fair visitor who didn't know what the Leo Castelli / Serra poster was for.
10. Barbara Hepworth monologue, *Women Should Be In Charge*, 20 May 2011, ICA , London.
11. Barbara Hepworth monologue, *Women Should Be In Charge*, 20 May 2011, ICA , London.
12. Stevens, Gary, "Ta Da!", in Mel Brimfield, Camden Arts Centre, April–June 2010. File Note # 54.
13. *This is Performance Art*, script.
14. Forsyth, Bruce, *The Generation Game*, 1980s. Show song.
15. McLean's after-dinner speech at the Henry Moore Institute's tenth anniversary party in 2003, staged to coincide with the exhibition Sculpture in Twentieth-Century Britain.
16. Cork, Richard, "Bruce McLean", 5 November 1971, in *Everything Seemed Possible: Art in the 1970s*, London and New Haven: Yale University Press, 2003, p. 37.
17. Jon Wood in conversation with Bruce McLean, "Fallen Warriors and a sculpture in my soup: Bruce McLean on Henry Moore", *Sculpture Journal*, Liverpool University Press, 17.2, 2008, pp. 116–124.
18. For another assessment of this connection, see: Jon Wood, "With Hidden Noise: Sculpture, Video and Ventriloquism", in *With Hidden Noise: Sculpture, Video and Ventriloquism*, Leeds: Henry Moore Institute, 2004, pp. 14–26.

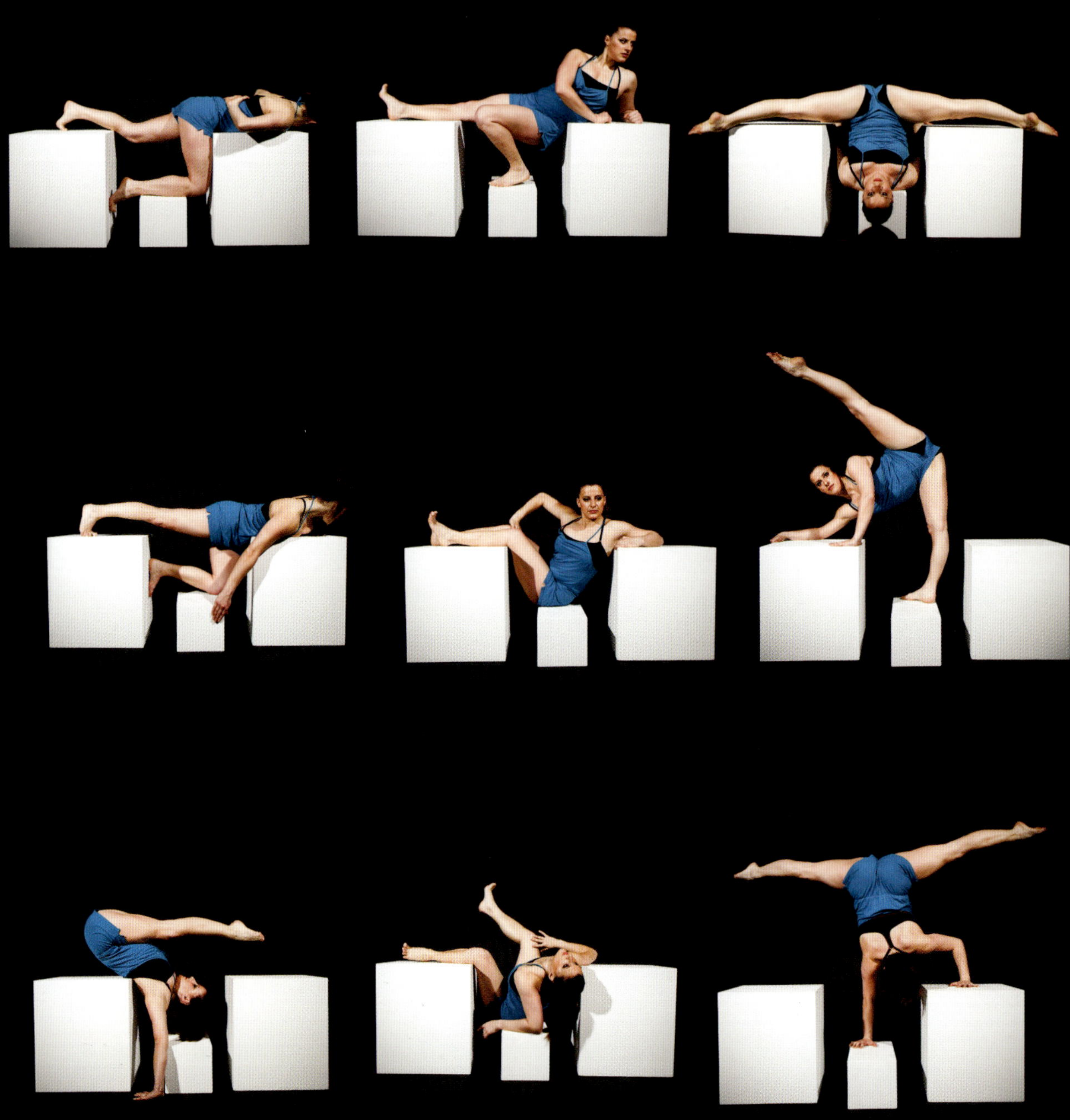

Mel Brimfield, produced in association with Alice Capitani and Edward Moore, *BODY/ROCK*, 2010, choreographic score, C-print, dimensions variable. Image courtesy the artist and Ceri Hand Gallery.

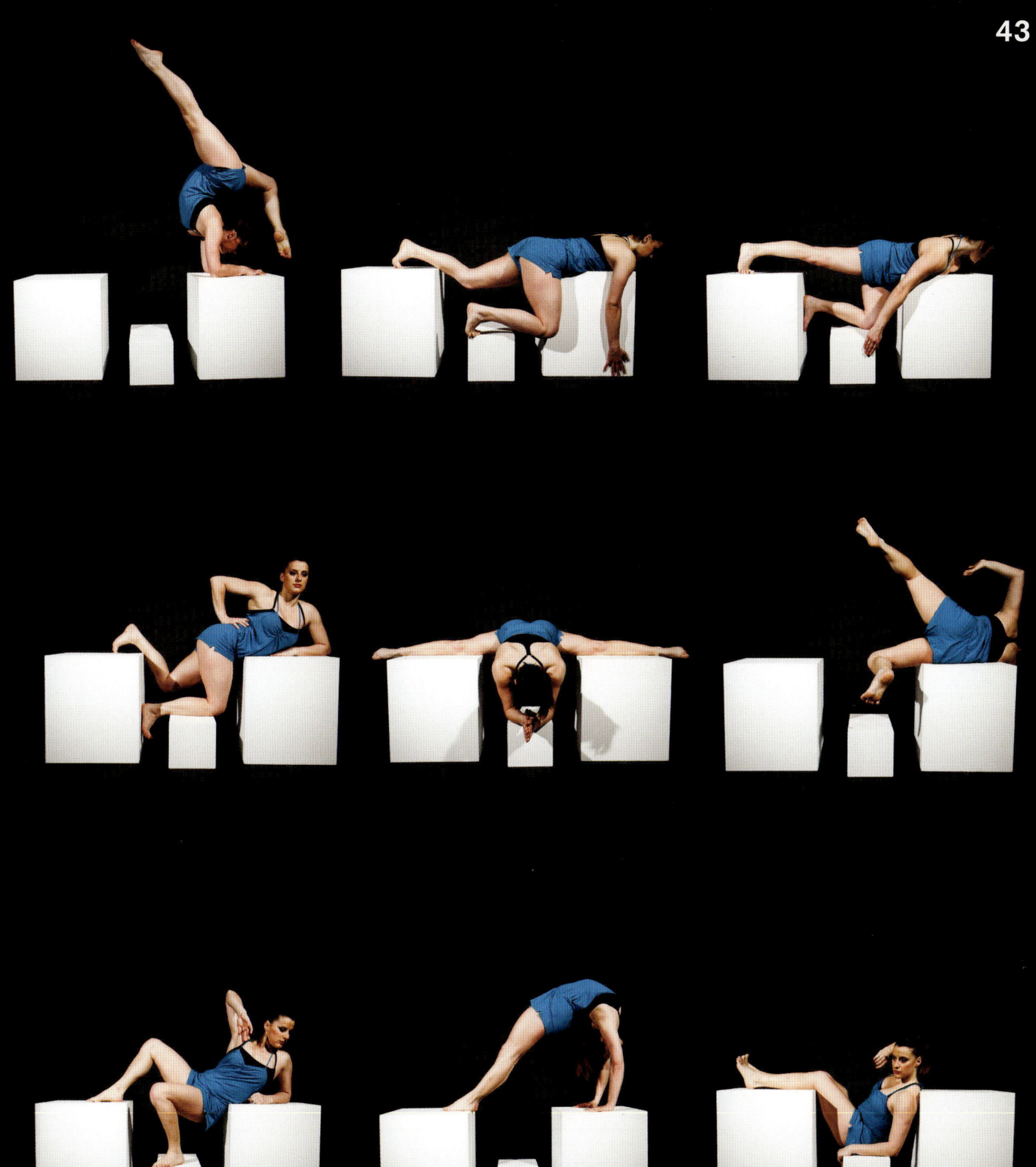

THIS IS PERFORMANCE ART—PART ONE: PERFORMED SCULPTURE AND DANCE

CAMDEN ARTS CENTRE AND YORKSHIRE SCULPTURE PARK

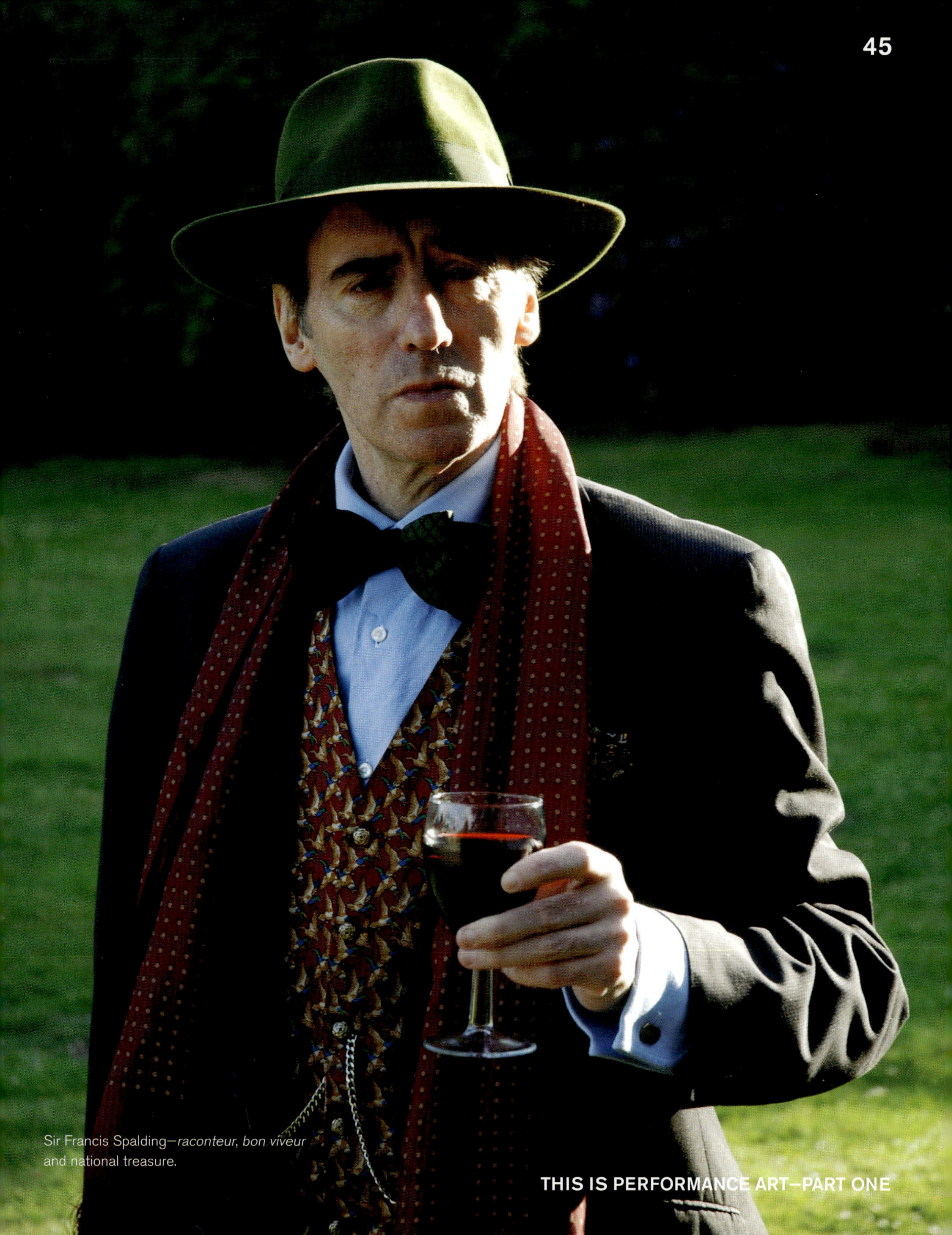

Sir Francis Spalding—*raconteur, bon viveur* and national treasure.

FILM TRANSCRIPT

Welcome to *This Is Performance Art*. Sir Francis Spalding has been lucky enough in the course of his illustrious career to rub shoulders with some of the key protagonists in Performance Art History, and has made it his business to preserve for the nation something of the dazzling panoply of the aesthetic wonders contained therein. This is the first in a landmark television series that seeks to instigate a revolutionary model for the assimilation of Live Art. Today's episode will concentrate on mapping a hitherto uncharted territory—that is the development and extraordinary mainstream proliferation and influence of Performed Sculpture and Dance within contemporary culture, with particular focus on the work of two of its leading proponents.

It seems logical to begin our voyage of discovery by considering that most legible of performed sculptural modes, namely ventriloquism. The transition of this cheap vaudeville technique to arch conceptual form is a fine example of the kind of mobility frequently achieved within the genre.

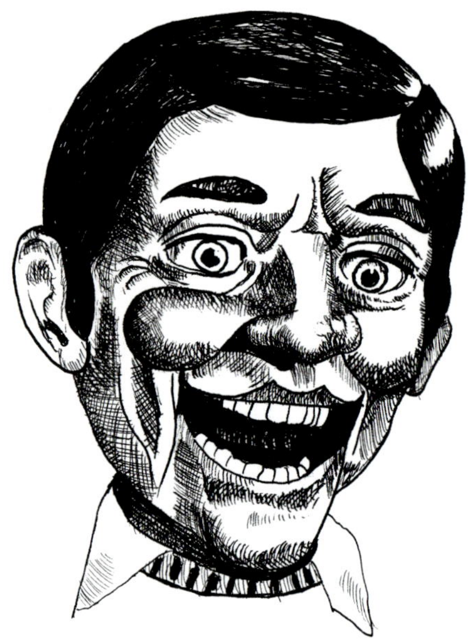

Of course, any discussion of the subject must necessarily open with the extraordinarily influential work of Joseph Beuys. The essence of his professionalism amounted to more than the appeal of his rare but irresistible grin, flawless ukelele technique, and heavily accented broken English. From the tip of his battered grey felt hat to the frayed hem of his hopelessly stained fishing jacket, he radiated a kind of sagging melancholy that audiences could relate to. Much is made of his profound understanding of primitive symbolism and certainly he was much in demand as a session musician. It is perhaps unsurprising, then, that throughout his illustrious career, his extraordinary talent for voice-throwing would always find its most effective outlet when allied with his considerable animal training skills. In fact he got his break on the popular BBC children's television series *Animal Magic,* where as the avuncular host, he supplied the jovial voiceovers to footage of various animals from Bristol Zoo.

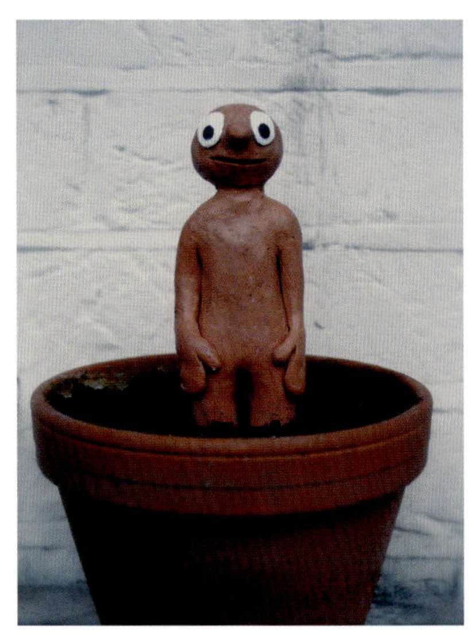

The first incarnation of his act was a skilful compilation of songs, jokes and anecdotes, bravado, sentiment and razzamatazz littered with a breathless string of garbled interjections and asides referencing humanism, social philosophy and juggling. Tabloid hack and celebrity gossip columnist Rosalind Krauss recalls the impact of *Explaining Pictures to a Dead Hare* on the assembled clutch of jaded onlookers who were to witness it at Kentucky's famed VentHaven Ventriloquist Convention:

> So he shuffles onto the stage with his head like, coated in gold leaf and honey, dragging a large trunk and with one foot strapped to a ski. So far, so normal, right? Then he takes his seat, opens up the trunk and pulls out his dummy just like always, but it's a freakin dead hare and he's just mumbling at it. I was electrified, because it was totally disjunctive in this situation. I mean, it had nothing to do with ventriloquism as I understood it, you know? There was this momentary question: Is he going crazy? Is this the moment? Are we witnessing it? Are we going crazy? The vent's dummy has to speak, right? That's the whole point. But then you realised the inherent tragedy of attempting, and failing to animate a

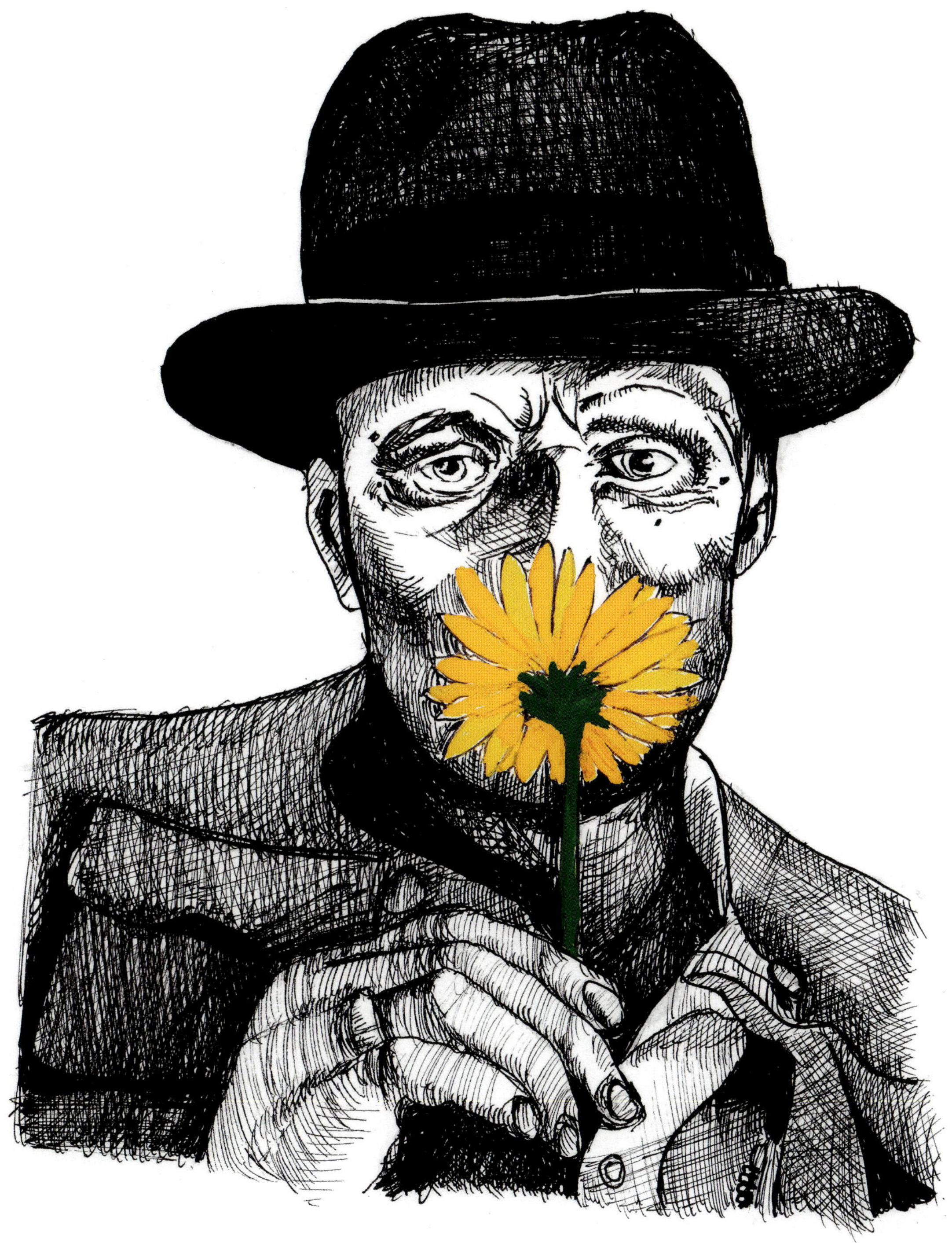

Ventriloquist Joseph Beuys radiated a kind of sagging melancholy that audiences could relate to.

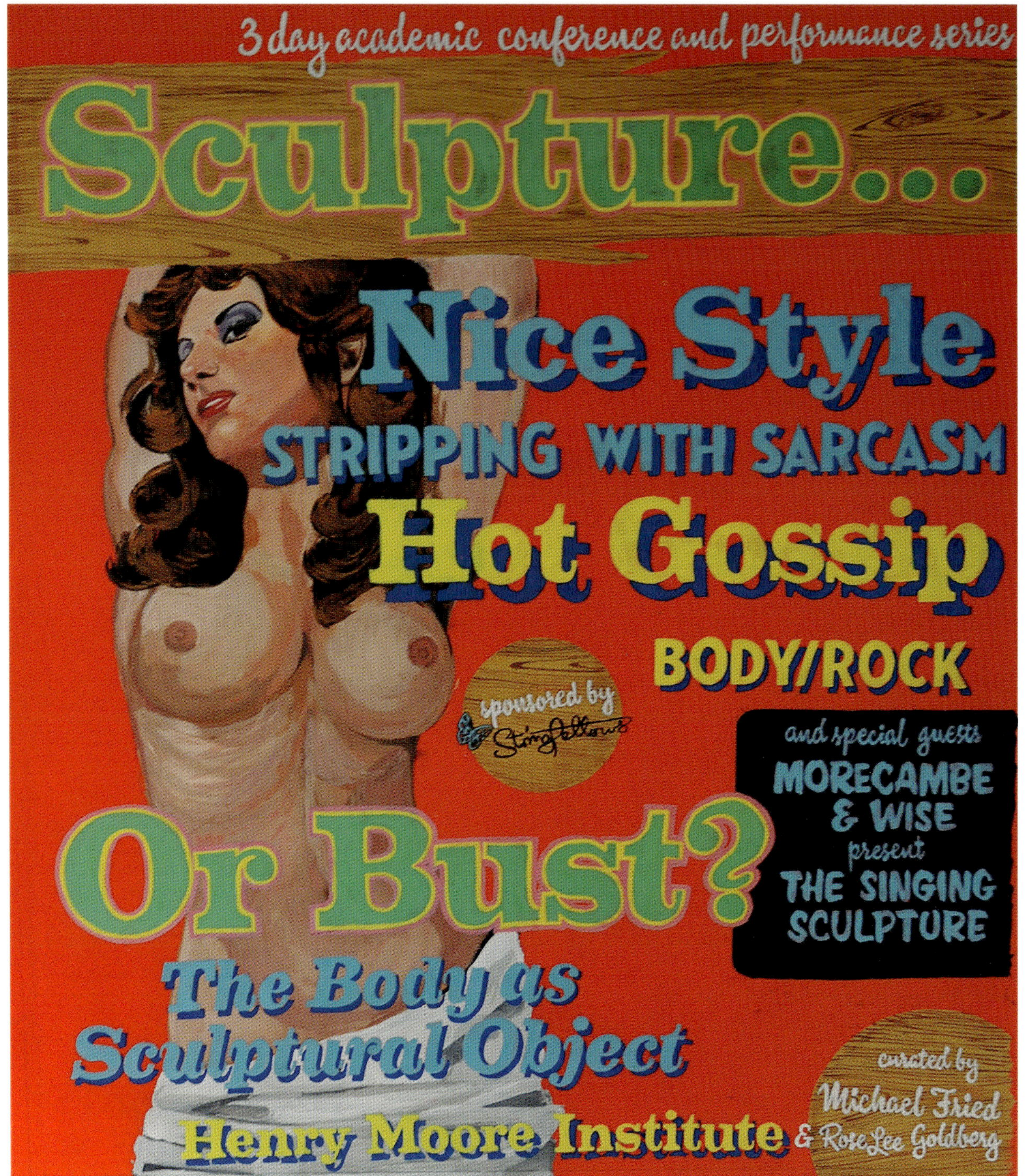

Mel Brimfield, *Sculpture or Bust*, 2010, Mixed media, 18.3 x 15.6 in. / 46.5 x 39.5 cm.
Image courtesy the artist and Ceri Hand Gallery. Private collection.

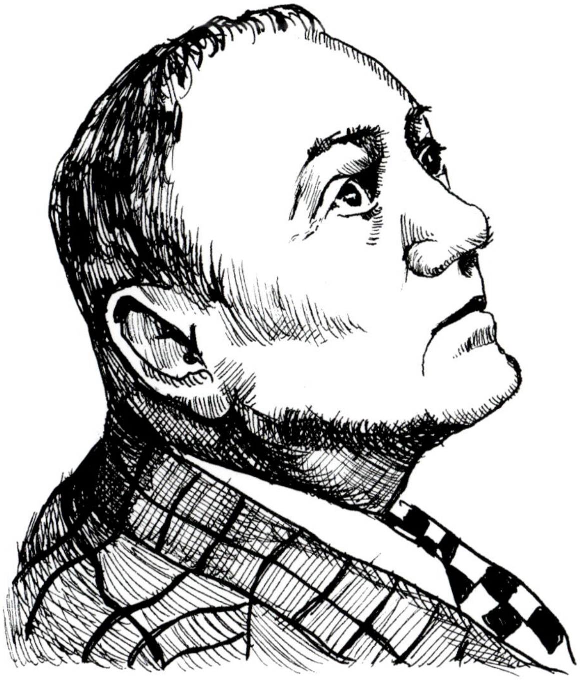

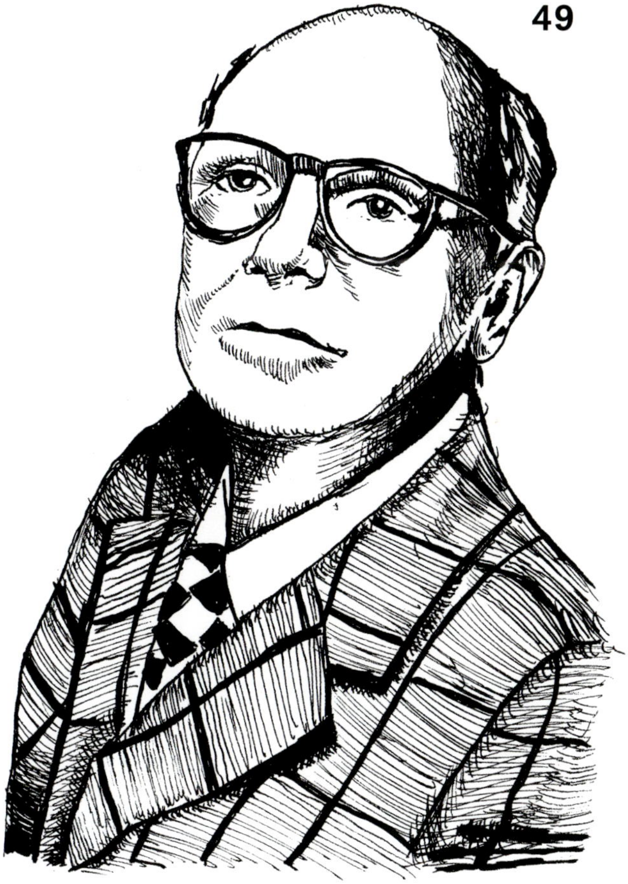

Collaborative performance artists Ernie Wise and Eric Morecambe.

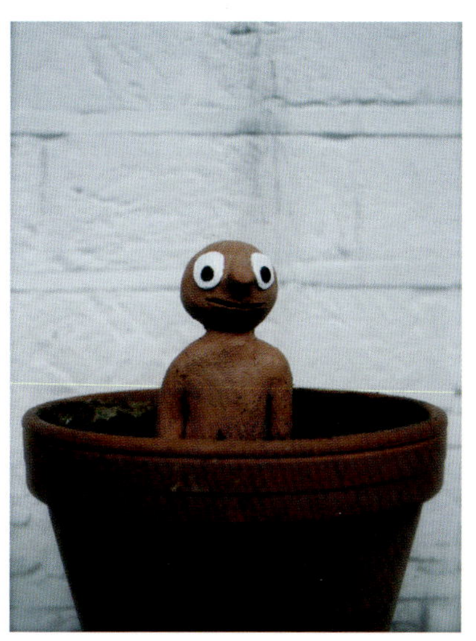

> dead creature, this motionless forever mute object—he was talking to it, and nothing was happening. The whole thing had me weeping and laughing all at once. That single gesture broke open the whole decorum of ventriloquism—completely unforgettable.

The inoperable dummy was to become a familiar motif within a new strand of self-reflexive ventriloquy on the circuit. Collaborative performance artists Eric Morecambe and Ernie Wise were already well known for their experiments in performed sculpture, and had submerged their individuality into a Siamese-twin-like persona shortly after meeting at St Martin's School of Art. The pair first appeared with a giant dummy at the three-day Henry Moore Institute 'Sculpture… or Bust?' conference which sought to interrogate new perspectives on the much-vaunted critical rejection of sculpture represented by live art—Krauss again:

> There was no escaping the total materiality of that thing, you know—they insisted on it throughout the whole performance with every move they made. It was just furreeeakin huge. They're hefting it about and its arms and legs are flailing all over the place, and it's completely dysfunctional and ridiculous—and

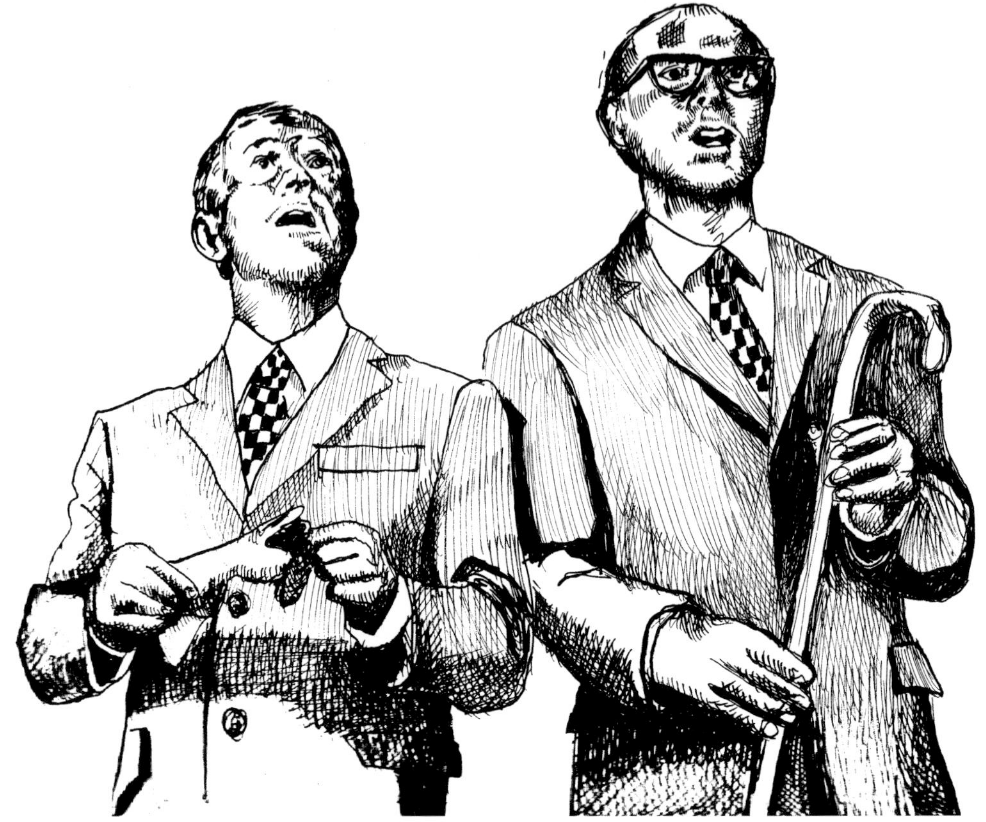

Ernie Wise and Eric Morecambe—inventors of the 'Living Statue' technique.

> then it hits you—pow—you know you're looking at a sculpture. And Eric's up and down the ladder trying to work the jaw, but it won't work, you know, and it won't speak. At five hours and 36 minutes, the piece was maybe a bit long, but the last hour or so was a total kinesthetic shot in the arm for anybody who had any doubts about the raw power of introducing a sculpture to the stage. When that dummy finally fell to pieces in their hands, there was a standing ovation. Just pure joy.

The pair are of course, also notable for the development of radical performative modes of sculpture-based street entertainment. "On leaving college and being without a penny", Wise later recalled, "we were just two physical presences, Morecambe & Wise." So it was, Morecambe added, that "we put on metallic make-up and became sculptures. Two bronze sculptures. We had a regular busking pitch." This 'Living Statue' technique has of course become something of a cliché in live art circles, but at the time of its first unveiling at the opening of the Milton Keynes shopping centre, it was construed to be something of a revolutionary conceptual exercise. In addition, the duo were to score a sweet, sweet profit in loose change, rumoured to be in excess of a monkey.

The displacement of the sculptural object by the human body was a recurrent theme in early 1960s performance work, and in the following decades, a new generation of ventriloquists were to take the cue of the early groundbreaking experiments I have outlined to ram the point home. From the ingenious yet terrifying ultra-realism of Ian Tough's *Wee Jimmy Krankie* robot dummy to the

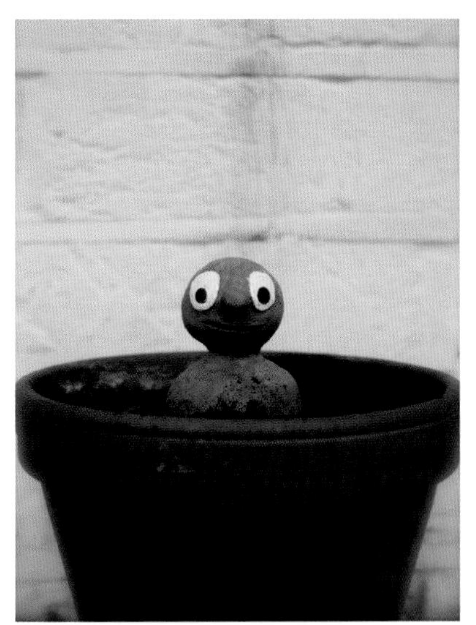

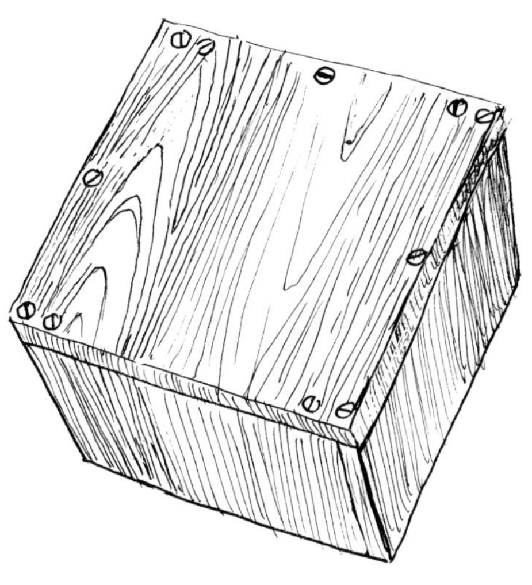

Robert Morris' *Box With the Sound of its Own Making*.

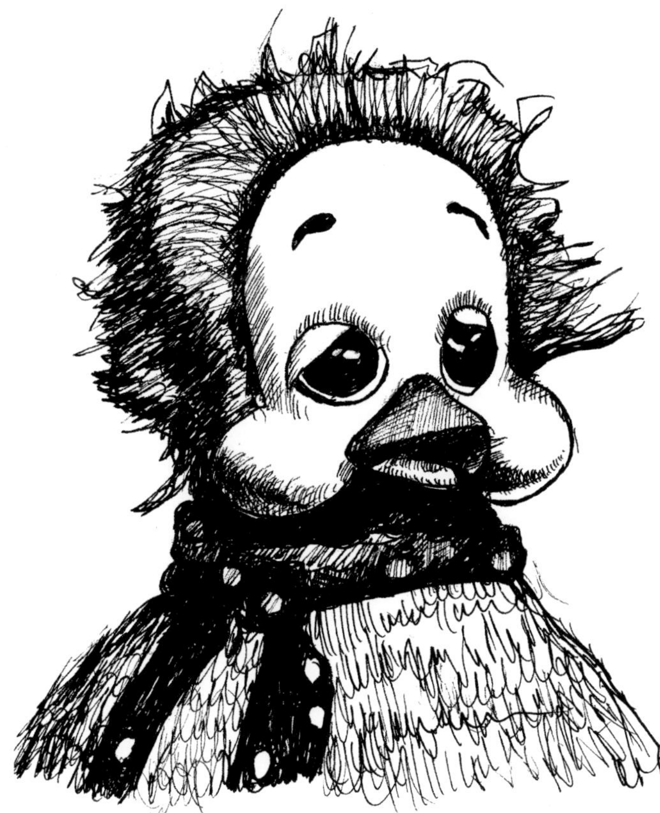

Orville.

uncanny self-portraiture demonstrated in Robert Morris' early performance work, increasingly life-like dummies began to assume a peculiar autonomy from their operators. By contrast, from the disturbingly onanistic overtones of Bob Flanagan's fetishised hand here in the guise of *Rosy Palm and her Five Lovely Daughters*, to the slew of performers themselves posing as unaccompanied dummies the unravelling of the form continued past the point of no return, like the proverbial dog chasing its own tail. It became clear that the time for simple wonderment at an illusion well-executed had passed, to be replaced by an extreme hard-edged conceptualism that was mercifully to strip the last vestiges of entertainment and humour from the form. The move was to prove unpopular with the general public however, as is perhaps most memorably evidenced by the well documented media furore that was to greet the announcement that Robert Morris' *Box With the Sound of its Own Making* had triumphed over the evergreen Keith Harris and Orville for the hotly contested ventriloquists spot at the 23rd Royal Command Variety Performance.

Minimalism was to remain a key reference point in the story of performed sculpture, if only as a mode of unfashionably object-centric sculpture-making to kick against.

One man can lay more of claim than most to toppling the unwieldy macho edifice from its dusty plinth. I refer of course to Bruce McLean. His path to global stardom proves what the human spirit can accomplish

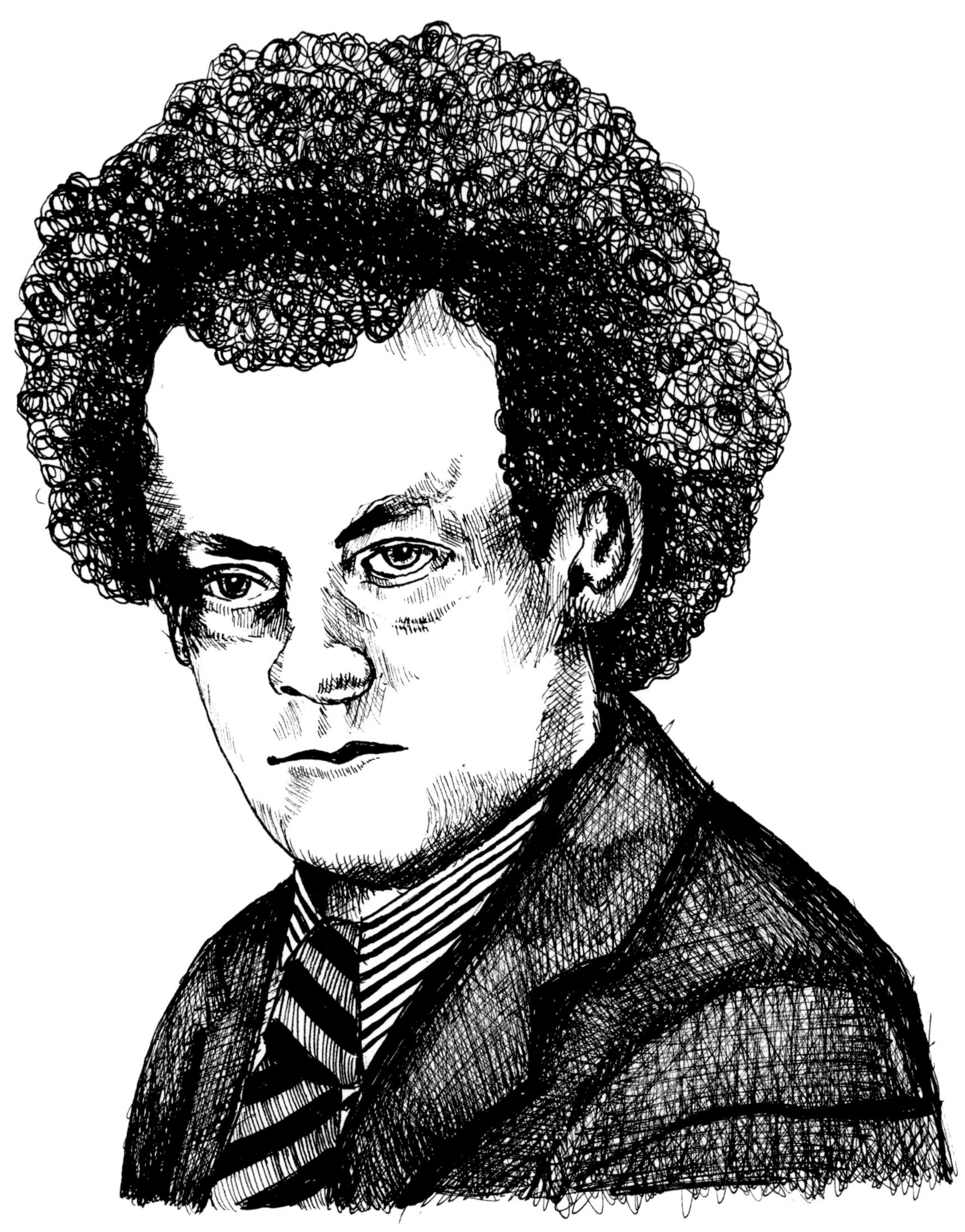

Donald Judd was slightly boss-eyed.

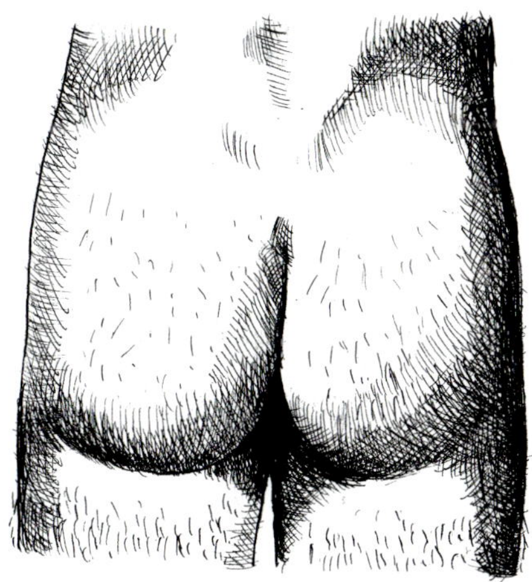

Bruce McLean.

when relentless drive and determination converge with dreams. His long and arduous journey from two-bit pub stripper collecting tips in a bucket to becoming one of the world's most accomplished and innovative artists is an inspiration to all who face overwhelming obstacles and challenges along the road to success. From the moment that influential Marxist dance quarterly *Two Left Feet* published the now-legendary centrefold of the young artist's virtuoso conceptual strip-tease under the provocative title *Beef (Jerky)*, his course was set.

"He was like Burt Reynolds, but without the moustache", recalls first wife Trisha Brown, then one of the idealistic young firebrands blazing a choreographic trail towards a dance revolution at the Judson Dance Theater. She laughs "I'd like to say I was impressed by the way he took on the pompous monumentality of plinth-based sculpture—I mean—I was, for sure—but mainly, he had a tush to die for. I couldn't put that magazine down. He was so damned hot—just suddenly the face of the moment. The behind of the times, I guess! Wow, that's terrible. Don't quote me."

Indeed, a lucrative contract with Levi's was to cash in on McLean's newfound notoriety. He was to deliver an unforgettable beefcake performance in the now infamous laundromat commercial—yes, stripping to his boxers in order to stone-wash his blue jeans to the strains of "I Heard It Through the Grapevine" was revealed to be a smart career move, earning the hunky youngster a large paypacket, and a string of high profile love affairs to boot with artworld notables including Rose Lee Goldberg, Martha Rosler and Olivia Newton John.

Few artists have succeeded without a sense of driving egotism, and McLean was no exception. His first tentative steps towards performance frequently aroused heated public debate, and often sheer confusion—the rigid stability which for decades had insisted that sculpture must be defined by the actual presence of an object was looking increasingly floppy under his unforgiving searchlight of progress. His first recorded performed sculptural work was a slap in the face for the prevailing Minimalist orthodoxy, a thrillingly anarchistic attack that was to begin a decade of tit-for-tat point scoring and bitter feuding between the Old and New schools.

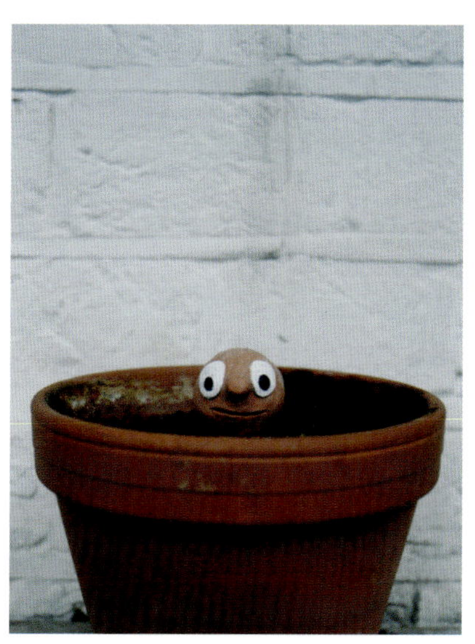

The subject of the intervention was hard-drinking failed philanderer and cheap suit haranguer Donald Judd, a man described by his own gallerist as "a man of nugatory intelligence and much unpleasantness", and by his first wife as "a nervous ugly man, swollen with petty tyranny". on the occasion of the opening of his colossal 60,000 acre theme-park in Marfa, Texas, Judd revealed a fierce temper and bull-headed resistance to new ideas by throwing an extraordinary tantrum when McLean, then a research assistant at the BBC, released helium into the recording studio during the interview. The eminent sculptor gnashed his teeth, stamped his feet and tore at his thinning hair in a hilariously Rumplestiltkinesque fit of fury. Michael Fried was later to celebrate the action in his infamous "Art and Objecthood" essay for *Private Eye:*

> Mclean has effectively slipped a giant Whoopee cushion under the ponderous backside of Minimalism, at a stroke puncturing the gargantuan egotism of Judd's dull literalist theatre. There's one artworld heavyweight who's lost a few pounds. It was like covering a toilet bowl with clingfilm and waiting for the inevitable. In art historical terms, it was a pivotal moment.

The incident was, of course, to lead to McLean's immediate dismissal from the BBC, but afforded him instant promotion to enfant terrible status. In fact, there was something about the rare mix of raw artistic talent, throbbing sensuality and humour evidenced in McLean's work that was to chime with the spirit of an age. It was the climax of the disco decade. Sex was free, and hedonism had become mainstream. Dry conceptual attitudes to sculpture were about to yield to a full-frontal attack of wry eroticism in a seismic cultural shift whose aftershocks would be felt for decades.

At the absolute epicentre of the whirlwind, the Judson Dance Theater was to play a key role in introducing the public to the thrilling New Wave of Performed Sculpture. Rejecting the confines of modern dance practice and theory, this young and vibrant company of like-minded avant-garde experimentalists began to seek out new methods of composition. Their frequently wild improvisatory workshops celebrated interdisciplinarity and more often than not drew in musicians, visual artists and theatre practitioners with explosive yet uncertain results. Absorbing aspects of ordinary pedestrian movement, the natural world and city life, they tested connections between private subject matter and theatrical expression to the limit, and reconsidered the relationship of the dancer and the prop. To critics of the avant-garde, this radical blurring of the boundaries between art and everyday life, this arrant celebration of the banal, signalled a vulgar lack of taste and the utter disintegration of art, perhaps even its disappearance. I cannot exaggerate my rage at this mixture of arid intellectualising and naive oversimplification. Influential and often controversial showbiz historian Clement Greenberg was a familiar face amongst the barflies propping up Judson's notorious cabaret bar, and a stalwart champion of the developing movement—he recalls the early days:

> Well, it was a tawdry, mucky little dive—you could barely see the stage for cigarette smoke most nights, and your feet'd stick to the carpet like they were glued. Still, it was a popular hangout for artists, and if you could tolerate lukewarm beer, and wine you wouldn't tenderise meat with, it was a giggle. Most nights there'd be some dreadful music or other—and there was usually a god-awful pianist in a moth-eaten wig and a tatty frock doing cocktail standards between the acts—she could barely keep her teeth in, the poor dear. It was the nudes that kept them coming back though.

Indeed, in a quaint and peculiar hangover from Lord Chamberlain's strict theatre licensing laws of the 1940s where nudity was permitted onstage only

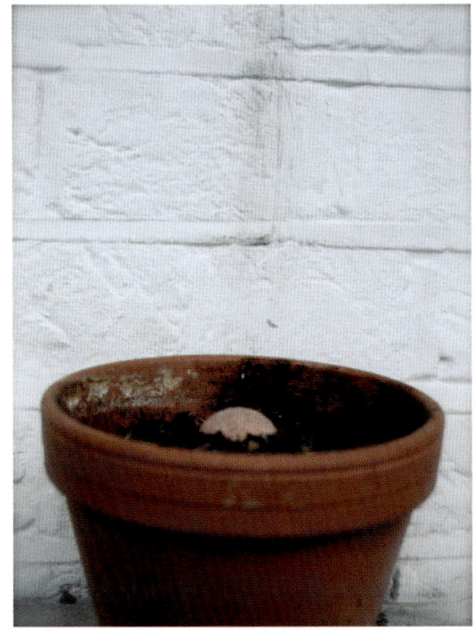

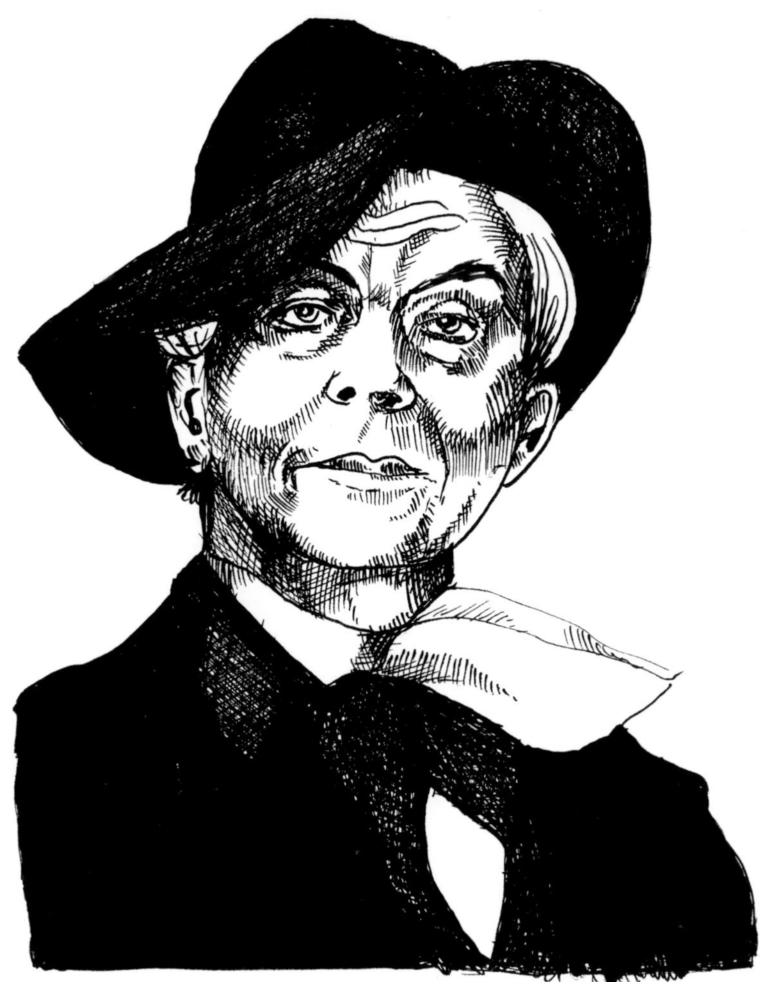

insofar as nobody moved, a troupe of *tableaux vivant artistes* were retained by the management on the condition that they took it all off three times a night and four on Sundays. Bruce McLean was to find his inspiration amidst the nimble feminine pulchritude of the group, although a series of ill-starred romantic entanglements with its various members would slow his artistic progress to a crawl in the early days—Greenberg again:

> I remember Bruce, of course. Who wouldn't? He started off as a bartender at Judson, and he just had this extraordinary magnetism, a kind of dynamic physicality—I must confess, I did rather tend to order the smoky bacon crisps from him purely on the basis that they were kept on the bottom shelf. I wasn't alone. He practically caused a riot with the first pieces he directed for the girls—just breathtakingly simple.... The curtain comes up and there's a whole series of plinths scattered around the stage, and the girls, fully clothed, mindst you, are draped over them and posing. And then there's a whole series of curtain drops and raises, and each time there's a reveal, they've changed position and shed a few

Controversial showbiz historian Clement Greenberg.

> garments. He called it *Strip of Timber* because of the wooden attitudes the girls would adopt on curtain up. The crowd went wild, of course.... For me, though, it was the later burlesque pieces that really hit home. He started incorporating young men into the *tableaux*, and then it really just came alive—in the end, it was an all male troupe, and all the better for it, in my opinion. It was frightfully sexy, but watertight as Conceptual Art. They started performing as Nice Style—the World's First Pose Band—I saw *all* of their performances at Judson Dance—they were usually themed.... There was *Strip—The Paintwork*, *Stripping with Sarcasm*, *Stripping Tap* and *Strip Lite*. Oh yes—and *Strip of Bacon*, *Stripping Yarns*, *Air Strip*, *Strip/Search*, and *Comic Strip. And Striply Come Dancing.*

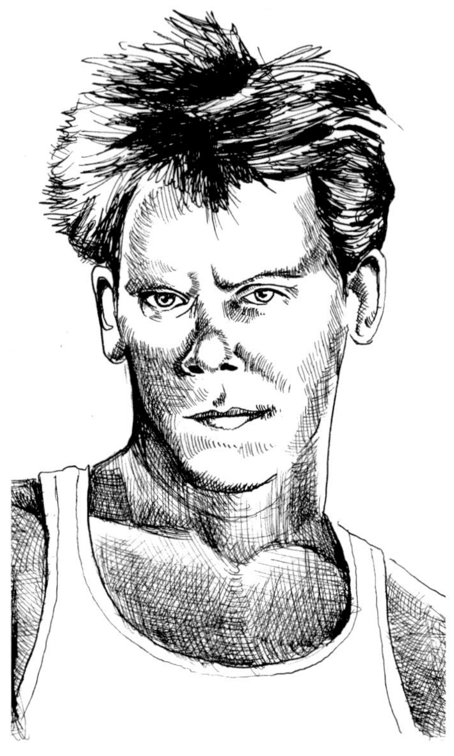

Hot-headed maverick Bruce Nauman.

There was something in McLean's infectious, energetic exuberance that was to open the door to a halcyon era at the theatre. Beginning his career as a member of Nice Style, hot-headed maverick Bruce Nauman quickly struck out on his own to produce a series of startling experimental choreographic video works in his warehouse studio that were to garner international acclaim following their screening at Judson. Following McLean's lead, an early work titled *Dancing in an Exaggerated Manner around the Perimeter of Donald Judd* issued a furious challenge to the all-pervasive Minimalist stranglehold on critical discourse. The pure white heat and vitality of his thrusting style contained a continuum of dynamic tension and release within a rigorous Conceptual framework of space investigation. It is at this early stage that the oft-repeated corridor motif first appears in Nauman's work, as an architectural cage frustrating, constraining and directing his body to test the limits of his environment. Recalling the dry Conceptualism of Mel Bochner's performative 'measurement' of objects, materials and spaces, Nauman injects a dose of virile masculinity into his videos of sliding, climbing, jumping, swinging, hanging and falling about the limits of his studio—there's a parallel here to Richard Serra's macho lead flinging, and a witty reference to his *Hand Catching Lead* film in the repetitive and relentless athleticism of Nauman's *Body Catching Air.* A later film in the studio series *Bouncing Four Balls Between the Floor and the Ceiling with Changing Rhythms* was to be the basis of a Golden Lion award winning performance at the 1982 Venice Biennale. It was the choreographic work that firmly positioned avant-garde juggling techniques and balancing feats within the lexicon of performed sculpture.

Another notable artist working in a similar vein to appear during this period was a gutsy young female dancer bent throughout her tragically short career on carving her name upon the mighty slabs of sculptural history, which incidentally are held in trust by the Henry Moore Institute in a temperature-controlled aircraft hangar in Newport Pagnell. I refer, of course, to Alex Owens, that vibrantly sexy poster girl for the Body Sculpture art movement and popular exercise phenomenon, that gifted entertainer and ferociously intellectual artist—outrageous, flamboyant and always sensational.

She was something of an unlikely art world heavyweight, a long-legged, doe-eyed *ingénue* innocent of the brute machismo of the late 1960s art scene. Nevertheless, driven by the twin engines of gargantuan ambition and the sheer pyrotechnic iconoclasm of youth, she burst onto the parched landscape of desiccated minimalist orthodoxy like a welcome monsoon of ultra-feminine sensuality. Possessed of a Herculean energy, she burned the candle of her genius at both ends to shed a light to rival the most brilliant stars in the artistic firmament. But like all fierce visionaries, she was nevertheless living on borrowed time, running on empty and about to go over the cliff.

I first met her in 1974, but her wacky antics, lilting voice and whooping laugh—together with a reputation for having the filthiest mouth in the art world—had made her a legend long before then. By the time I first saw her on a mixed bill at the Putney Hippodrome, she had already succeeded in scissor-kicking her way into the national consciousness via a series of audacious conceptual performances and bold sculptural works that were to turn this critic's outdated notion of ideal feminine beauty on its head. Her amazing mastery of technique was thrilling to behold, and marked her out from the other lesser sculptors that night—amongst a complex animated set of spinning plates, and dressed in a drab floral apron and smock, the artist balanced a series of increasingly large domestic objects on her face, including a sink plunger, vacuum cleaner, armchair, and 12 piece Wedgewood dinner service, all whilst hula hooping and comically gurning with a trim grotesque flexibility. The piece was an utter triumph, a complex critique of commodified versions of women's roles in society—the comical symbolism of the increasingly oppressive household objects bearing down on the hapless Owens was not lost to the suitably appreciative audience.

For her third and final encore, she performed a now legendary juggling routine, where her extraordinary ability to throw progressively more complex geometric shapes throughout was made all the more gripping by being simultaneously combined with the energetic choreographic spectacle of a fast-paced on-the-spot Irish themed jig in an ironic nod to Michael Flatley's 'Feet of Flame'. The atmosphere was palpably electric as she began with the simple elegance of *Throwing Three Balls in the Air to get a Equilateral Triangle* and progressed through to the set piece *Throwing Four Balls in the Air to get a Square* then determinedly onwards to the delicately nuanced emotional highpoint of *Throwing Ten Balls in the Air to get a Star.* The unforgettable and hilarious climax to the work couldn't fail to bring the house down—I refer, of course, to the devastating *Throwing Twelve Balls in the Air to get an Icosahedron.* The audience erupted into a spontaneous standing ovation that was to last some 23 minutes. I gave her the greatest tribute a critic can possibly bestow on an artist: I laughed so hard I wet my pants. In the years that followed, I made it a point to see her performances again and again.

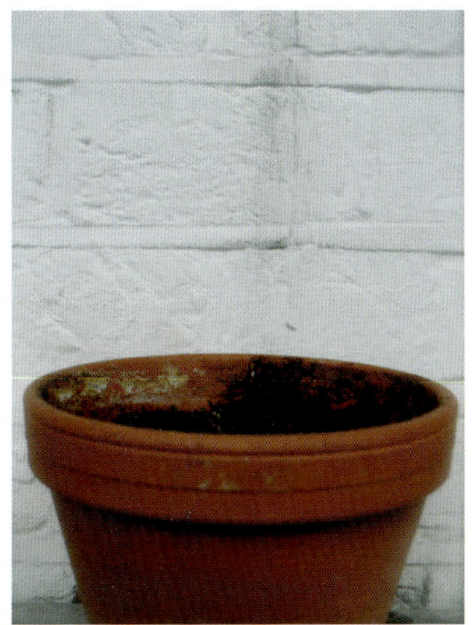

My trousers remained dry, but I never stopped laughing, and marveling… and thinking. The theme of juggling and balancing was to become something a recurrent motif in subsequent performances by Owens, both for live audiences, and for the camera. The iconic *On Board* was contrived through a complex balance between weight and gravity—the artist suspended her body

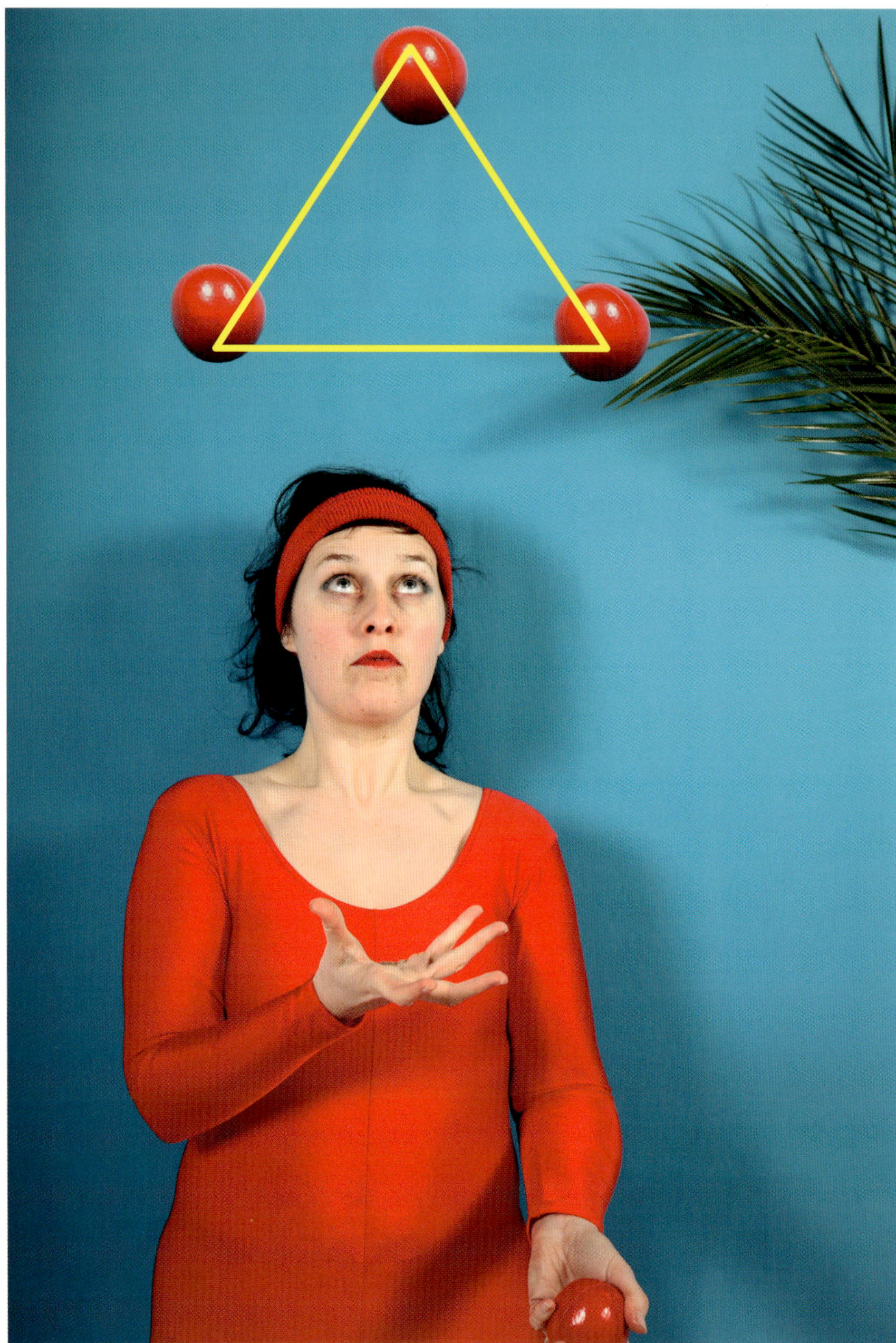

Mel Brimfield, produced in association with Joanna Neary and Edward Moore, *Throwing Three Balls in the Air to get an Equilateral Triangle*, 2010, C-print, Acetate overlay with electrical tape, 12 x 8 in. / 20.32 x 30.48 cm. Image courtesy the artist and Ceri Hand Gallery.

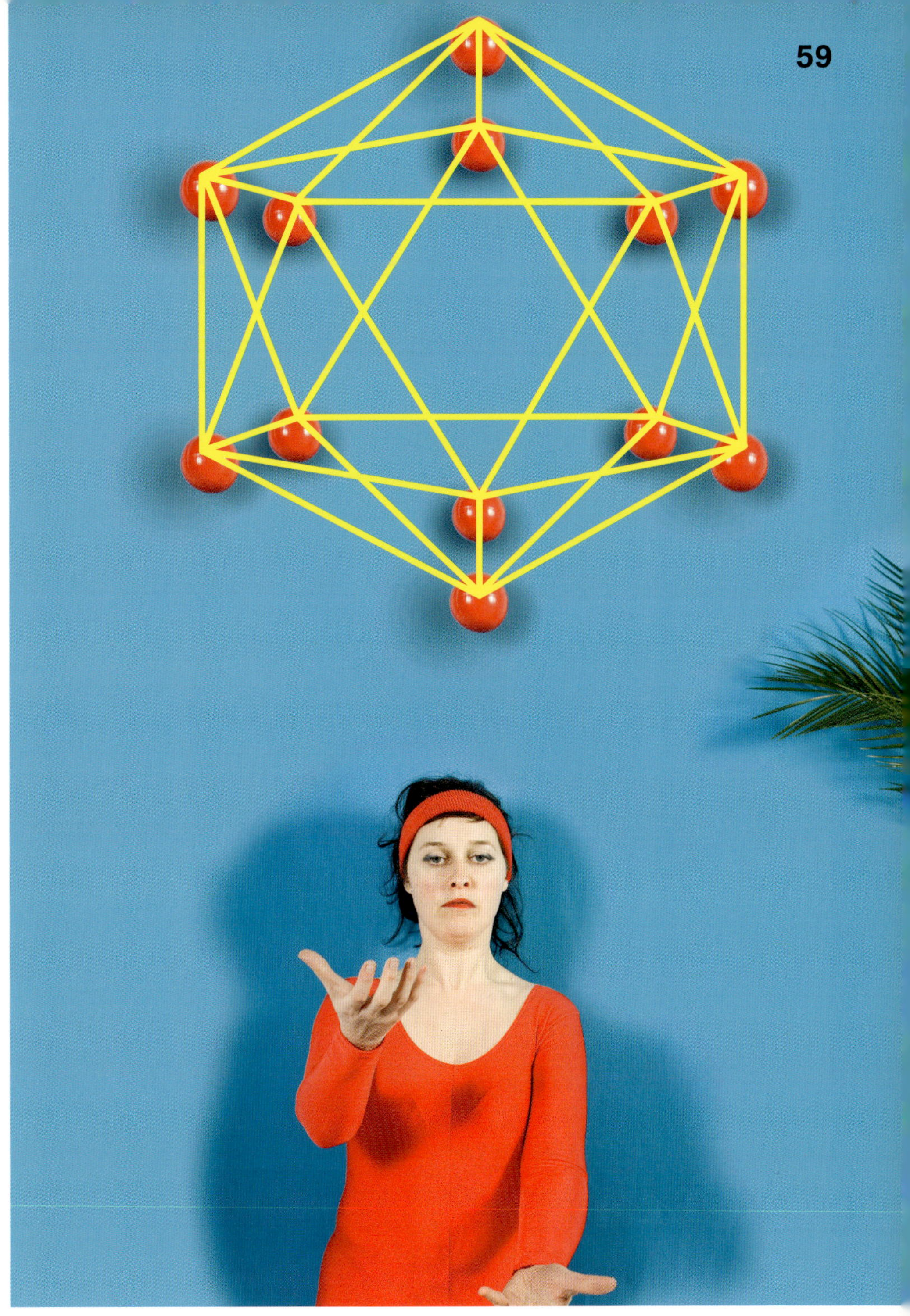

Mel Brimfield, produced in association with Joanna Meary and Edward Moore, *Throwing Twelve Balls in the Air to get an Icosahedron*, 2010, C-print, Acetate overlay with electrical tape, 19.4 x 12.9 in. / 49.28 x 32.86 cm. Image courtesy the artist and Ceri Hand Gallery.

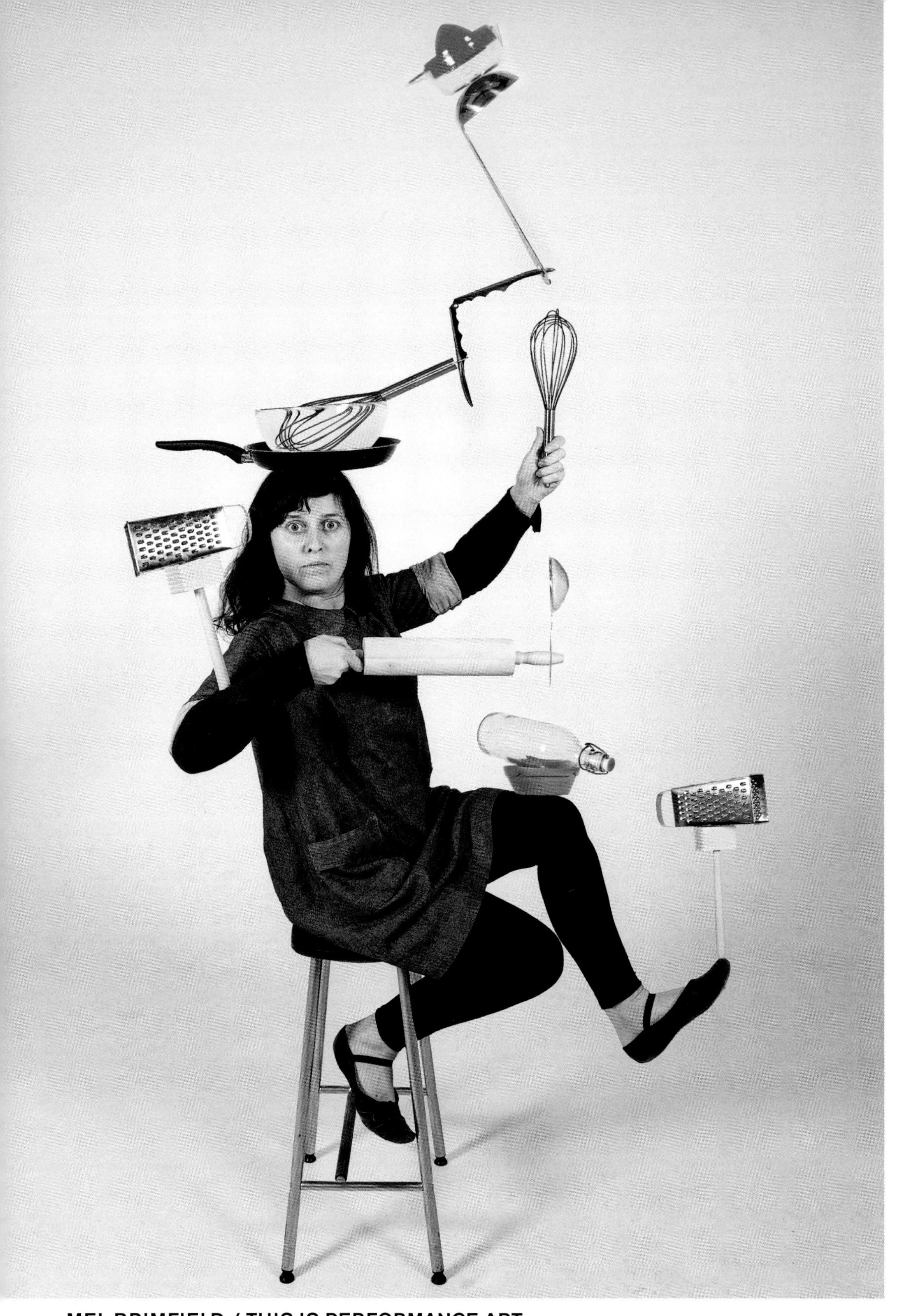

MEL BRIMFIELD / THIS IS PERFORMANCE ART

using only an ironing board, creating a minimal, graphic image that is at once humourous and unsettling. The static photograph belies the performative nature of the activity presented, and reads as both an impressive physical feat, and a symbolic representation of the domestic oppression of women.

The Semiotics of the Kitchen similarly challenges the taken-for-granted role of happy housewife and selfless producer, subverting the familiar signs of domestic industry and food production in a work of hilarious feminist parody. Indeed, her continued experiments with object and sculpture-based performances revealed an increasingly polemical stance towards the site of the feminine body—in an extraordinary series of transformations over eight years, Owens was to undergo rigorous and often excruciating exercise and weight-lifting regimes, intending to rewrite a critical history of Western civilisation upon her body. In one of her most notorious actions, titled *Out of Arm's Way*, she spent 12 months building the strength and muscle tone of only her right arm until it resembled the exact dimensions of Arnold Schwarzenegger's corresponding limb in box-office smash *Conan the Barbarian*. These extremes of shaping and modifying physicality as sculptural project reached a zenith when in a final radical act, Owens persuaded a group of like-minded female sculptors to join her in becoming morbidly obese through a dedicated programme of gluttony and inactivity to form revolutionary feminist dance troupe The Roly Polys.

From the outset, their work was the subject of hot controversy within the media. Like Bruce McLean before them, the girls were catapulted into the limelight via a breakthrough photoshoot for the cover of the all-time best-selling Fat Feminist Issue of *Two Left Feet*. Conceived as a celebratory paean to their newly acquired fleshly super-abundance, and flipping the V's to Western art historical traditions of shapely female nudes arranged for an appreciate male gaze, the piece combined extraordinarily limber dexterity with technical finesse and baroque flourish. The chubby octet experimented with avant-garde choreographic techniques first seen at the Judson Dance Theater; adhering firmly to chance methodology and task-oriented rule games to extend the range of movement outside of traditional guidelines, the group devised a suitably off-the-wall approach to presenting a series of performed sculptures for the camera.

The work was performed on a large plastic mat spread on the floor, marked with four rows of large vividly coloured circles on it, with a different colour in each row—emerald green, canary yellow, sky blue and scarlet. The title of the piece was *Twister*, presumably echoing the complex arrangements of overlapping and interlocking limbs, themselves arbitrarily dictated by a kind of rudimentary spinner. In a peculiar postscript, The Roly Polys were forced to enter into a complex series of extended intellectual property litigations when global games manufacturer Hasbro seized upon the format to launch a toy fad phenomenon the likes of which hadn't been experienced since the invention of the hula hoop—they settled out of court for an undisclosed sum, and in so doing, lit the touch paper that was to fire the public imagination towards acceptance of performed sculpture as a mainstream format.

Mel Brimfield, *The Semiotics of the Kitchen*, 2011, C-print, 29 x 19.5 in. / 73.7 x 49.5 cm. Image courtesy the artist and Ceri Hand Gallery. Private collection.

Indeed, offers flooded in during the following two years from all corners of the art and entertainment worlds, comprising invites to devise new work for performances, exhibitions and photoshoots, adding up to an extraordinarily prolific period for the troupe. Owens herself was to become the particular focus of intense media scrutiny. As choreographer Trisha Brown recalls, "There was something about her. She just had this amazing mastery of technique. It's pretty hard to put a sock on when you're standing on your head, but she could do it, you know? She knocked me out from day one."

Perhaps the defining moment of Owens' career was the tightly choreographed piece that was to mark the extraordinary metamorphosis of the Roly Polys into the new 'Hot Gossip' troupe—it was co-commissioned by BBC Two and the Tate as part of the influential *Out of the Box* programme of live dance broadcasts referencing minimalist sculpture. *Cubular Belles* stands as a work of joyous certainty, performed by an artist at the peak of her powers. Again, the Henry Moore Institute were to host the landmark event—Sir Francis Spalding was, of course, in the audience for the transmission, and wrote the following rave review for *Two Left Feet*:

> Miss Owens amply filled her trademark sea green and pastel aqua shellsuit as she powered onto the floodlit stage to the self-evident delight of the invited A-list studio audience, whose stamping, whooping and hollering didn't let up for a full seven minutes. Bowing briefly to accept the accolade, the feisty fatty proceeded to execute three perfect bulk-juddering-back flips to the strains of "Let's Get Physical" into the midst of her fellow shellsuit-clad Roly Polys, already onstage and jogging rapidly on the spot, and holding large cube structures rigidly above their heads. Using a headset mic, Owens bellowed instructions to her crew in the manner of a manic aerobics instructor, such as 'Find it—feel it—do it—work—and work—and work—that's right—let me hear your body talk.' In perfect syncopation, the troupe combined leg movements going through a range of extraordinary pretzel mutations and high fast extensions with serialised marching passages, flat-arm flings, long jet-stride walks, vibrations and wide zingy turns on and around the cube structures in a wildly energetic high impact 'workout'-like routine.

On cue, at the beginning of each chorus, these highly regulated sections dissolved into something altogether freer, with the troupe whipping the cubes out from under their own feet to rush upstage and central to add a block to a slowly-forming giant Rubik's Cube. In one of the most talked-about finales in choreographic history, the tubby dancers formed a line in front of the now complete sculpture, and in one smoothly executed yank ripped off their own Velcro-fastened shellsuits, now revealed to be massively padded to give the illusion of obesity. Underneath, their newly toned athletic bodies resplendent in scarlet satin lycra unitards provoked an astonished and spontaneous standing ovation, especially when one after the other, the dancers turned and bent over—each perfectly

Mel Brimfield, *Cubular Belles*, 2010, Gouache on paper, 19.3 x 14.2 in. / 49 x 36 cm. Image courtesy the artist and Ceri Hand Gallery. Collection of Leeds Art Galleries.

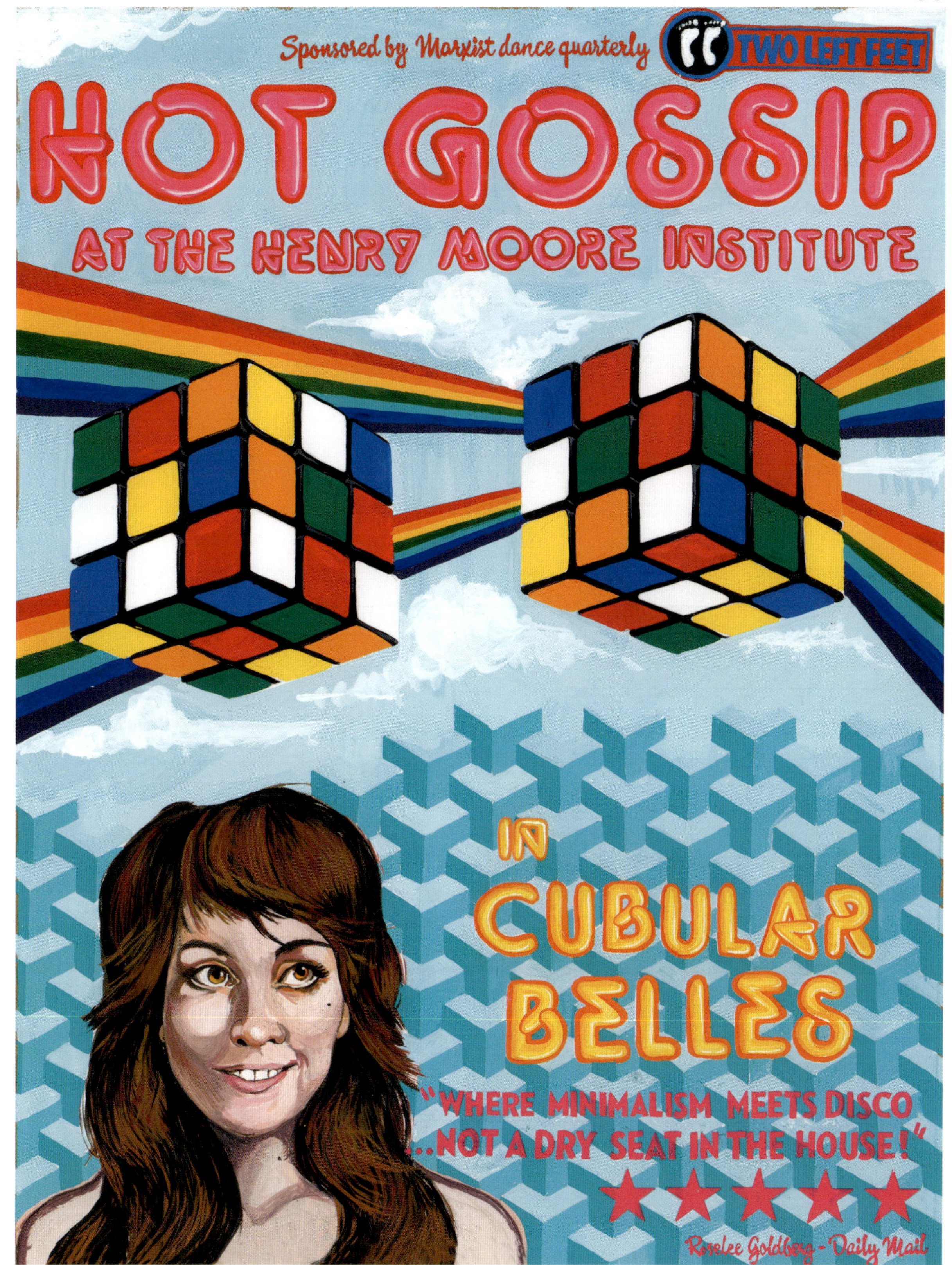

THIS IS PERFORMANCE ART—PART ONE

shaped backside carried a letter—when lined up, those backsides spelled out both "Hot Gossip", and a new dawn in performed sculptural history. In a dramatic change of pace, and to the accompaniment of a solemn funereal dirge, Owens closed the performance by wheeling a giant trolley full of fat representing the troupe's collective weight loss across the stage, some 402 pounds, demonstrating both staggering upper body strength and strong emotion in her grunty physical exertions.

The ensuing media furore was unprecedented, with angry feminists on both sides simultaneously celebrating and decrying the action—opinion was sharply divided as to the conceptual integrity of the troupe's transformation. Joseph Beuys was an unexpected advocate of the new direction—indeed, the influence of the *Cubular Belles* piece is evident in his own experiments with fat as a medium in the months following his attendance of the performance. In the following months, Owens was to publish the revolutionary *Body/Sculpture* exercise plan that was to establish her reputation as both an exercise guru and an interstellar art superstar. In a series of beautifully produced photographs functioning both as cutting edge aesthetic experiments in performed sculpture, and as clearly diagramatic instruction for effective weight-loss, toning and muscle strengthening, Owens was to irrevocably change the public perception of the artists role in society.

The physical and emotional demands of her gruelling practice were inevitably to take their toll. As a consequence of the excrutiating yo-yo weight gains and losses neccessitated by her unwavering artistic vision, she was left with a weakened heart, and died whilst jogging shortly before the release of her final book *The Complete Book of Running*, still, incidentally, the best-selling non-fiction hardcover ever. The flame of a phenomenal talent was finally resolutely snuffed. I have contributed the screenplay for the forthcoming biopic of Alex Owens, directed by Hans Namuth—it is scheduled for a summer release. I leave you with a clip where the artist, played to devastating effect by Jennifer Beales, first makes the connection between Minimalism and dance. See you next week....

This is Performance Art—Part One: Performed Sculpture and Dance, produced and screened at Camden Arts Centre, and exhibited at Yorkshire Sculpture Park, 2011. Written by Mel Brimfield, voiceover performed by Brian Dewan and Sir Francis Spalding.

Mel Brimfield, produced in association with Joanna Neary and Edward Moore, *Pose Work for Balls,* 2010, Colour photograph, 44.1 x 24.8 in. / 112 x 63 cm. Image courtesy the artist and Ceri Hand Gallery.

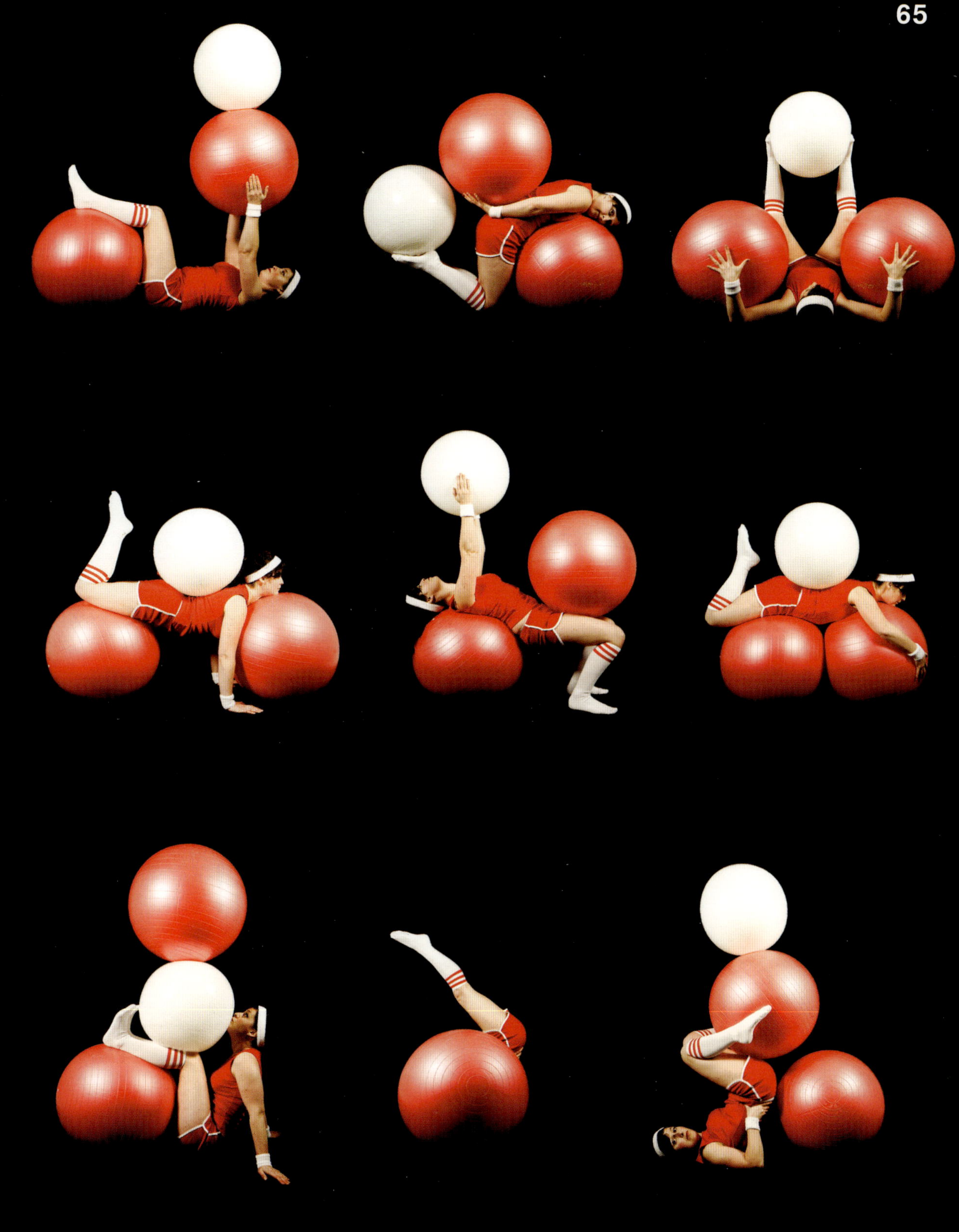

A conversation between Mel Brimfield and Ceri Hand

Ceri Hand: Why do you involve such an extraordinary range of performers in your work?

Mel Brimfield: On a basic level, it's down to enthusiasm—I'm always looking for people to join in. I'm irresistibly attracted to virtuosity of all kinds, and can't help but try and recruit it when I come across it. Sometimes it takes years to figure out the right shape of project to propose to a potential collaborator, and in the meantime I keep on adding to a rolling wish list of future conspirators. I operated as a freelance curator making large-scale interdisciplinary projects for a good seven or eight years before I began making my own artwork again—I stopped after I finished my MA at Chelsea in 2000. During that time I made short films, recordings and broadcasts, performances and publications with scores of artists, actors, writers, comedians and dancers. I became fairly adept at structuring legible formats that allowed for considerable risk-taking, and variable outcomes. I think the expansiveness of my approach was something that people responded to—certainly, the ambition and scale of those projects has stood me in good stead since. I've gone on to work with many of the participants in a more involved way, so it was a really good testing ground. It's made me pretty fearless about putting on big productions.

CH: The Socialist magician, the Italian Olympic gymnast, the colliery band, the Karen Carpenter tribute act, the troupe of dancing girls, the ventriloquist, your list of past collaborators looks like an episode of *Opportunity Knocks!*

MB: Yes—in many ways, I do see myself as a cigar-chomping showbiz impresario booking 'the talent'. The idea of Variety Theatre is somehow quite central to most of my practice. Formally, the notion of bringing together lots of disparate acts on a mixed bill appeals. There are all sorts of tantalising publicity photographs and lovely ephemera relating to amazing acts that toured the same turn for years—I love the aesthetics of those materials; the typography, the design, the costumes and props, the language of the promotional blurb. There are really only a small amount of audio and film fragments to sift through—they document the tail end of Variety as radio and TV took over, so you largely have to rely on anecdotal accounts. There's a parallel there to the notoriously slippery history of performance art, and the way it's impossible to form an objective overview when the documentation is so partial. That similarity is one of the things that make my fictional histories at least partially plausible.

CH: You reference the ways in which live art is institutionally assimilated very specifically in the *This Is Performance Art* series. It reads less like critique, somehow, and more like a suggestion of an alternative approach to the process. Is it your intention to open up dialogues in that area?

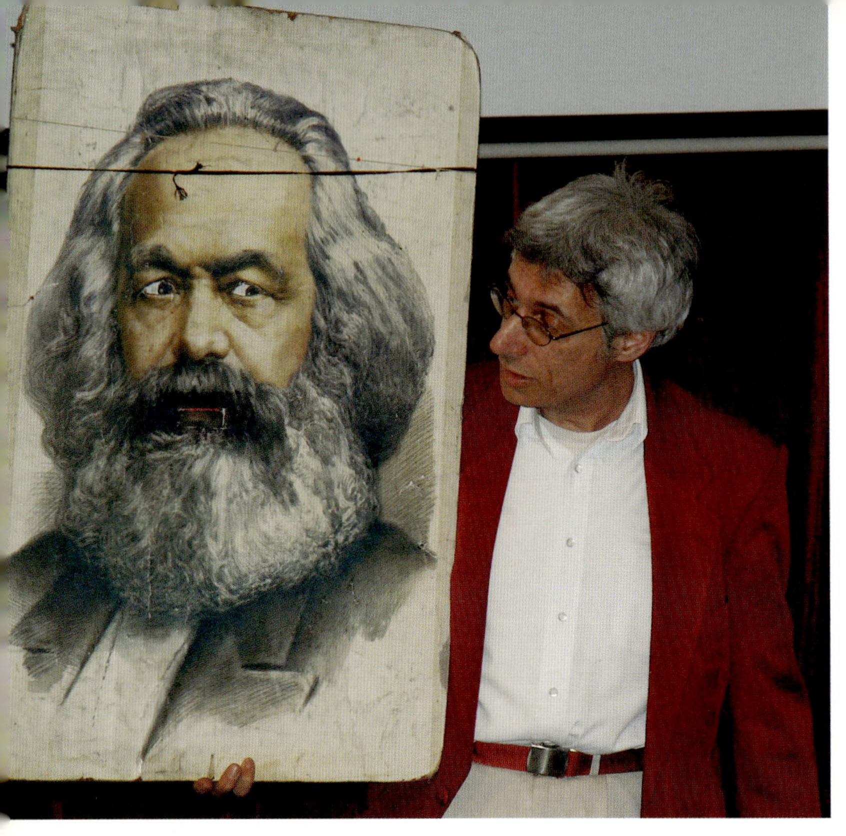

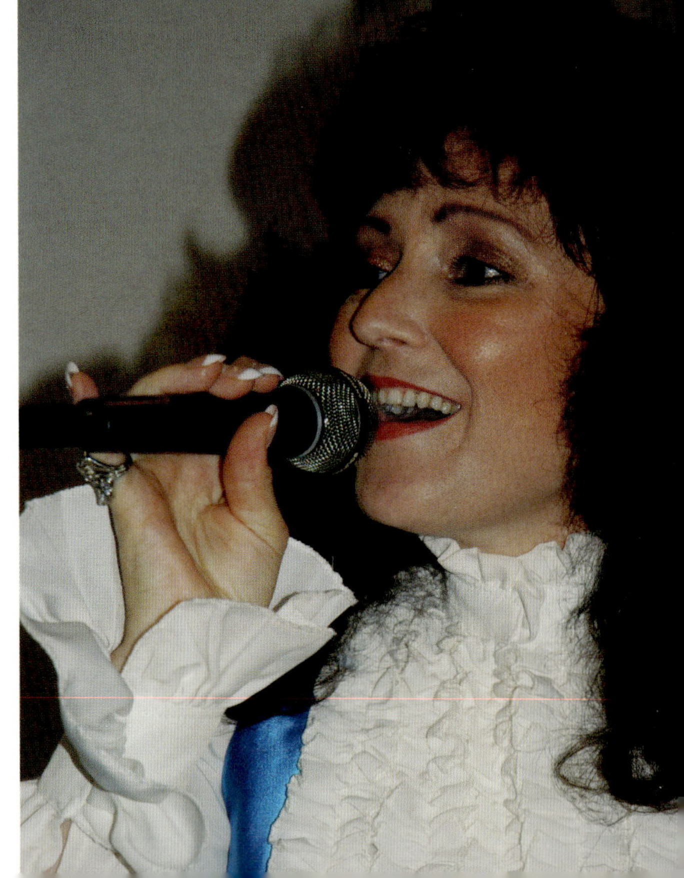

TOP

Socialist magician Ian Saville performs *The Karl Marx Card Prediction Trick* at the Brown Mountain Cabaret of Curiosities fundraiser, 2009.

BOTTOM

Karen Carpenter impersonator performs at the opening of The Golden Record—Sounds of Earth at the Collective Gallery, Edinburgh Festival, 2008.

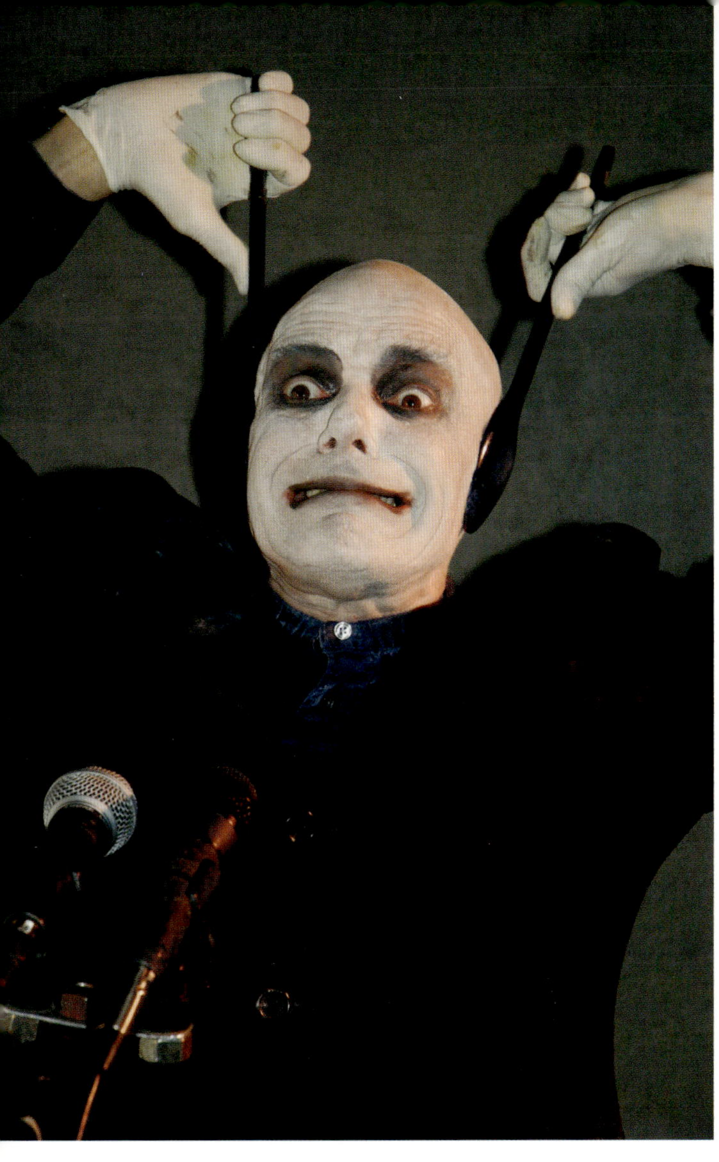

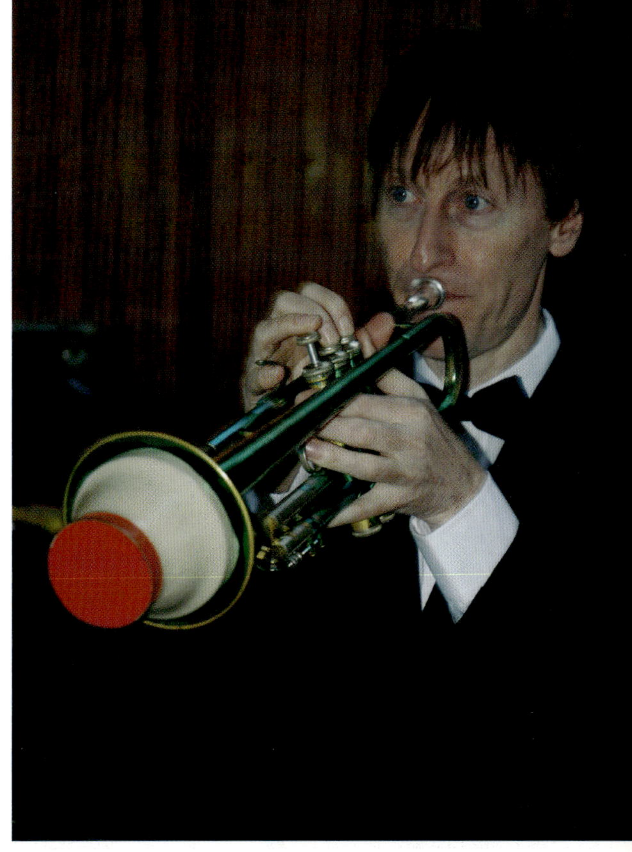

TOP

Andrew Bailey demonstrates *The Russian Space Programme—The Early Years* in a video for The Golden Record—Sounds of Earth, The Collective Gallery, Edinburgh Festival 2008.

BOTTOM

Composer and musician Paul Higgs, is the musical director for the *This Is Performance Art* live series.

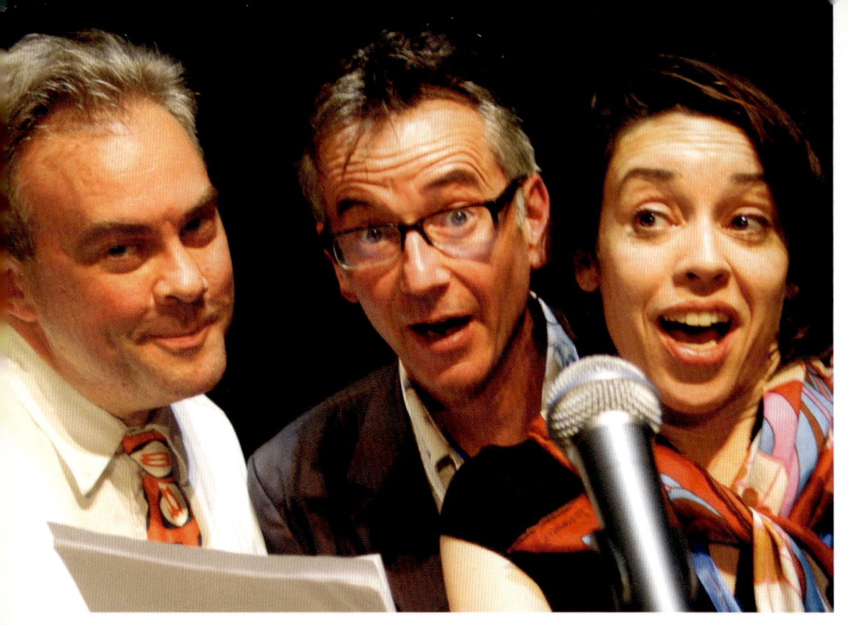

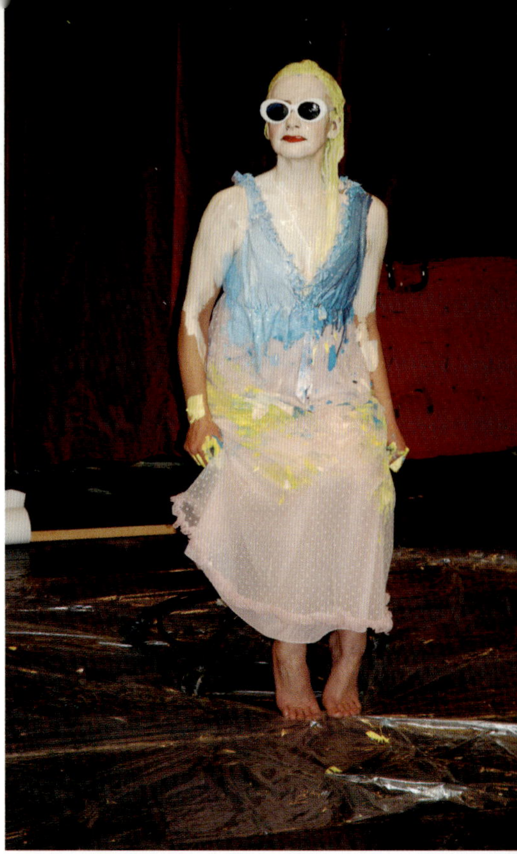

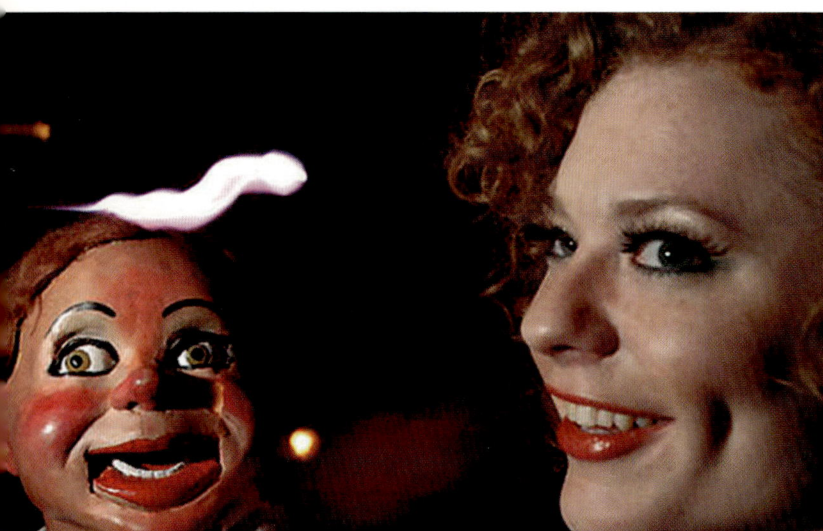

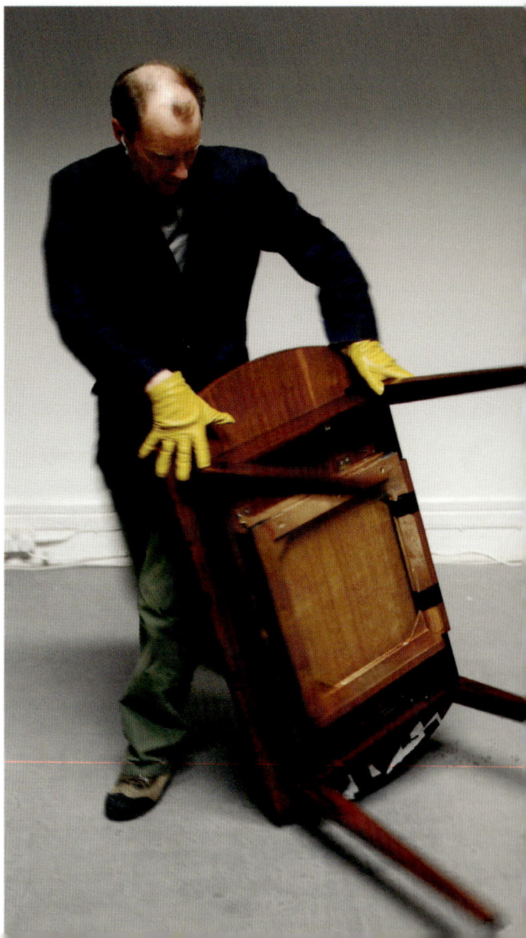

MEL BRIMFIELD / THIS IS PERFORMANCE ART

MB: Discussions of the appropriateness of the ways in which performance histories are evaluated has been a big part of critical discourse for a long time—in the middle of that is the thorny issue of performance documentation, and I'm very interested in those discussions, and particularly in art and theatre practice that addresses it. I read Peggy Phelan's *Unmarked* text at an early stage in my research, like everyone else—there's one phrase that had particular resonance for me: "Performance's only life is in the present. Performance cannot be saved, recorded, documented or otherwise participate in the circulation of representations: once it does so, it becomes something other than performance." It was the provocation for a lot of what followed for me, especially in the development of a devising technique for performance that's actively based on figuring and refiguring documentation of it before, during and after the staging. I'm making her 'something other', I guess—I want to change the ways in which those 'circulations of representations' operate. There's a lot of research activity around performative approaches to documentation anyway, of course.

CH: Your method is a bit like making a performance backwards, isn't it? You imagine the documentation and art historical context for it as a direct part of the making process. You're inserting more fragmented evidence into the continuum, and joining up cultural moments that might initially appear to have nothing in common in the process?

MB: That's the aim, and also as a practical collaborative structure for working with a really wide variety of performers belonging in different fields, and used to different devising techniques, it works. I set up *This Is Performance Art* as a structure to support comprehensible development of the interdisciplinary performance work I wanted to make—it makes the parameters of the work clear to the collaborators and the audience. It seemed that aping the curatorial strategies of institutions and their interpretative materials was an economical way of foregrounding the understated links with activism, theatre, comedy, music and dance in live art history. I'd become quite frustrated with what I saw at the time as a total focus in the UK on body, gender and identity politics, in both institutional accounts of performance history and the commissioning of new live work; there seemed to be a fairly big division between gallery artists and live artists. I'd set up Brown Mountain College of the Performing Arts with writer Sally O'Reilly and producer Ben Roberts in an effort to think about curatorial modes that might address the lack of appropriate platforms for development of interdisciplinary work. It was through our various projects that I began to realise that I was becoming preoccupied with making elaborate contexts for staging other people's work, and not interested so much in the curating and presentation of that work as an end in itself. The structure of *This Is Performance Art* definitely stemmed from that experience.

CH: Sir Francis Spalding has, from the beginning, seemed to occupy a central position in your thinking about the project. In fact, you've built up a kind of repertory company for *This Is Performance Art* that he's in the middle

OPPOSITE TOP LEFT

Artist Brian Dewan, poet John Hegley and actress Chris Entwisle perform *The Yellowjacket* at The Traverse Theatre, as part of *The Comic Book* performance programme, presented in association with The Collective Gallery, 2008.

OPPOSITE TOP RIGHT

Artist Boo Ritson performs at the Brown Mountain College Cabaret of Curiosities fundraiser at the Royal Academy of Art, 2008.

OPPOSITE BOTTOM LEFT

New York ventriloquist Carla Rhodes and Cecil describe termites to aliens in a short film made for The Golden Record—Sounds of Earth, the Collective Gallery, Edinburgh Festival, 2008.

OPPOSITE BOTTOM RIGHT

Artist Jefford Horrigan in rehearsal for The Brown Mountain Festival of the Performing Arts, Slade Research Centre, London, 2008.

of—is there a particular reason for featuring some collaborators repeatedly in your various productions?

MB: Sir Francis is an important device for introducing the context and art historical pointers for my work in a legible way—humour for me is an essential part of hanging a lot of complicated ideas and references together with economy, so the use of stereotypical characters and recognisable formats is part of that. He's an overblown grotesque, a sort of Alan Partridge of cultural commentators. He's an inflated amalgam of Ned Sherrin, Kenneth Tynan and Kenneth Williams. He's insufferably self-congratulatory, and is continually peppering his commentaries with half-remembered anecdotes, misunderstood critical theories and absurd metaphors; the scripts for the character are purposefully over-written and pompous. All in all, he's the most familiar kind of mouthpiece for delivery of authoritative histories, so he's the common element to all of the presentations in the series. It's exciting when collaborations develop into more long-standing creative relationships—Tony Green is the actor who plays Sir Francis, and being able to anticipate his range makes the script-writing much more effective—he has an extraordinary range of voices at his disposal. Composer Paul Higgs has been the musical director on all of the largest of the productions so far, and we'll continue to work together—he's a superb arranger, pianist, trumpet player, all round genius, really—and his background in theatre makes him key to the process of devising, rehearsing and working out the staging, and managing musicians. He contributes a lot to the distinctive high level of production I feel it's necessary to achieve for the performances. The Beaux Belles for *This Is Performance Art* are a bit like Hot Gossip for Kenny Everett, or The Roly Polys for Les Dawson. It's gloriously camp to have a troupe of dancing girls cropping up repeatedly, and it's a Variety convention. Adopting the polished aesthetics of mainstream entertainment formats also underlines the serious intent of the project to examine other performance histories than those traditionally posited by the conventional live art canon. I think there's quite a broad range of curators, theatre producers and festival programmers interested in blurring those distinctions now—it's interesting to think of audiences merging and what that might mean for artists.

CH: It seems apt that you mention Alan Partridge—the way you cram together figures from lots of cultural fields at once reminds me of chat shows at times....

MB: I reference old-fashioned showbiz puffery of various kinds frequently, and there certainly was a lot of it on TV chat shows when I was growing up—Terry Wogan, Russell Harty, Michael Parkinson... I find the overtly staged nature of the 'chat' appealing. The guests are there because they have something to plug, and perhaps a couple of specific anecdotes to tell, and the host has to steer the conversation between those points and make it all sound as natural as possible. The greasiness of it all lends itself to spoofing fairly irresistibly, and Partridge is funny partly because he's so bad at doing

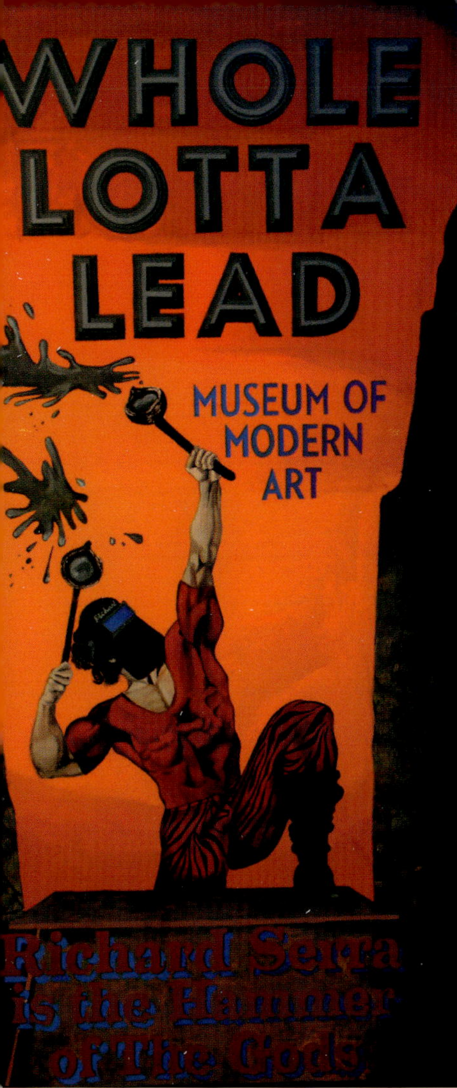

Mel Brimfield, *Whole Lotta Lead*, 2010, Gouache on board, 45.7 x 27.6 in. / 116 x 70 cm. Image courtesy the artist and Ceri Hand Gallery.

it with any degree of skill. Sir Francis is similarly unable to exercise any degree of objectivity in his accounts of performance history, and is caught up in the mythologies and gossip circulating around the artists involved in it. His tone is borrowed from low-end showbiz memoirs and hyperbolic press releases, but applied to 'serious' arts broadcasting formats—in developing the style of *This Is Performance Art*, I've been very influenced by landmark arts broadcasting like *Monitor*, *Face To Face* and *The South Bank Show* too—it's the kind of programming that sets out to be educational, but can't help but be part of the machinery of mythologising artists and their place in culture, especially retrospectively. As soon as a biographical or psychological aspect is introduced to coverage of an artist's work, those formats start to run on parallel tracks to the populist chat show in a way.

CH: You're underlining the idea that these mythologies have some kind of cultural value, perhaps, in some of your exaggerated fictionalising?

MB: Yes—perhaps the role of myth here is to introduce some sort of continuity—these recurring stories lend a kind of knowable frame through which we can start to contextualise new cultural phenomena. Or maybe it just comes down to natural or prurient interest in other people's lives—it's hard to say, but the persistence of certain myths is undeniable. For instance, the idea of the tragic alcoholic/drug-addled/promiscuous/mentally ill genius living on the fringes of society and suffering for his or her art is amongst the most persistent… Van Gogh, Hemmingway, Pollock, Modigliani, Emin… Winehouse! I suppose as a subject matter it inevitably starts to back into celebrity culture, but that's not particularly relevant to the work. It makes my fictions more plausible to use exaggerated versions of those myths.

CH: You seem particularly intent on puncturing the bubble of macho posturing that often goes with the myth of being a 'great artist'. So in your account, Richard Serra is an almost cartoon-like figure of masculinity: over-muscled, oiled up, clad in leopard skin strides and massive motorcycle boots, waving crucibles full of molten lead about… you even go as far as to cast a male stripper as Serra for a series of photographs.

MB: There's something about massive serious sculpture that I find particularly funny, also the fact that most often it's men who make it. I suppose it's partly because you really have to mean it—the elaborate fabrication processes, the transport, the budget needed for it all, the unveiling. What if it's rubbish when it's finished? Some of it must be, and everyone involved must know it. The potential for artists' hubris is enormous, and that's an appealing comic situation. It all reminds me of the bit in *Spinal Tap* when the miniature Stonehenge descends onto the stage. I'd been looking at photos of Serra at work on his lead-throwing series at Leo Castelli's warehouse, and they seemed to suggest the cheesy romantic idea of the artist as conduit of violent creative passion, and the studio as some sort of theatre of dramatic conflict. The reality of it is mindnumbingly dull, of course. It made me think of scenes from naff fantasy illustration like Boris Vallejo (who I love) with buff adventurers at the forge burnishing their swords—it's weird how quickly images of hyper-masculine bodies veer into campery, completely devoid of any plausible heterosexual content—sexualised images of women can't be funny very easily. I was stuck then with the idea that The Sculptor was a good stripping character—the leather apron, the boots, the gauntlets, the mask—and that presenting Serra that way really underlines the ludicrousness of that ultra-macho action man figure in sculptural history. And then of course there's an obvious similarity to Hans Namuth's photographs of Jackson Pollock.

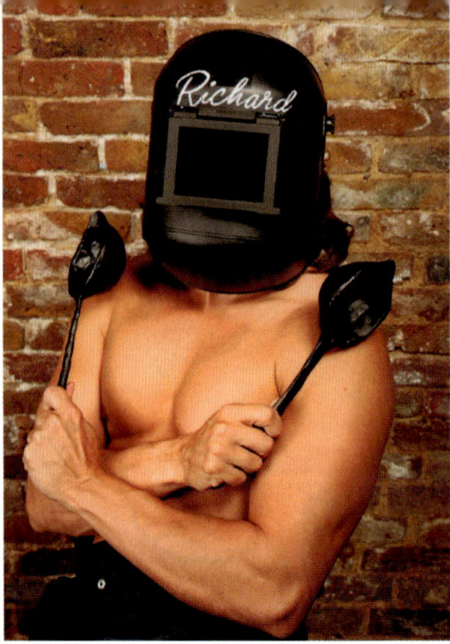

Male stripper Sexecute Nick Molloy as Richard Serra.

CH: Namuth's series really represents some of the most enduring images of a great artist at work in the studio, doesn't it? He's presented as a force of nature, flinging paint around with great intensity, hard-drinking, chain-smoking, black T-shirt, denims and work boots, leaning on the running board of his pick-up truck looking brooding and melancholy....

MB: It's back to the tragic genius bent on self-destruction myth, isn't it? I've been obsessed with Pollock since my very earliest days as an art student. It's not his work, though that comes into it in a roundabout way... it's the extraordinary volume of hilarious hyperbolic biographical writing around him, even in supposedly straight academic texts—I've collected a whole stack of them over the years, beginning with that famous 1950s *Life* magazine article titled "Is He the Greatest Living Painter in the US?"—that's where those Namuth photographs were first published; it's interesting that they're right up in the top hits when you do a Google image search on Pollock, ahead of a lot of his most famous paintings. I'm particularly drawn to the various accounts of how he 'invents' the drip technique and singlehandedly changes the face of Western Art—obviously it's a construct—there were other painters who dripped before, it was a logical progression of Abstract Expressionism, etc., etc.,—but the romantic conviction a lot of writers bring to it is a delight. They have it variously as the result of a late-night drunken rage brought on by lack of drawing skill or intelligence or even an inability to get it up, or a response to early memories of his macho father pissing patterns onto a flat rock, as the gesture of a cowboy frontiersman lassoing an imaginary steer—all real. I love the daftness of presenting an identifiable pivotal moment where everything clicks into place in a narrative—it's so clearly illusory, and yet somehow the neatness of it is really appealing when you're faced with the sloppy mess of history. I remember watching Ed Harris' Pollock biopic and really waiting for that inevitable 'first drip' scene. The same brilliant quotes come up over and over again too—like Hans Hofmann suggesting he should work more from nature, and him apparently replying "I don't paint nature. I AM nature." Or someone asking him "How do you know when you're finished with a painting?" and he says "How do you know when you're finished making love?" Brilliant—like a cross between the Marlboro Man and Swiss Tony.

CH: You have an in-depth knowledge of comedy, performance art and TV history. What happens if the audience for your films and performances doesn't share it? If some of the references are lost on them, do you think there's a danger of excluding some of them?

MB: I find it interesting that I get asked this kind of question a lot. There are many modes of practice that rely for meaning on references to highly specialised literature, critical theory, film and theatre forms. I'm very directly co-opting the materials and formats of mainstream entertainment, and that isn't supposed to be obscure; maybe it's doubly uncomfortable to insist on squashing so-called low brow or trashy forms up against exaggerated versions of the formal institutional machinery at work in the assimilation of live art within a gallery context. I try and hand the content and the context over to the viewers, and plant very obvious gags to offset the more obscure references throughout—the scripts are really carefully structured that way. If you don't get one reference, there are another 50 to follow in quick succession that might hit home.... Whatever the reason, there's still something about introducing a distinct narrative structure to film and performance that sits uneasily with current art audiences, which is why I can't help but carry on doing it.

CH: Comedy plays an important role in your work—you directly appropriate clips from TV programmes, some well-loved, others irredeemably terrible; you apply some of the structural formats common to comedy scripts to your writing, and you have frequently worked directly with comedians. Why is it so central to your thinking?

MB: I think partly it's to do with detecting a certain itchiness in the artworld about direct humour—it's common to both live art and gallery based practice. It's made me convinced that if you could actually achieve laugh out-loud comedy within a visual art setting that is simultaneously loaded with content, and coming from an irrefutably solid conceptual standpoint, you'd really be onto something. I'm set on pushing at that uncomfortable spot, aiming at the sort of space occupied by projects such as Andy Kaufman's "Intergender Wrestling" film *I'm From Hollywood*, and Chris Morris' *Brasseye* series. They seem fairly close to certain activist strands of live art practice to me, and they do something that lots of other excellent comedy and drama doesn't. I'm coming from the other end, but it seems a feasible target to point toward, especially if I continue to work with people who have such a high level of performance skill. Invariably survey shows about humour in art aren't funny, and having tried and failed myself, just inserting comedians into a gallery setting alongside artists is often a pointless exercise, no matter how carefully orchestrated or conceptualised. So it can't come from curators and programmers, only from direct, committed collaborative practice-led activity between artists from different fields.

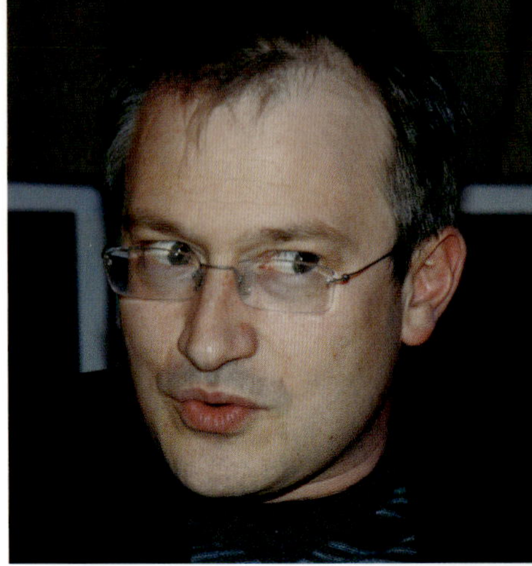

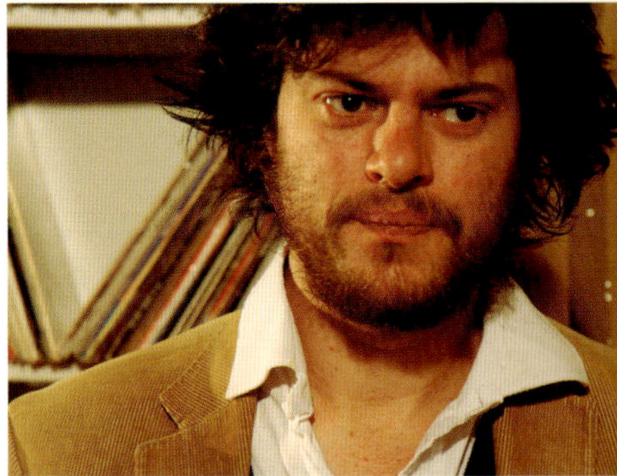

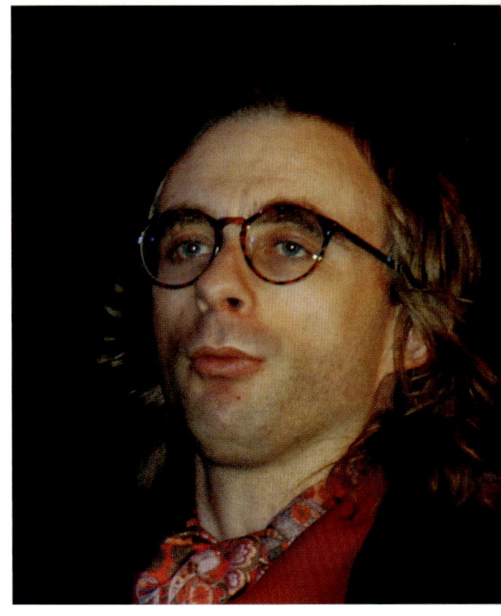

CH: Your writing increasingly seems to hold the key to that process—it frames, contains and feeds into all aspects of your work with other practitioners, and there's a strand of it that seems to be moving more directly to writing for actors. What sources are you drawing on to hone those skills? Where does the style of it come from?

MB: Learning to do it properly is proving to be a frustratingly slow process. As well as being driven by a youth full of watching sitcoms, crap gameshows, terrible 1980s films, and an abiding obsessive interest in stand-up of all kinds, theatre and TV drama also come into it. I respond to the ludicrous wordplay and pointed use of weird outdated vernacular and the veiled nastiness in the work of 1960s playwrights like Pinter and Orton in particular. I like the sham old-fashioned respectfulness of tone to the writing about celebrities in *Hello*, *OK!* and *People* magazines, and the crazily over-loaded sentence structures they employ. I've been looking a lot at the self-reflexive plot structuring of *Curb Your Enthusiasm* and *Extras*, and amidst piles of dreadful old showbiz biographies and compilations of theatrical anecdotes and reviews, I've got biopics and docudramas about artists, writers, comedians and actors. Increasingly, the simplicity of the monologue as a form is compelling—all the narrative, characterisation and drama packed entirely into one sustained individual performance… Hugo Blick and Rob Brydon's *Marion and Geoff*, Alan Bennett's *Talking Heads*, Bob Newhart's one-sided conversations like "The Driving Instructor" and "Introducing Tobacco to Civilisation"… those 'An Audience With…' formats that were particularly popular in the 1980s—the Kenneth Williams one in particular—and De Niro as Rupert Pupkin in *King of Comedy* talking to himself in his homemade studio set with cardboard cut-out stars. Dennis Potter is someone I go back to again and again, especially *Karaoke*, which isn't seen to be one of his best. It's my favourite, though—structurally, it's pleasingly complicated and legible at the same time, and all the tangled self-reflexivity in it doesn't take anything away from the brilliant characterisation and story-telling. There's a central writer character who stands in for Potter—Daniel Feeld, played by Albert Finney—and that character has written a film called *Karaoke* which is in the process of being edited together. He starts hearing snatches of the dialogue in the real world shortly after having been diagnosed with advanced pancreatic cancer (Potter had a few months to live himself when he wrote it), and a whole soup of juxtaposed metafictional storylines start to reveal themselves in various complicated ways, all over-lapping and undercutting each other, never entirely establishing themselves as part of the 'true' narrative or not—either of the fictional film or the drama based around it.

CH: Is there something about karaoke as a metaphor that appeals to you? It seems to crop up as a tangential theme in quite a lot of your work?

MB: It's true—it's because the space for bringing any creativity to the interpretation is so miniscule—the lyrics, the arrangement of the music,

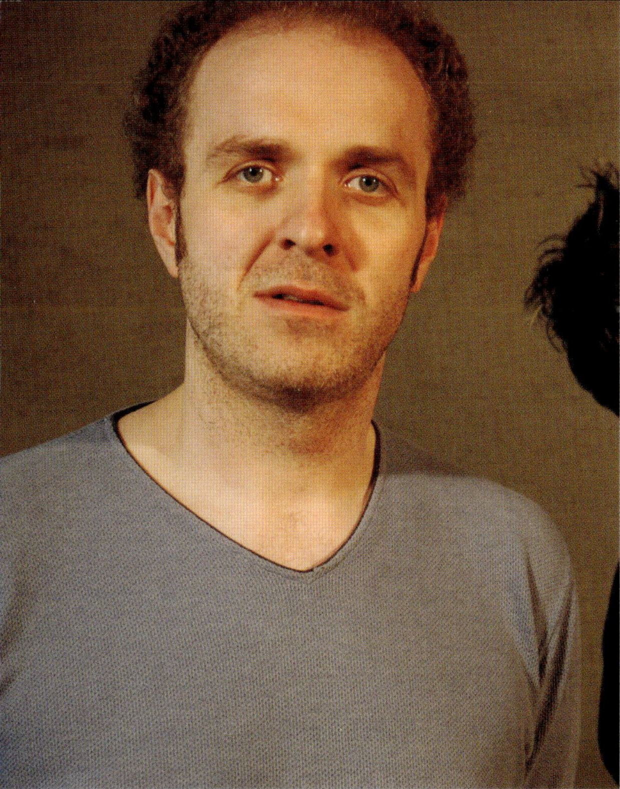

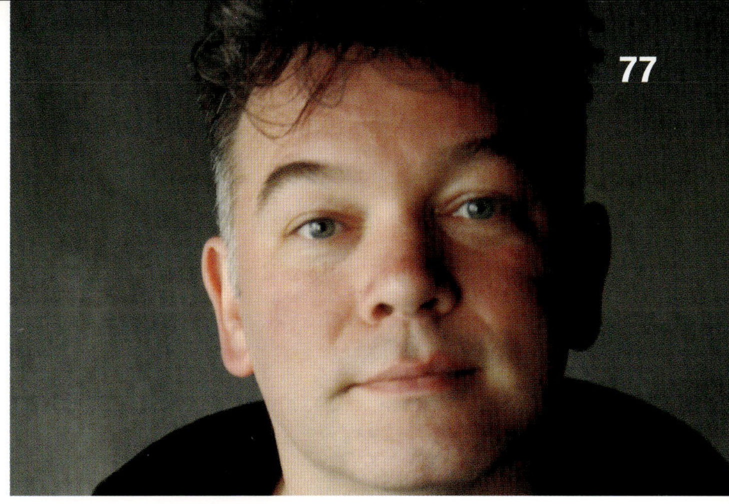

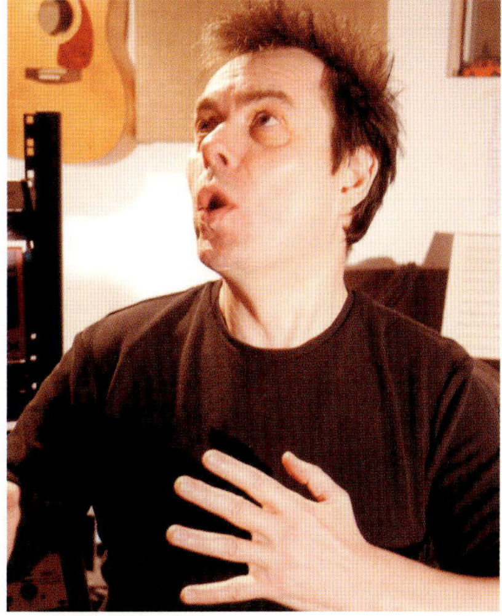

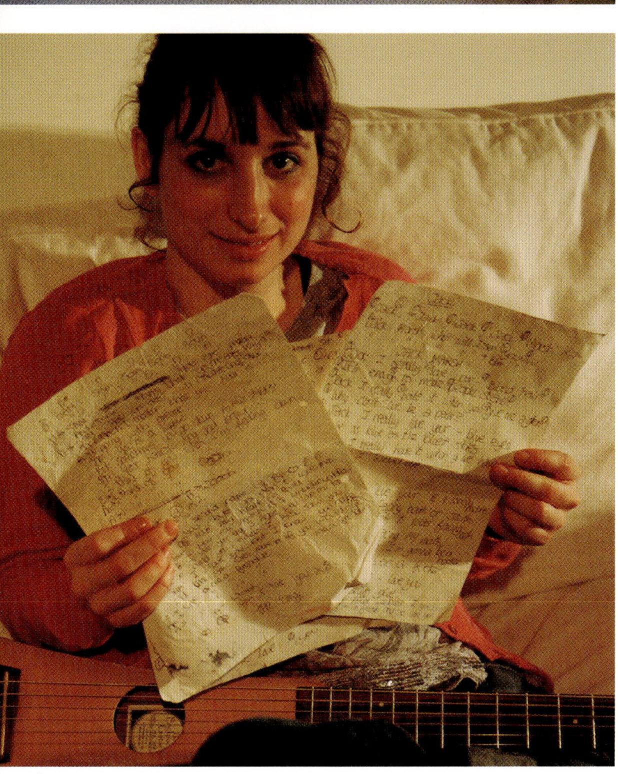

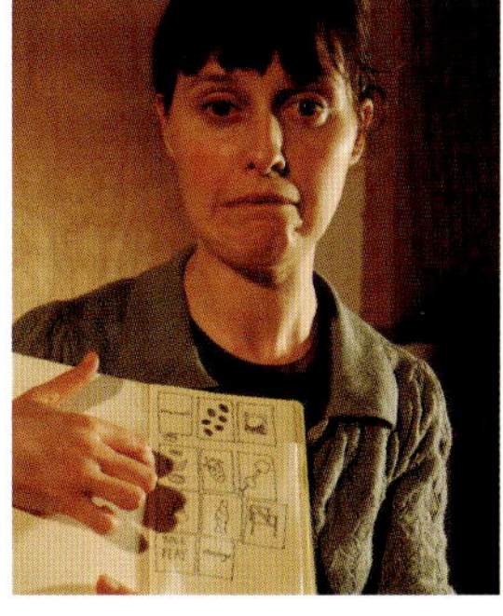

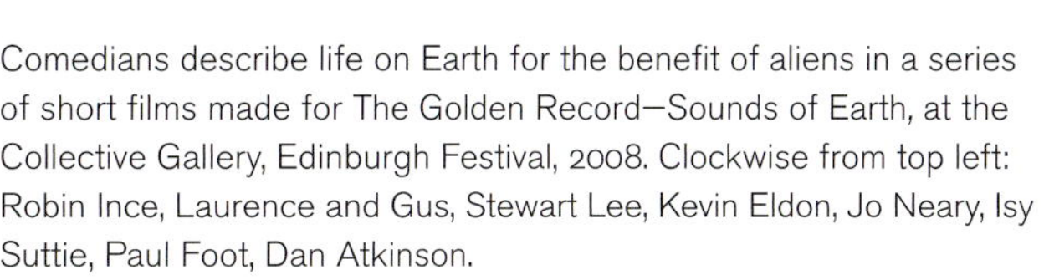

Comedians describe life on Earth for the benefit of aliens in a series of short films made for The Golden Record—Sounds of Earth, at the Collective Gallery, Edinburgh Festival, 2008. Clockwise from top left: Robin Ince, Laurence and Gus, Stewart Lee, Kevin Eldon, Jo Neary, Isy Suttie, Paul Foot, Dan Atkinson.

A CONVERSATION BETWEEN MEL BRIMFIELD AND CERI HAND

the timing, everything—entirely prescribed by someone else. But there's something eminently gratifying for the audience about being able to tabulate exactly how far the original is being emulated or not in a performance. There's definitely something of that in my approach to constructing the material for the pseudo-archive of *This Is Performance Art*; often I'm referring to one or more art historical or cultural moments simultaneously, substituting one for the other, or adopting a recogniseable formal structure or aesthetic and applying it to inappropriate content.

I saw Bob Golding in Tim Whitnall's *Morecambe* last year—it had something to do with the narrowness of karaoke for me. I found it to be a peculiarly melancholy experience, although it was undeniably brilliantly performed, well written and beautifully staged. You felt the audience eagerly leaning in towards those parts of the show where Golding's eerily accurate impression most obviously kicked in. Those were the bits that got the biggest laughs and provoked the rounds of spontaneous applause. I was reminded of *Stars In Their Eyes*, that TV programme that Matthew Kelley used to present, with members of the public appearing as pop celebrities. They'd go through a door, there'd be a puff of smoke and they'd reappear as the pop star they were about to imitate, always in elaborate (but often laughable) costuming and makeup. The intro would start up and they'd sing the first few notes, and without fail, the audience would applaud wildly—the applause was based entirely on the degree of accuracy with which the contestants were able to mimic the original performance. Even when I was young, it struck me as a weird talent. Inevitably, they would slip in and out of sounding 'right' as well.

I arranged a live radio recording event as part of my *Radio Radio* project with three David Bowies who'd all been on the programme once. It was a complete accident—I contacted Granada TV and asked if they'd forward my request on to people who'd appeared as a whole list of stars, and it just so happened that the first three to get in touch were Bowies. I asked artists Paul Rooney, Die Kunst and The Ken Ardley Playboys to arrange their signature tunes, with the only proviso being that the Bowies must be able to sing it in the way they were accustomed. I remember being at the sound check when the first of them, Tony Perry, started singing "Wild Is The Wind", and it actually made me cry and laugh with delight simultaneously because it was exact—I found it inexplicably moving that he was so right. I remember thinking that Bowie himself wouldn't be able to reproduce the vocal line that appears on the record so accurately anymore, which when you think about it, is a really melancholy thought. It has a strange status—it's an audio recording of a live event for later radio broadcast, and it slides in and out of being an entirely plausible Bowie bootleg if you weren't there. If you were, the visual wrongness of all of the impersonators was particularly pleasing. Now I think it was one of my earliest stabs at performative documentation.

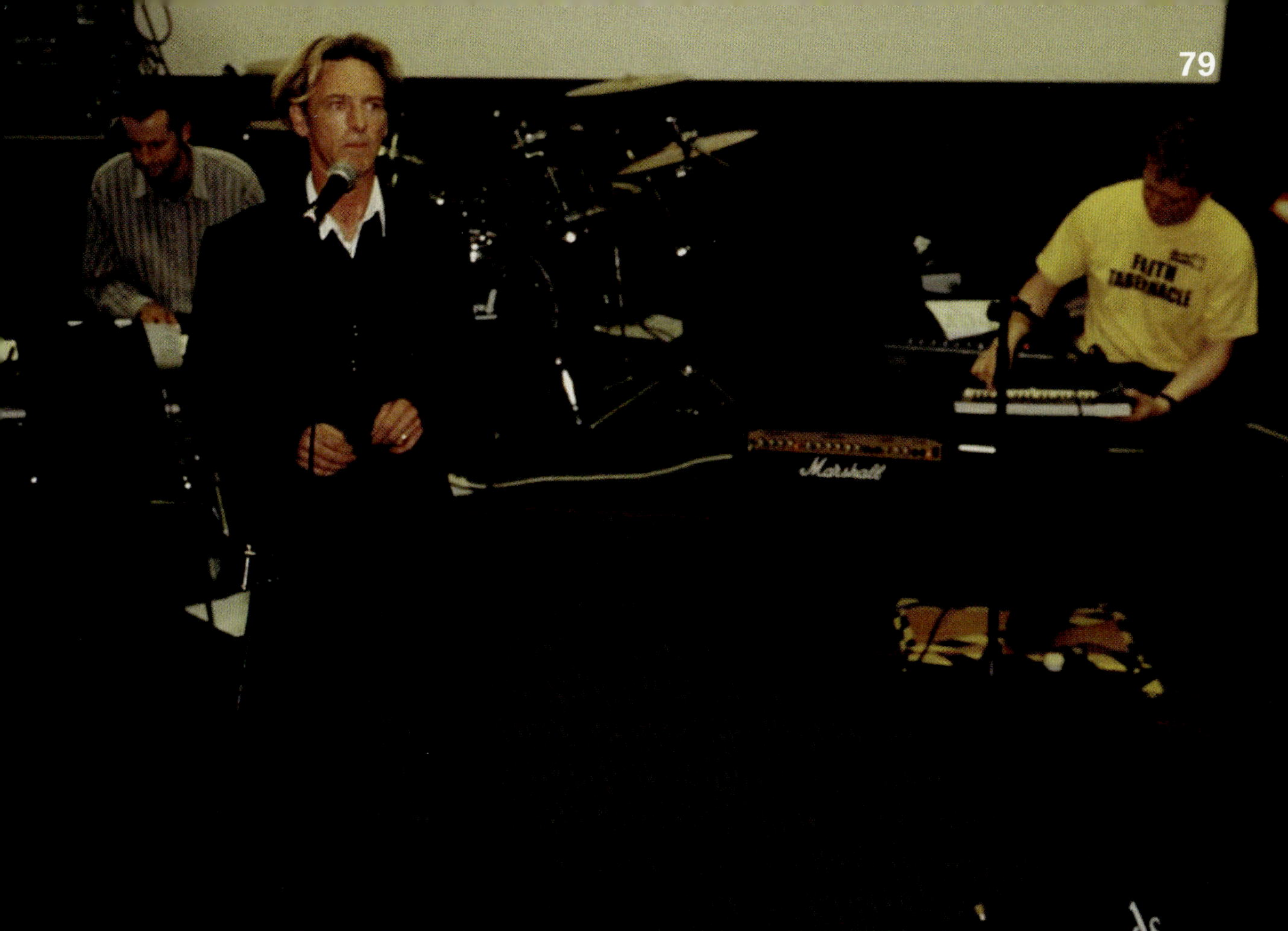

"Tonight Matthew, I'm going to be… David Bowie!", a live radio recording for *Radio Radio* at Chelsea College of Art lecture theatre, Millbank, 2004.

CH: You seem to be actively showing us the results of an ongoing series of cultural excavations. In fact, your practice ends up being a kind of performed cultural historiography in itself, rooted in quite genuine delight at finding points of comparison in wildly divergent sources.

MB: I'm very serious about finding legitimate ways of working with virtuoso performers from all sorts of backgrounds, and presenting it to audiences in a way that might cause a disruption of accepted distinctions between disciplines. Recently, I also couldn't help but notice an eerie similarity between a film I saw a while ago of a naked 1970s model operating the different parts of Robert Morris' *bodyspacemotionthings*, and a dance sequence in *Can't Stop The Music*, the film about the formation of the Village People, featuring the Construction Worker character thrusting his way hotly around an identical set with a load of women who look like they belong in a Robert Palmer video. He looks uncannily like the poster for Morris' *Labyrinths* show too—where he's wearing aviators, helmet and lots of baby oil. I'm not sure what it means, but it's not nothing.

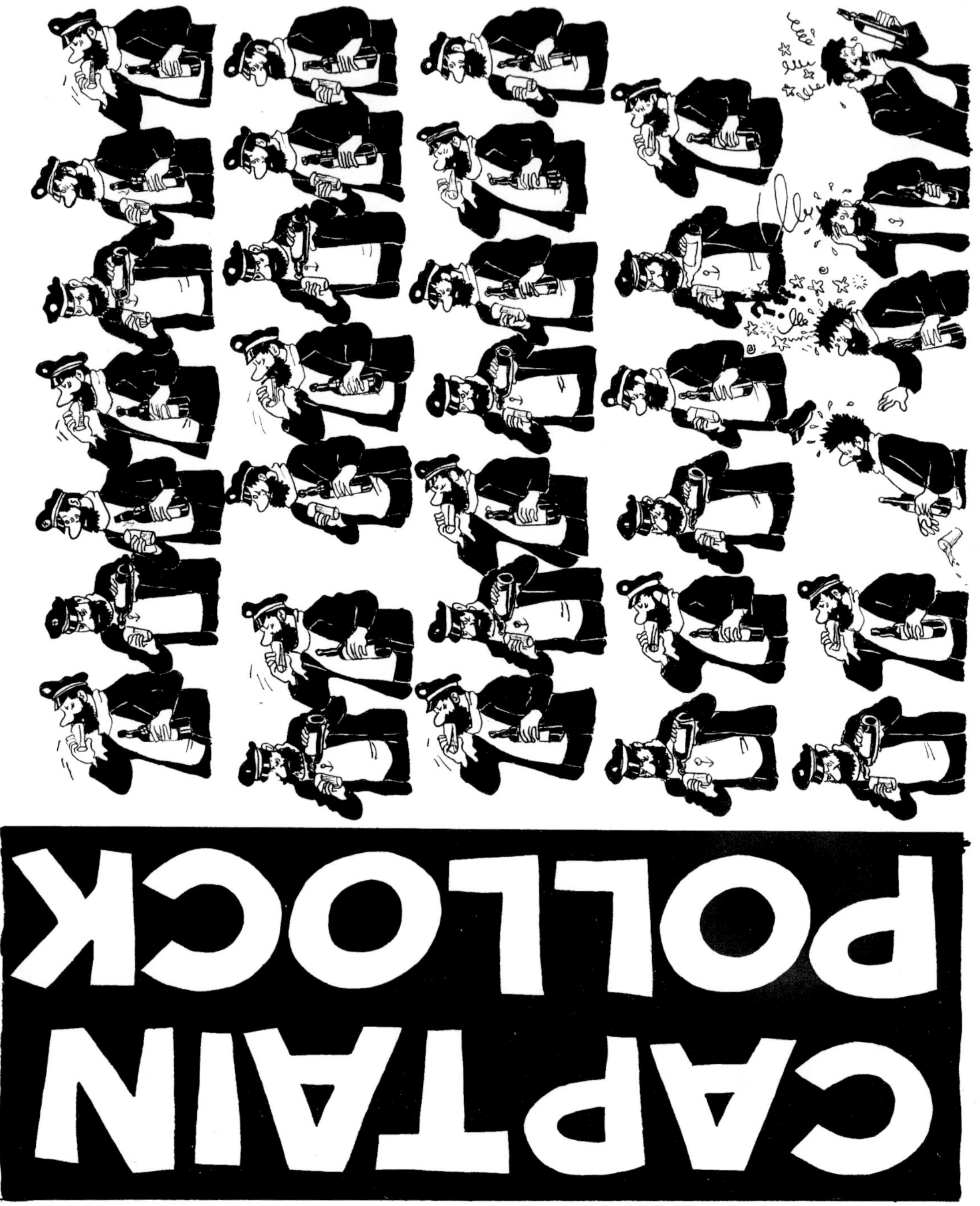

Mel Brimfield, *Captain Pollock*, 2007, Ink on paper, 16.5 x 11.7 in. / 42 x 29.7 cm.
Image courtesy the artist and Ceri Hand Gallery.

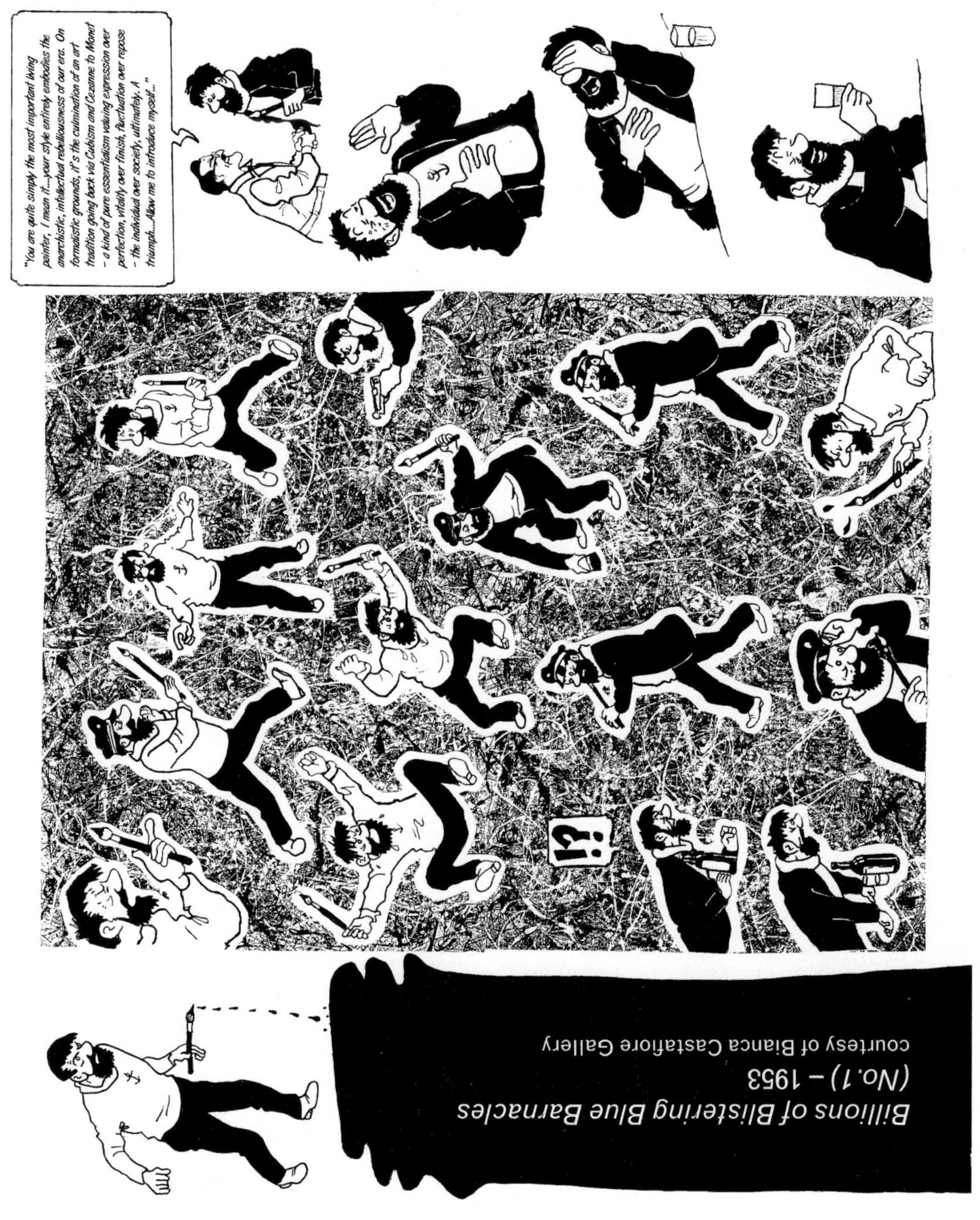

Billions of Blistering Blue Barnacles
(No.1) – 1953
courtesy of Bianca Castafiore Gallery

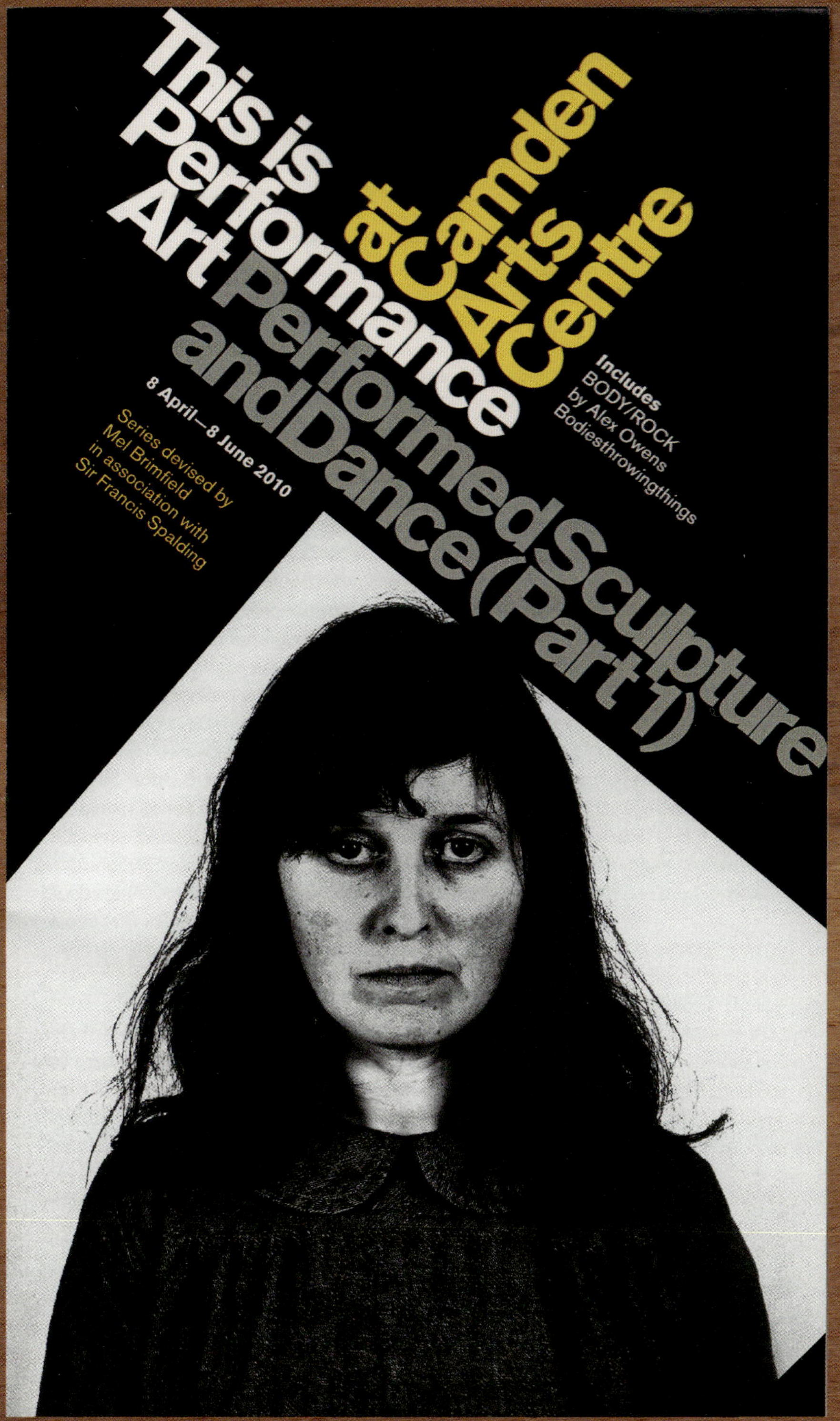

Souvenir programme for *This is Performance Art* at the Camden Art Centre, 2010.

An Introduction

Allow me to introduce myself; I am multi-award-winning cultural commentator Sir Francis Spalding, raconteur, bon-viveur,—and dare I say it, national treasure. I have been lucky enough in the course of my illustrious career to rub shoulders with some of the key protagonists in Performance Art History, and have made it my business to preserve for the nation something of the dazzling panoply of the aesthetic wonders contained therein. It came as no surprise, then, when I received a somewhat drunken late-night distress call from tearful Camden Arts Centre Director Jenni Lomax demanding that I act as figurehead for an innovative and thrilling programme of restaged seminal performances, publications and TV broadcasts at the gallery. Though her speech was slurred, I was able to piece together these key facts: one—that Melvyn Bragg had pulled out of the project owing to 'ill-health', (certainly, recently published tabloid photographs of the man leaving the offices of a renowned Harley Street hair transplant specialist would seem to support this claim—get well soon, Melvyn); two—that the series would surely stand as a landmark in arts broadcasting, and as a revolutionary institutional model for the assimilation of live art and its history; and three, that Matthew Collings could go and stuff himself if he thought for a minute that she'd stump up for the exorbitant payout insisted upon by his grasping agent for replacing Bragg.

From such troubled acorns, mighty oaks have nevertheless flourished. I have been working tirelessly, and for very little renumaration, I might add, with the curators here at the Arts Centre to bring you the launch of an ongoing series which explores the impact and legacy of performance art from the 1940s to today, and which insists on searching through the hitherto unexplored nooks and crannies of theatre, activism, comedy, music and sport for the very seeds of its inception and for evidence of its continued importance. I give you— This Is Performance Art. A 32 part BBC2 series will air in autumn, condensing some 60 years of its rich history into 16 short hours of essential primetime viewing, every Sunday at 4:30am from September onwards.

Tonight we proudly present a screening of the first episode that covers the extraordinary mainstream proliferation and influence of Performed Sculpture and Dance within contemporary culture, with particular focus on the work of leading light Alex Owens, a fiercely gifted and often over-looked artist.

Indeed, we are revisiting two of Owens' pioneering live performances —controversial Genital Panic revue staged at legendary performance art hub The Windmill Theatre in the 60s. The displacement of the sculptural object by the human body was already a hot topic in critical discourse of the time; Genital Panic combined groundbreaking modes of conceptual burlesque, dummy-less ventriloquy and aerobic exercise workouts as literal Body Sculpture. Body/Rock was performed as part of the programme by Owens and her Hot Gossip troupe to universally rapturous acclaim, though only scant documentary evidence and contradictory anecdotal accounts of the work remain in the Windmill Theatre archive. Tonight's presentation of the work is based entirely on these incomplete fragments, interpreted by a crack team of performers and musicians under the direction of myself and producer Mel Brimfield, who is widely acknowledged to be the world's foremost authority on the practice of Alex Owens. And we are all, of course, familiar with the second work on the bill, namely Owens' Bodiesthrowingthings—it was the choreographic work that firmly positioned avant-garde juggling techniques and balancing feats within the lexicon of performed sculpture. As the roof-raising finale to Genital Panic, it was instantly hailed as a classic, and set a precedent for the appearance of reappraised vaudeville techniques within live art contexts.

In anticipation of the usual barrage of questions, it is necessary to conclude by touching on the complicated litigation surrounding the publication of the 'libelous' Genital Panic souvenir programme. The offending pages are in fact reproduced at the rear of this programme, together with an account my own unfortunate part in the proceedings, so widely and consistently misreported. It is my fond hope that this will finally set the record straight, as I have no intention of discussing the matter further publically.

Programme and Cast

Bodiesthrowingthings

Sir Francis Spalding welcomes the audience, and introduces the UK premiere of *This Is Performance Art—Performed Sculpture and Dance.*

Sir Francis introduces the first of our performances, an interpretation of Bodiesthrowingthings, originally performed by Alex Owens as part of the Genital Panic revue at The Windmill Theatre.

Performed by:

Clever Peter

Richard Bond

Edward Eales-White

William Hartley

Dominic Stone

Assisted by The Beaux Belles

BODY/ROCK

Sir Francis returns to introduce the second performance, a restaging of *BODY/ROCK*, as originally performed by Alex Owens and Hot Gossip at the Genital Panic revue at The Windmill Theatre.

Musical Director—Paul Higgs
Choreography advisor—Tom Roden (New Art Club)

Performed by

The Dancers

Alice Capitani—Soloist
The Beaux Belles:
Lexi Bradburn
Heather Hot
Ann Pidcoc
Jo Stobbs
Amy Thornhill
Gemma Whelan

The Band

Paul Higgs—Keyboard
Gwyneth Herbet—Vocals
Steve Richardson—Bass Guitar
Geoff Haves—Guitar
Rocco Webb—Drum

The performers, Joanna Neary, Brian Dewan, John Hegley and Ed Moore
Ben Roberts and all at Camden Arts Centre

The estates of Alex Owens, Peggy Googleheim and Vivian Van Damm
The Windmill Theatre Archive

Genital Panic section reproduced with kind permission of
Pump House Gallery

Programme designed and printed by Ryan Gillard 2010
Mel Brimfield, courtesy of Ceri Hand Gallery

BODY/ROCK

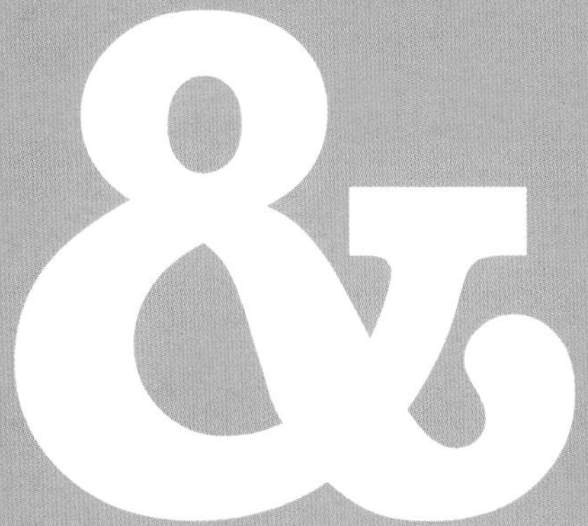

BODIESTHROWINGTHINGS

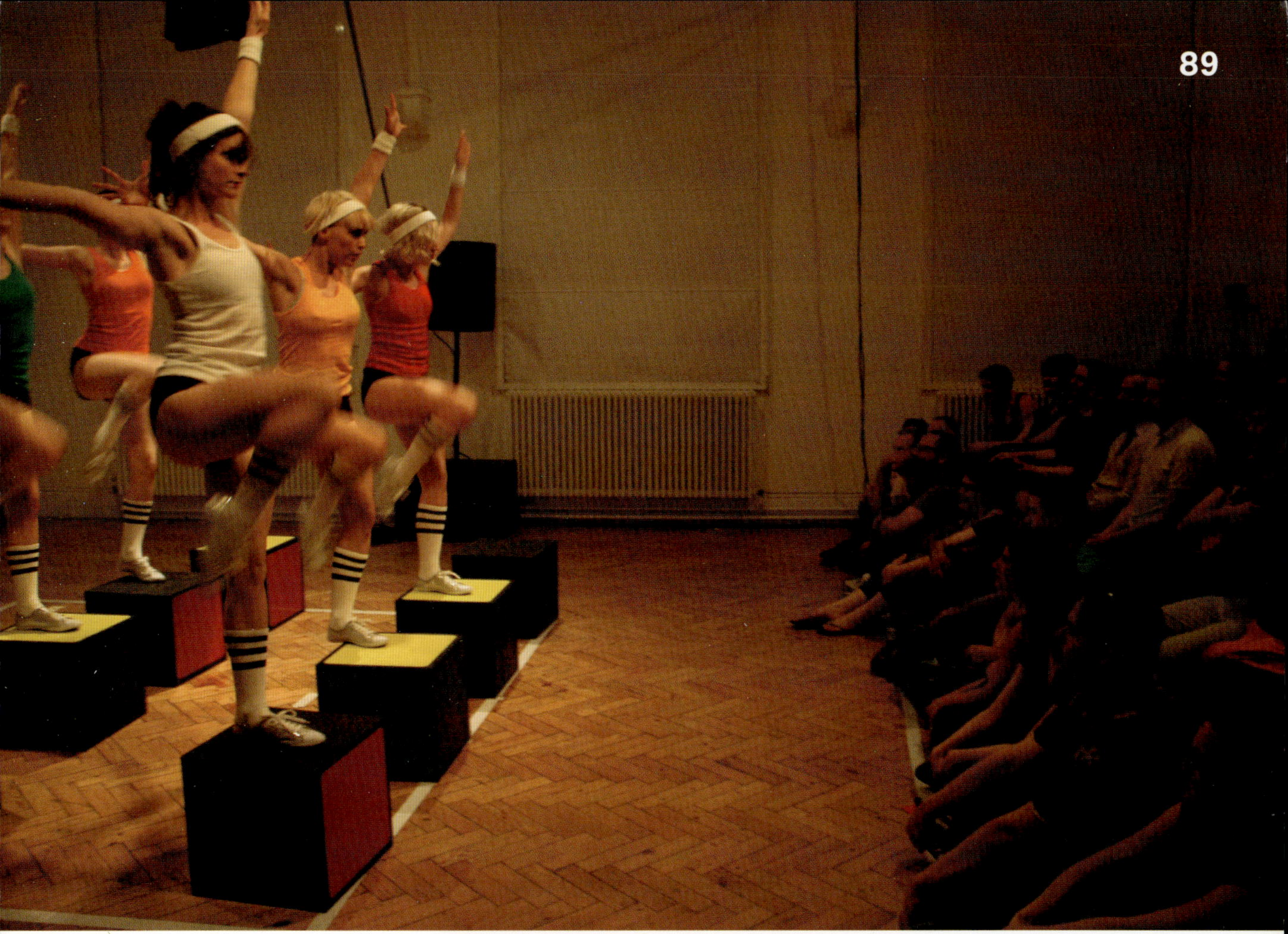

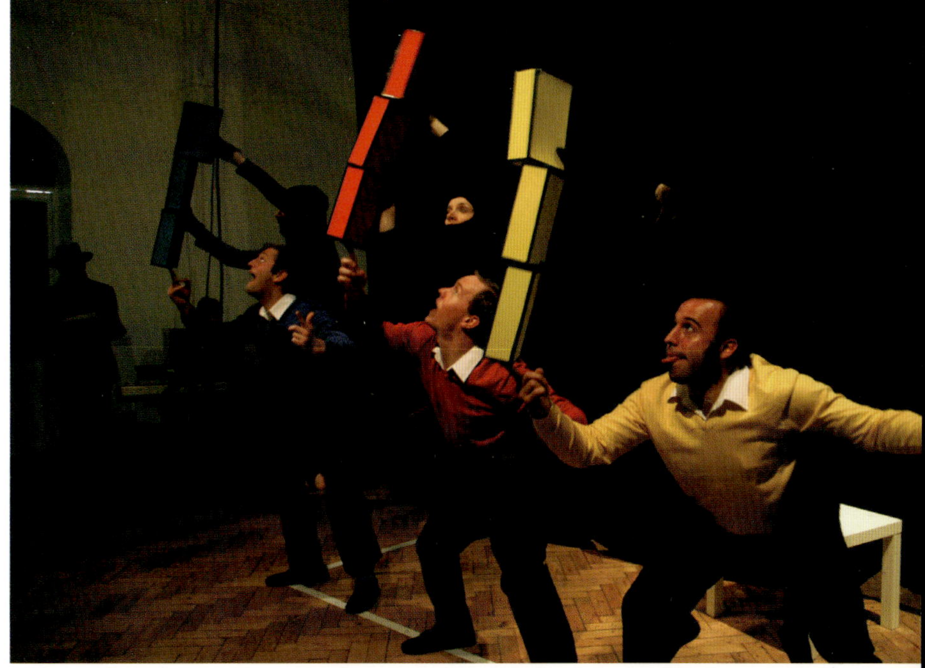

The Beaux Belles, Alice Capitani and Clever Peter perform *Body/Rock*, Camden Art Centre, London and *Bodiesthrowingthings* at the end of Brimfield's Camden Art Centre artist's residency. Photos: Peter Dodd.

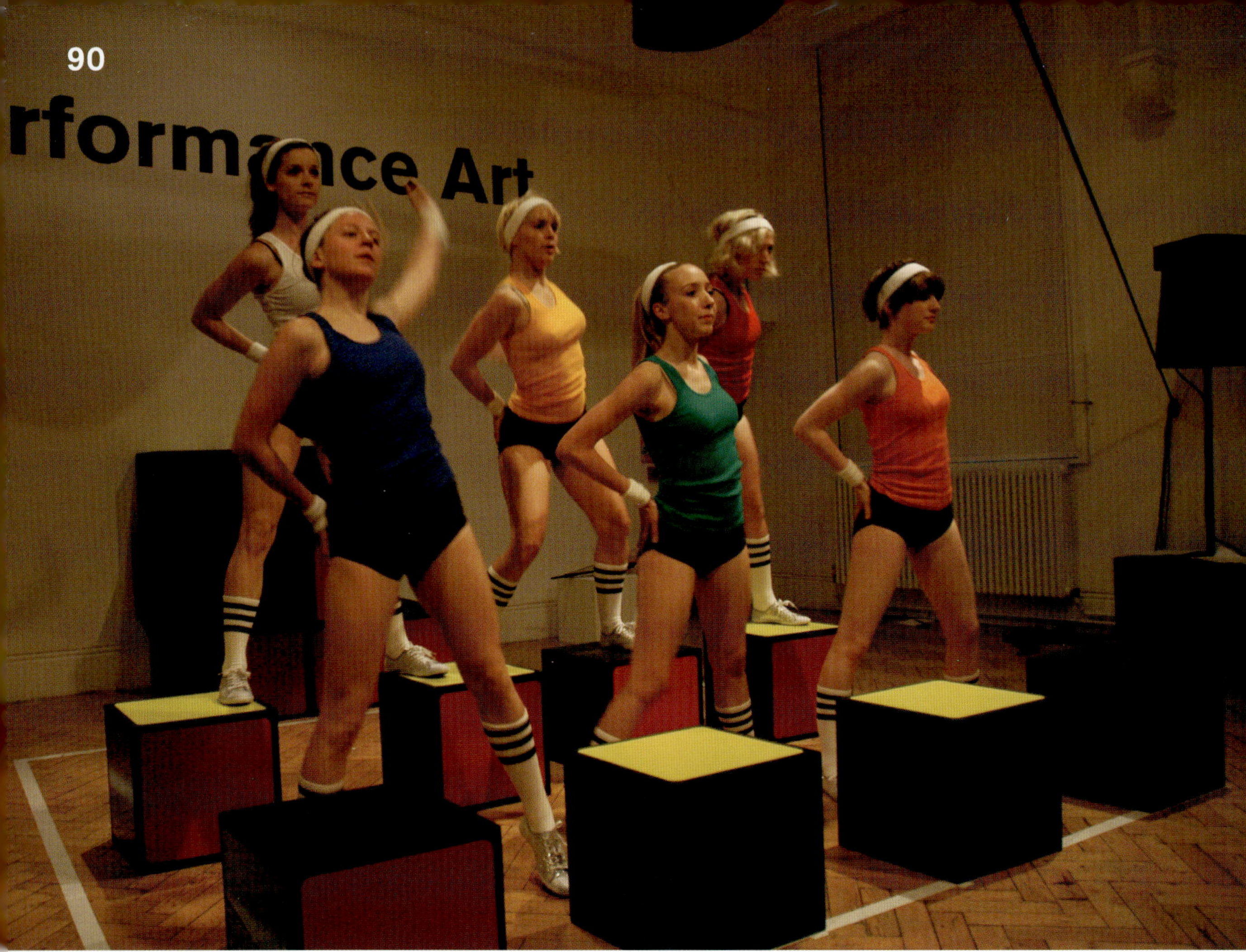

MEL BRIMFIELD / THIS IS PERFORMANCE ART

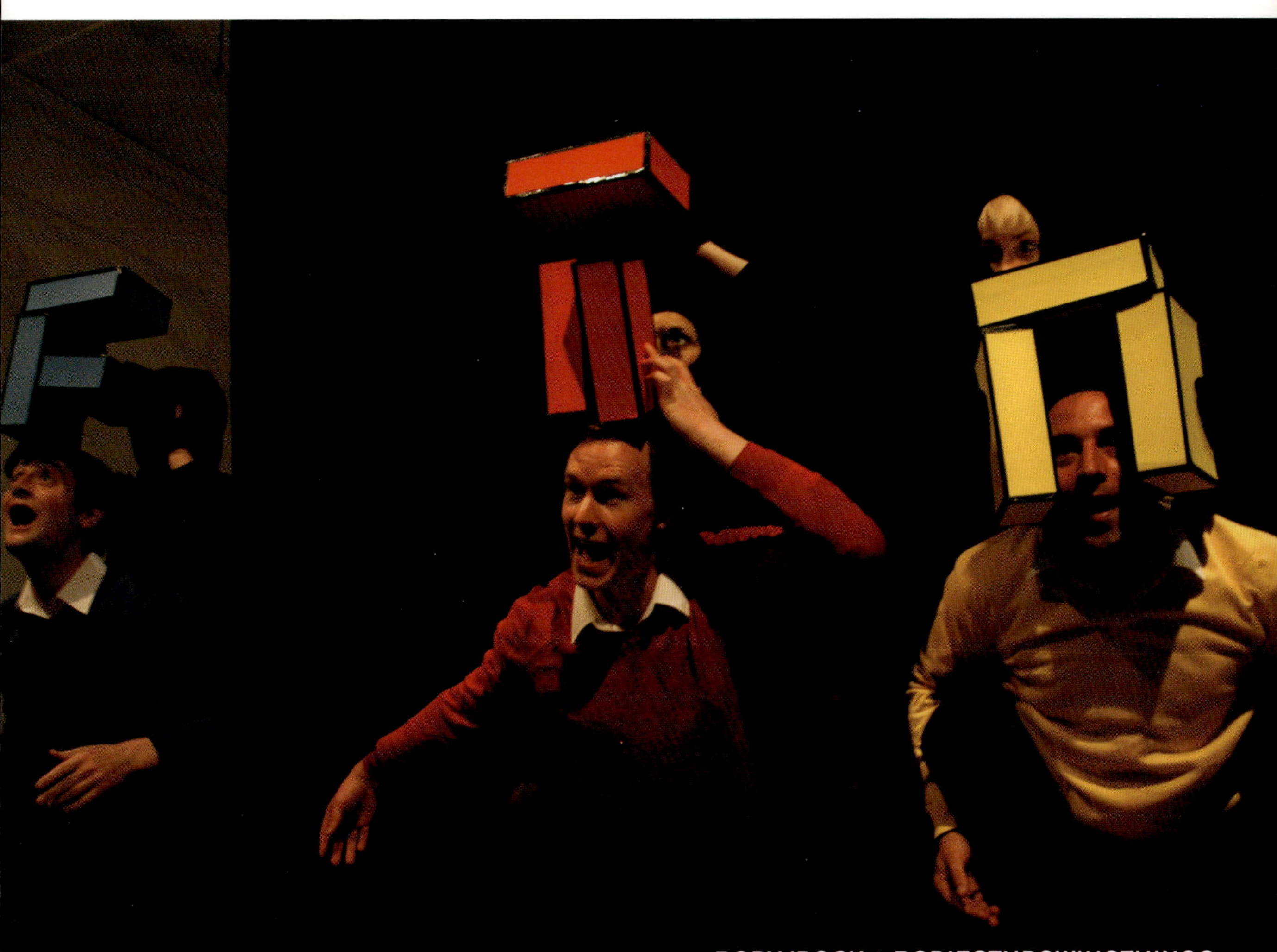

BODY/ROCK & BODIESTHROWINGTHINGS

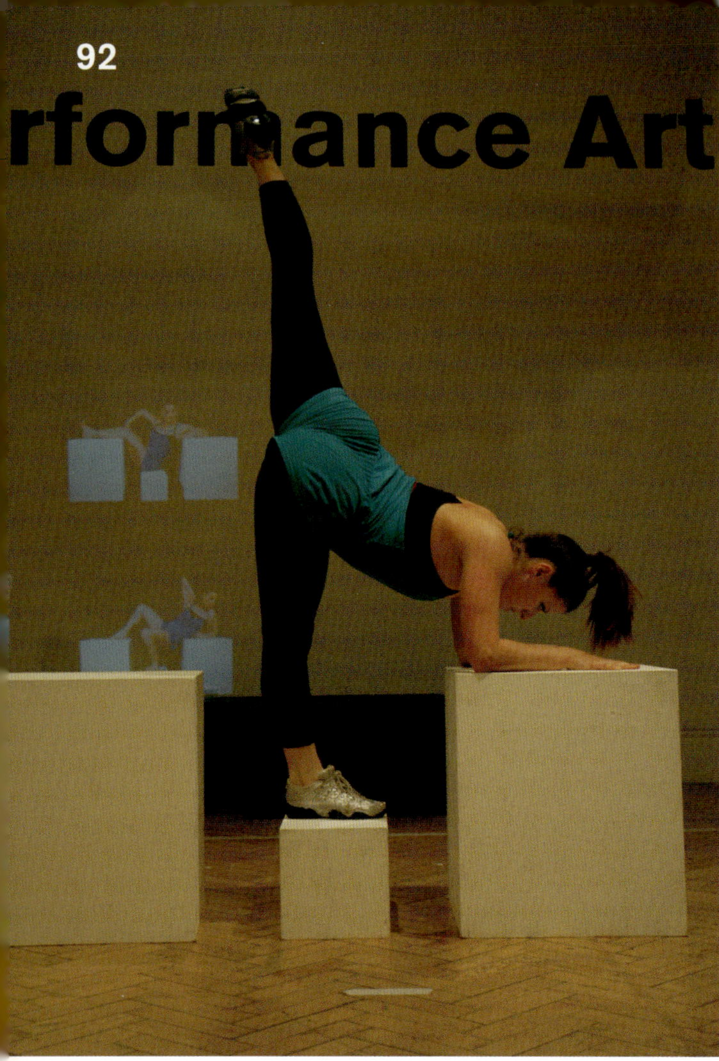

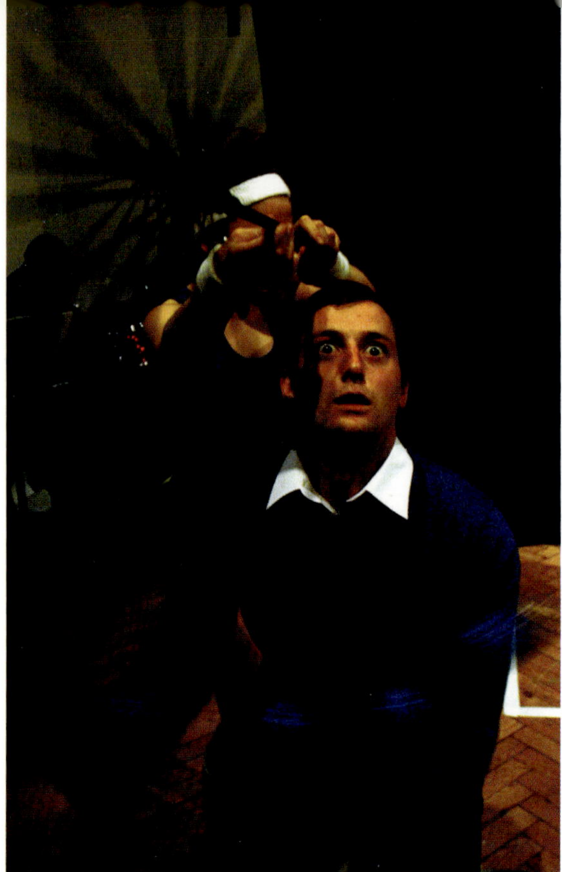

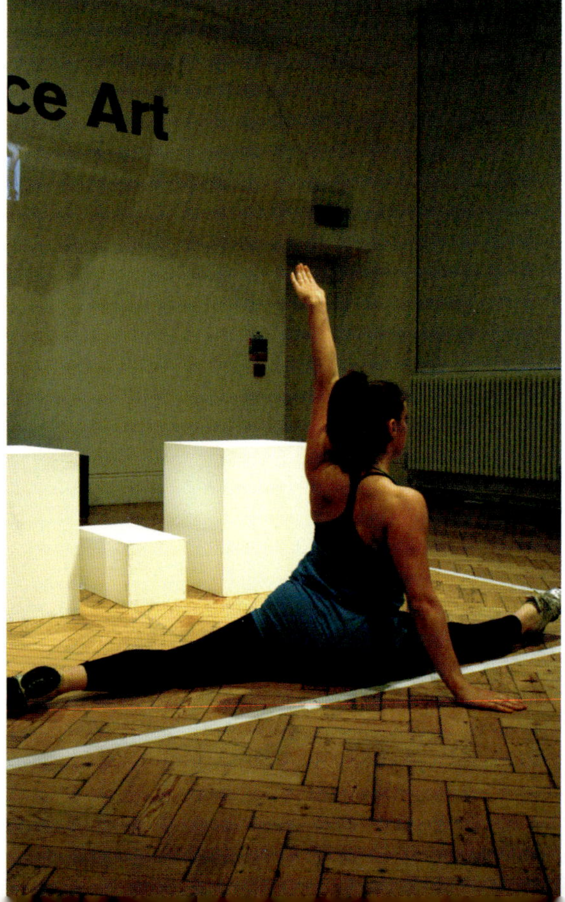

MEL BRIMFIELD / THIS IS PERFORMANCE ART

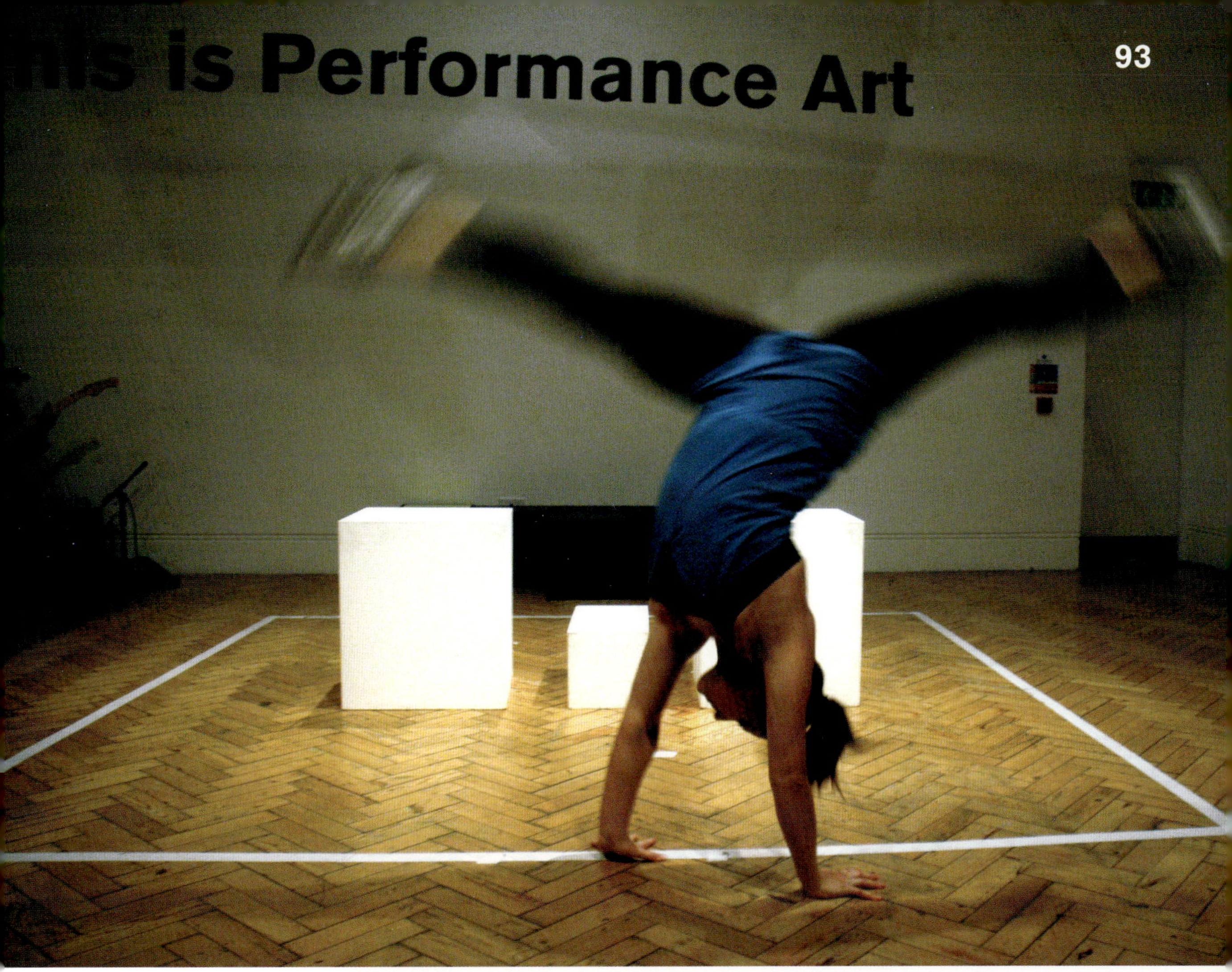

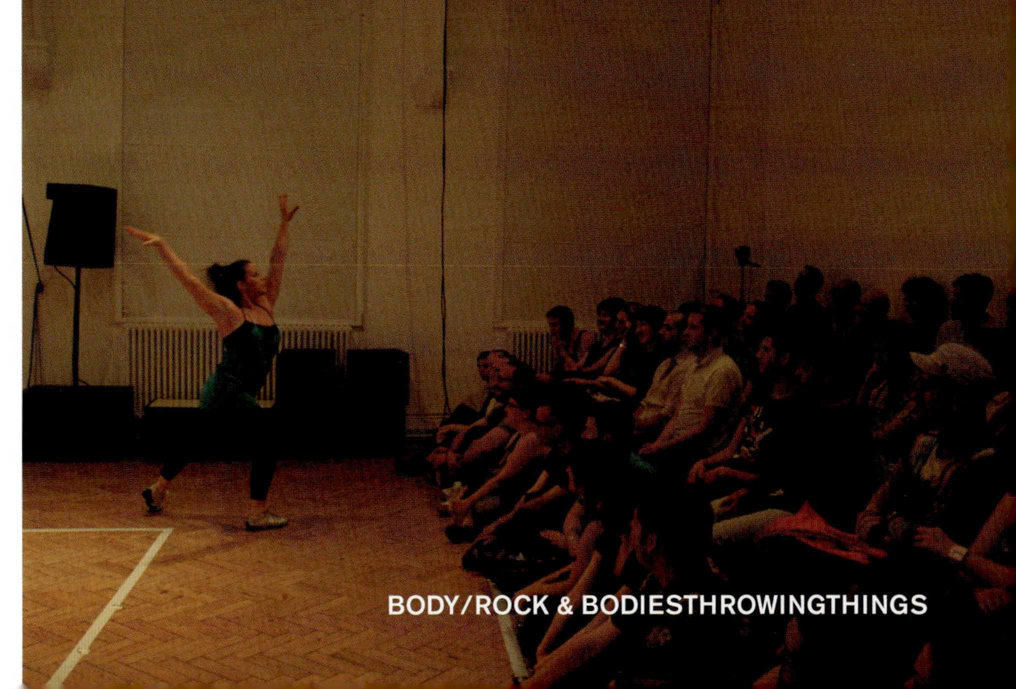

BODY/ROCK & BODIESTHROWINGTHINGS

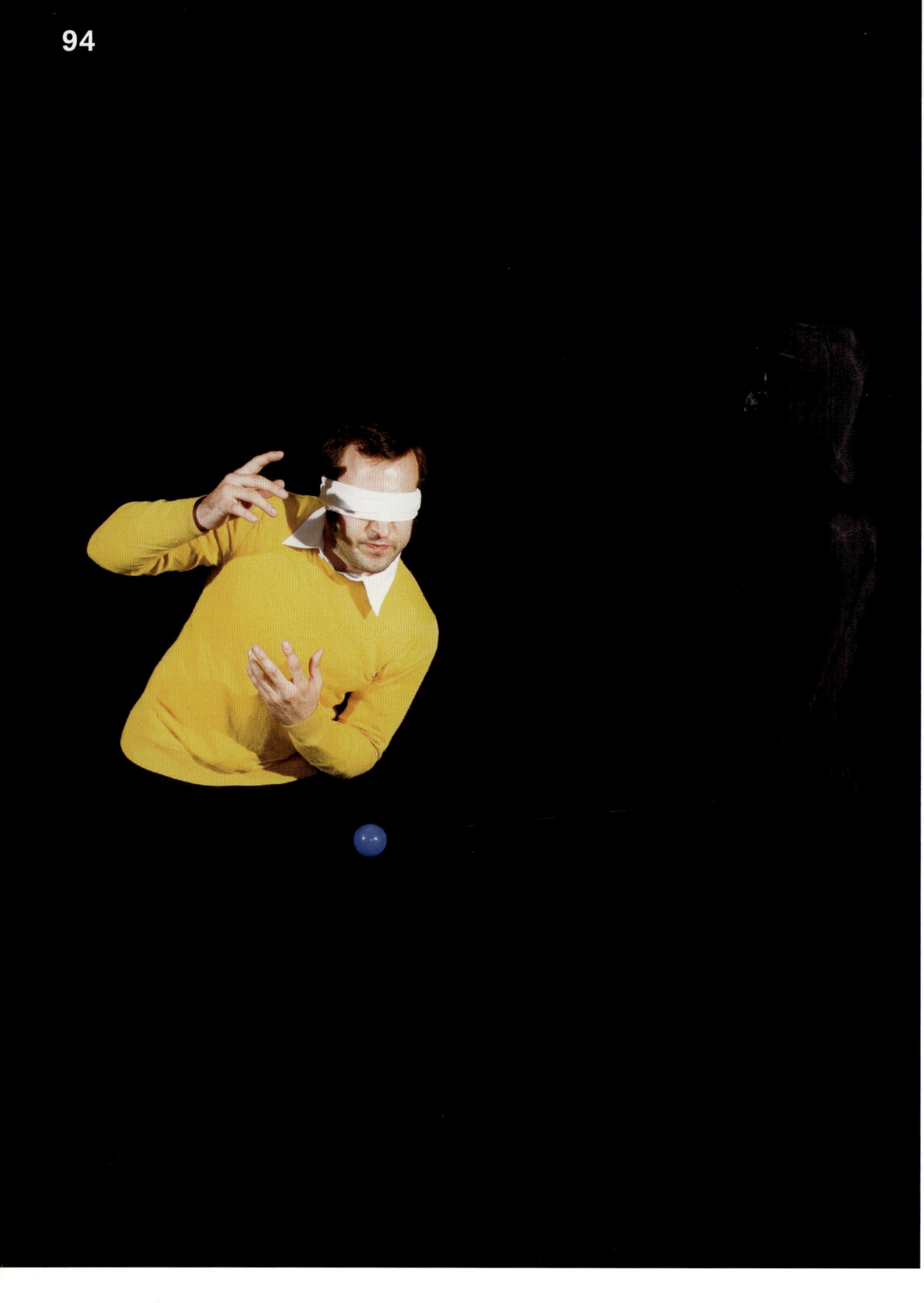

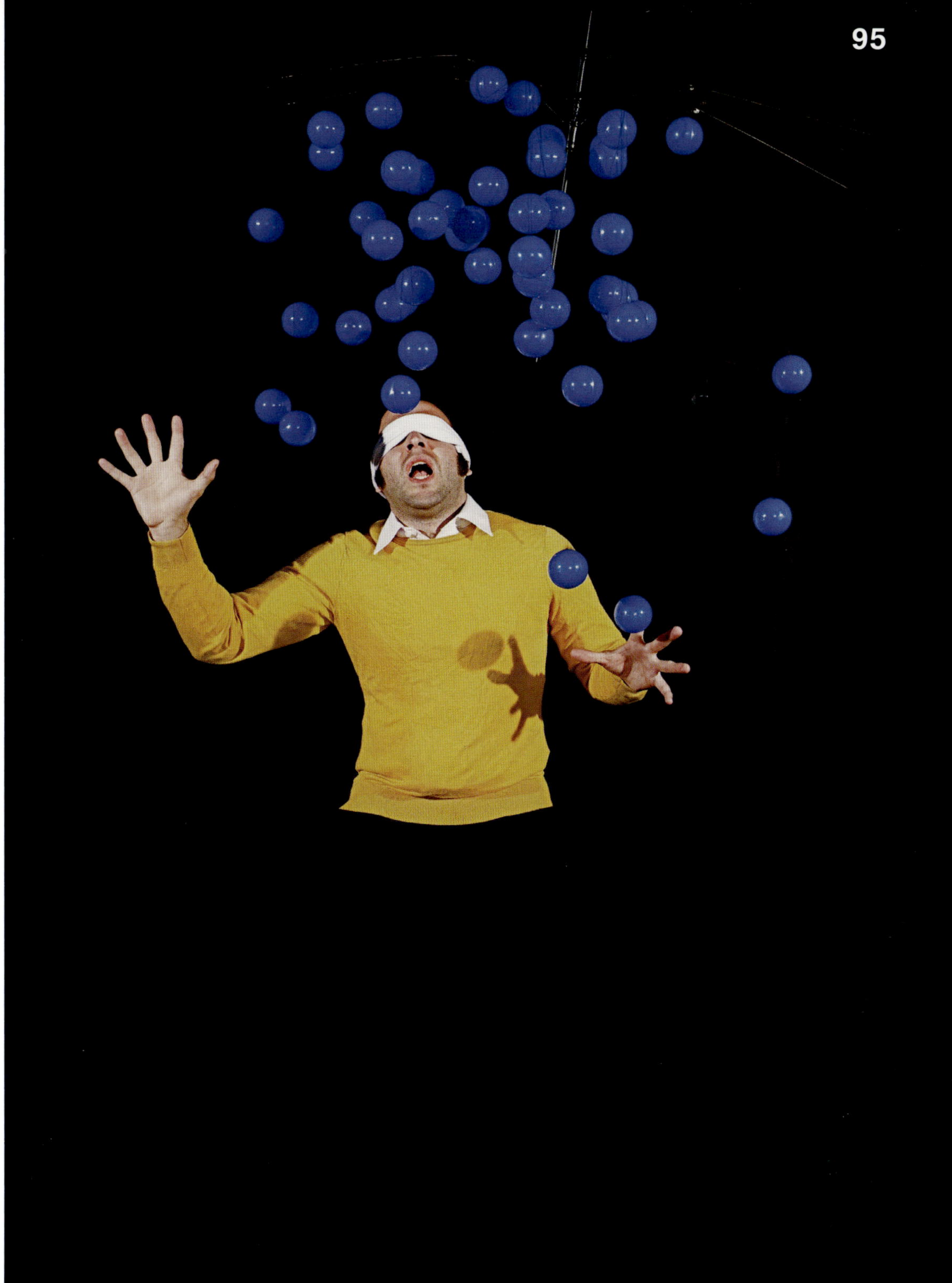

Blindfolded Catching, 2010, 11.4 x 17.2 in. / 29.4 x 43.7 cm. Image courtesy the artist and Ceri Hand Gallery. Produced in association with Will Hartley, Jo Stobbs and Edward Moore.

GALLERY 2
Ventriloquism | Rooms 7–12
This part of the exhibition charts the development of that most legible of performed sculptural techniques, namely ventriloquism. Following on from the demise of Variety theatre, it became clear that the time for simple wonderment at an illusion well-executed had passed, to be replaced by an extreme hard-edged conceptualism that was mercifully to strip the last vestiges of entertainment and humour from the form. The move was to prove unpopular with the general public however, as is perhaps most memorably evidenced by the well documented media furore that was to greet the announcement that Robert Morris' **Box With the Sound of its Own Making** had triumphed over the evergreen Keith Harris and Orville for the hotly contested ventriloquists spot at the 23rd Royal Command Variety Performance.

Room 9 – Joseph Beuys' **Explaining Pictures to a Dead Hare**
As he shambled onto the stage at Kentucky's Vent Haven conference with his head coated in gold leaf and honey, dragging a large trunk and with one foot strapped to a ski, there was no indication that seasoned ventriloquist Joseph Beuys had planned anything unusual for his performance. However, when his dummy was revealed to be a dead hare, the atmosphere was suddenly electric. The inherent tragedy of attempting, and failing to animate a dead creature, a motionless forever-mute object was clear. Krauss again: '...he was talking to it, and nothing was happening. The whole thing had me weeping and laughing all at once. That single gesture broke open the whole decorum of ventriloquism – completely unforgettable.'

Room 12 – Morecambe and Wise
The inoperable dummy was to become a familiar motif within a new strand of self-reflexive ventriloquy on the circuit emerging in the 60s. Collaborative performance artists Eric Morecambe and Ernie Wise were again to make their presence felt with the introduction of a giant dummy at the three-day Henry Moore Institute **Sculpture...or Bust?** conference, which sought to interrogate new perspectives on the much vaunted critical rejection of sculpture represented by live art – exclusive documentation of the performance is presented in Room 12. The scale of the dummy, and the artists' comic inability to work the thing was to present its materiality as an inalienable fact. Tabloid hack and celebrity gossip columnist Rosalind Krauss was prompted to describe the piece as '...a total kinesthetic shot in the arm for anybody who had any doubts about the raw power of introducing a sculpture to the stage.'

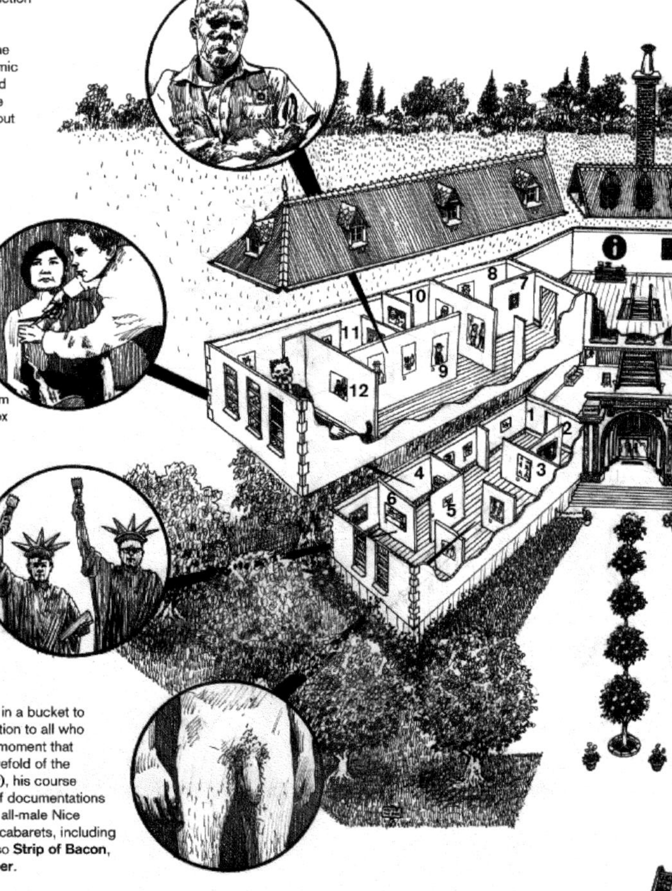

Room 4 – Yoko Ono's **Cut Piece**
Yoko Ono's thrillingly subversive **Cut Piece** burlesque routine was first performed as part of the **Destruction in Art Symposium** at the Windmill Theatre in London, and was to establish the plucky ingénue as the leading avant-garde stripper of our age, bar none. Casually kneeling on the floor in a draped garment, she invited audience members to begin cutting until she was naked, but for a pair of rhinestone encrusted tassled pasties, to the accompaniment of the David Rose Orchestra smashing their instruments to smithereens. Only one pasty (the left) and a dented trombone were retrieved from the bonfire set by curator Gustav Metzger to destroy all evidence and documentation of the symposium's activity at its conclusion – both are presented in Room 4. Notably, it was through this work that Yoko was to meet third husband and long-term collaborator John Lydon, then lead singer of progressive Punk Rock combo The Sex Pistols, also on the bill at DIAS.

Room 6 spotlight – **The Singing Sculpture**
Collaborative performance artists Eric Morecambe and Ernie Wise are best known for their development of radical performative modes of sculpture-based street entertainment. Although their Living Statue Technique has since become something of a cliché in live art circles, **The Singing Sculpture** as unveiled at the opening of the Milton Keynes Shopping Centre in 1970 was construed to be something of a revolutionary conceptual exercise. Rare documentation of this landmark performance is screened for the first time in Room 6.

Room 5 spotlight – Bruce McLean and Nice Style – The World's First Pose Band
Bruce McLean's long and arduous journey from two-bit pub stripper collecting tips in a bucket to becoming one of the world's most accomplished and innovative artists is an inspiration to all who face overwhelming obstacles and challenges along the road to success. From the moment that influential Marxist dance quarterly Two Left Feet published the now-legendary centrefold of the young artist's virtuoso conceptual striptease under the provocative title **Beef (Jerky)**, his course was set. This groundbreaking photographic work is presented alongside a series of documentations of later collaborative tableaux vivants and choreographic pieces, produced with his all-male Nice Style burlesque troupe for a series of themed Judson Dance Theatre and Windmill cabarets, including **Strip – The Paintwork, Stripping With Sarcasm, Stripping Tap** and **Strip Lite**. Also **Strip of Bacon, Stripping Yarns, Air/Strip**, and **Strip/Search**. And **Comic Strip** and **Strip of Timber**.

GALLERY 1
Tableaux Vivants and Conceptual Burlesque | Rooms 1–6
Performance art is, in the popular imagination, inextricably linked with nudity – and for good reason. Britain's antiquated censorship laws required that until the late 1980s, all public performances be submitted for approval to Lord Chamberlain and his Watch Committee. In a peculiar quirk of legislation, nudity was permitted, but on the condition that naked performers remained motionless – as the memorable headline of one tabloid's report of the new laws put it, 'If it moves, it's rude'. Entrepreneurial variety impresario Vivian Van Damm and multi-millionaire computer programmer and arts patron Peggy Googleheim took their cue to programme an extraordinary series of avant-garde cabarets based on the presentation of nude tableaux vivants at the Windmill theatre. Functioning simultaneously as both sculptural installations and high-end strip shows, these revolutionary works pulled controversial formal debates into sharp focus – had the sculptural object finally been displaced by the body? This portion of the exhibition examines the impact of a generation of sculptors bent on questioning the laughable objectcentricity of traditional modes of practice.

The Bothy Gallery

Drawing by Edward Ward, words by Mel Brimfield, 2011, 33 x 23.4 in. / 84 x 59 cm. Laser print. Image courtesy the artist and Ceri Hand Gallery.

This Is Performance Art – Part One: Performed Sculpture and Dance
Curated by Francis Spalding OBE

Room 17 – AUDITORIUM
The **This Is Performance Art** TV series is screened in its entirety throughout the course of the exhibition. Presented by bon viveur, raconteur and national treasure Sir Francis Spalding, this landmark moment in arts broadcasting explores the impact and legacy of performance art from the 1940s to today, and insists on searching through the hitherto unexplored nooks and crannies of theatre, activism, comedy, music and sport for the very seeds of its inception and for evidence of its continued importance. This 32-part BBC 4 production will air in autumn, condensing some 60 years of its rich history into 16 short hours of essential primetime viewing, every Sunday at 4:30am from September onwards.

THE PEGGY GOOGLEHEIM MEMORIAL TEA PAVILION AND GIFT SHOP

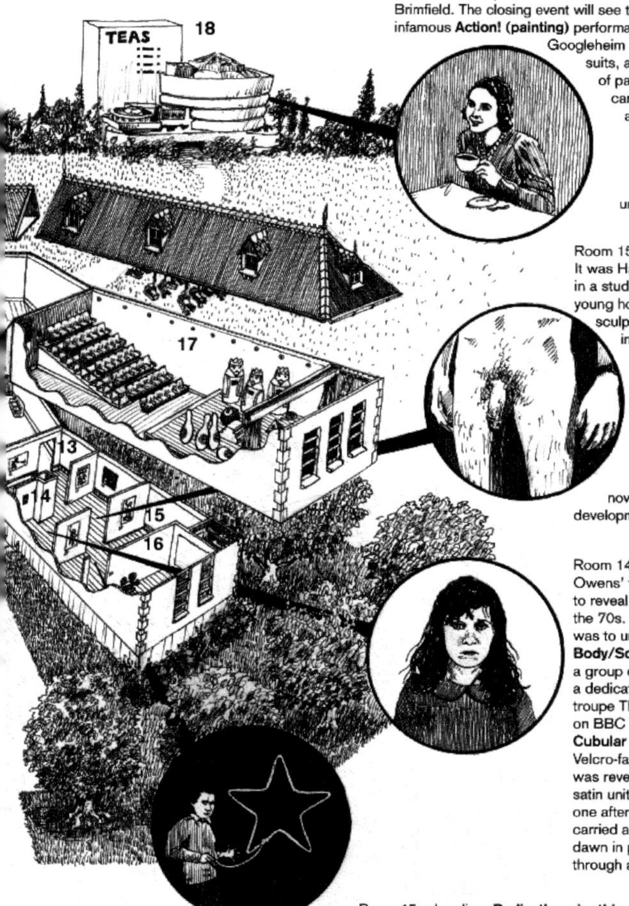

TEAS 18

17

13

14

15

16

In addition, a programme of live performances revisiting influential moments in the history of Performed Sculpture and Dance will punctuate the screenings, curated by Sir Francis and Mel Brimfield. The closing event will see the restaging of three-time Olympic black-belt Cato Fong's infamous **Action! (painting)** performance as presented by the Gutai formation squad at the Googleheim Museum in 1964. Dressed in large moulded foam rubber suits, and attached to bungees, the participating artists carried buckets of paint up greasy poles and over rolling logs towards giant canvases whilst being fired on incessantly by paint cannons and paint-filled custard pies toted by the audience. In a peculiar postscript, Fong was forced to enter into a complex series of extended intellectual property litigations when ITV seized upon the format to launch the popular It's A Knockout games tournament series – they settled out of court for an undisclosed sum.

Room 15 – Richard Serra Rolling Stone magazine spread
It was Hans Namuth's photographs of Richard Serra at work on his **Throwing Lead** series in a studio at the Leo Castelli warehouse that were to establish the ripplingly muscular young hotshot as a household name. Published as an eight-page spread in prominent sculpture journal Rolling Stone, under the headline 'Is he the greatest living sculptor in the United States?', the photographs are a paean to both masculine animal magnetism, and the raw physicality and drama of the sculptor's art. His naked torso is smeared with oil and soot, and glistens in the dim light of the foundry furnace against a backdrop of exposed brickwork and rusty steel – he is barely aware of the rude interruption of Namuth's probing lens as his studded gauntlets firmly grip the handles of his twin crucible ladles, full to the brim with molten lead. In a flurry of impetuous speed, the artist furiously hurls lariats of the fluid metal at the wall, a blur of superhuman energy and cathartic outpouring, before withdrawing, spent and cooling, a burnt out crater between explosions. These now iconic images, displayed in Room 15, stand for a seminal moment in the development of performed sculptural history.

Room 14 – Hot Gossip Posters
Owens' free-wheeling experiments with object and sculpture based performances began to reveal an increasingly polemical stance towards the site of the feminine body throughout the 70s. In an extraordinary series of physical transformations over eight years, the artist was to undergo rigorous and often excruciating exercise and weight lifting regimes – her **Body/Sculpture** series was to reach a zenith when in a final radical act, Owens persuaded a group of like-minded female sculptors to join her in becoming morbidly obese through a dedicated programme of gluttony and inactivity to form revolutionary feminist dance troupe The Roly Polys. The group are of course best known for their frequent appearances on BBC TV music chart show Top of The Pops, and for the thrilling finale of their **Cubular Belles** piece in which their final metamorphosis was to be revealed; casting aside Velcro-fastened massively padded shellsuits in one smoothly executed yank, their obesity was revealed to be a thing of the past. Their newly toned athletic bodies resplendent in satin unitards provoked an astonished and spontaneous standing ovation, especially when one after the other, the dancers turned and bent over – each perfectly shaped backside carried a letter – when lined up, those backsides spelled out both Hot Gossip, and a new dawn in performed sculptural history. Room 14 highlights the group's meteoric rise to fame through a private collection of posters and historic magazine covers.

Room 15 – Juggling: **Bodiesthrowingthings**
Bruce McLean and his Nice Style troupe didn't just innovate within the field of conceptual burlesque, though the appropriation of inappropriately gaudy mainstream entertainment formats continued to inform their cutting edge dance works. Room 15 presents documentation of **Bodiesthrowingthings,** a collaborative performance born out of a series of choreographic workshops at the Judson Theatre. It adopted some of the more challenging aspects of avant-gardism in the 60s, in particular the widespread and conspicuous use of ordinary gestures, actions, rhythms and objects as the base material of performance. Deliberately assembling a troupe of artists entirely lacking in even the basic technical skills required for it, McLean devised a complicated routine incorporating trick cycling, advanced juggling and balancing feats, and rope spinning. Performing in front of a black curtain, the dancers were in fact assisted by prop handlers who were clad head to toe in black – balaclava, gloves, etc. The handlers were clearly visible in the tiny performance space, removing any pretence at theatrical illusion – the result was an exhilarating and conceptually complex piece of performed sculpture that privileged the choreographic manoeuvring of objects over and above the tired vaudeville 'act' apparently presented to the audience.

GALLERY 3
Alex Owens and reappraised Vaudeville techniques | Rooms 13–16
This section of the exhibition focuses on the extraordinary and tragically short career of renowned polymath Alex Owens. She was something of an unlikely art-world heavyweight, a long-legged, doe-eyed ingénue innocent of the brute machismo of the late 60s art scene on her arrival. Nevertheless, driven by the twin engines of ambition and the sheer pyrotechnic iconoclasm of youth, she burst onto the parched landscape of desiccated minimalist orthodoxy like a welcome monsoon of ultra-feminine sensuality. Combining high-energy jazz choreography, aerobics and strident feminist politics with masterful use of re-appraised vaudeville techniques including juggling, balancing and paper-tearing, the young firebrand was to single-handedly rewrite the lexicon of accepted sculptural practice. Room 15 also displays material demonstrating the muscularity of much contemporary activity in the field for context, focusing on the work of Richard Serra as a key example.

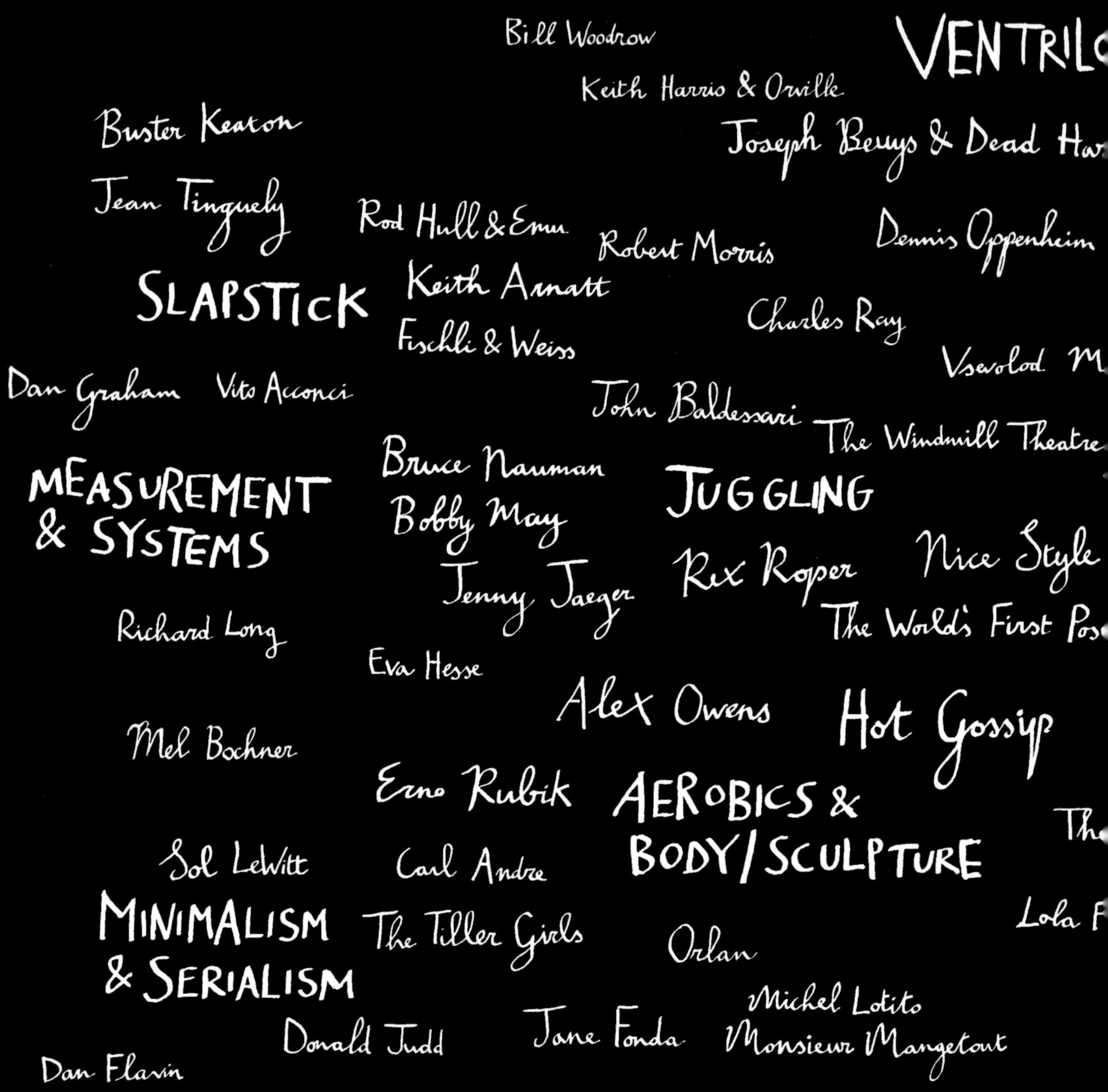

Bill Woodrow

VENTRILO

Keith Harris & Orville

Buster Keaton

Joseph Beuys & Dead Ha

Jean Tinguely

Rod Hull & Emu

Robert Morris

Dennis Oppenheim

SLAPSTICK

Keith Arnatt

Charles Ray

Fischli & Weiss

Vsevolod M

Dan Graham

Vito Acconci

John Baldessari

The Windmill Theatre

Bruce Nauman

MEASUREMENT & SYSTEMS

JUGGLING

Bobby May

Nice Style

Rex Roper

Jenny Jaeger

The World's First Pos

Richard Long

Eva Hesse

Alex Owens

Hot Gossip

Mel Bochner

Erno Rubik

AEROBICS & BODY/SCULPTURE

Th

Sol LeWitt

Carl Andre

MINIMALISM & SERIALISM

The Tiller Girls

Lola F

Orlan

Michel Lotito

Monsieur Mangetout

Donald Judd

Jane Fonda

Dan Flavin

This Is Performance Art—Part One: Performed Sculpture and Dance diagram.

M

Oskar Schlemmer The Muppets

ne Detroy & Marquis the Chimp Pablo Picasso Sophie Taeuber

Alexander Calder

ecambe & Wise & Gilbert & George

The Blue Blouse Group

BLEAUX VIVANTS Robert Longo Tommy Cooper

Hugo Ball

Jane of The Daily Mirror

The Cockettes PROP & COSTUME

Joan Rhodes

ghty Mannequin Judson Dance Theatre Franz West Lygia Clark

Lionel Blair

BURLESQUE

VALIE EXPORT Gustav Metzger

uce McLean Yoko Ono Destruction In Art Symposium

Richard Serra ACTION PAINTING Hans Namuth

lys

Niki de Saint Phalle

John Cage Georges Matthieu Lucio Fontana

Jackson Hancock

unningham CHANCE Cato Fong and The

Gutai Formation Display Team

ff Capes It's A Knockout

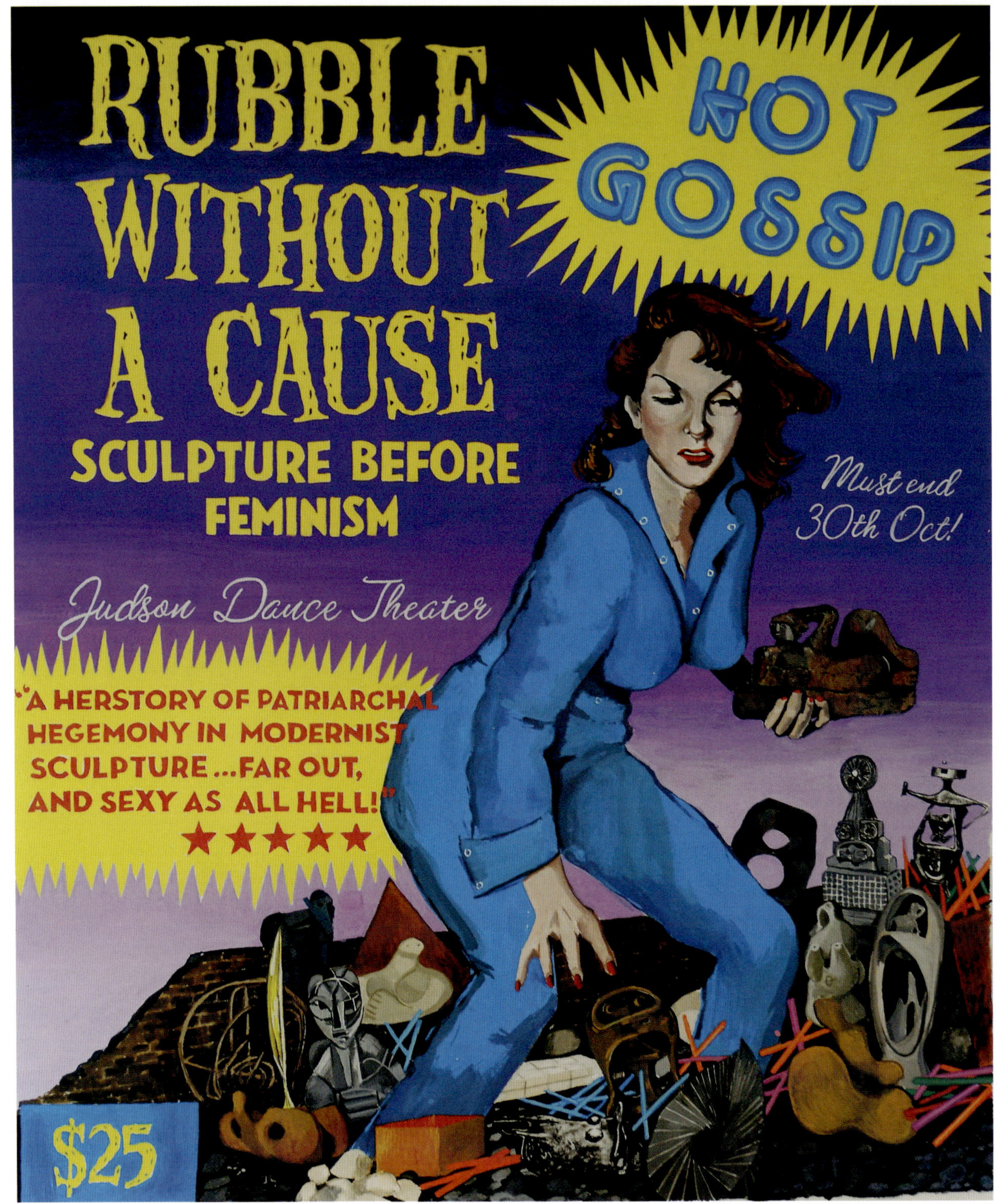
RUBBLE WITHOUT A CAUSE
SCULPTURE BEFORE FEMINISM
HOT GOSSIP
Must end 30th Oct!
Judson Dance Theater
"A HERSTORY OF PATRIARCHAL HEGEMONY IN MODERNIST SCULPTURE...FAR OUT, AND SEXY AS ALL HELL!"
★★★★★
$25

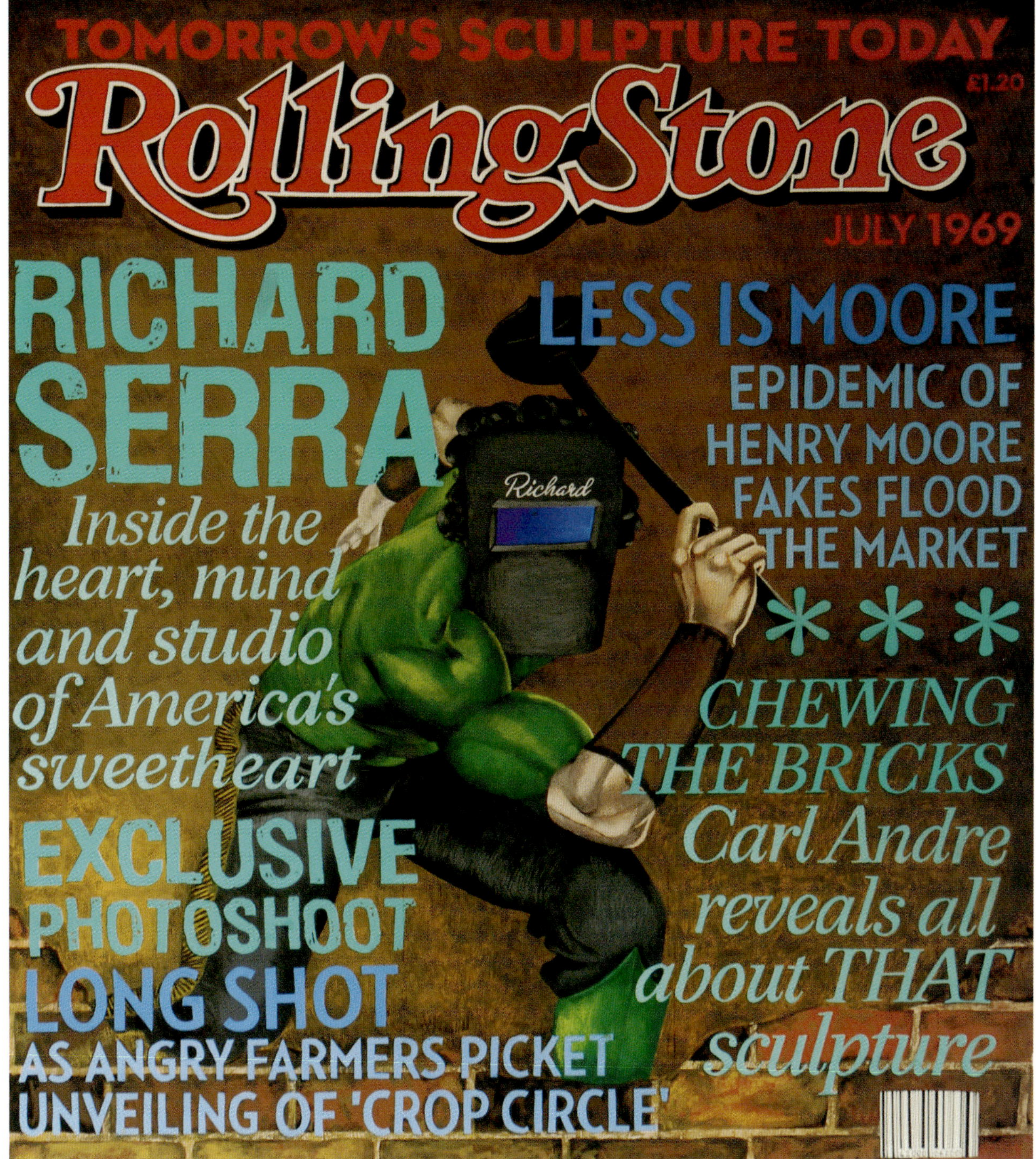

OPPOSITE

Mel Brimfield, *Rubble Without* a Cause, 2010, Gouache on board, 24.8 x 20.9 in. / 63 x 53 cm. Image courtesy the artist and Ceri Hand Gallery.

ABOVE

Mel Brimfield, *Rolling Stone, July 1969*, 2011, Gouache on paper, 34.6 x 40.2 in. / 88 x 102 cm. Image courtesy the artist and Ceri Hand Gallery.

OVERLEAF

Mel Brimfield, *Action! (Painting)*, 2011, C-print, 38.6 x 57.1 in. / 98 x 145 cm. Image courtesy the artist and Ceri Hand Gallery.

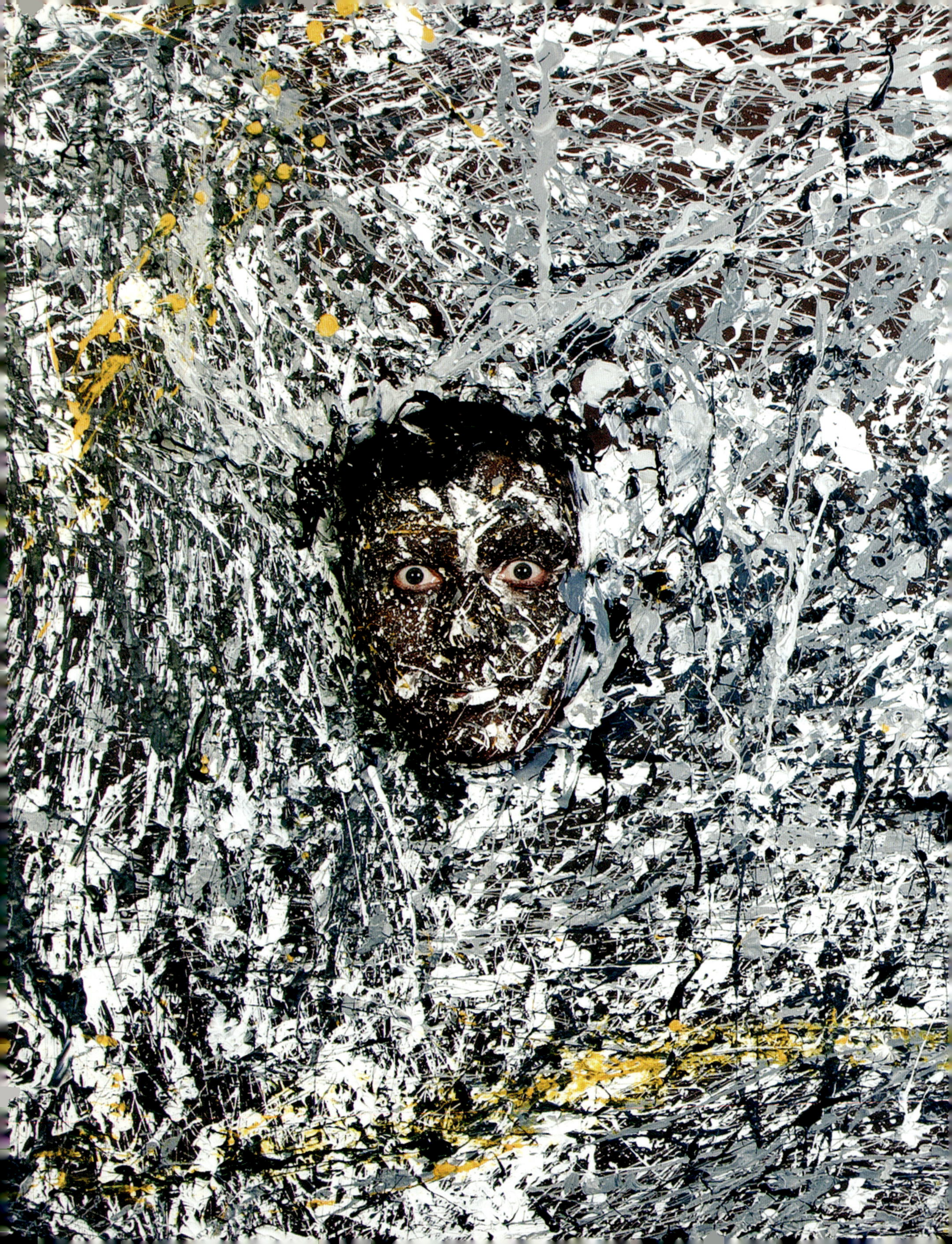

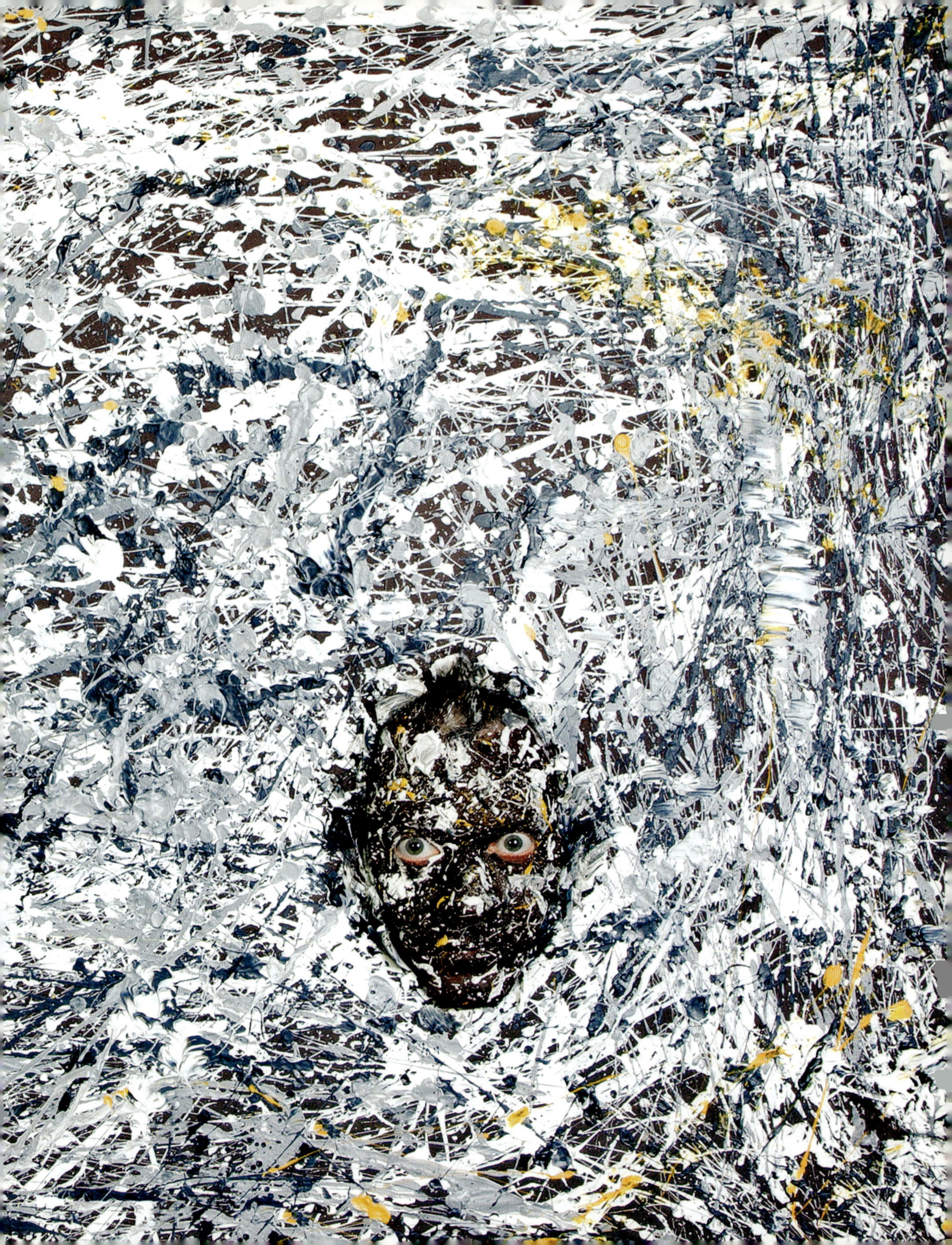

Mel Brimfield, *Monument (Living Sculpture)*,
2011, C-print, 33.1 x 47.2 in. / 84 x 120 cm.
Image courtesy the artist and Ceri Hand Gallery.
Private collection.

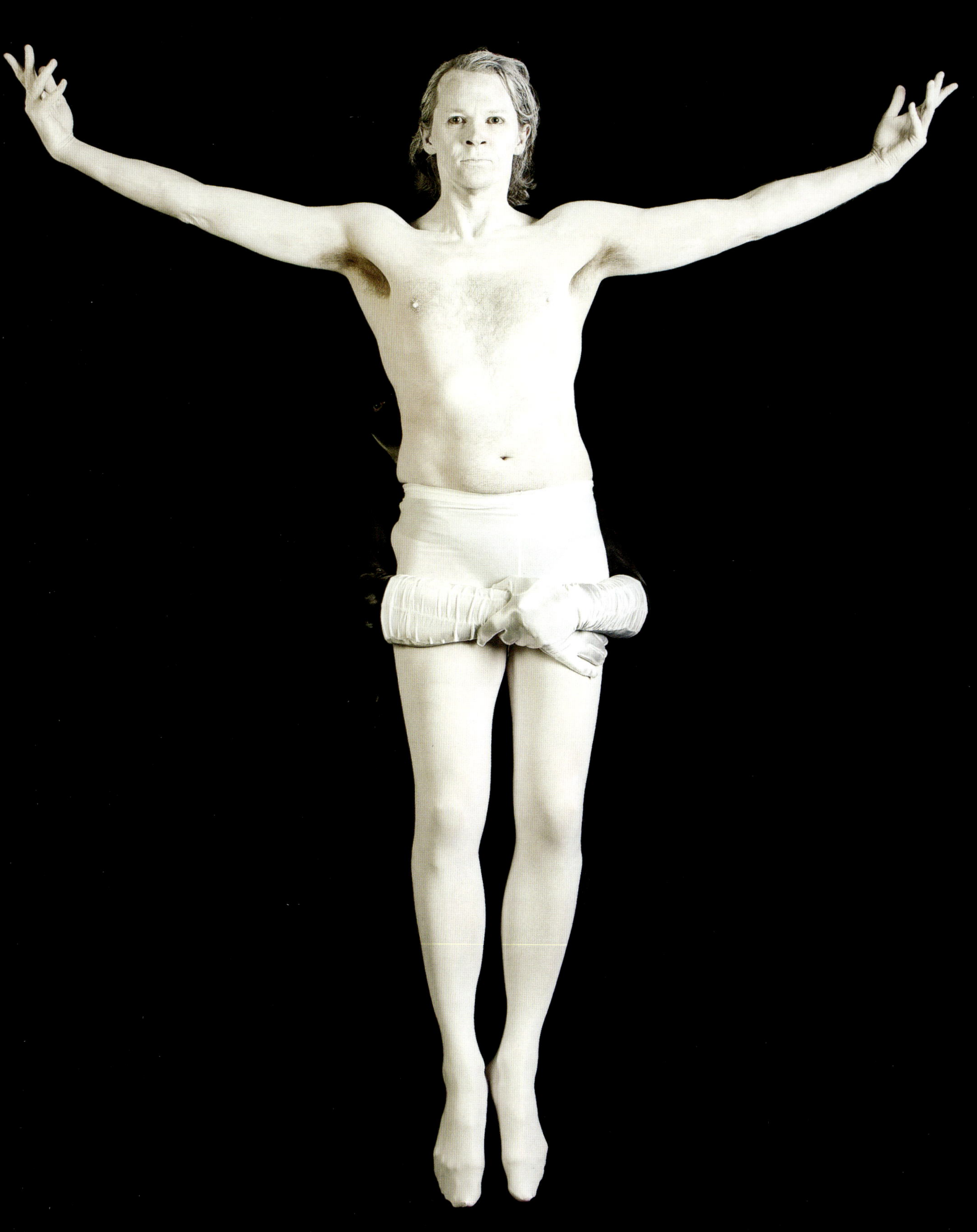

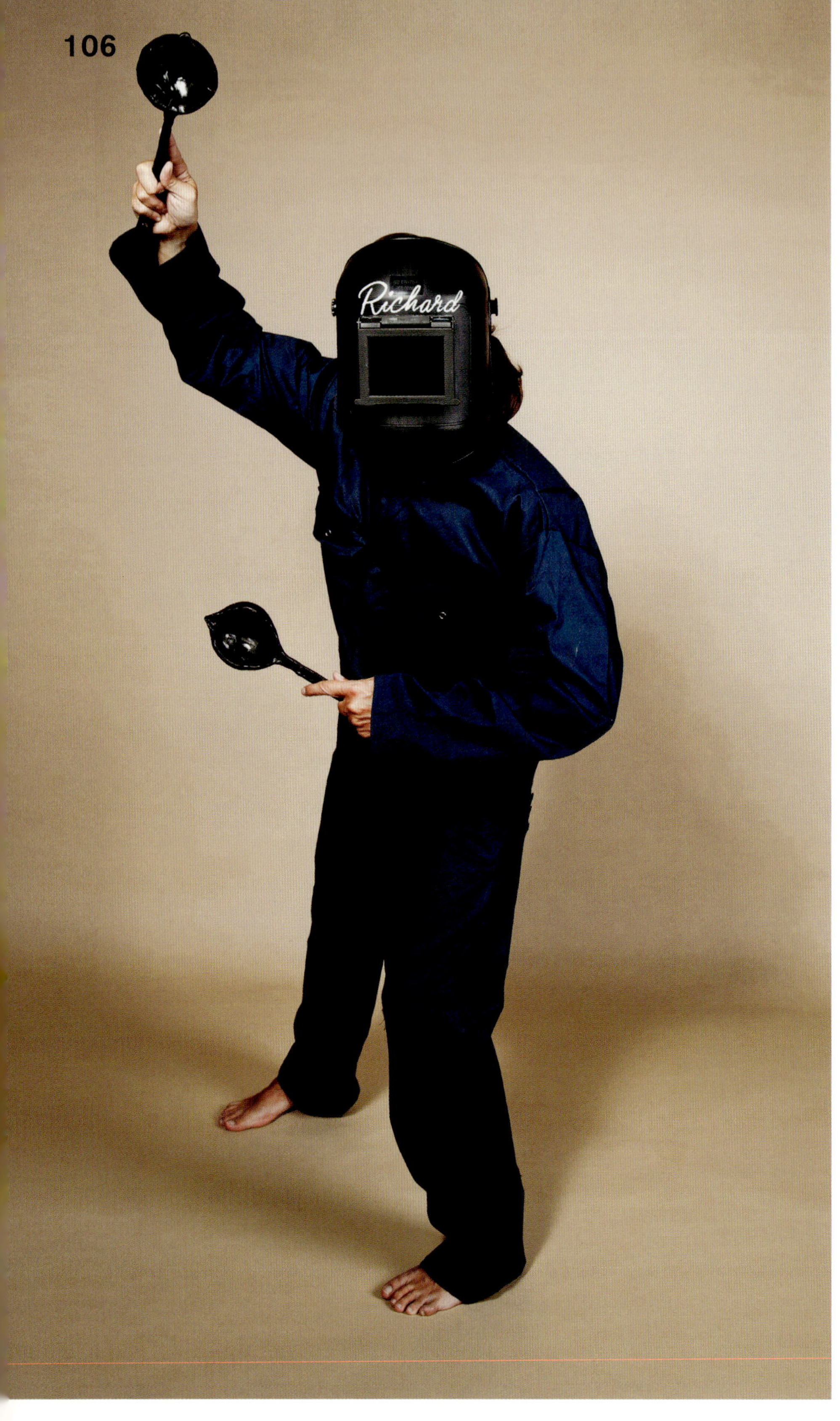

Mel Brimfield, *Cut Piece (Richard Serra)*, 2011, two C-print colour photographs, each 83.2 x 45.5 in. / 211.3 x 115.6 cm. Image courtesy the artist and Ceri Hand Gallery.

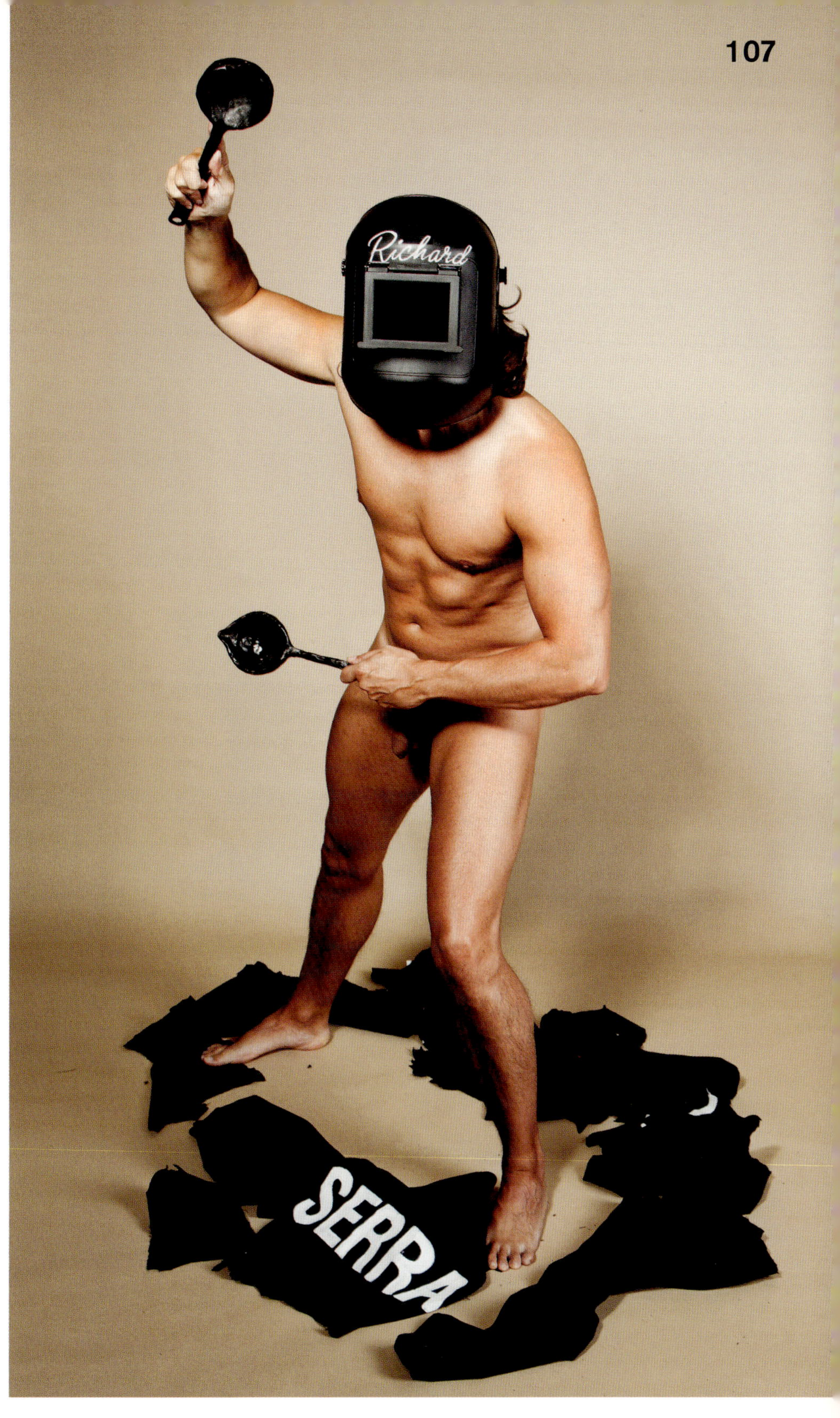

YORKSHIRE SCULPTURE PARK EXHIBITION

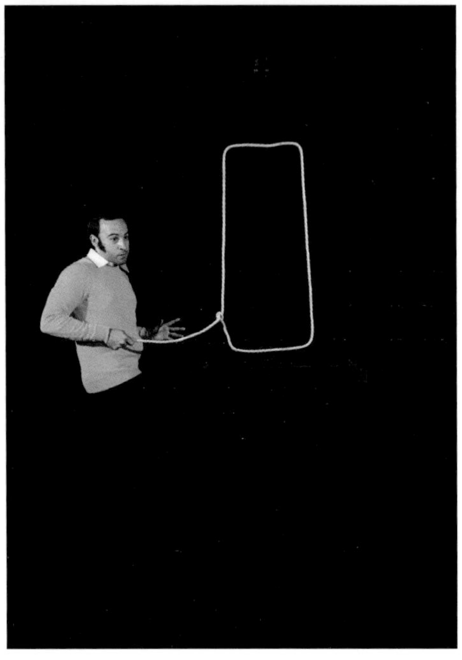

Mel Brimfield, *Bodiesthrowingthings*, 2010, three C-prints, 10.5 x 8 in. / 27 x 20 cm. Images courtesy the artist and Ceri Hand Gallery. Private collection.

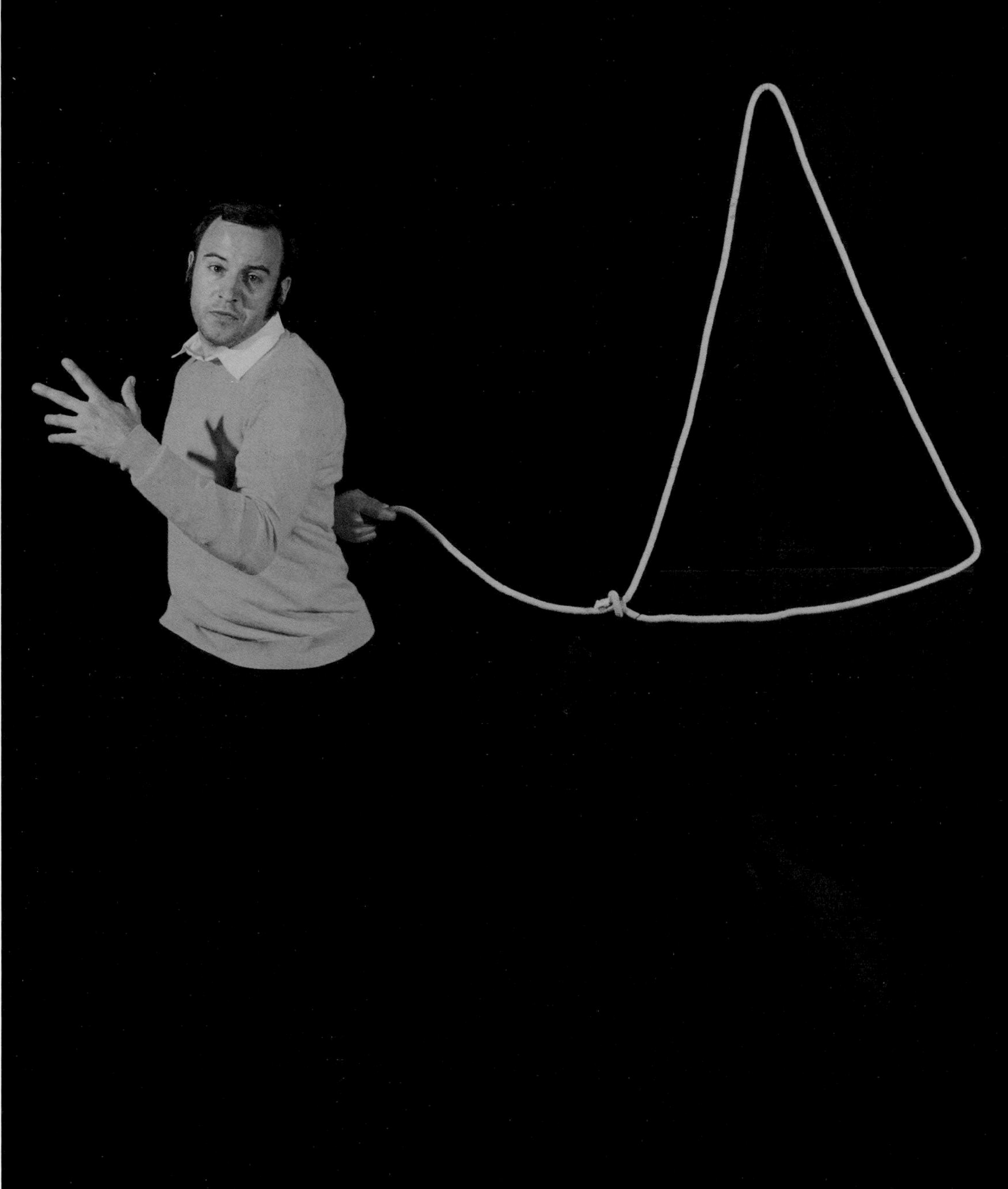

THE BREAKFAST SCULPTURE

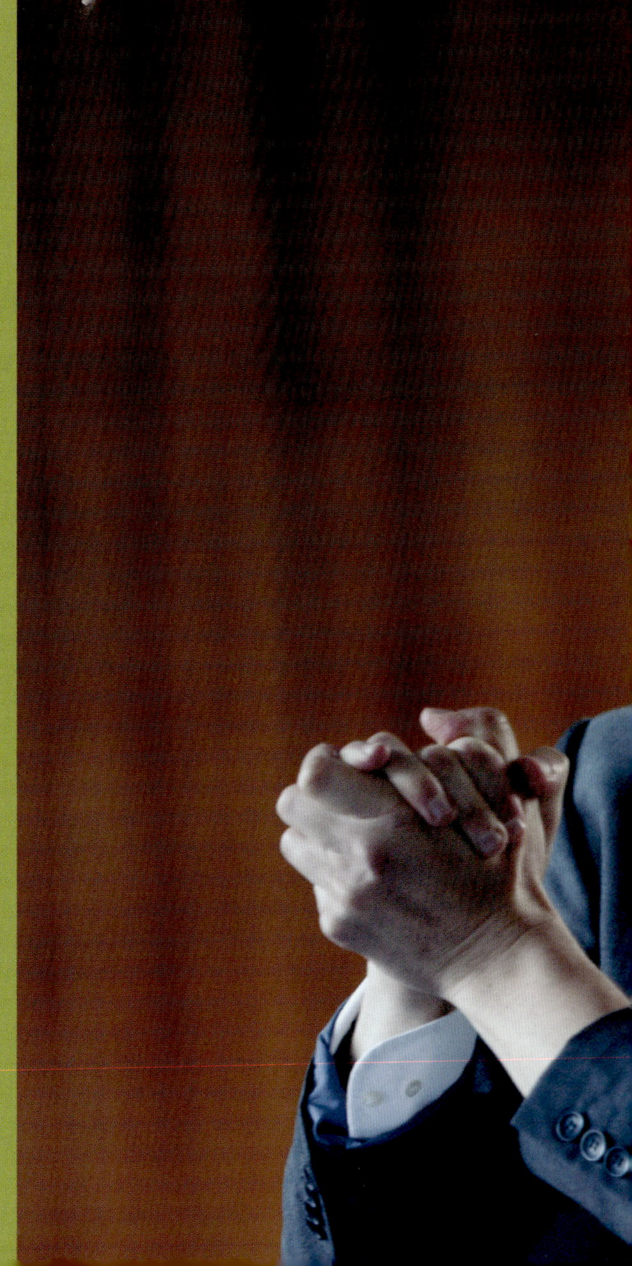

Tom Roden and Pete Shenton perform *The Breakfast Sculpture*, a 'restaging' of a fictional conceptual burlesque work by Nice Style—The World's First Pose Band, at Yorkshire Sculpture Park, 2011. Photos: Jonty Wilde.

A collaboration with dance theatre company New Art Club (Tom Roden and Pete Shenton), composer Paul Higgs and Dinnington Colliery Band at Yorkshire Sculpture Park

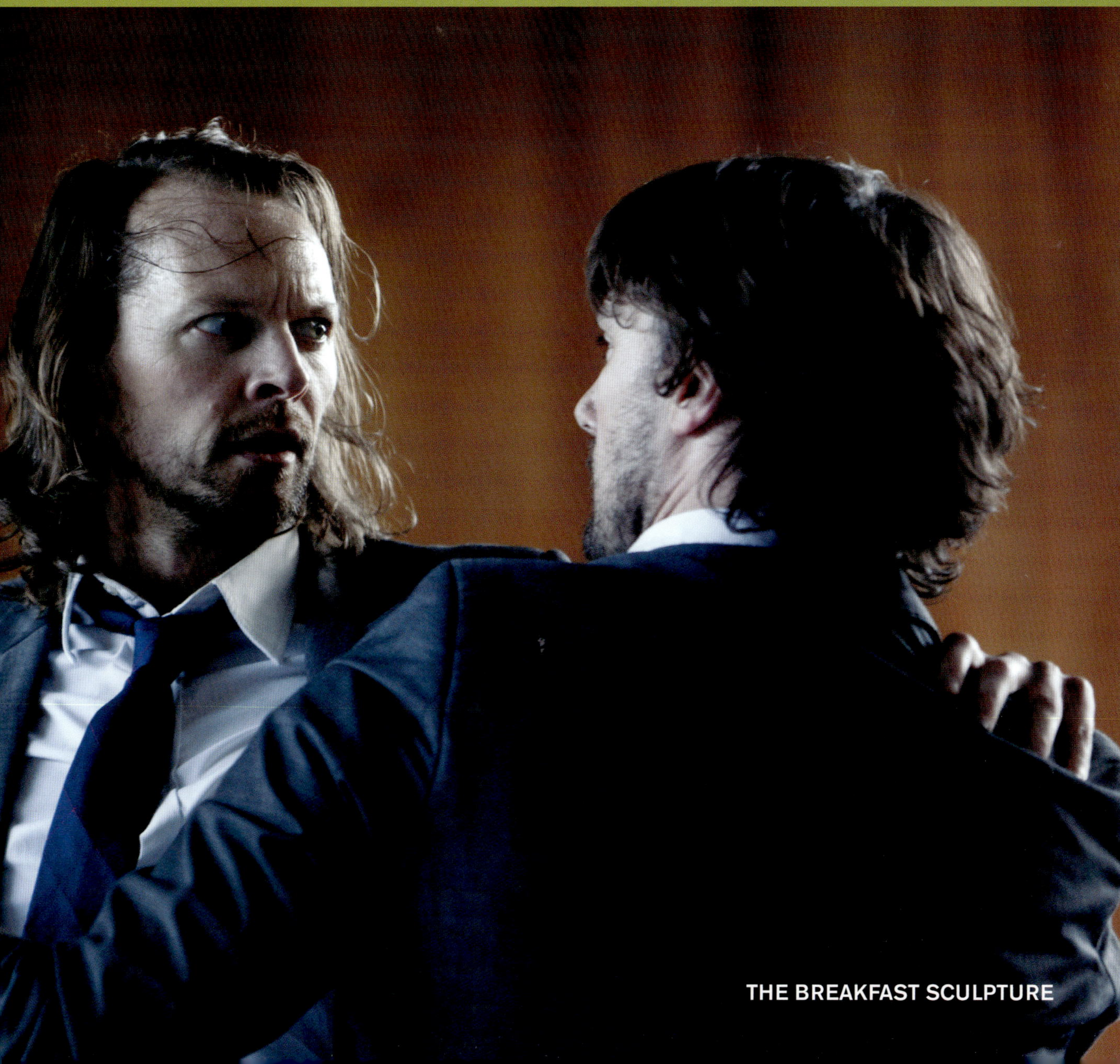

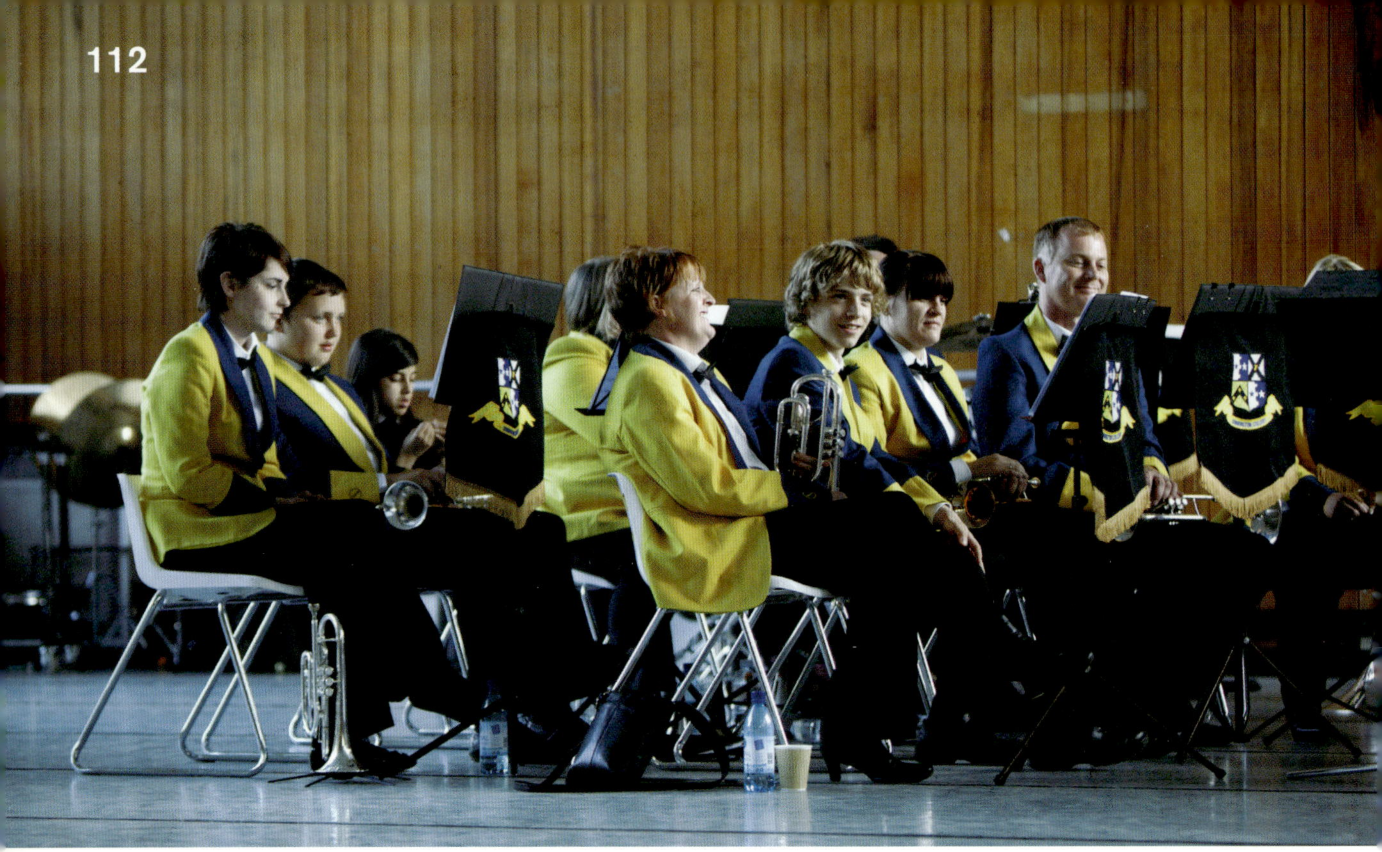

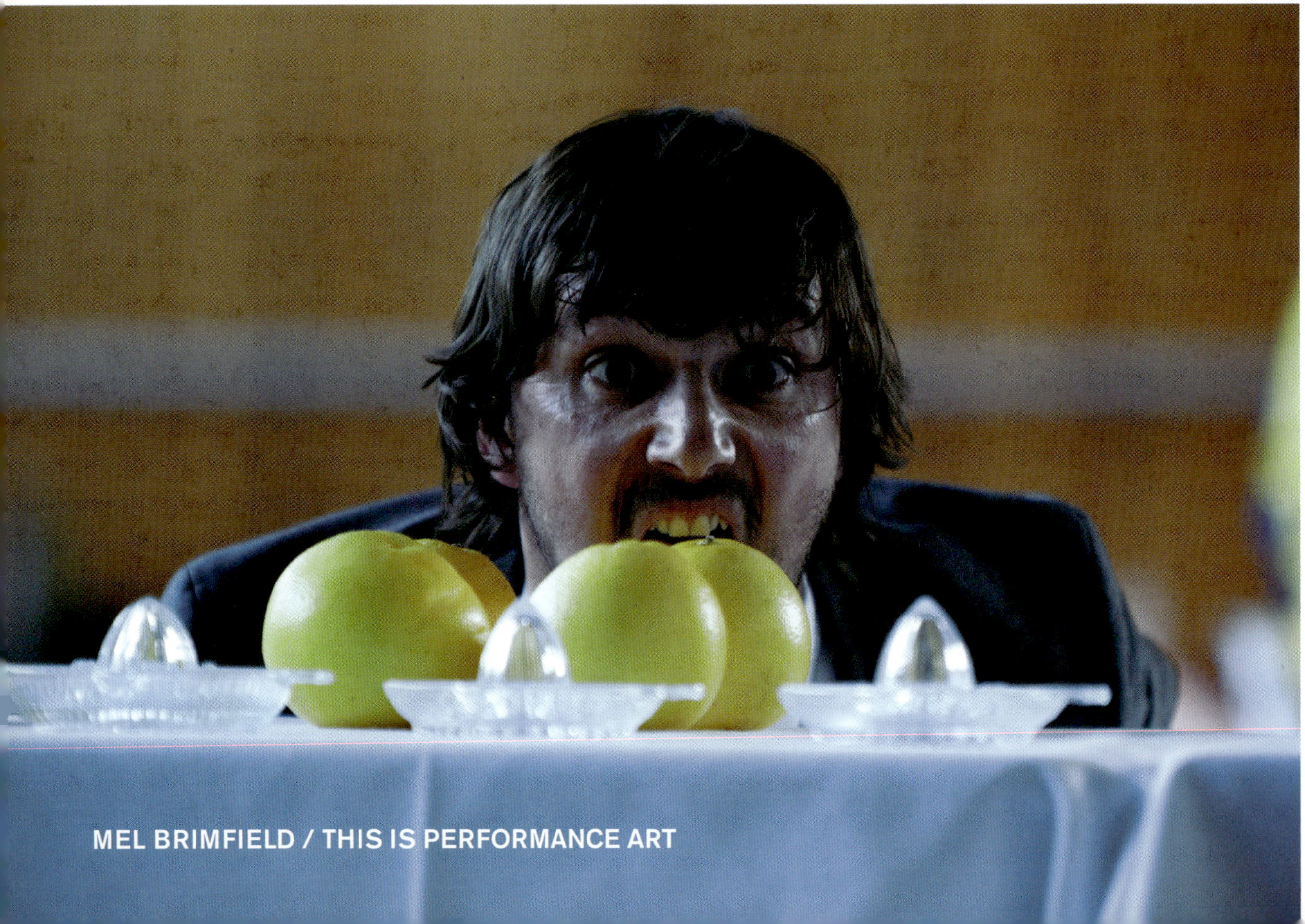

MEL BRIMFIELD / THIS IS PERFORMANCE ART

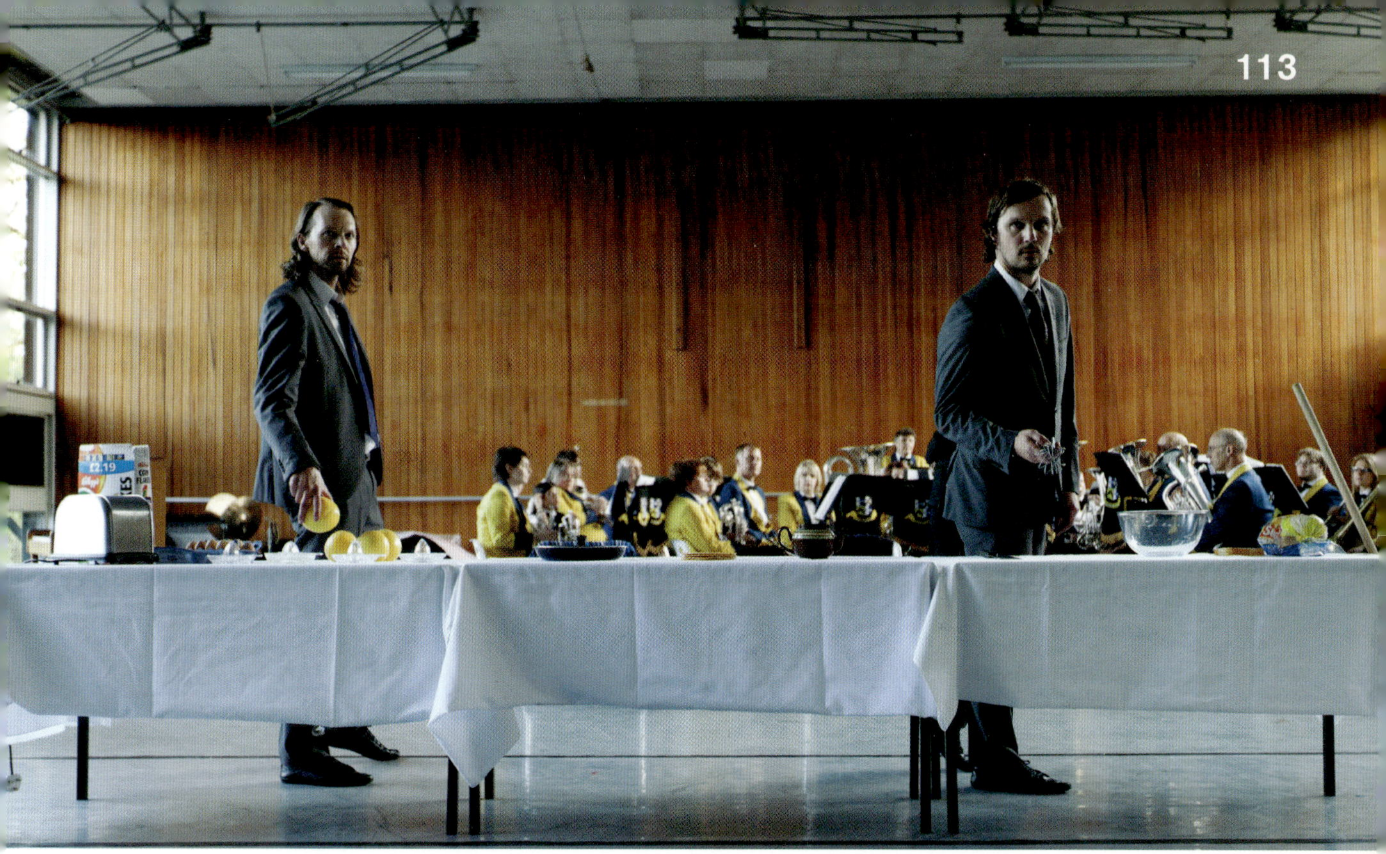

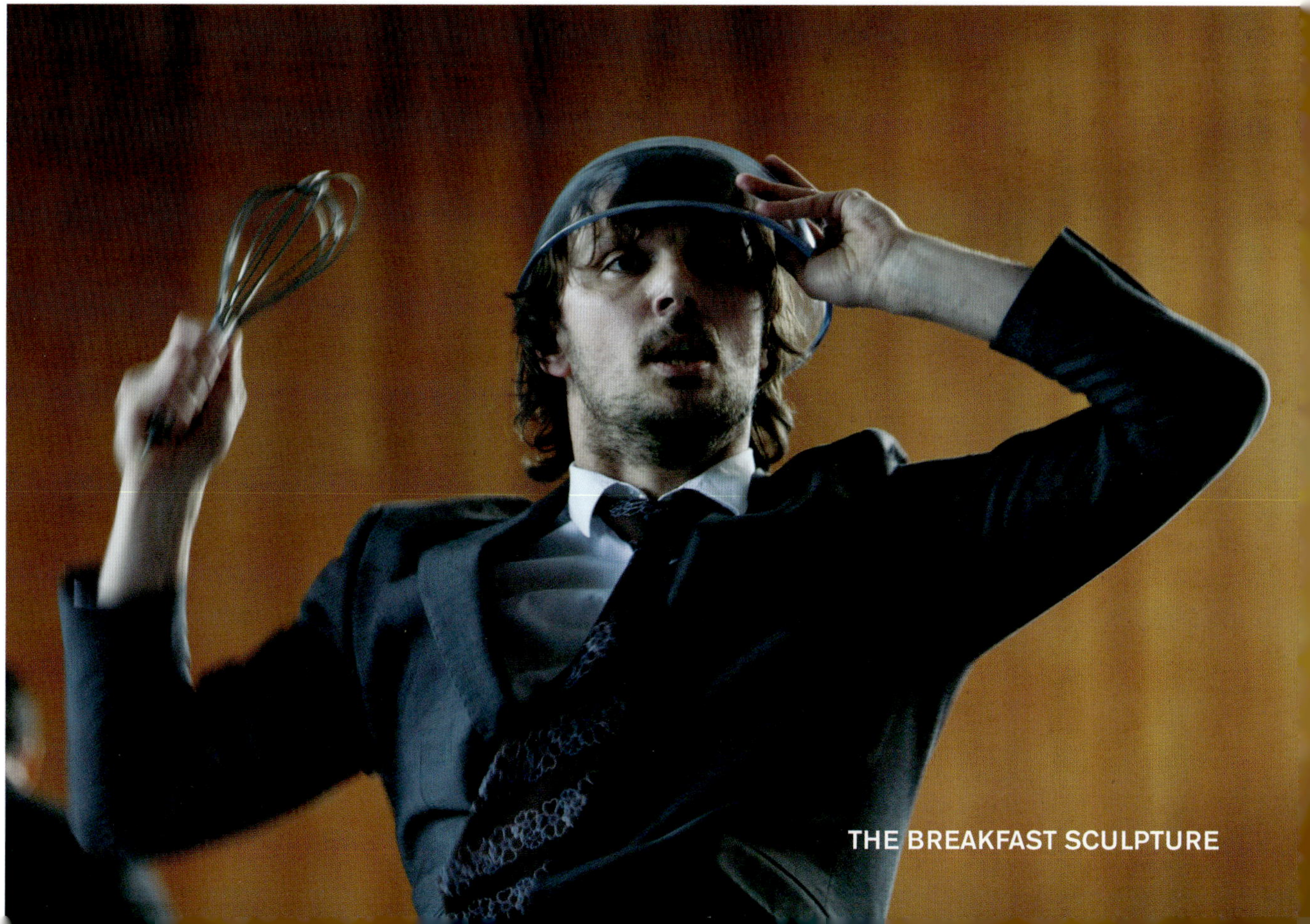

THE BREAKFAST SCULPTURE

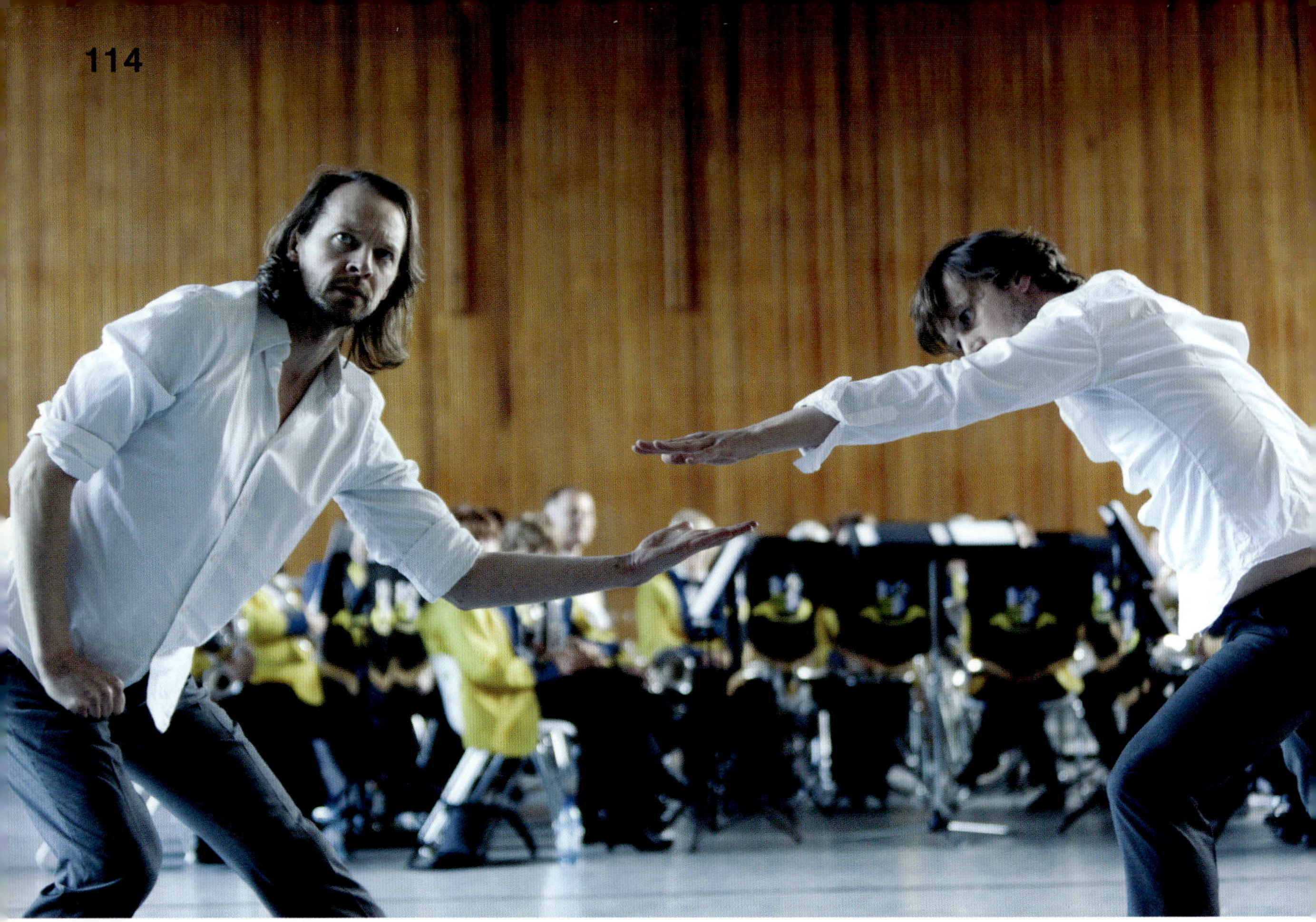

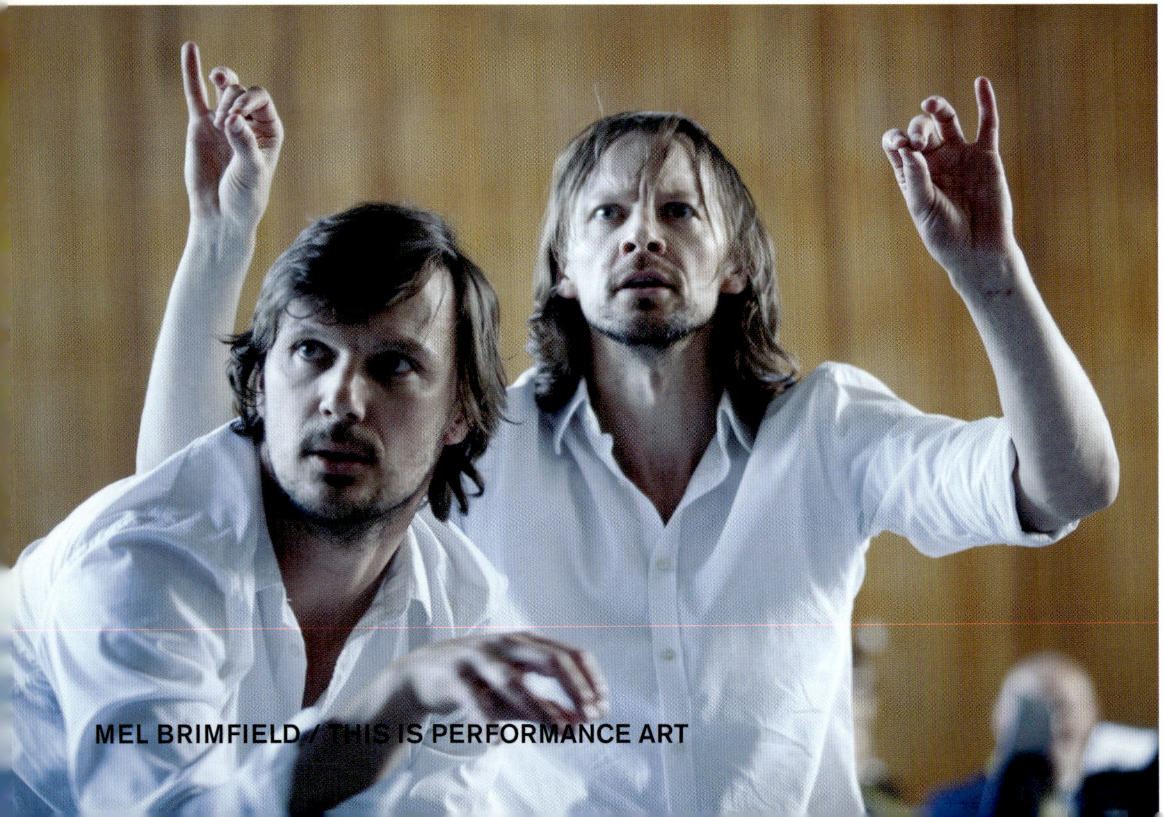

MEL BRIMFIELD / THIS IS PERFORMANCE ART

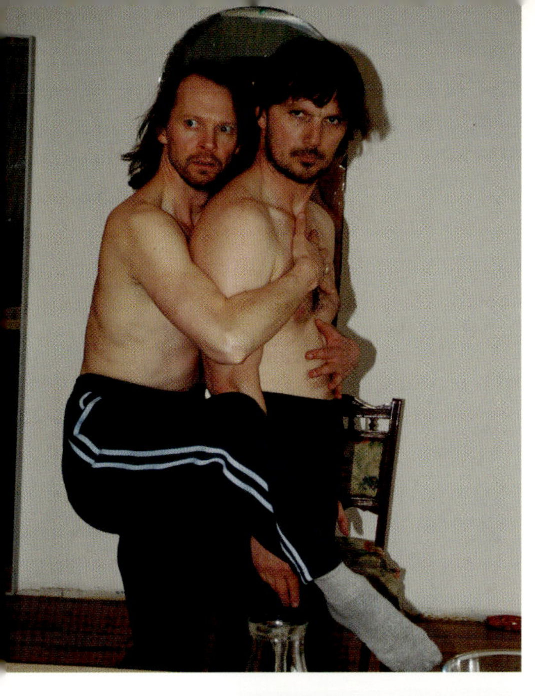

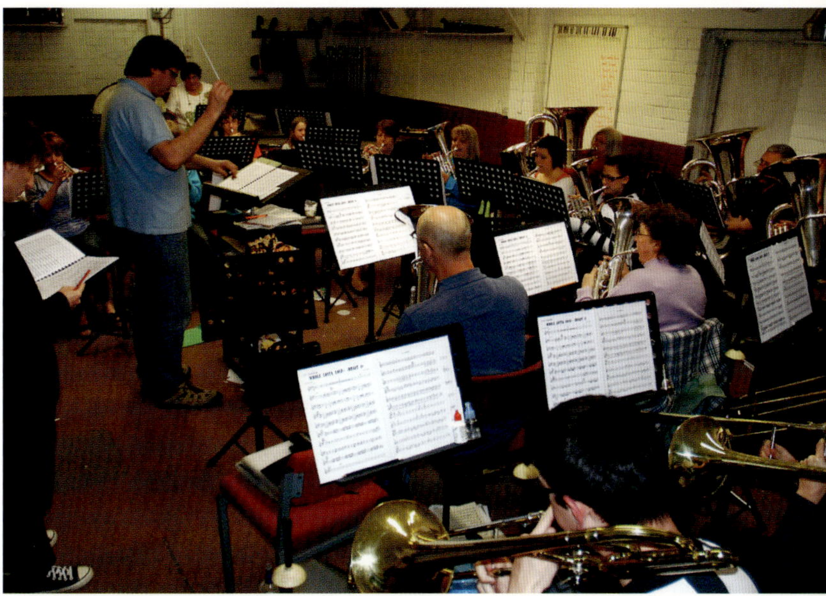

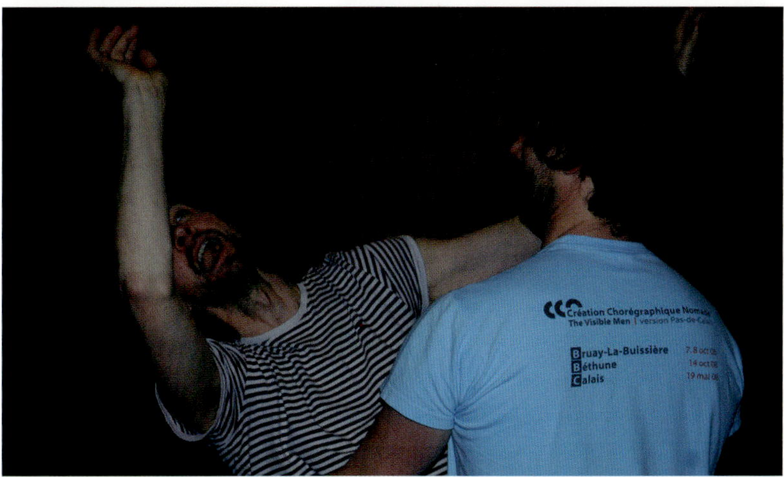

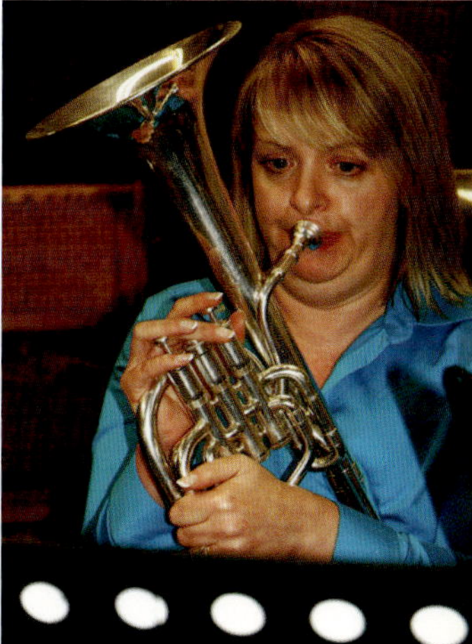

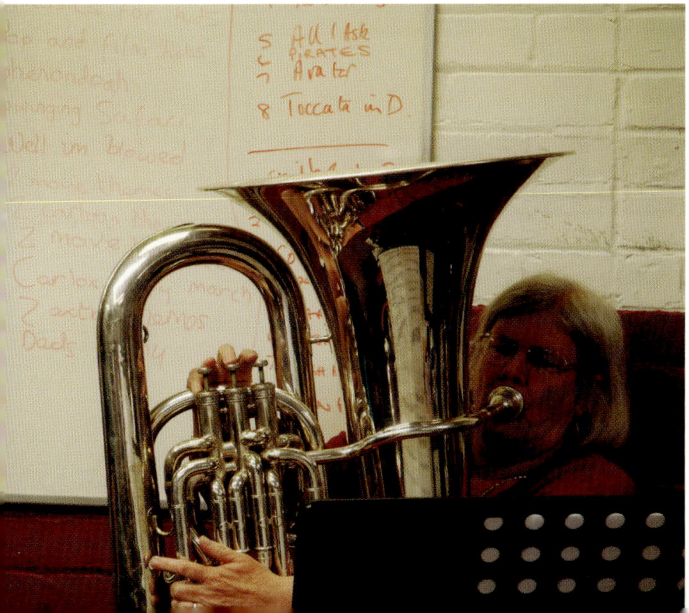

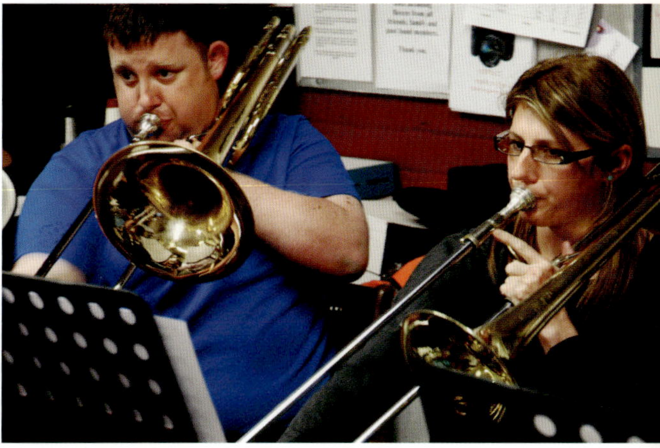

Rehersal photos for *The Breakfast Sculpture*.

Barbara Hepworth > Henry Moore

Good evening. For those of you who do not know, I am Dame Barbara Hepworth PhD QVC WRVS CBA. I detest all forms of pomp and ceremony, and yet one must not shirk one's responsibilities as a national treasure. I am honoured to appear before you tonight, albeit somewhat reluctantly, as an after-dinner speaker, and I'd actually like to start proper by expressing my appreciation for our hosts—we are, of course, here to celebrate the centenary of the longest running feminist arts organisation in the UK, namely Women in the Arts, or WITA, as the well known acronym would have it. They just go on and on and on and on, and I for one, applaud their persistence and tenacity.

Their diverse portfolio of projects has fearlessly and consistently broken new ground in many cultural arenas. The vital importance of their work cannot be overstated, and tonight's celebratory programme of lectures, performances, and musical recitals proves it. Joanna Lumley joins us first on the main stage to read the award-winning 32-part serialisation of her *Mountain Women and Spoon Boxes of Daghestan* travelogue for BBC Radio Four's *Woman's Hour* was of course produced by the broadcasting arm of WITA, and she'll share extracts with us this evening. We'll be treated next to an extraordinary *mélange* of Innuit throat singing, interpretative dance and bongo rhythms from the Earth Exchange Theatre Cooperative, before moving on to a lecture by popular science commentator Dr Susan Greenfield. When few gave credence to her pioneering application of mathematical principles to the interpretation of modern cinema, it was WITA who petitioned for the publication of her early work. I refer, of course, to the seminal essay *Here's Looking at Euclid—Geometry and the Films of Humphrey Bogart*, now rightly acknowledged as a classic and reprised for this evening's event. And finally, popular beat combo The Fucks will be wrapping up proceedings by building their own sonic cathedral with bricks of experimental death disco leaded with a vaulted roof of flipscat, spackbot and techno beats—heady stuff. I'd also like to ask you to raise a glass to the Friends and Patrons of WITA—it is through their visionary support and generosity that tonight's running buffet became a reality.

And now—to me. I have been described as a genius, and as the epoch-defining voice of British Art, but for all of the numerous accolades I have collected, and continue to collect, I prefer the humble title of sculptor. I am an artisan, allied to the sons of toil by dint of sheer hard manual labour and an affinity with the Earth, and I wouldn't change it, even if I wanted to. I've been asked to talk to you tonight about my muse and formative influences, perhaps even to offer advice to those young women foolhardy enough to dream that they might one day carve a reputation for themselves with urgent chisel upon the mighty slabs of sculptural history. It is my belief that one is born a sculptor; one cannot 'become' a sculptor, anymore than one can just 'become' a shop assistant. Certainly all of my early memories are of form, shape, colour and texture—I had an extremely close relationship with my father, and have a strong memory of riding in his car as a very small child. The hills were sculptures—the roads defined the form. Above all there was the sensation of moving over the contours, the fullnesses and concavities, through hollows and over peaks. Feeling, touching, seeing, through mind and hand and eye. This sensation has never left me. I am the form, and I am the hollow, the thrust and the contour. In fact, the very first word I uttered was "Papa", which later I was fascinated to discover is an obscure Maori term for a kind of soft blue-grey clay of marine siltstone or sandstone. Who knows where I could have picked up such a word, but it doesn't actually surprise me that even at the age of six, I was already attuned to the throb of the soil.

The process I undergo when making a sculpture is as much a mystery to me as it is to you. The maddeningly fleeting will-o-the-wisp of inspiration seems to flutter into sight unbidden. I have formulated ideas for sculpture whilst fingering nubbly avocados, whilst vaselining cracked winter lips, whilst petting a variety of sheep, cats, children and bullocks—even once whilst contemplating the frank heft of a ruddy-faced laundress' low-slung bosom. The source is as unquantifiable as Wales. One theme is consistent; I must be amongst the earthy Northern people of my youth—on a recent visit to Wakefield, I was to strike up a conversation with a lone drinker in the lounge bar of a typical spit and sawdust public house. His face was scarlet from years of continual alcohol ingestion, and as he described his failed marriage, enforced redundancy and ruined heath, I was moved to tears—the chiaroscuro effect of the failing tobacco stained light upon his baggy, bloated, caved-in face was extraordinary. I set to sketching an impression of his bulging features on the back of a handy beermat immediately. The importance of light in relation to form will always interest me. Many and various are the inspirations of great artists.

Inevitably, people will insist on asking me about the nature of my relationship with that endearing old duffer Henry Moore, almost before they step over the threshold of my studio to look at my fucking work. Dear, dear bumbling Henry. I always thought that he was something of an unlikely so-called genius behind closed doors, I must say—he was hampered thoughout his life by poor motor skills and an almost complete inability to hold a mallet or chisel in his ham-fisted grip, but he didn't let it hold him back; such marvellous spirit despite his obvious shortcomings. He was the son of a mining engineer, and indeed his working class roots were only too audible in his speech—at points the guttural cadence of his thick Northern brogue rendered his speech impenetrable to the general ear. Elocution lessons certainly helped, but much of what he said remains a lovely mystery to us all. Perhaps in many ways it is as well for him—he wasn't the brightest, but then, there are times when a low wattage bulb is just what you need.

How to convey an impression of what I saw in the studio when I first visited him at work in Much Hadham all those years ago? It was incredibly beautiful in its own way—like watching a caveman attempt speech for the first time. I am anything but a woman of sentiment, and the workings of brutish machismo are entirely foreign to my sensibility; yet that morning, absurd though it sounds, my heart was almost broken. I caught glimpses of a near human intelligence in his lumbering ineptitude as he lunged and hacked wildly at the gargantuan granite block filling his workspace. The savage and misshapen figure revealed was incontrovertibly feminine. Somehow this fact was to move me to the most profound melancholy. I resolved then and there to direct his career if I could—to find an audience for his pathetic broken outpourings.

We hiked to his local hostelry for lunch, and as we passed through the bleak countryside in taciturn silence, Henry mutely accumulated chunks of driftwood, pebbles, rocks and shells for his collection—I gasped when he delicately pressed a tiny mouse skull into my palm with his shovel like brown paws at the stile. Later, over several questionable pints of cloudy ale and a pair of limp cheese and pickle sandwiches, he surprised me by embarking on an impassioned diatribe about the state of British sculpture. Downing whisky chasers like a sailor on shore leave, and pounding the sticky table for emphasis, he launched into some manner of foul-mouthed tirade against the art establishment that was clearly fit to make the saltiest navvy blush. It was, of course, impossible in the main part to decode the meaning of his slurred and grunted Northern coloquialisms, but the maniacal hubristic glint in his eye was unmistakeable—indeed, the clustered locals retreated to the four corners of the pub to avoid it. The only phrase I could make out with difficulty was "Calls himself Cambridge educated? He couldn't write fuck on a dusty blind" in relation to his good friend Roland Penrose. But that was Henry for you—pensive, slack-mouthed and dribbling one minute, and filled with the strange destructive fire of primitive rage and creativity at the next.

Were we ever romantically involved? Of course. I slept with everyone. As a vibrant Bohemian spirit pioneering for my sex, it was my duty. He was a surprisingly gentle, if uninventive lover, and let's just say that his bizarre compulsion to magnify modest maquettes into vast public sculpture was somewhat clarified for me following the experience. But I have no regrets. Do I feel that his gender was the only thing standing between me and an assured place in history as the most significant sculptor to emerge from the early twentieth century? Do I wish I'd never introduced him to influential critic Herbert Read? Not at all—no-one could begrudge daft old Henry the oodles of cash and status that came with being the international ambassador for British Modernism. Obviously, only a man could be trusted with such a weighty responsibility. On that note, as to the vexed question of which of us first introduced the hole to the modernist sculptural form, only ask yourself "Who had a vagina?" I will say no more on the subject.

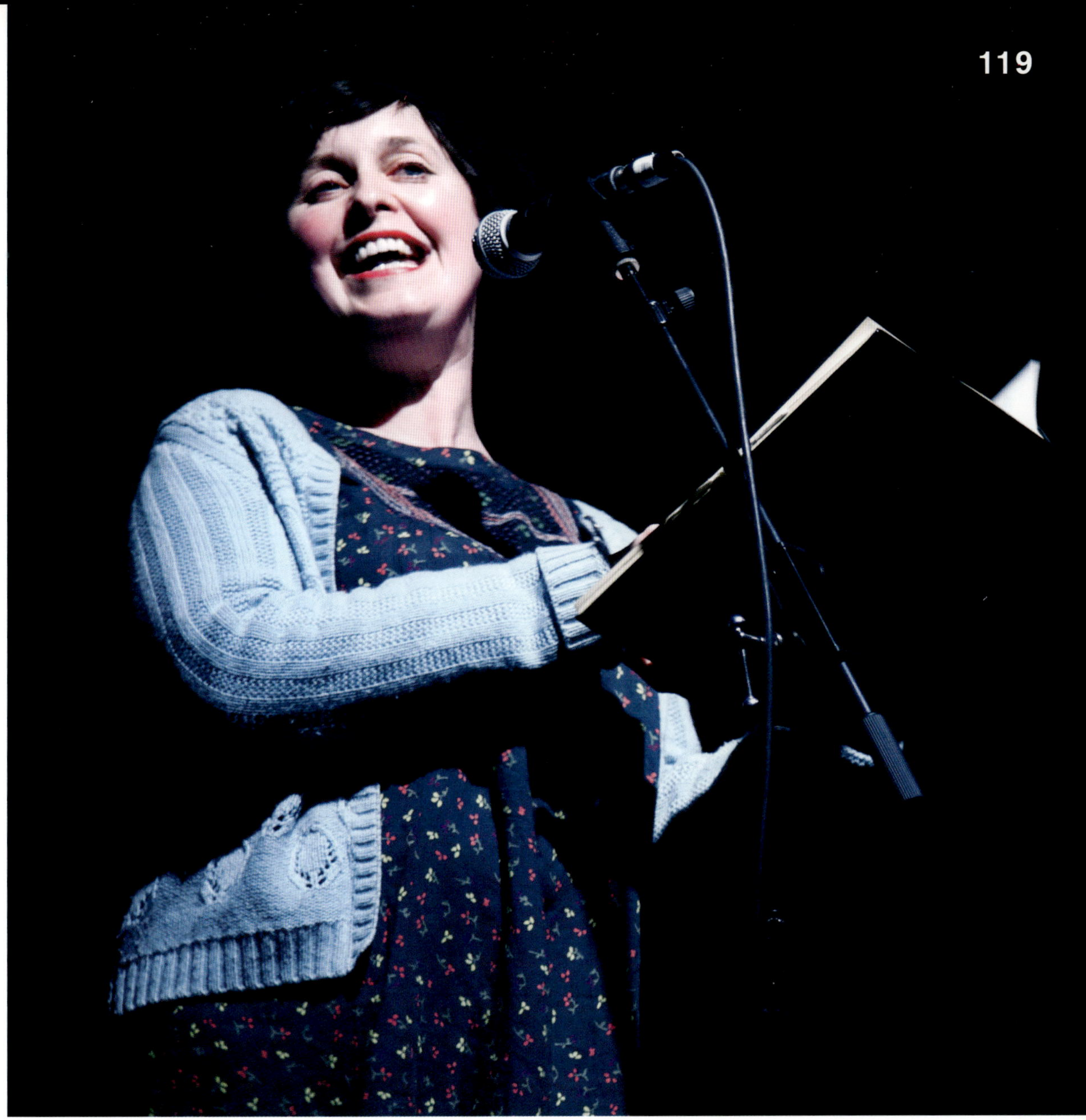

Joanna Neary is Dame Barbara Hepworth in *Barbara Hepworth > Henry Moore* performance at Bob and Roberta Smith's Women Should Be In Charge at the ICA, produced by Home, 2011. Photo Jim Banks.

I do hope you will enjoy the rest of your evening—it only remains for me to congratulate Roberta Smith on her recent election to the Women In The Arts chair. It was a surprising appointment to many, given the fact that for years, she has languished very much in the shadow of her less talented brother Bob. The acrimonious breakdown of their working relationship has been well documented in the press, and I see no reason for raking over the coals. Suffice it to say that a woman is much like a tea bag—it's only when she's in hot water that you realise just how strong she is. Thank you, and good evening.

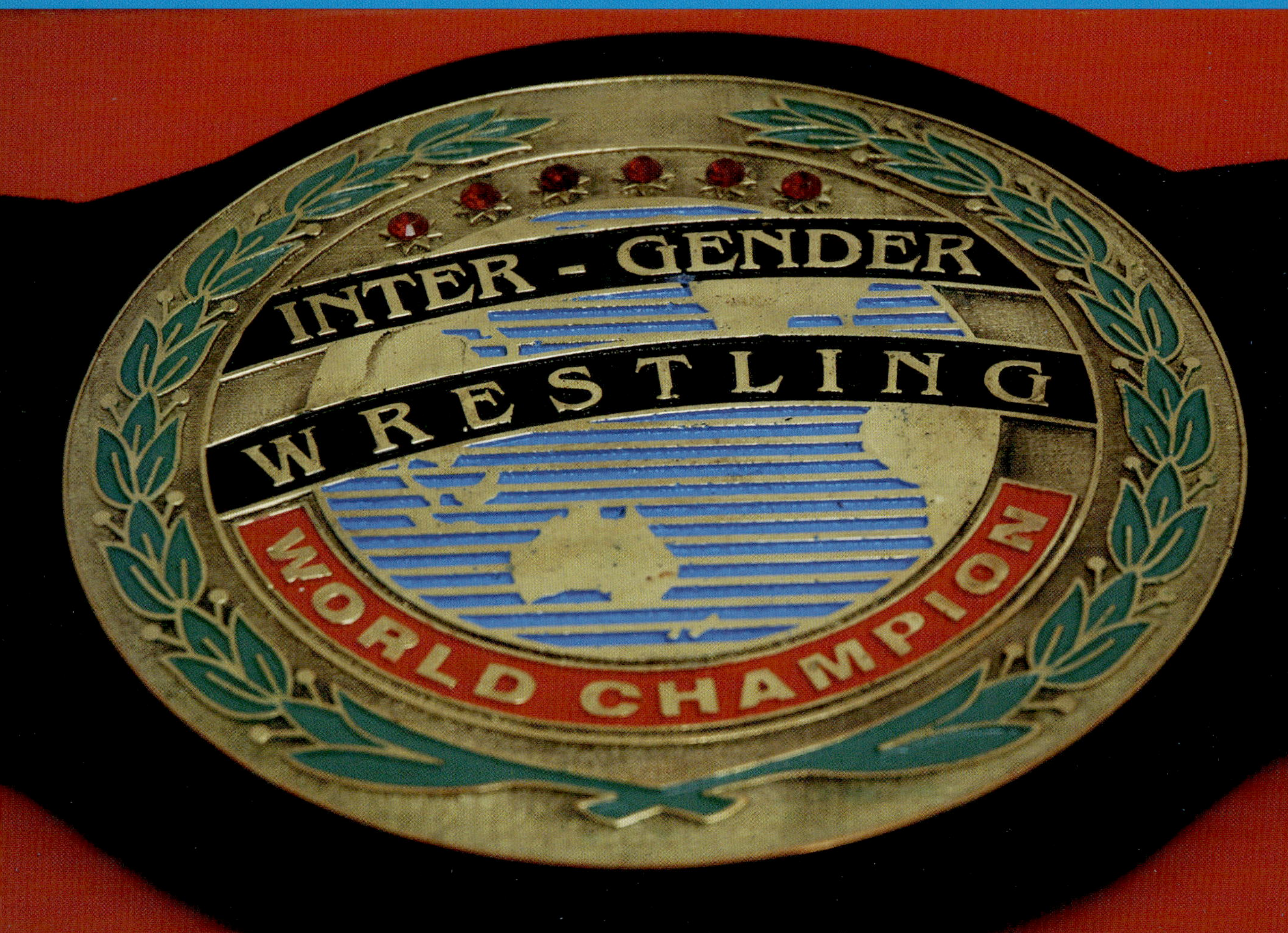

Mel Brimfield, *Inter-gender wrestling championship belt*, 2008, Brass, leather and gems, 49.2 x 10.2 in. / 125 x 26 cm. Image courtesy the artist and Ceri Hand Gallery.

This is Performance Art

26th April 2011

Series devised by Mel Brimfield in association with Sir Francis Spalding

at The London Word Festival

Simon Munnery
Isy Suttie
Lore Lixenburg
The Beaux Belles
Josie Long
Rachel Pantechnicon
Helen Lederer
Tony Law
Kevin Eldon
Oompah Brass
Tim Wells

Intergender Wrestling Part 2

INTERGENDER WRESTLING

An Introduction by Sir Francis Spalding

Hello there, I'm a human being. What are you? You people disgust me. That's right—I'm talking to you. There's something shameful about the frenzied mob mentality you tend to find amongst collected 'grapple fans' at a meet—one is reminded unpleasantly of gaggles of toothless peasants egging on the hangman. Being something of an aesthete myself, I naturally recoil from all forms of violence, organised or otherwise, and indeed you can only imagine my revulsion when called upon to host this tacky theatre of brutality. But one must not shirk one's responsibilities.

I have been working tirelessly, and for very little remuneration, I might add, with artist Mel Brimfield to bring you *This Is Performance Art*, a series of groundbreaking broadcasts, exhibitions and restaged seminal performances exploring the impact and legacy of live art from the 1940s to today; the programme insists on searching through the hitherto unexplored nooks and crannies of theatre, activism, comedy, music and sport for the very seeds of its inception and for evidence of its continued importance. Tonight, in association with the London Word Festival, we examine the extraordinary wrestling career of performance artist Andy Kaufman, in a disgusting and flagrant display of machismo the like of which hasn't been seen since Ken Russell ordered Oliver Reed to grapple nude with Alan Bates, in front of a roaring log fire in 1969, (although the spectacle of The World's Strongest Men gruntingly hauling juggernauts up a hill on a rope never fails to induce fits of hysterical laughter round my way). I do hope you'll enjoy your evening's 'entertainment'. It saddens me to think of the vulgar pantomime of violence that must surely be enacted here this evening, but evidently that's what it takes to fill the theatres these days. I myself shall be passing the evening with a good book and a bottle of '45 Mouton-Rothschild in the Green Room avoiding the whole stinking heap of it—and in the meantime, if you so much as look at me, I'll stomp a mudhole in your ass and walk it dry, numbnuts.

The Contenders: Simon Munnery

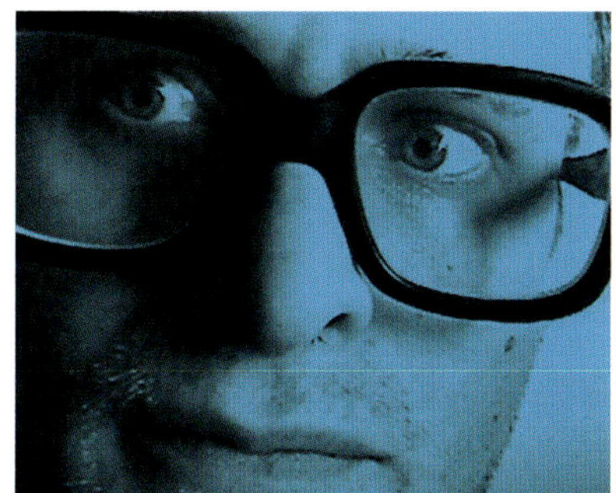

Your defending 'champion' this evening is athlete, provocateur and occasional comedian Simon Munnery. I met this chicken-legged, pigeon-chested cock for a glass in the Coach and Horses last week to discuss the event, and was immediately struck by the maniacal hubristic glint in his eye. Make no mistake, he means it. He shared some of his frankly shocking opinions with me on the subject of gender inequality—I have to admit a grudging admiration for the man who can loudly ask the question "Does pornography degrade women? Or does it merely raise the standard by which they are judged?" without batting an eyelid in the midst of a pub full of ugly feminists. Expect pyrotechnics when he brings it to the ring, and look out for his signature twisting half in-half out treble tiger feint Muzurka drop!

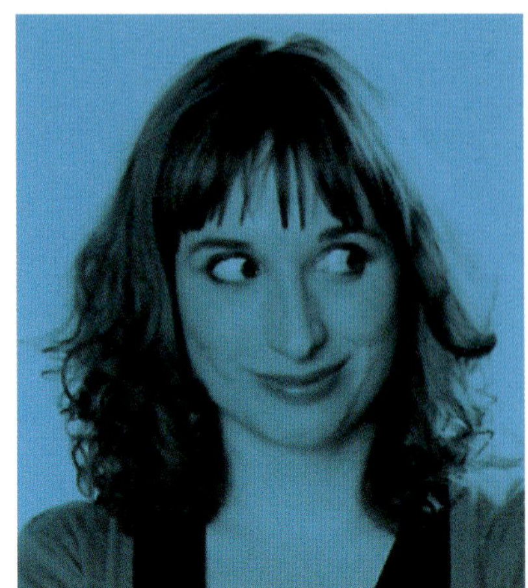

ROUND ONE: ISY SUTTIE

Fresh-faced *ingénue* Isy Suttie is, at first glance, an unlikely challenger. Since scooping the hotly contested 1985 BBC Young Musician of the Year title at the tender age of 11 with a haunting rendition of Saint-Saëns' *Havanaise* on the triangle, this gap-toothed prodigy has scarcely been out of the public eye. She was to win the hearts and minds of the nation with her triple-platinum selling number one hit single "There's No-one Quite Like Grandma" shortly after her BBCYMOTHY success, and subsequently came of age in the full glare of the media spotlight via a series of gritty heavyweight West End roles to become one of the most respected actresses in the business. Although unavailable for comment in the run-up to the match, owing to the punishing rehearsal schedule for her role as Fanny Shufflecock in the Chichester Festival Theatre's forthcoming revival of *Oops, There Go My Bloomers*, Suttie is known to have adopted a gruelling training regime and special diet for some months in a bid to clinch the title. Munnery's comments? "Wear brown trousers and a shirt the colour of blood—you're going down."

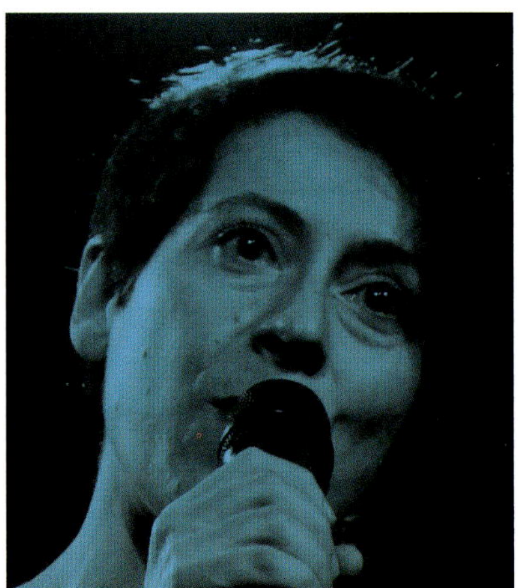

ROUND TWO: LORE LIXENBERG

Copper-bottomed opera diva Lore Lixenberg has certainly got a good pair of lungs on her, (and her voice ain't half bad either, as abject vulgarian Munnery might be inclined to say). I was lucky enough to be allowed access to the voluptuous mezzo soprano's dressing room on the first night of her triumphant return to the Drury Lane Theatre for a three week run of her abbreviated one woman *Ring Cycle*. There are those idiotic naysayers who claim that at 12 hours and 32 minutes, the performance runs a little short, but I was to find myself fully sated by her economical and spirited rendition. Bravo! Adding my paltry floral tribute to the mass of bouquets already festooning her dressing table, I sat down to discuss the ins and outs of her rigorous wrestling preparations. Smiling enigmatically, she cleared her throat, took a sip of champagne, and proceeded to unleash an ear-bleeding B flat over high C for some three minutes. It appeared our interview was at its conclusion. I brushed the glass fragments from my trousers and left the theatre with a smile playing upon my lips. It is good to know that at least some culture will be in evidence at this wretched event.

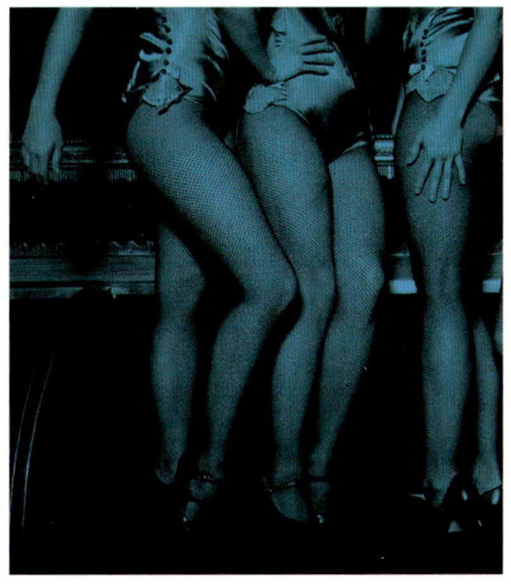

ROUND THREE: THE BEAUX BELLES

Weighing in at a massive 43 stone, the five-headed, ten-legged ideal of nimble feminine pulchritude that is tag team and smokin' hot all-star super troupe The Beaux Belles have a considerable advantage over Munnery—they can dance! I caught up with the girls at the Pineapple Studios during an energetic rehearsal session for the forthcoming *This Is Performance Art* re-staging of Richard Serra's controversial 1973 *Whole Lotta Lead* musical. We chatted of this and that over a Chai Latte, or six, and although it was hard to keep a track of their delightful twittering, (calling to mind for me an aviary full of tiny brightly coloured chaffinches clustered around a seed tray), I gathered that the ladies were confident of victory. Giggling good-naturedly, they insisted upon demonstrating some of their more advanced wrestling moves. I was to sustain a series of rather unpleasant injuries during this genial roughhousing session—Munnery should incorporate shin pads, goggles and some manner of cricket box into his sparring costume. Bless them; they don't know their own strength! Somewhat disoriented after the experience, I was embarrassed to discover on reaching the Tube station that I had some how misplaced my wallet, pocket watch, mobile phone and Oyster card—most embarrassing.

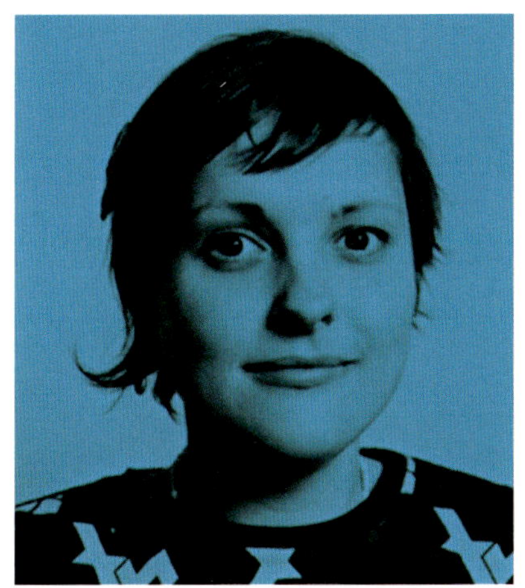

ROUND FOUR: JOSIE LONG

Outspoken rhetorician and polemicist Josie Long unusually combines a career in stand-up comedy with extraordinary feats of athleticism and academicism. Being something of a keen amateur boxer, biathlete and championship baton twirler, she keeps herself in tip-top condition by jogging on the spot for up to seven hours a day. Indeed, she insisted on doing so throughout our interview in a grimy South London 'Music Pub', as over a number of virtually undrinkable pints of cloudy Scrumpy and a brace of pickled eggs, we discussed the forthcoming bout in detail. Downing whisky chasers like a sailor on shore leave, and pounding the sticky table for emphasis, the anachronistically baby-faced Ms Long launched into a foul-mouthed tirade against arch-rival Munnery fit to make the saltiest navvy blush. Indeed, the majority of the long-bearded leather-clad patrons around us dissolved to the four corners of the pub in order to avoid it. She departed shortly after her fifth pint, but not before graciously signing my personal copy of her most recent runaway bestseller *Greek Rural Postmen and their Cancellation Numbers*, (as the long awaited follow up to the critically acclaimed *Oral Sadism and the Vegetarian Personality*, it doesn't disappoint, let me assure you).

ROUND 5: RACHEL PANTECHNICON

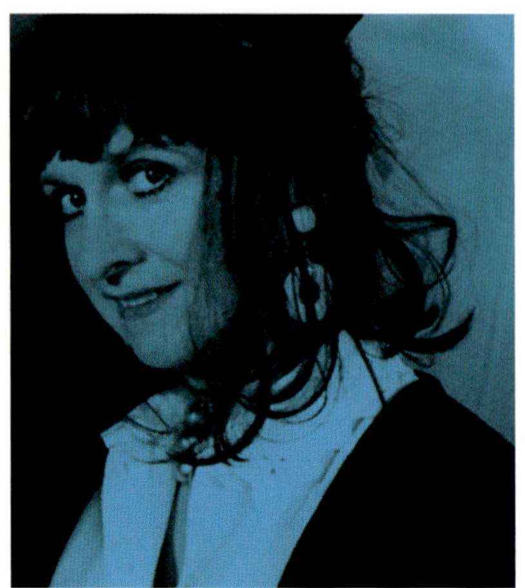

Rank outsider Rachel Pantechnicon is familiar to us all as the erstwhile spokesperson for Tena Lady feminine hygiene products. It's not all bladder weakness and incontinence for the glamorous poetess, however—she is, of course, best known as the writer-cum-illustrator of the multi-award winning children's books *Cheesegrater Leg-Iron Lion* and *Michelle in the House of Crisps*. When I caught up with the comely brunette for a welcome G and T at The Poet's Society Café last week, her somewhat gnomic remarks concerning strategy for the bout revealed little in the way of legible sporting tactics. She drew my attention to an ordinance survey map of Waltham Forest and the surrounding areas—by outlining certain key geographical features, it's possible to reveal an astonishing likeness of Private Godfrey from popular BBC series *Dad's Army*, although how this is likely to influence the outcome of the wrestling match is unclear. Pressing a worn copy of Euclid's *Elements* into my hands, and muttering cryptically about parallelograms and leylines, she exited, leaving me none the wiser....

ROUND 6: HELEN LEDERER

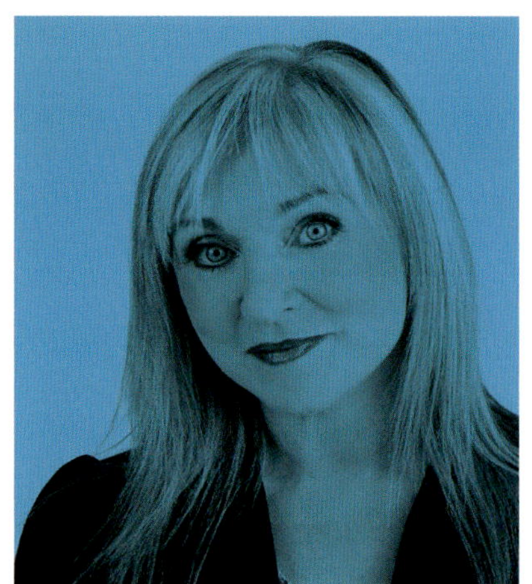

That veteran showbiz legend Helen Lederer should feel compelled to participate in this tawdry affair is a source of lingering regret for me... Pearls before swine. Nevertheless, it is a pleasure to bear witness to the exceptional talent of this stellar performer under any circumstance; it is her sheer versatility that never fails to knock my socks off. From her early days as a gifted hoofer and pop-opera singer, she thrilled variety audiences with the horn-like improvisational ability of her exciting four-octave tenor voice and unerring sense of comic timing. Indeed, it quickly became clear that her outstanding raw talent would win out as she worked her way through the chorus rank and file to take her rightful place in the limelight. She brings an intoxicating blend of bleak intensity, vulnerability and verisimilitude to any role that she inhabits, as was evidenced by her Fairy Godmother in last year's *Cinderella* at The Churchill, Croydon. Quite rightly, she refused to grant a pre-match interview. As an aside, it is fascinating to note that it was Lederer's Czechoslovakian great-great-grandfather who was to originate and give his name to the design of knee-length leather shorts commonly associated with Bavarian national dress.

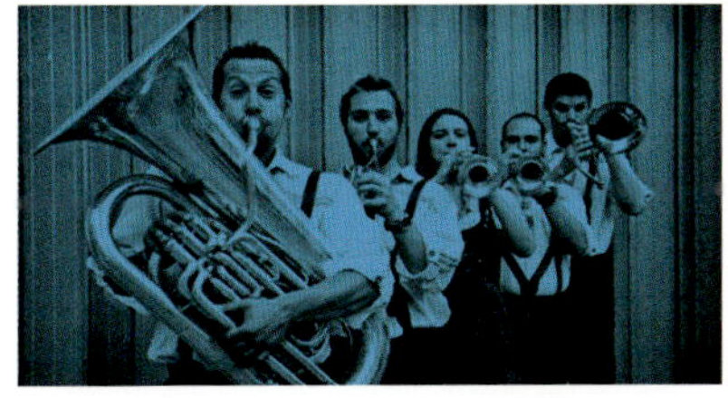

THE ENTERTAINMENT: OOMPAH BRASS

Fetchingly clad in their trademark Ledererhosen and dirndls, award-winning five-piece Oompah Brass will bring a blast of Alpine glamour to tonight's proceedings, treating the assembled to a medley of traditional Bavarian tunes including "Bohemian Rhapsody", "Ace of Spades" and "Smells Like Teen Spirit".

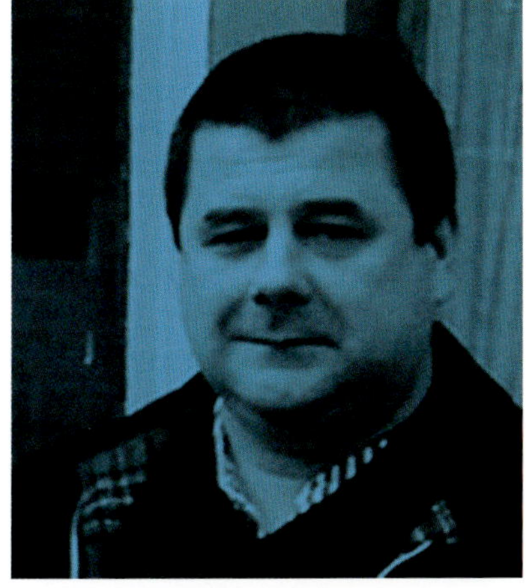

THE REFEREE: TIM WELLS

Caught up with referee Tim Wells trampoline-side in the middle of an intensive coaching session at the Poplar Boys Club Wrestling Arena and Paddling Pool in the week before the event. Accredited by the highly respected UGRIP and BSPAC Wrestling Federations, he is also a Forward prize-winning poet who has performed at an impressive array of prestigious sporting venues internationally. He wouldn't be drawn into idle speculation as to the outcome of the tournament, but commented "I never predict anything, and I never will, but as I see it, the tide is very much in Lederer's court."

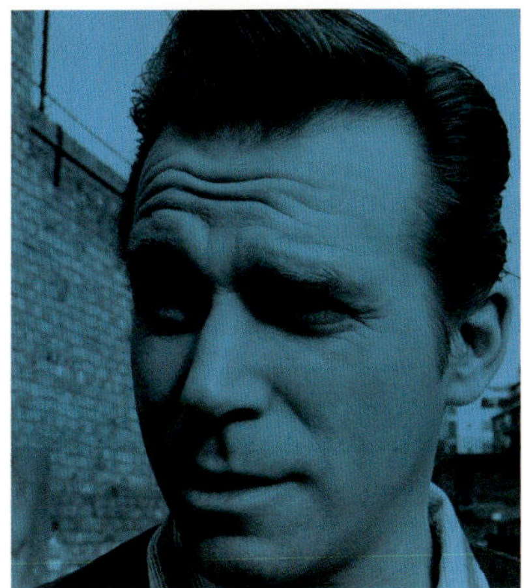

THE COMMENTATORS: TONY LAW AND KEVIN ELDON

Lantern jawed sausage dog breeder and retired rodeo cowboy Tony Law is a regular commentator on the BBC, Five Live and QVC. No one even minds that he's Canadian, or if they do, they just have to suck it up. He is joined by rubber-faced polymath Kevin Eldon, who needs no introduction.

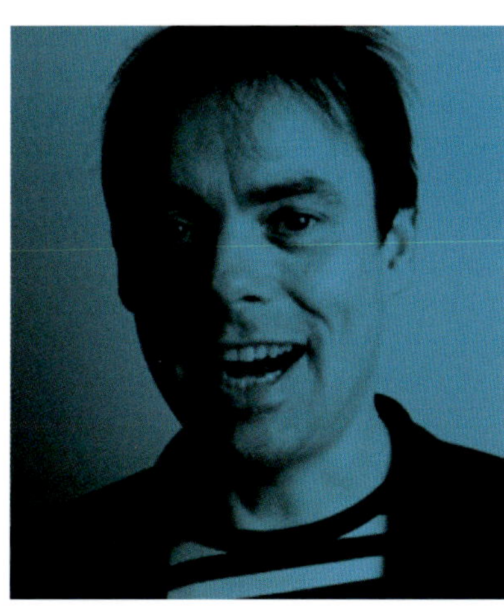

SIMON MUNNERY ADDRESSES THE WOMEN

Recently I've been thinking about bras a good deal. Who hasn't? They're everywhere these days: on television, advertising hoardings, women's bodies. Men's bodies sometimes; I am wearing one now, as a form of research. And I am a man. Oh yes—and determined to remain one, despite the provocation. Bras intrigue me, they delight me, but most of all they puzzle me. How do you get them off? How do you get them on? Why wear one in the first place? And what's going on with lace? Eh? It is just material with holes in it; less cloth for more money. Harmless enough, some might say, but that money could have been used for hospitals. And what, pray, will be the evolutionary impact of the bra in the long term? Has the bra enabled larger breasted women who would naturally have died out—by toppling or ostracisation—to live longer and have more sex, hence more offspring, thereby raising the average breast size of the population? Or is the recorded rise in average breast volume simply a result of the fundamental law of supply and demand? After all, nature abhors a vacuum. Surely—and research may well back this up—some relation must exist between mammary capacity and for example intelligence. Perhaps an inverse relationship: The same nutrients can't go to two parts of the body. When they look back at us, will they say "Twas as if they willed their own demise"?

Hooters, tits, ya yas, bouncy castles, call them what you like, you can't get away from them—but what is so attractive about breasts? Is it because there are two of them and that represents good value? For thousands of years, millions of months from a woman's perspective—think what that means—men have venerated women's bodies. We put them on pedestals. Why? Was it so we could look up their skirts? Does pornography degrade women? Or does it merely raise the standard by which they are judged? And who shot JR? A woman no doubt, but that is unusual. Generally—and I use the word advisedly, perhaps ill advisedly, time will tell—it is men that do all the murder and commit all the crime. Yes, yes, yes; but who gave birth to the swine? Who raised them to be as they are? Women, that's who. I rest my case.

I have no interest in history, it's all water under the bridge in my book, but it was Germaine Greer, I believe, who kick-started the feminist movement in the 1960s by symbolically removing her bra and setting fire to it. She then went on to write a series of bestsellers about the incident: *Why I Burned my Bra*; *How I Burned My Bra*; *My Bra, Burning*; *May I Burn Your Bra Too?*; *Bras Aflame, Girls, Come On* and so on, which established her as an author of high repute. Of course like all pivotal events in the collection of lies we call history, it happened by accident to some extent, and chance played its part—perhaps she was undressing while fiddling with matches, multitasking like they do—ineffectively—but it happened to the right person at the right time and she was able to capitalise on it. Good on her. Don't be a stick in the mud—learn how to surf. Ride the Zeitgeist. Eat your dinner. Don't talk back to your mother, etc..

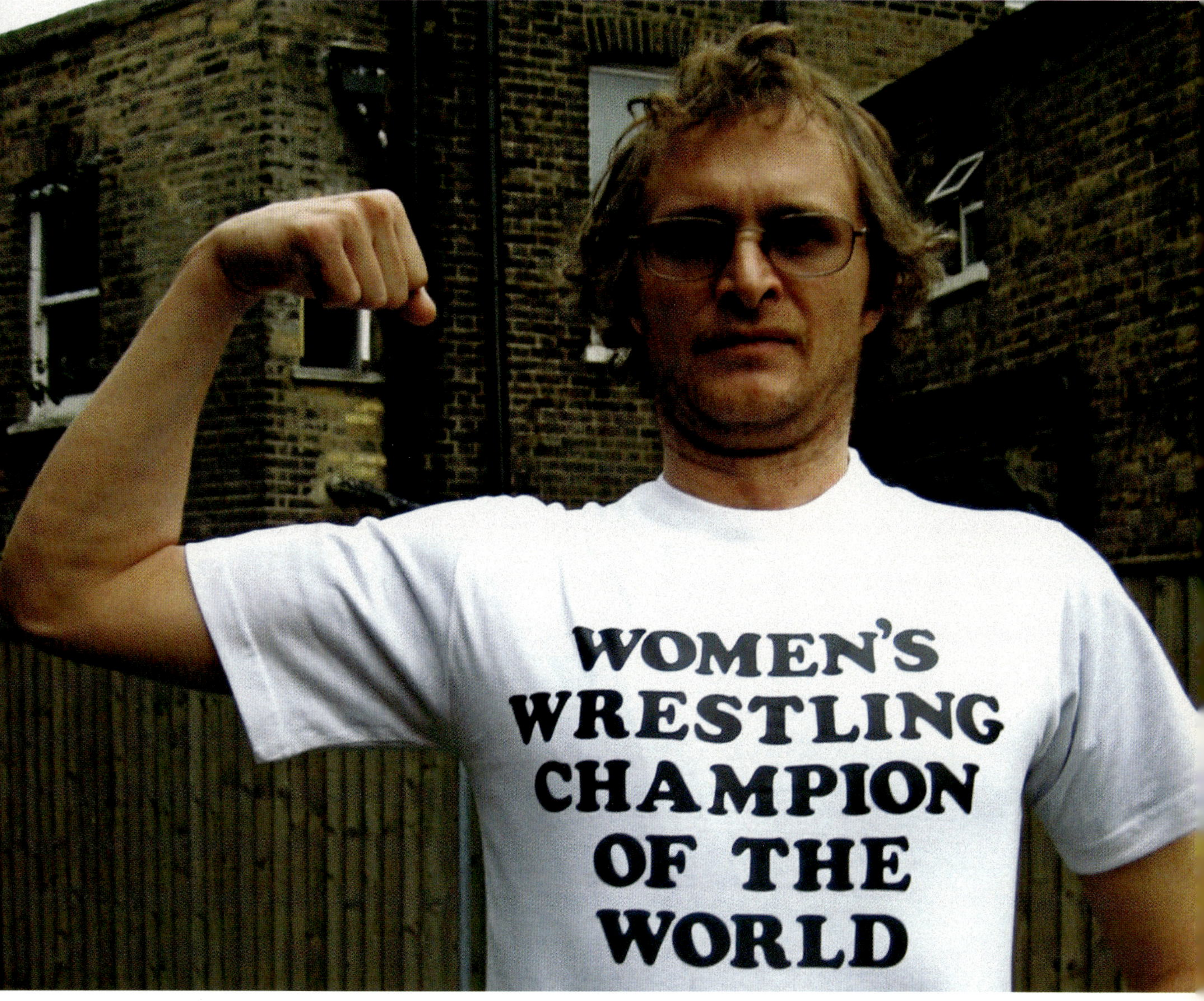

INTERGENDER WRESTLING

The Feminist Movement seems bizarre in retrospect, now that it's over. "All men are bastards" they claimed. But why? Could it be because all women are whores? But one cannot blame Germaine for this, or anything, given her gender.

I've been studying women for a long time now, using binoculars mainly, sniffing apparatus, and sound recording devices which I secrete in their toilets. Nothing to report; I have been unable to hear the audio playback due to the blood thumping in my ears. Yet despite my studies, women remain a mystery to me. Who are they? What do they want? If you ask a woman what she wants she'll say sex, but then you give it to them and they say "Yes, but that wasn't it, quite." Why do they want sex anyway? They're not very good at it and they don't enjoy it. And their vaginas are too big.

And what do women do, generally? I've made a list: shop, gossip, and moan. It's not an exhaustive list—one could add, of course, chores and witchcraft—but those are the main three. On the other hand perhaps moaning has a positive value: It was the Reverend J Malthus, I believe who wrote "What are woman's moans but the engine of industrial change? For what is more natural than for the nagged man to repair unto the tavern and plan the future?"

It is said "A woman's work is never done", to which I would add only one word—properly. Recently I conducted a time and motion study on my wife: lots of time, very little motion. And it set me thinking, aside from child rearing, what have women ever achieved? A comparative list of 'great inventors of the past' may prove enlightening. Men: Isaac Newton—who invented the laws of mechanics which make the game of pool possible; Sir Michael Faraday—who invented electricity, without which we couldn't have big screen sport; Albert Einstein—who invented the space-time continuum which enables horse racing; and William Hill. And there are many others. But on the list of Great Female Inventors of The Past there is only one name: Marie Curie. And what did she invent? Cancer.

"No woman no cry" sang Bob Marley, correctly: No women—no crying; one woman—some crying; several women—much crying; a nation of women—Woman's Hour. Why do men die before their wives? Could it be because they want to? Horses sweat, gentlemen perspire, women sweat and perspire, and shit and piss and menstruate, but you'd never guess that to look at them with their faces.

GREAT INVENTORS OF THE PAST

MEN	WOMEN
1. ISAAC NEWTON invented the laws of mechanics that make the game of pool possible.	1. MARIE CURIE invented cancer.
2. SIR MICHAEL FARADAY invented electricity, without which we wouldn't have big screen sport.	
3. ALBERT EINSTEIN invented the space-time continuum which enables horse racing.	
4. WILLIAM HILL	

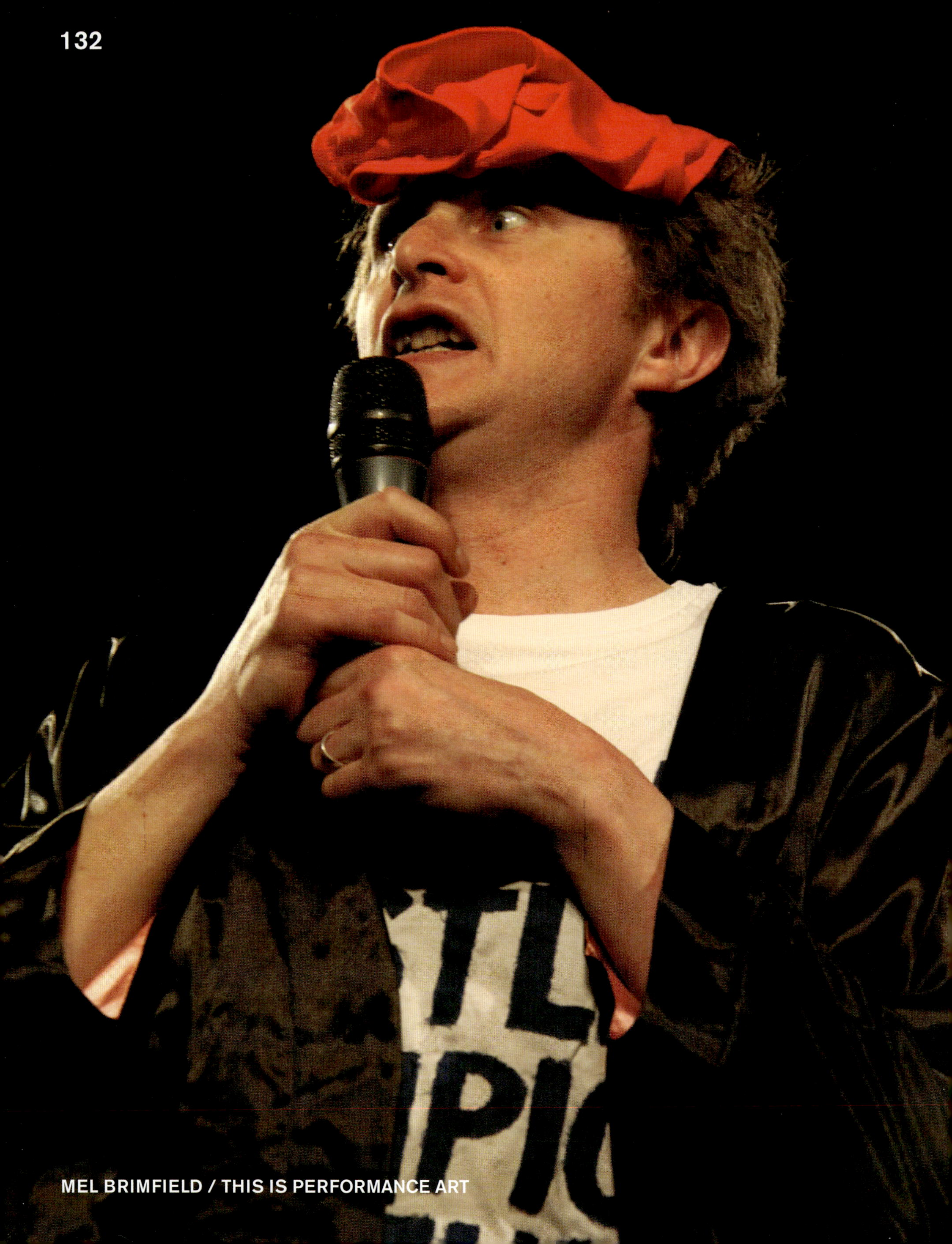

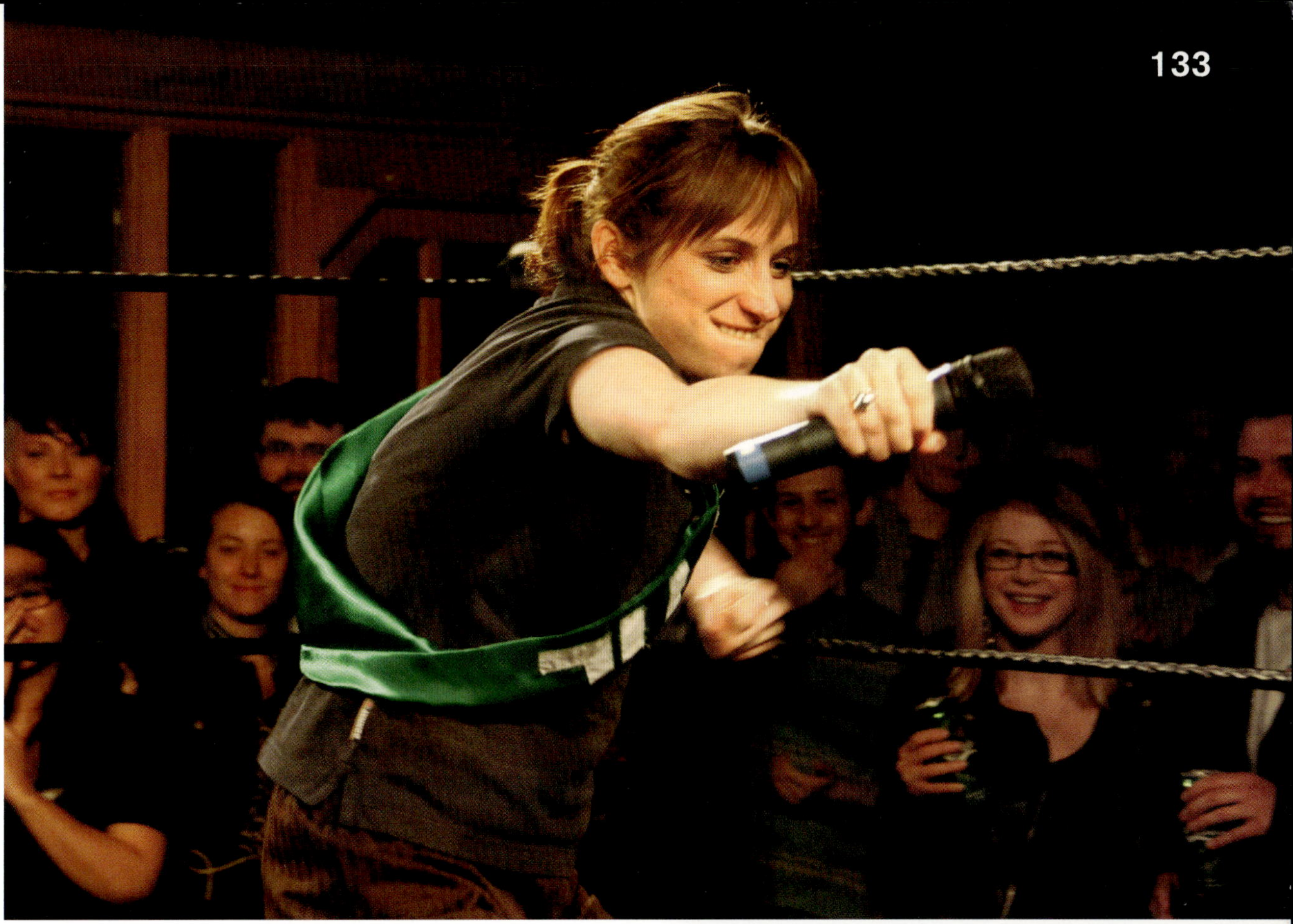

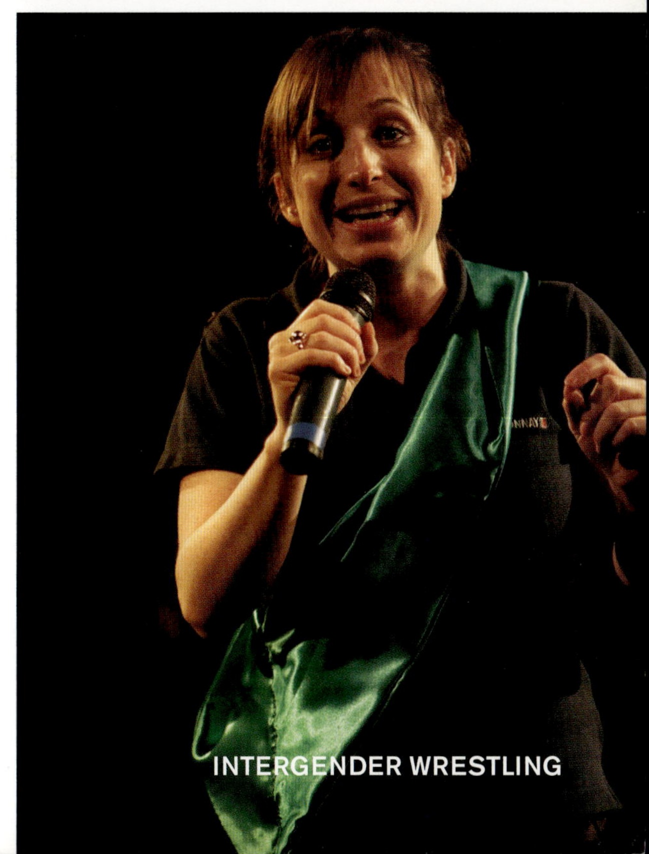

INTERGENDER WRESTLING

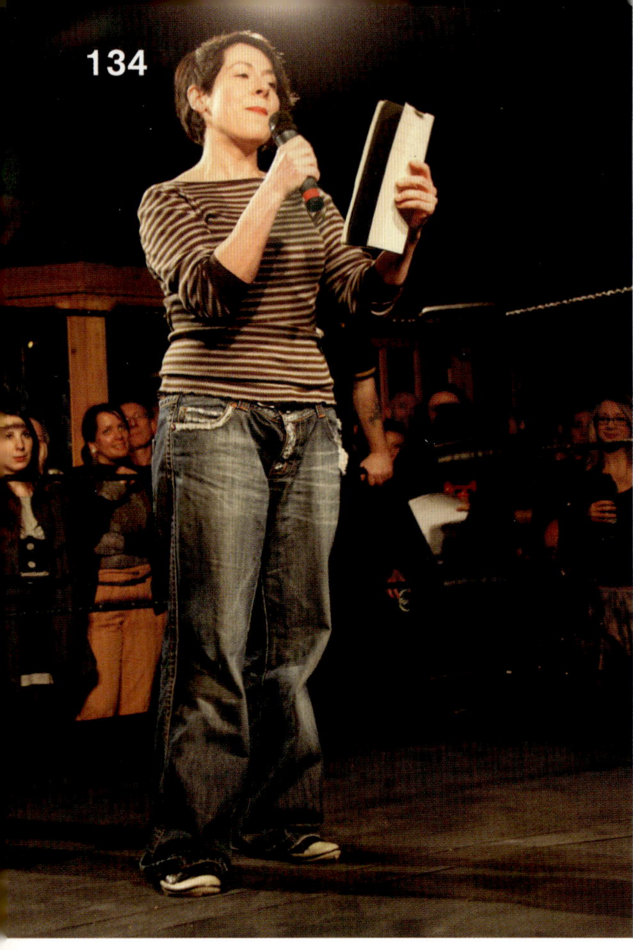

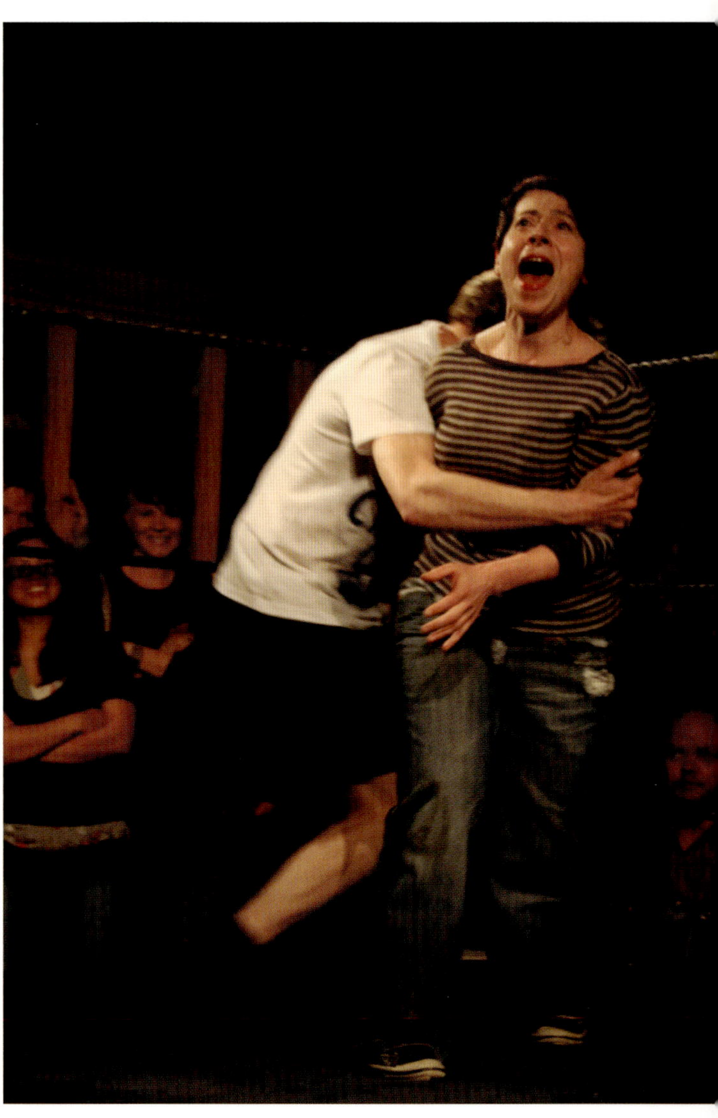

MEL BRIMFIELD / THIS IS PERFORMANCE ART

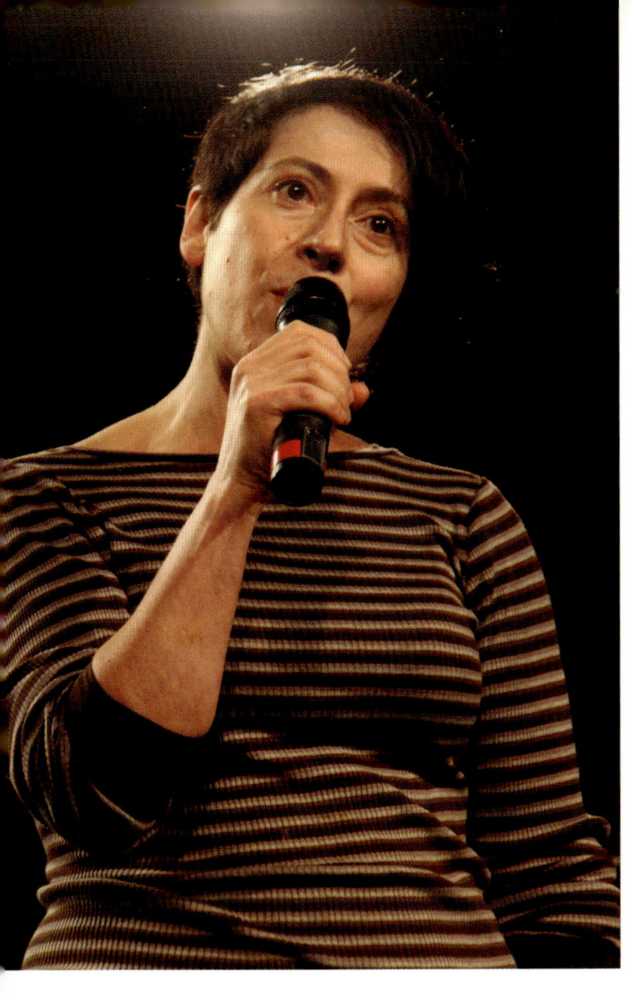

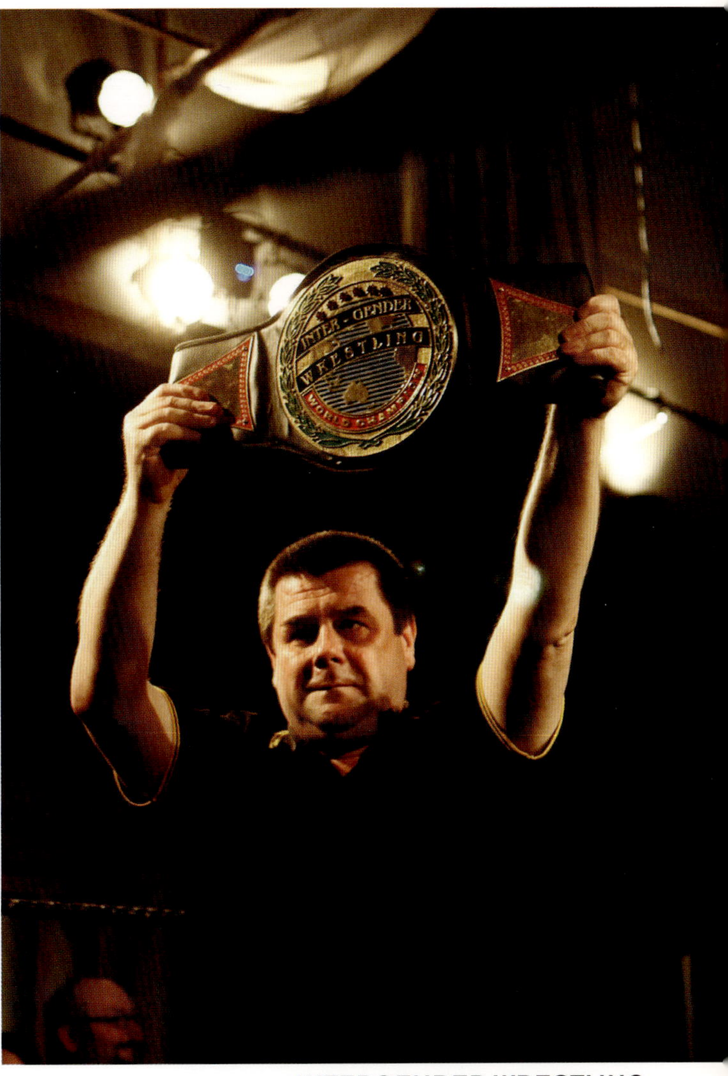
INTER-GENDER
WRESTLING

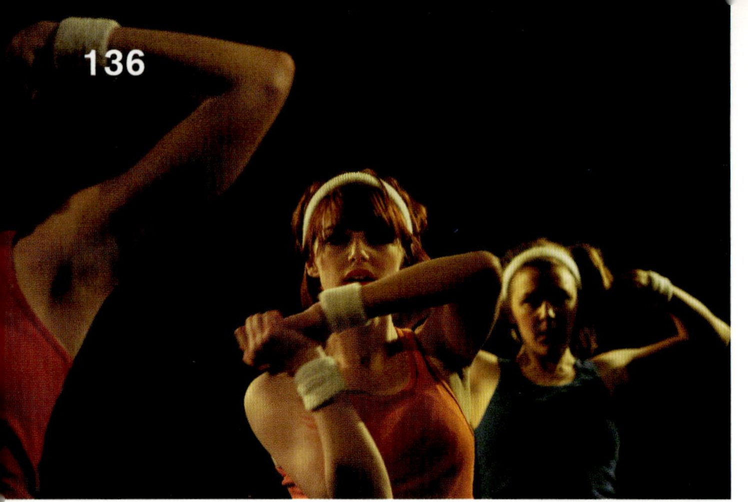

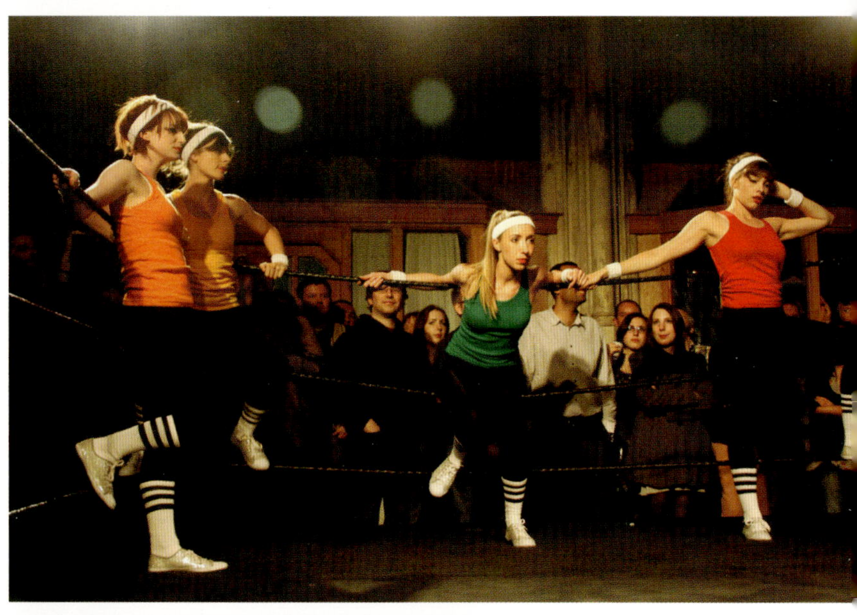

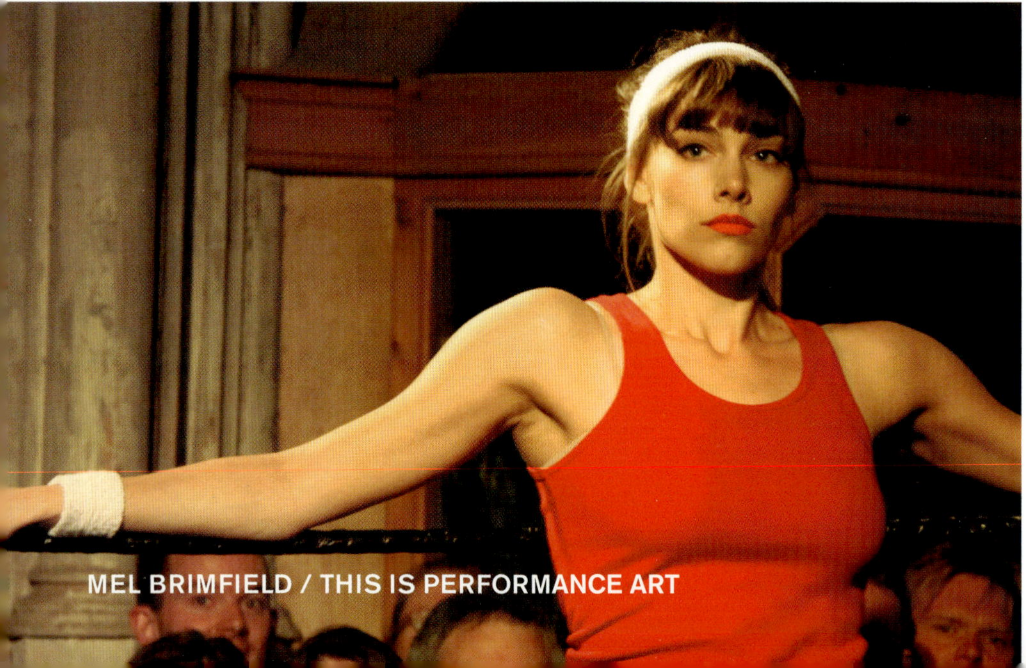

MEL BRIMFIELD / THIS IS PERFORMANCE ART

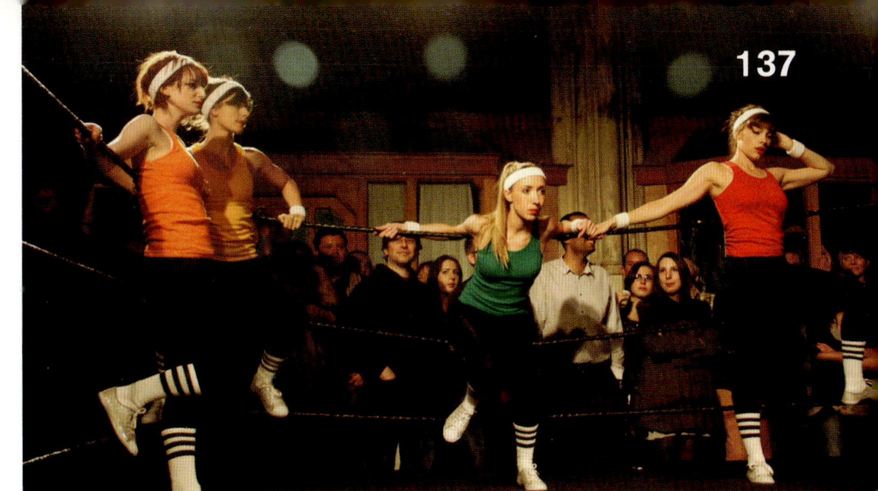

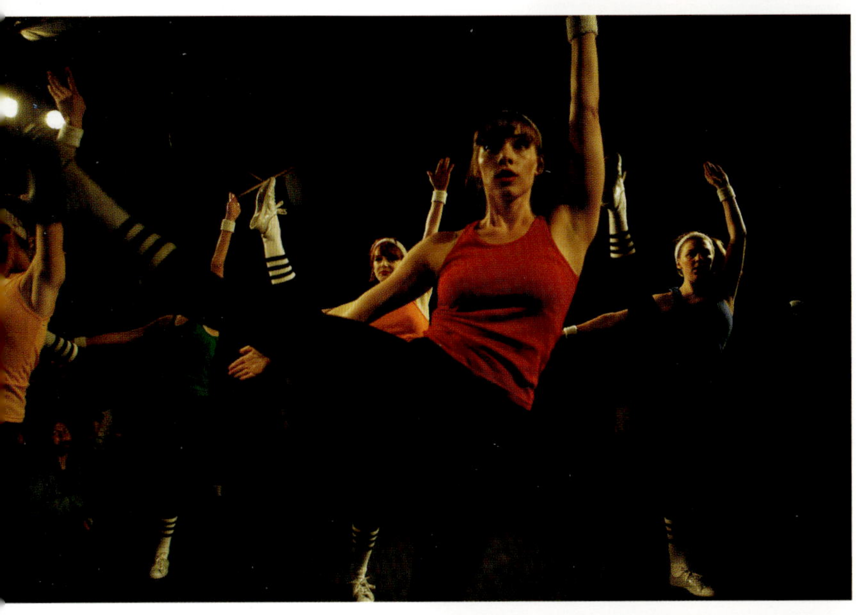

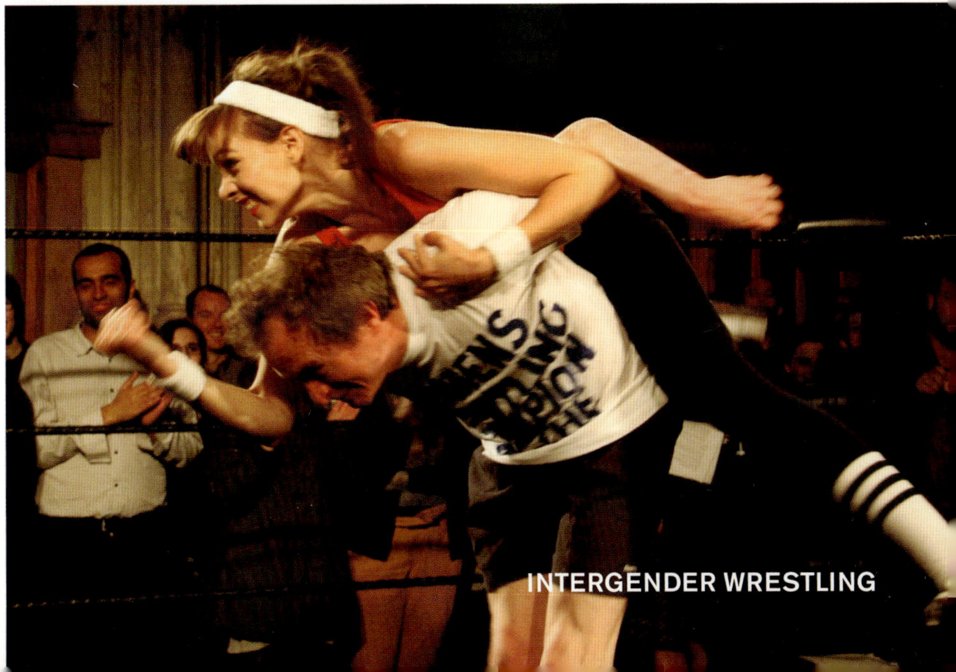

INTERGENDER WRESTLING

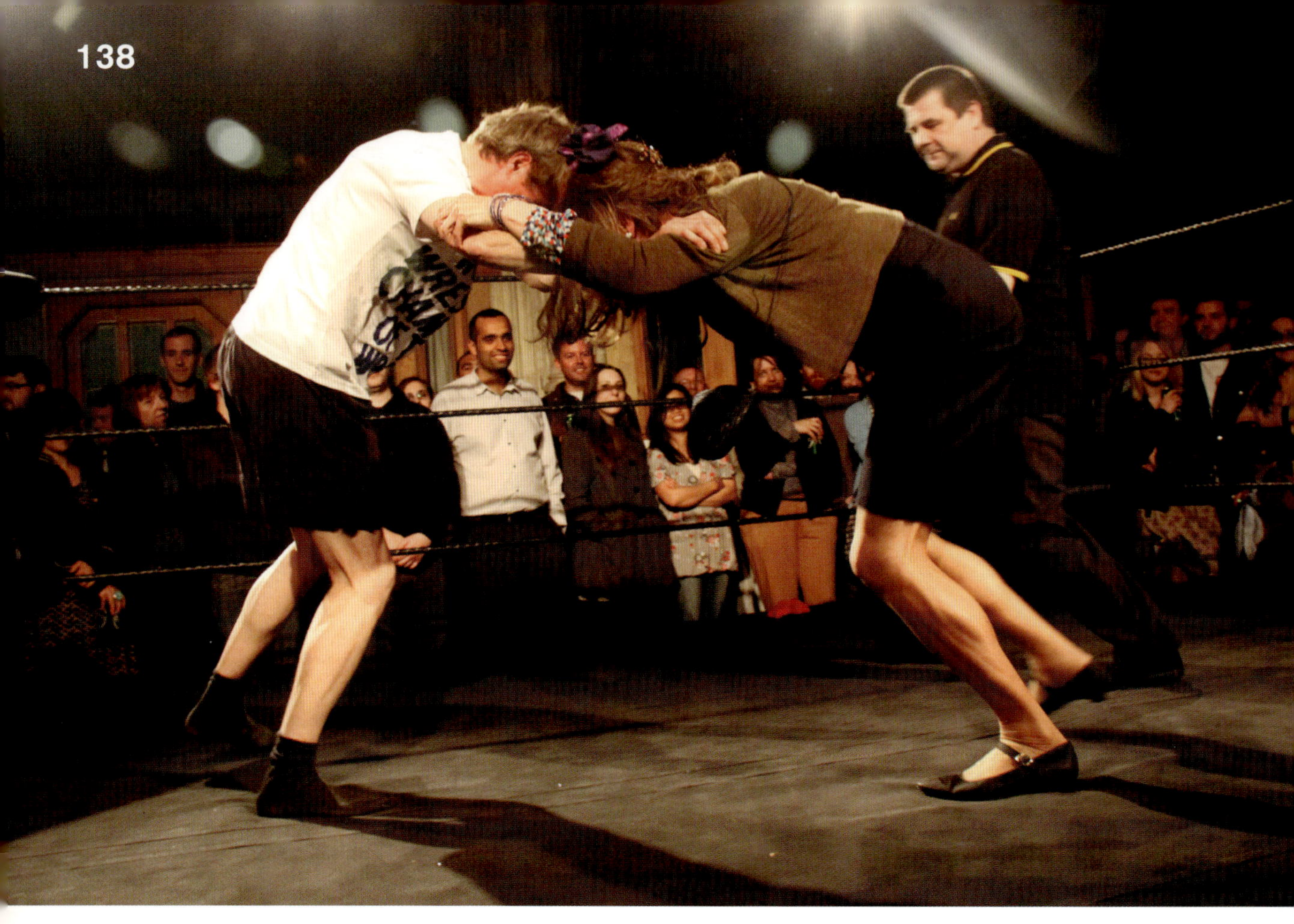

MEL BRIMFIELD / THIS IS PERFORMANCE ART

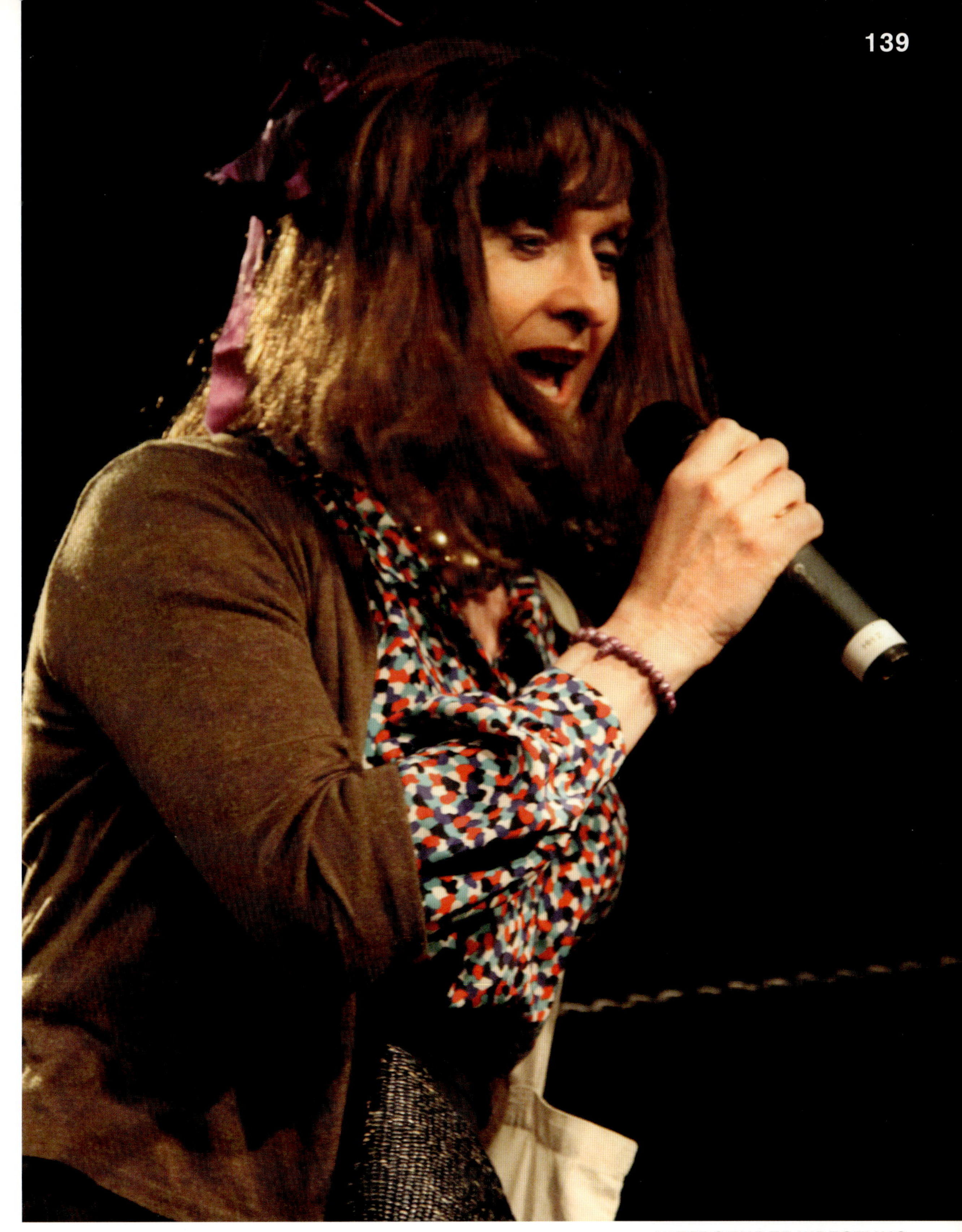

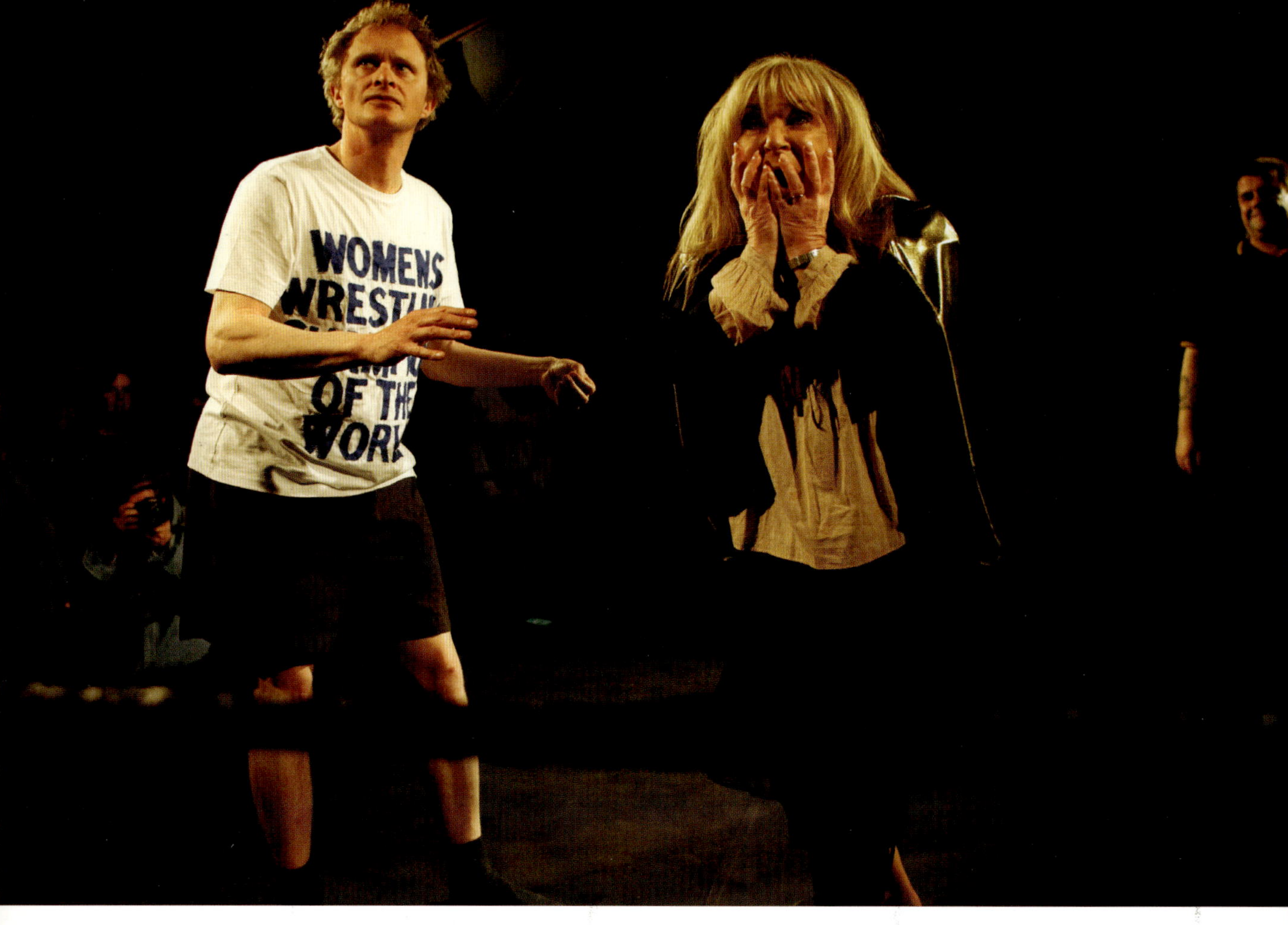

MEL BRIMFIELD / THIS IS PERFORMANCE ART

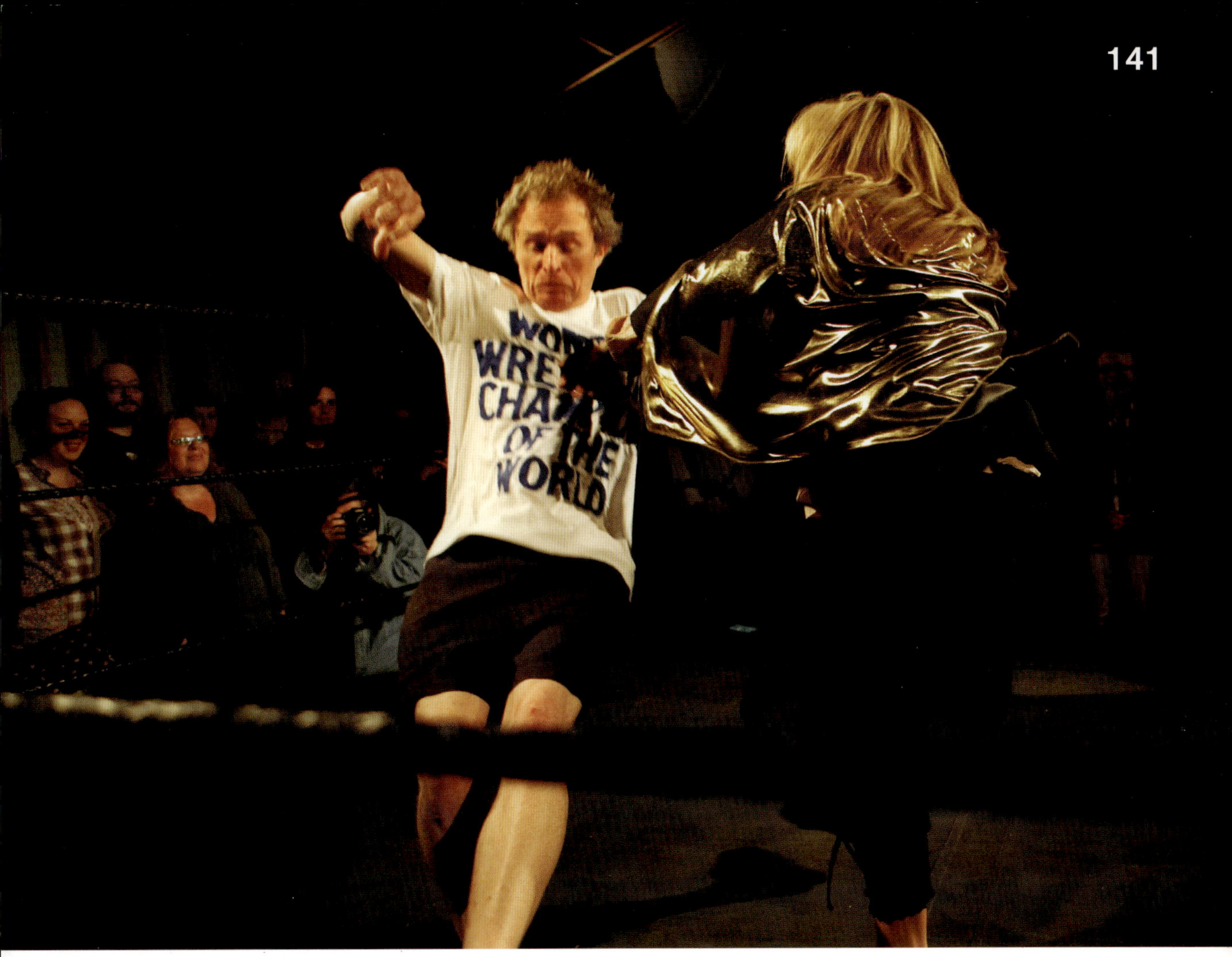
OF THE
WORLD

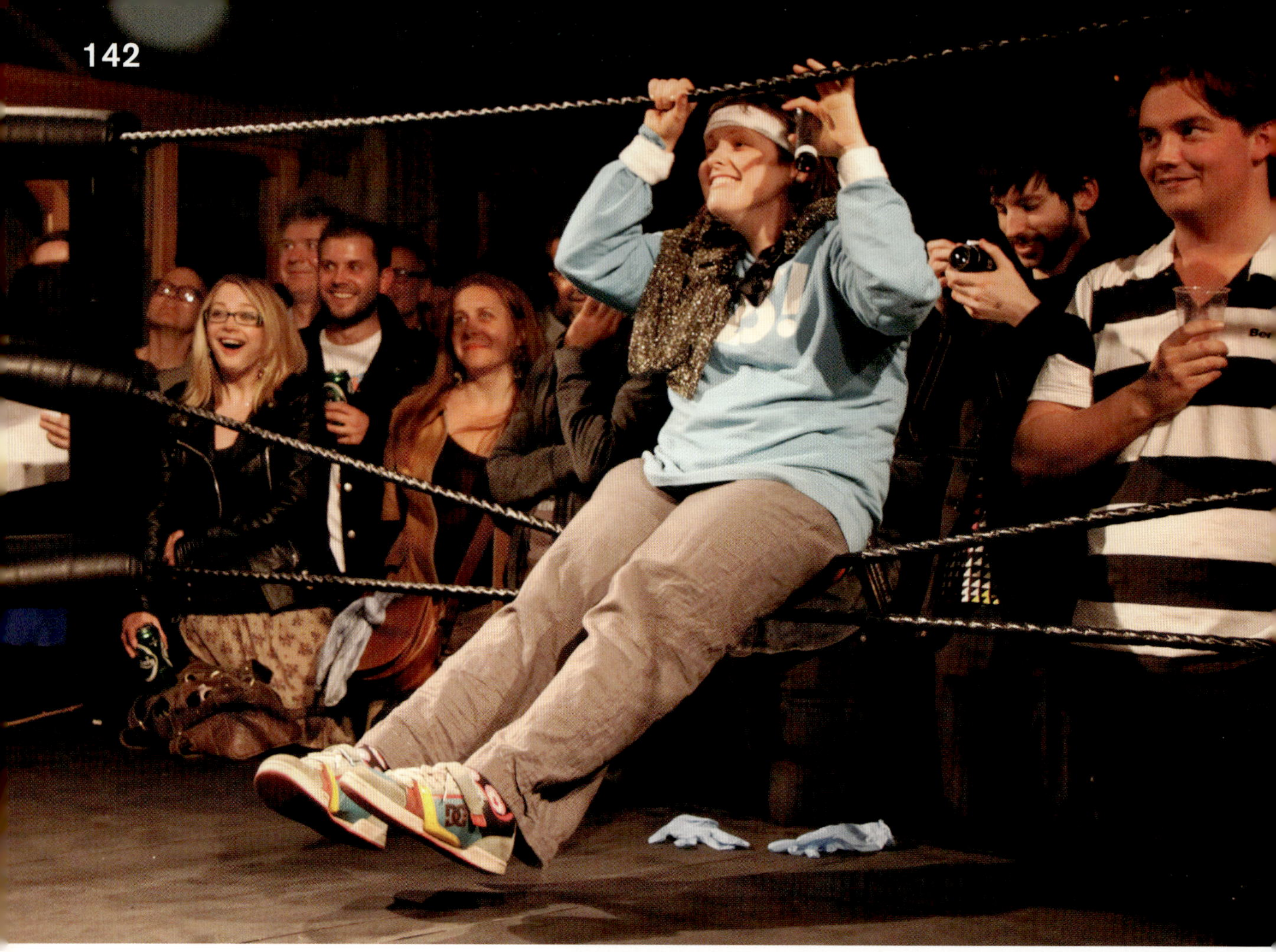

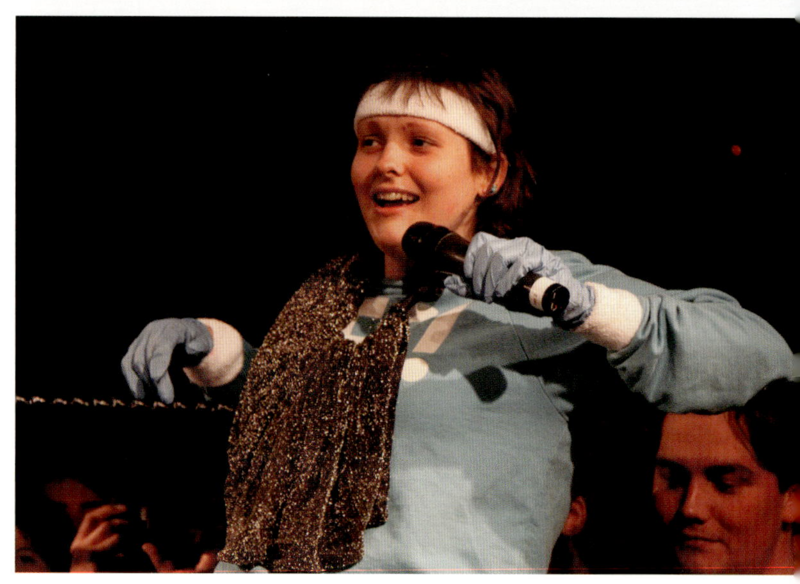

MEL BRIMFIELD / THIS IS PERFORMANCE ART

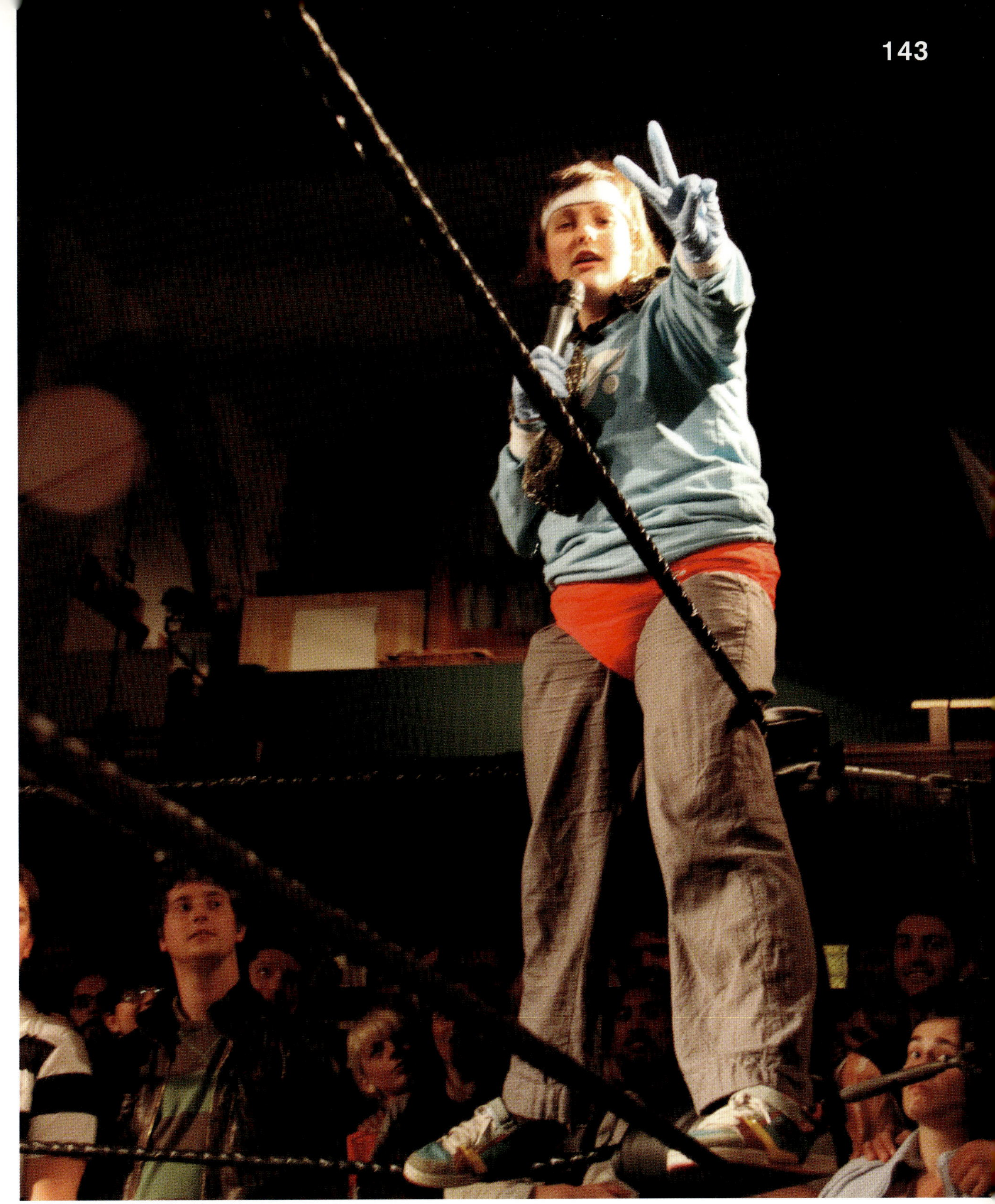

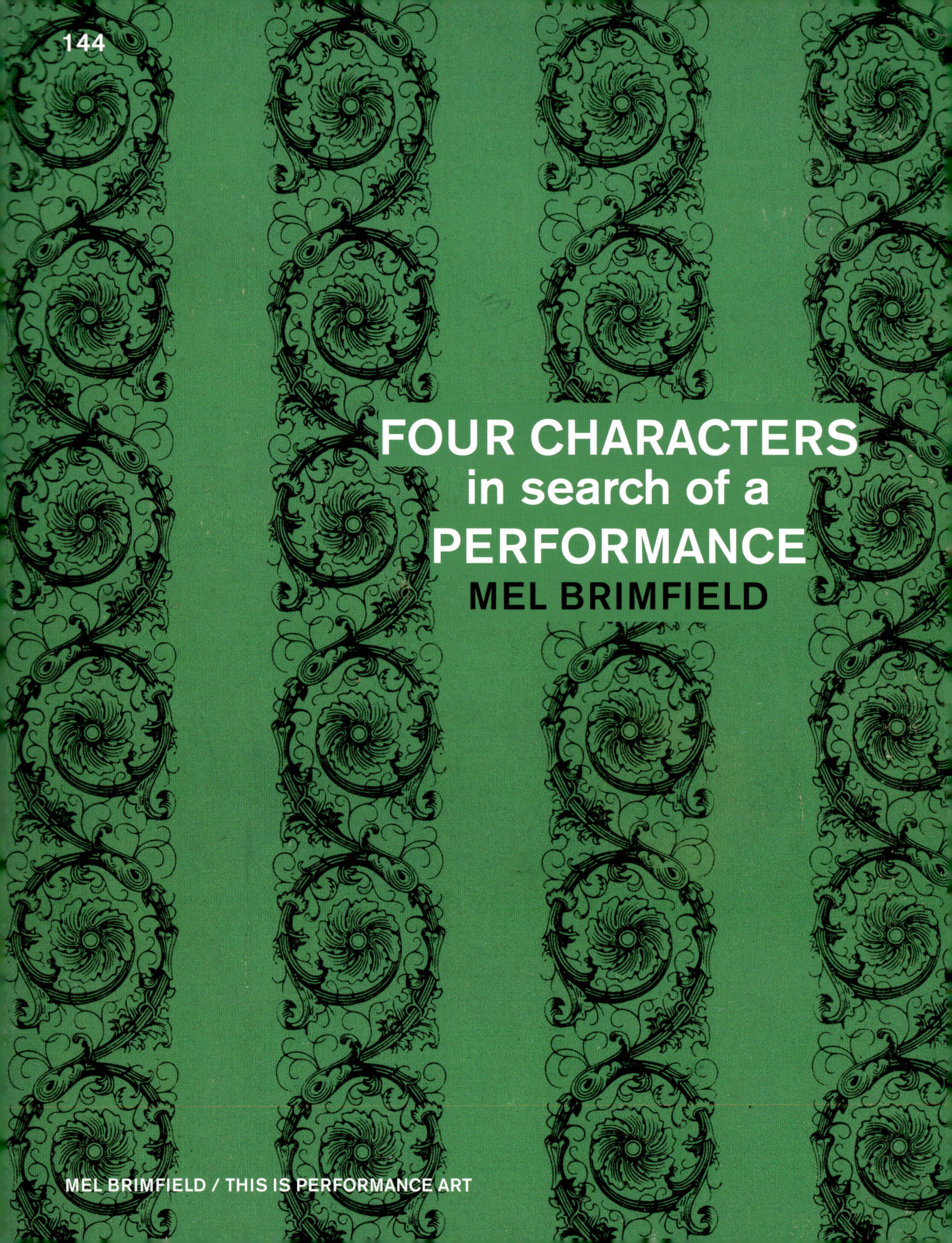

FOUR CHARACTERS in search of a PERFORMANCE

MEL BRIMFIELD

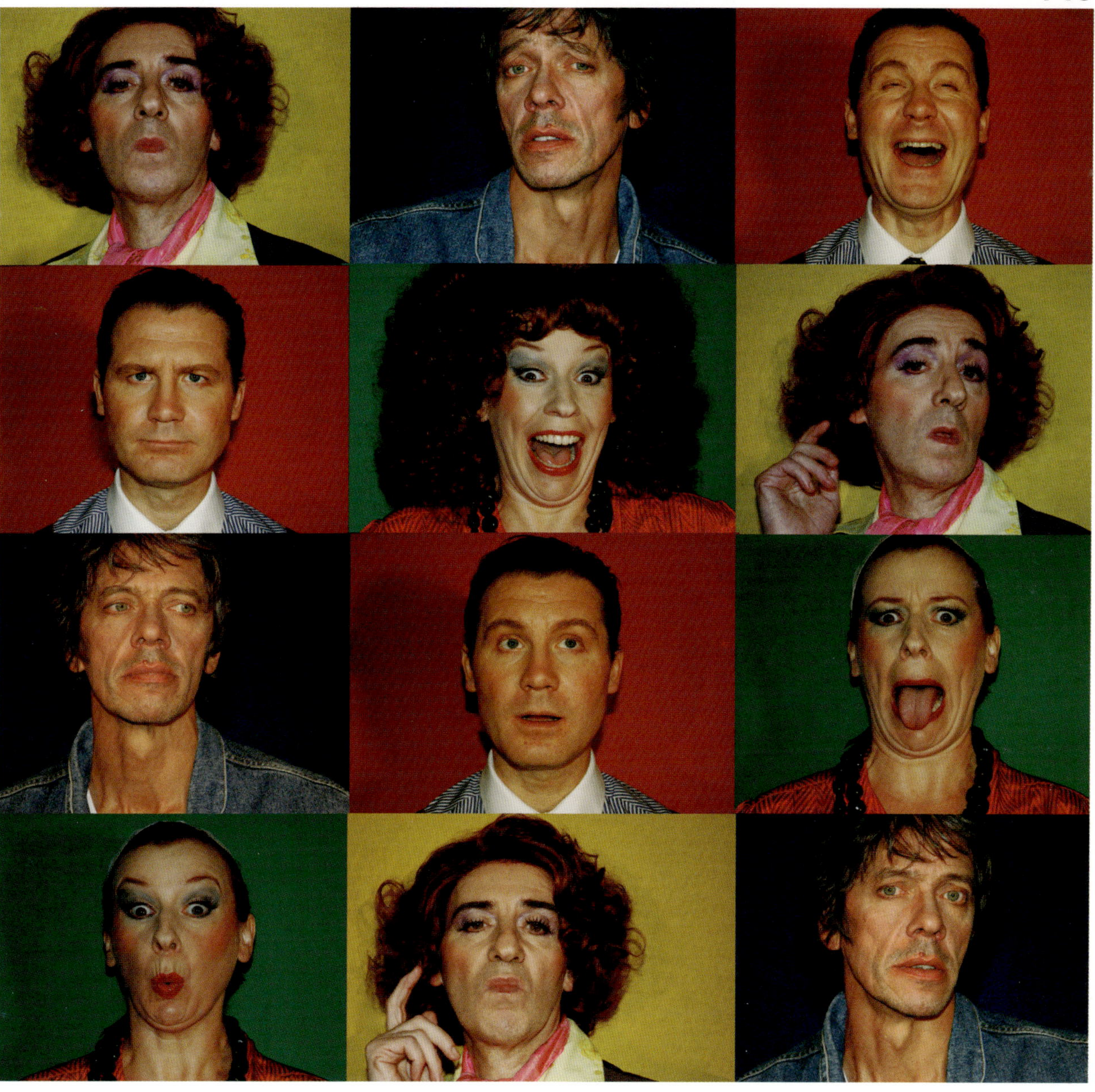

Four screen film installation commissioned by Jerwood Visual Arts for the LOCATE exhibition curated by Sarah Williams, 2010. Shown with new commissions by Aura Satz and Sarah Pickering.
Mel Brimfield, *Four Characters in Search of a Performance*, 2010, Digital film, 32 minutes.
Image courtesy the artist and Ceri Hand Gallery.

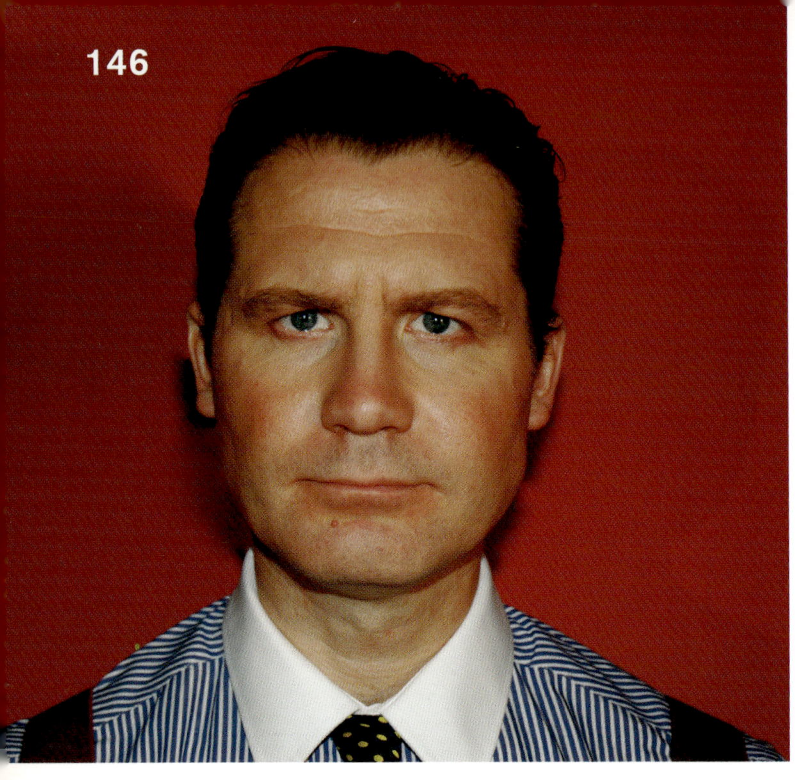

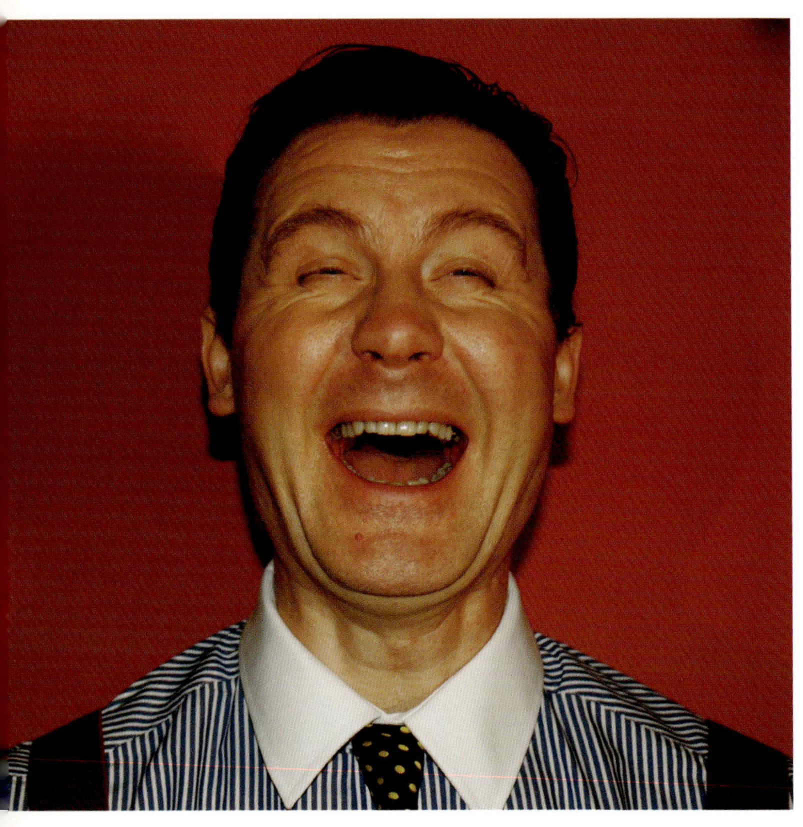

THE COLLECTOR

Is based visually on Michael Douglas' *Wall Street* Gordon Gekko character. He wears a fitted blue shirt with white collar and cuffs, and a sedately patterned tie, and has aggressively slicked back hair with plenty of gel in it. Appears in front of a bright red background. Performed by Ian Shaw.

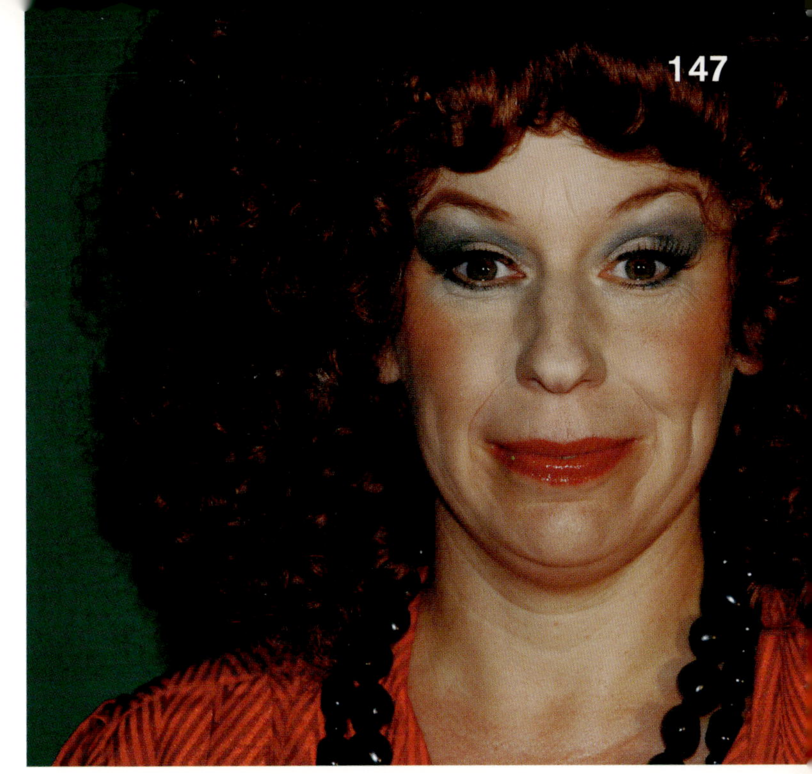

THE GIRLFRIEND

Begins by wearing a wig cap, and heavy foundation, but no other make-up. She has make-up tissues tucked into her collar, and a towel around her shoulders. Elements of her costume and make-up are added, tested and discarded throughout the script until she resembles an Annie Sprinkle style character just in advance of her main speeches at the conclusion of the piece. Appears in front of bright green background. Performed by Esther Coles.

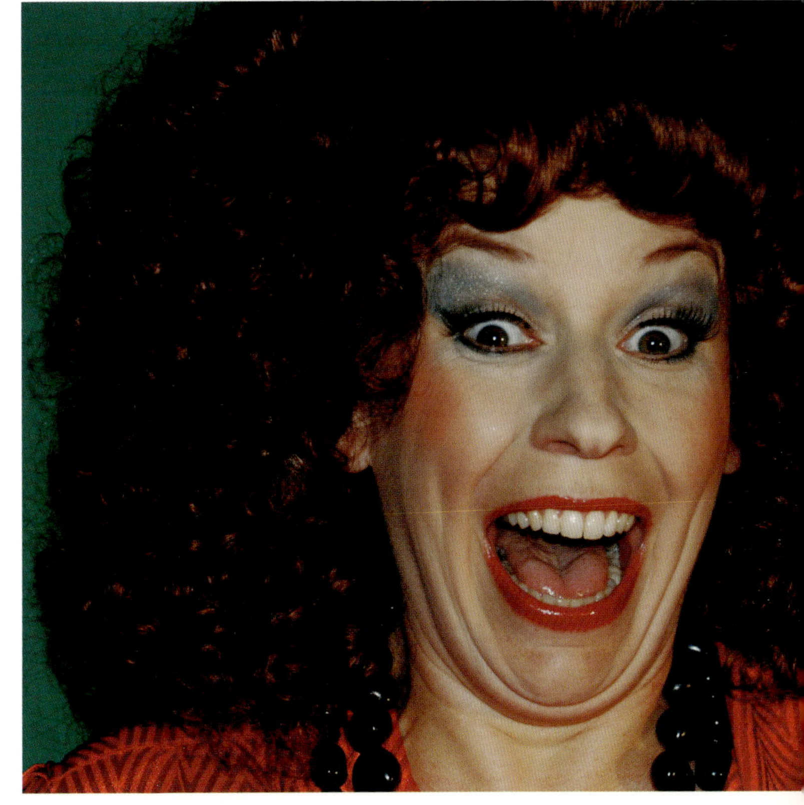

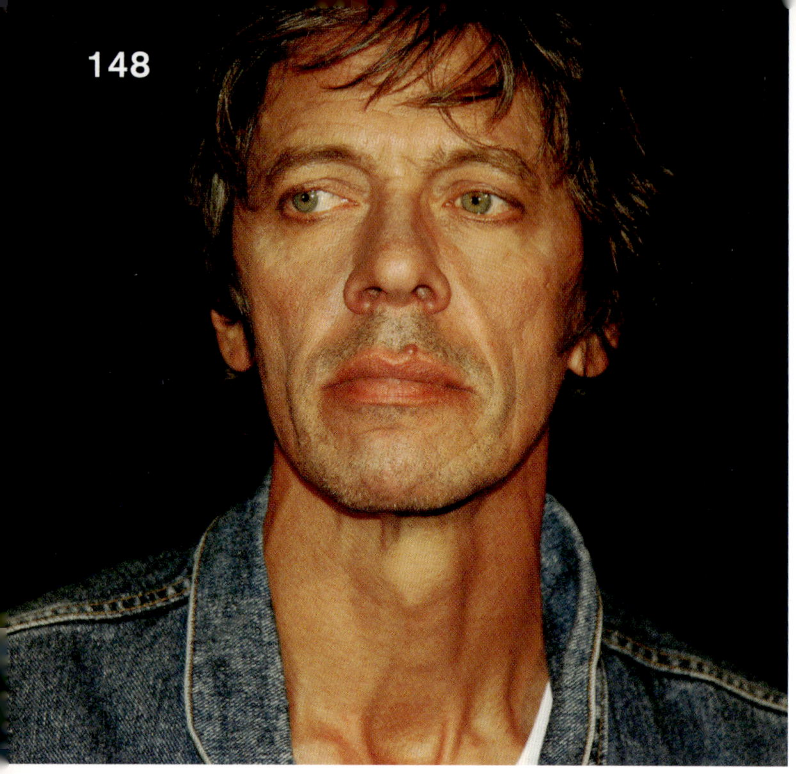

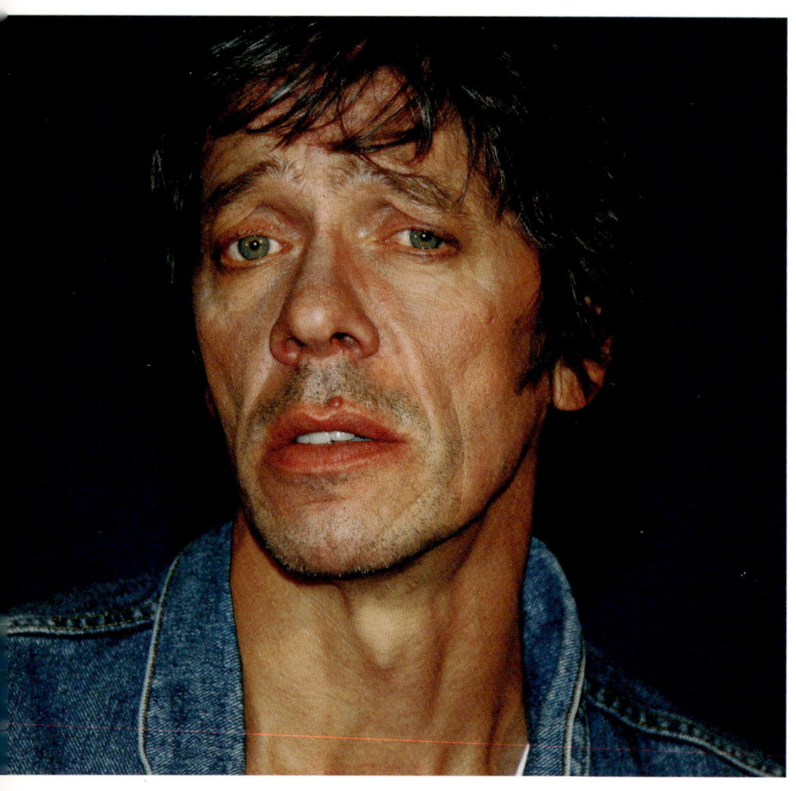

THE PHOTOGRAPHER

Is wearing a dirty denim jacket and grubby white T-shirt. He has greasy longish hair. He looks like a stereotypical roadie/sound technician. Appears in front of a bright blue background. Performed by Alastair Kerr.

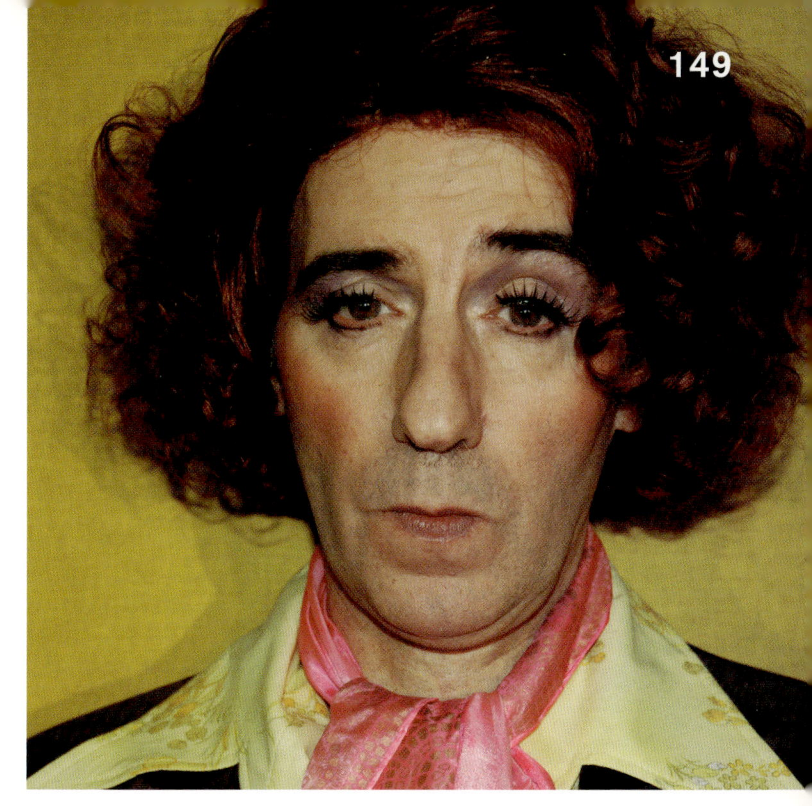

THE CRITIC

Is wearing a Henna wig in the style of John Hurt's portrayal of Quentin Crisp in *The Naked Civil Servant*. He has a clearly made-up and powdered face, dark velvet jacket and satin shirt, and a chiffon scarf around the neck. Appears in front of a bright yellow background. Performed by Sir Francis Spalding.

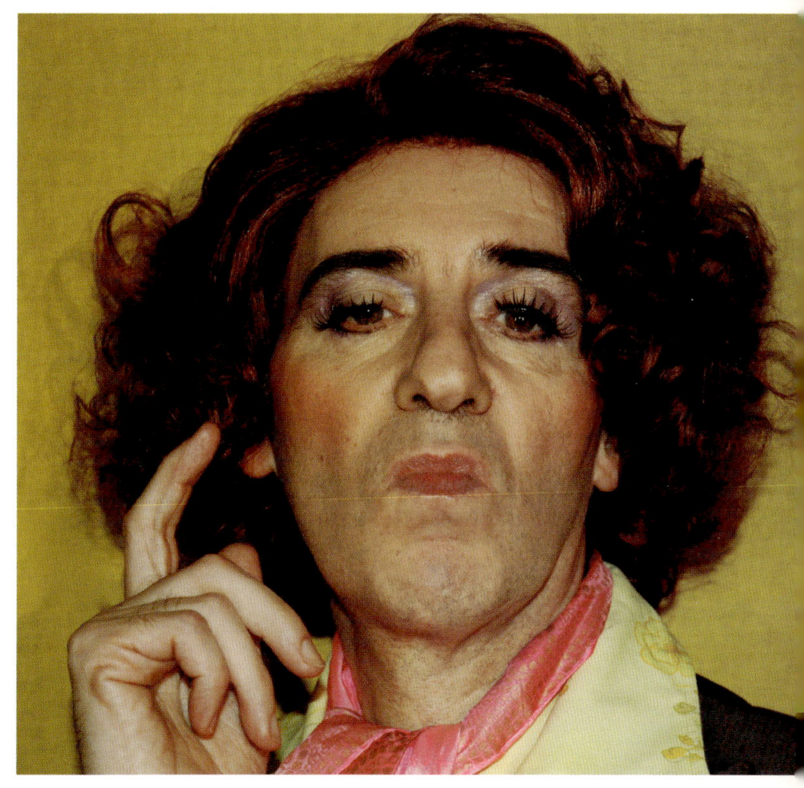

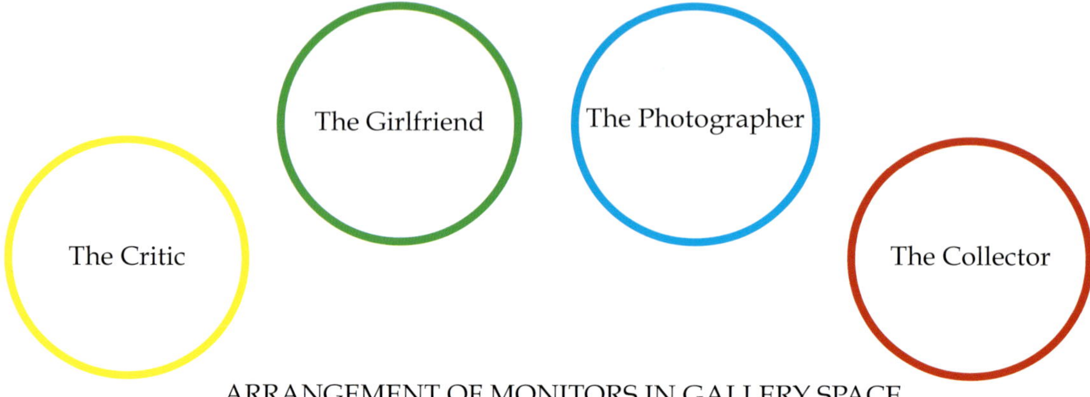

ARRANGEMENT OF MONITORS IN GALLERY SPACE

There is an empty stool in the centre of a small stage with a black back curtain. A stand behind the stool supports a two metre square stretcher covered with a brightly coloured fabric, which serves as a backdrop. Each actor is filmed on the same set. The colour of the backdrop is different for each character. The action begins on all four monitors with the same reasonably wide shot. A strong spotlight falls on the stool. At the same moment on each monitor, the actors appear on screen to take a seat – THE CRITIC *and* THE GIRLFRIEND *come in from the left, and* THE PHOTOGRAPHER *and* THE COLLECTOR *come in from the right. They settle into a relaxed position looking straight ahead at the camera. A slow close-up into each performer follows, at the same speed on each monitor.*

Throughout the script, 'Main Action' indicates the primary focus, usually when the performer is in Character and delivering a monologue – the other corresponding numbered sections are usually for the actions performed by the other Actors during these speeches. Where no action is indicated for either the Actor or Character, he or she will assume a rest position, looking straight ahead at the camera.

During Main Action 1, THE COLLECTOR *is practising a series of facial expressions. He runs through smug, amused, furiously angry, vacant, etc.. He keeps pausing and going back to a neutral expression. He consults his script on occasion. These are expressions that we will see on his face at various points through his speeches – until the end of Main Action 1.*

During Main Action 1, THE GIRLFRIEND *is performing a series of ludicrous silent facial warm-up exercises – it must be clear that this is what she is doing. She pauses occasionally to roll her head in a pronounced way and to massage her neck. Pulls at cheeks, odd mouth shapes, etc. – until the end of Main Action 1.*

During Main Action 1, THE PHOTOGRAPHER *sits still, looking directly at the camera, occasionally adjusting his collar, but in a relaxed way, blank face – until the end of Main Action 1.*

MAIN ACTION 1: THE CRITIC *(Very camp and prissy.)* It seems to me that this is a rather pointless exercise, all in all—I'm not sure what it is that we're trying to achieve. It's just not possible to work out what the performance was. An extraordinary statement, you might think, from one who was actually there in the audience, but there you have it. You'd be hard-pressed to find two people with the same account. Or in fact who'd be willing to talk about it at all—it's derailed a few academic careers along the way, I can tell you. There's agreement on a few particulars. One: that it was a filthy, deranged and wrongheaded spectacle from its inception. There's always periodic interest in trying to run it up the flagpole as some sort of landmark artistic statement, but then there always is in that kind of prurient muck. It was a rotten thing, a nasty little exercise spun out with a disgusting degree of relish and refinement of detail. Two: that it was a dreadful mistake to stage the thing in the round—the sight-lines were atrocious, rendering the majority of the action as completely invisible to one section of the audience or other at all times. Idiotic.

THE CRITIC *stops, visibly relaxes, moves out of sight to the right, reappears with a glass of water. Sips from it, tips head back and gargles for an extended period. Stops, swallows, puts glass off screen, rests, looks impassively at camera, testing profile, pursing lips patting hair, etc., until the end of Main Action 2.*

MAIN ACTION 2: THE COLLECTOR *laughs hysterically for an uncomfortably extended period. It's forced, and he's visibly strained by the exertion. He pauses, looks perplexedly just past the camera, and as if responding to direction from an unseen producer, changes the laugh to a much smaller one—silent shoulder shaking with unpleasant heavy out-breath, rests for Main Action 3.*

> *During Main Action 2 and 3* – THE GIRLFRIEND *stops her warm-up exercises, and just before the end of* THE COLLECTOR'S *laughter, leans forward, bobs out of view and comes back in a pair of thick-lensed glasses. Blinks at camera with massively magnified eyes until the end of* THE CRITIC'S *Main Action 3.*

> *During Main Action 2 and 3* – THE PHOTOGRAPHER *is still sitting impassively, steadily looking at the camera, through the course of Main Actions 2 and 3.*

MAIN ACTION 3: THE CRITIC It's become something of an obsession for me, I'm afraid. Piecing together the fragments of it and re-constructing the thing, I mean. Imagine that the shards of a shattered mirror had each captured part of something and were reflecting it oddly tilted in space and severed from context. *(Pauses.)* It's a bit like that. Some of the most tantalising morsels turn up in the form of a series of commands for cuts and revisions issued by the Lord Chamberlain's office—a gaggle of his censors unexpectedly turned up for a dress rehearsal the day before curtain up. For those of you who don't know, for decades, all performances presented for the public were subject to censorship by the Lord Chamberlain and his Watch Committee. It seems farcical now, of course—but it was quite the problem at the time. Artists could spend months in fevered correspondence with the office bargaining over the most pedantic directions and strictures. Some live work was scandalously eviscerated in the process. I managed recently to winkle a copy of the original Licensing agreement (Holds sheaf of papers.) for the performance from some private archives—it's a quite fascinating document—examples:

(Puts glasses on, clears throat and adopts officious upper class accent.) The License is issued on the understanding that the following alterations are made to the script: Act 1, Page 16—For "The Vicar's got the clappers", substitute "The Vicar's dropped a clanger."

Act II, Page 8—The mock priest must not wear a crucifix on his snorkel. It must be made immediately clear that the book the priest handles is not the *Bible*.
Page 23—Omit all references to the Prime Minister's undergarments.

*During Main Action 4—*THE CRITIC *sips water until the end of Main Action 4.*

*During Main Action 4—*THE COLLECTOR *goes off camera, and reappears with a glass of water. Sips water until the end of Main Action 4, where he gargles in low tone in unison with* THE CRITIC *and* THE GIRLFRIEND

MAIN ACTION 4: THE GIRLFRIEND *removes glasses, and loudly and seriously does a series of vocal exercises in strident BBC announcer style voice—everything is over-enunciated with lots of face movement, and picks up a faster and faster tempo as she proceeds.*

Red Rubber Red Rubber Red Rubber Red Rubber
Red Rubber Red Rubber Red Rubber Red Rubber
(Opens eyes and mouth very wide for a beat or two.)
Red leather Yellow leather Red leather Yellow leather
Red leather Yellow leather Red leather Yellow leather

> THE GIRLFRIEND *begins to pull extreme happy and sad facial expressions, still in facial warm up mode, then dips out of sight for moment, comes back up still with glass, and gargles in medium tone in unison with* THE CRITIC *and* THE COLLECTOR.

MAIN ACTION 5: THE CRITIC Act 3, Page 10—Omit "... clockwork Virgin Mary made in Hong Kong, whistles the twist".
Page 13—Omit "Balls of the Medici": "testicles of the Medici" would be acceptable.
Page 15–Omit "Piss off, piss off, piss off", substitute "Shut your steaming gob".

(Shakes head while removing glasses, back to prissy voice.) Extraordinary, and bearing absolutely no resemblance to my own experience of the work.

THE CRITIC *stops, sips water, gargles in high tone in unison with* THE COLLECTOR, *picks up script, reads until end of Main Action 7.*

MAIN ACTION 6: THE PHOTOGRAPHER *is attempting to fix an appropriate accent – begins with Liverpool accent, with different emphases for repetitions.* Extraordinary chiaroscuro... chiaroscuro... extraordinary chiaroscuro *(Scottish accent)* extraordinary chiaroscuro... extraordinary chiaroscuro effects *(Birmingham accent)* extraordinary chiaroscuro effects... extraordinary chiaroscuro... chiaroscuro... chiaroscuro, chiaroscuro, chiaroscuro chiaroscuro... extraordinary chiaroscuro effects.

MAIN ACTION 7*:* THE GIRLFRIEND *breathes in, does The Lion facial yoga exercise – opens the eyes wide, sticks the tongue out as far as possible, and pushes the face forward – she holds that pose for about ten seconds and rests. Does the exercise again, indicates where she feels the stretch on her face. She again holds tongue out for long period, stops, pulls at cheeks to 'stretch out', back to varied facial exercises until end of Main Action 8.*

> *During Main Action 8.* THE CRITIC *looks steadily at the camera, makes small adjustments to posture, shifting in seat, etc.. Practises raising eyebrow quizzically and touching lip thoughtfully repeatedly. Refers to script at intervals – lips moving, etc. – it's a rehearsal of Main Action 11.*

MAIN ACTION 8: THE PHOTOGRAPHER *(Broad regional accent – Birmingham preferably, or Liverpool – he has a flat monotone, and is only really animated when describing technical equipment.)* The lighting conditions were fairly awful most of the time – I mean, at points, it was pitch black. Even so, I achieved some quite extraordinary chiaroscuro effects in my shots of the roller skating sequences, especially considering the speed that they went round the maypole, at any rate. I was using some pretty maverick techniques back then. *(Laughingly.)* I even used an N-Vision GT-14 monocular with Generation 3 Pinnacle tube, if you can imagine that! *(Shakes head in disbelief.)* Wild times. Hats off to Peter, you know, credit where it's due; it was a virtuoso performance. But to explain the artist's magic is impossible – it's as elusive as a snowflake in the hand. *(Pauses.)* That first act hurricane sequence was a masterpiece of imaginative stagecraft, and a subtle and fitting metaphor for the sharply delineated boiling sexual frustration of the central Vicar character. No-one was expecting it. Come to think of it, most of the audience couldn't see it. If you were stuck behind one of the towering fluorescent cock inflatables, it was hard to take in much at all.

MAIN ACTION 9: THE GIRLFRIEND *(Slowly and clearly enunciated, then speeds up.)* Peter picked a pecker Peter picked a pecker Peter picked a pecker Peter picked a pecker Peter picked a pecker. *(Again, slow and clear to begin, speeds up.)* Peter picked a peck of pickled peppercorns. Peter picked a peck of pickled peppercorns. Peter picked a peck of pickled peppercorns. *(Rests.)*

MAIN ACTION 10: THE COLLECTOR *emits a long note and then goes off camera until the end of* THE CRITIC'S *first speech in Main Action 11.*

MAIN ACTION 11: The CRITIC *(As practiced, raises eyebrow quizzically, and touches lip thoughtfully.)* Of course, the reviews are of no use whatsoever—the descriptive passages in them are wildly at odds. As for any shared idea as to the value or meaning of the thing, forget it. For sheer gnomic indecipherability, you can't beat professional pompous fathead Brian Sewell, and his account of the piece as published in Marxist dance quarterly *Two Left Feet* is inevitably a first stop for researchers. You couldn't hope to make up a more ludicrously overblown pile of old cobblers—here: *(Puts on glasses, adopts Sewell tones, consults sheaf of papers.)*

THE COLLECTOR *re-enters camera frame, settles on stool, begins to tie a pair of castanets to each hand.*

MAIN ACTION 11 CONTINUED: THE CRITIC Even as he shambled into the gallery, my heart was in my throat, and I am anything but a man of sentiment. In every faltering step, the audience were forced to read a devastating account of his troubled life, and this in advance of him uttering a syllable. It was inscribed in the patchwork eyebrows attached with makeshift indifference over wild mournful eyes, and the shaggily implausible bread-knife haircut and clumpy beard; his very trousers were somehow overlaid with an undiminished and heroic idealism—shiny about the knees, but painstakingly pressed and tightly belted. He was simply and abundantly alive. I was moved to the most profound melancholy.

And this a description of the artist walking into the room. God knows what he would have made of the rest of it, had he actually been seated in a position where he could've seen the stage. *(Pauses.)*

MAIN ACTION 12: THE COLLECTOR *operates castanets vigorously, in a variety of ways with different facial expressions. He appears to settle on one particular flourish, holds a pose for quite a long period, and then rests until end of Main Action 14.*

MAIN ACTION 13: THE GIRLFRIEND *(Very exaggerated face movements, each set of vowels is like one fluid word.) A, E, I, O, U… A, E, I, O, U… A, E, I, O, U… A, E, I, O, U. (Then rests until the end of Main Action 15.)*

MAIN ACTION 14: THE PHOTOGRAPHER Peter had given me absolutely no indication as to what was to unfold over the course of the performance. So I was flying blind, in effect, with regards documenting it. It was a pressure, because I was the only photographer allowed in. And when I asked for bit of direction at the outset, he said "It's more interesting if it's arbitrary." And I said "But to who, Peter? It was my understanding that like me, you have no patience with mediocre self-indulgent artists passing off a degree of potential failure or lack of control as some kind of valid performance methodology, and that the ill-conceived and unrehearsed products of such erratic conceptual idleness could ultimately only serve to undermine the importance of live art as a provocative stand against the gathering market forces that threaten to overwhelm our cultural life. So answer me—should I use a tripod or not?" He laughed, took my hand and replied "You are the camera. The legacy of the performance rests in your hands. Your perceptions, your experience, your understanding—to represent the work accurately, the honesty of that response must not be compromised by instruction from me. Besides—I see you've got a Sigma APO 300-800mm F5.6 IF HSM ultra-telephoto zoom lens; because it retains a constant fast aperture of f2.8 at all focal lengths, your ability to zoom quickly from a fixed position offers unparalleled versatility in composing an image. You'll be fine." *(He rests impassively until end of Main Action 16.)*

MAIN ACTION 15: THE COLLECTOR *(Very well-spoken, and smug – is on a mobile phone, laughing for an uncomfortably long time in the same way he's just been practicing. He keeps looking at the camera and gesturing as if to indicate that he won't be a minute.)* I'll call you later. *(hangs up, instantly sobers up as he faces camera)* I loathe performance art. Always have. It's pointless. There's nothing to buy, for a start. Or so you'd think. Wouldn't touch it with yours until I met my wife. So it was sheer bad luck that she insisted on dragging me along to the blasted thing in the first place. I don't know what it is, but she's obsessed. There's a Victorian bell jar on our mantelpiece that has a sugar cube in it. That's right—a sugarcube; and the unique selling point is that the devious cretin who sold it to her had apparently dipped the thing in his own blood. I wouldn't be so crass as to tell you what the daft cow paid for it, but suffice it to say that I felt like using his body to express some alienation and trauma myself when I signed the sodding cheque. And that wasn't the end of it—courtesy of my better half, we're now the proud owners of a Kilner jar full of toenail clippings, some pieces of scalp, hair still attached, in a reliquary, and the *pièce de resistance*: a tin of old shit. Literally. It's been in there since 1961—a masterpiece, according to the chiseling rat-faced pinhead of a dealer that keeps persuading her to buy the stuff. I said to her "It's starting to look like a forensic criminology lab round here, darling." She said… well, she said something unrepeatable actually, and fairly took the door off of its hinges on her way out. No, I basically deal in paintings. I don't have a particular line as such, but I won't have that rubbish in my collection. *(Raises eyebrow smugly.)*

MAIN ACTION 16: THE GIRLFRIEND (*Starts fast, slows down to be very clearly enunciated.)* My my my my my my my my my my my my my my my my my my my my my my my my my my... *(Continues mouth shape in silence through* THE COLLECTOR'S *next speech.)*

THE PHOTOGRAPHER *emits a long low note which harmonises with the end of* THE GIRLFRIEND'S *my my my my exercise. He stops before* THE COLLECTOR *speaks.*

MAIN ACTION 17: THE COLLECTOR One doesn't like to toot one's own horn, but it has been borne out time and time again that I have something of an exemplary eye.

MAIN ACTION 18: THE GIRLFRIEND *(Starts fast, slows down to be very clearly enunciated.)* Me me me me me me me me me me me me me me me me me me me me me me me me... *(Continues mouth shape in silence through* THE CRITIC'S *next speech.)*

THE PHOTOGRAPHER *emits a long low note which harmonises with the end of* THE GIRLFRIEND'S *me me me me exercise. Stops before* THE CRITIC *speaks.*

MAIN ACTION 19: THE CRITIC As to the tone of the thing, snippets from other reviews praise *(Consults sheets.)* "the artist's miraculous ear for colloquial eccentricities and gift for ribald parody" whilst others describe "a feast of carrion and squalor that runs the gamut from ill-advised toilet humour to out and out obscenity throughout". *(Still looking at the sheets.)* There's a reference here to an "improvised Spanish dance accompanied by a hauntingly vivid passage of Inuit throat singing". Well, I certainly remember a great nit in a mantilla lumbering about the stage brandishing castanets to the sounds of a woman evidently in the last throes of succumbing to a wonky lung at one point—I suppose that fits.

MAIN ACTION 20: THE GIRLFRIEND reappears with one eye made up—begins long drone in her throat, opens and closes mouth for "wawawawawawawa" sound repeatedly over the top until she runs out of breath—pants with exertion. *(It is still feasibly a warm-up exercise.)* Stool is wheeled sideways out of shot with her on it, after she has recovered and assumed a neutral position.

THE COLLECTOR *snaps castanets over the end of* THE GIRLFRIEND'S *drone (as he appeared to rehearse and settle on earlier in script), and pauses in 'flourish' position before resting.*

MAIN ACTION 21: THE CRITIC: Of course, we were plunged into darkness with alarming frequency throughout the thing, owing to technical failures of various kinds, so that it was impossible to identify what was intended and what was purely incidental. I found myself looking at a closed curtain for at least an hour at one point during the first act listening to assorted barnyard noises, muffled thuds, crashes and trumpet shrills coming from the other side. They really did have terrible problems with that curtain—it was up and down like a tart's drawers at the most inopportune moments. I can't emphasise enough just how abysmal all aspects of the staging were. And it's curious, but I can find no mention anywhere of the clutch of comic monologues that punctuated the piece—and to my mind, they really were amongst the best bits. Well, of the bits that I managed to see, anyway. They were delivered by a mysterious caped figure clad entirely in sateen lycra, given to gyrating his hips with an unpleasantly oleaginous blandness to hilariously droll effect throughout—he had the audience in hysterics.

MAIN ACTION 22: THE GIRLFRIEND *reappears with second eye made-up – she is performing another warm-up, exaggerated "h's" and facial expressions, hand on chest – the "ha's" end up sounding like the opening to Laurie Anderson's "O Superman".* He he he he he he he he he he he he he he ha ha ha ha ha ha ha ha ha ha ha ha ha ha ha ha ha ha ha ha ha ha ha ha ha ha....

Overlaps end of Main Action 22: THE COLLECTOR and THE PHOTOGRAPHER *complete the Laurie Anderson intro over the top of* THE GIRLFRIEND'S *"Ha's" – completely deadpan...Oh Superman.*

THE GIRLFRIEND *is wheeled off again when she has assumed a neutral position.*

MAIN ACTION 23: THE PHOTOGRAPHER *(Consults script – tests accent again.)* Post... post... post... post-coital lassitude.

MAIN ACTION 24: THE CRITIC, THE COLLECTOR and THE PHOTOGRAPHER *all heave a hefty sigh in unison. There's a long pause as they all look directly at the camera.*

MAIN ACTION 25: THE CRITIC: There are, in fact, lots of references to choreographic episodes of varying sorts throughout the published accounts, but it's more of the usual obfuscated bilge—did any of the audience know what they were looking at, or more crucially, why they'd bothered to come and look at it in the first place? *(Consults notes.)* The artist was, apparently, "like someone religiously determined to make an omelette with anything but an egg" in his approach to dance, whatever that means; to close the third act, "a trio of male dancers sporting only sombreros and knee pads engaged in a vigorous series of alternating squat thrusts and high-energy jet-stride walks to the brutal beat of a hastily improvised Oompah band" were immediately followed by "a troupe of men and women nude but for thick American tan tights and roller-skates, each hauling a taxidermied piglet on a skateboard around a maypole whilst strewing flowers, ketchup and mayonnaise onto the hapless front row". I sat through all four hours and 37 minutes of the performance, and cannot recall seeing anything that might remotely call to mind these descriptions. And the most uninterested of observers could not fail to have taken in these details, surely? *(Purses lips and raises eyebrows questioningly.)*

MAIN ACTION 26: THE GIRLFRIEND *reappears with lips made-up – she opens her mouth as if to do or say something, thinks better of it, closes mouth, looks sideways at* THE CRITIC, *then back to the front and is wheeled off sideways. The joke is that she has effectively been performing an aspect of* THE CRITIC'S *descriptions, and the last one is too complex.*

MAIN ACTION 27: THE PHOTOGRAPHER I muddled through as best I could, you know, but I seemed to be in the worst possible position to catch the action at any given moment throughout the entire production. There was just no knowing what was coming next and which lens to use for it. I was frantically cleaning mayonnaise out of my fisheye when the chorus line shimmied into view again for the finale, and it was with a sense of futility that I pulled out my back-up Minolta and fired off a roll. I knew I was on to a loser – *(Shakes head.)* the spectral sensitivity of the orthochromatic black-and-white film I'd loaded up minutes previously was a laughably poor match for the in-built light meter, and there simply wasn't the time to attach any filters or re-calibrate before they'd completely stripped the vicar and tossed the last caber. By the end, I must say there was a palpable air of what I can only describe as post-coital lassitude. You were left with an image of superhuman energy and cathartic outpouring burned indelibly into the retinas. Peter was, at the end, a lone spot-lit figure in the middle of the stage lying in a puddle of syrup, piss, flour and sequins, for all the world cooling like a burnt out crater between explosions. It was the last shot I took, and ironically enough, the only photograph of the performance to survive the studio fire.

MAIN ACTION 28: THE COLLECTOR I found myself in the car park smearing ketchup and mayonnaise all over my wife's vintage Balenciaga after the third act. I joked "Well, darling – I know you prefer Hellman's to that own brand muck, so I didn't skimp." I wonder if she had to aim a dollop of the stuff at my eyes – the vinegar did make it sting rather. And it was the ruin of my bespoke charcoal flannel three piece. Malicious, really. She knew I'd only just picked it up after the last fitting. And the reason I was dispatched to the filthy little corner shop for condiments to rub into our evening dress? You may well ask. We were late – my fault, needless-to-say, for having the temerity to insist on looking for a parking space where the Beamer was marginally less likely to be turned over by hooded drug addicts. I lost a set of hubcaps that night as it was. Well, anyway, by the time we'd collected our tickets—for front-row seats, of course; the thing had started. The boss-eyed jobs-worth on the desk told us that no late-comers would be admitted. So there was nothing for it but to throw back a couple of stiffish GnTs in the bar, and wait for halftime. In fact, there was nothing to do but drink. The cold shoulder was of course firmly in effect. I have to admit I was more than a little sloshed by the time they emerged for the interval a few hours later. And then the wife's dragging me outside, practically in tears because everyone would know we'd missed it because we weren't covered in ketchup like the rest of the front row. Hence the furtive car park daubings and the ruined Saville Row tailoring. Unbelievable.

MAIN ACTION 29: THE CRITIC *emits a long note.*

MAIN ACTION 30: THE COLLECTOR She insisted on buying up all the discarded crap left at the end of the bloody thing. I got back from the lavatory to find her cornered by that money-grubbing leech of a dealer again, and it was already too late. They were pursuing an animated discussion at the bar. The old goat was flannelling the little idiot with praise for her rare ability to appreciate the extraordinary value of performance ephemera. She said she was fascinated by the way the traces bracket off a place for the work, and hold open a site which is both empty and full of meaning. *(Pauses.)* Truth be told, there probably aren't many takers for the tatty sub-car boot trash pile I was forced to sign the cheque for by the end of their little chat, not forgetting the thousands tacked on for the art handlers. The idea that a team of dedicated professionals would don the cotton gloves to carefully sift through and crate up that junk—well, it would have had me in fits if I hadn't been the poor chump shelling out. Here's the list *(Consults paper.)* 17 pairs of soiled lederhosen (varying sizes), 36 glo-sticks, four straw donkeys, a burnt out Breville sandwich toaster, a bowlful of ball-bearings, three giant playing cards (the four of clubs, the jack of hearts and the 11 of diamonds if you're interested), 23 empty jars of mayonnaise—catering size, ditto ketchup, three sombreros... *(Goes to next sheet in pile, appears to read through, shaking head while* THE CRITIC *speaks.)*

MAIN ACTION 31: THE CRITIC Of course, a rich collector scooped up all of the flotsam and jetsam they left behind—he's a horrible vulgar turd of a man. I've always hated him. Still, there was quite the buzz *après*-performance. I must confess, I couldn't resist nipping out to the car when I heard the news—my niece's brat had dropped a mucky stuffed rabbit on the back seat the week previously. It was the work of the moment to trouser the thing, slip in through the stage door and plant it in amongst the stage detritus before beating a hasty retreat to the bar for a well-earned vodka tonic. I've seen that rabbit in no less than 13 major exhibitions in the last 20 years, along with the collection of other junk he bought that night.

I wrote the catalogue essay for the last one. I don't know what it means, but it gives me a quite delightful charge whenever I see the thing in a vitrine.

MAIN ACTION 32: THE COLLECTOR I don't know what I'm supposed to do about the massive inflatable sausage—it seems to have a slow puncture. For some unaccountable reason, when I mentioned this to my wife she laughed like a drain.

MAIN ACTION 33: THE GIRLFRIEND *reappears with the large curly wig on, and the towel/tissues, etc., have been removed to reveal a brightly coloured costume – she has a full face of make-up.* THE PHOTOGRAPHER and THE COLLECTOR *look right, and* THE CRITIC *looks left at* THE GIRLFRIEND. *She begins to raise and lower her shoulders and laugh heartily – it is another acting warm-up. All the characters laugh hysterically for an extended period, before stopping simultaneously, returning to a rest position and returning to look steadily at the camera.*

MAIN ACTION 34: THE GIRLFRIEND *sings a long loud high operatic note.* THE PHOTOGRAPHER, THE CRITIC *and* THE COLLECTOR *all emit the notes they have practiced elsewhere in the script to make a harmony. They all end at the same moment.... The light turns off simultaneously in each monitor.*

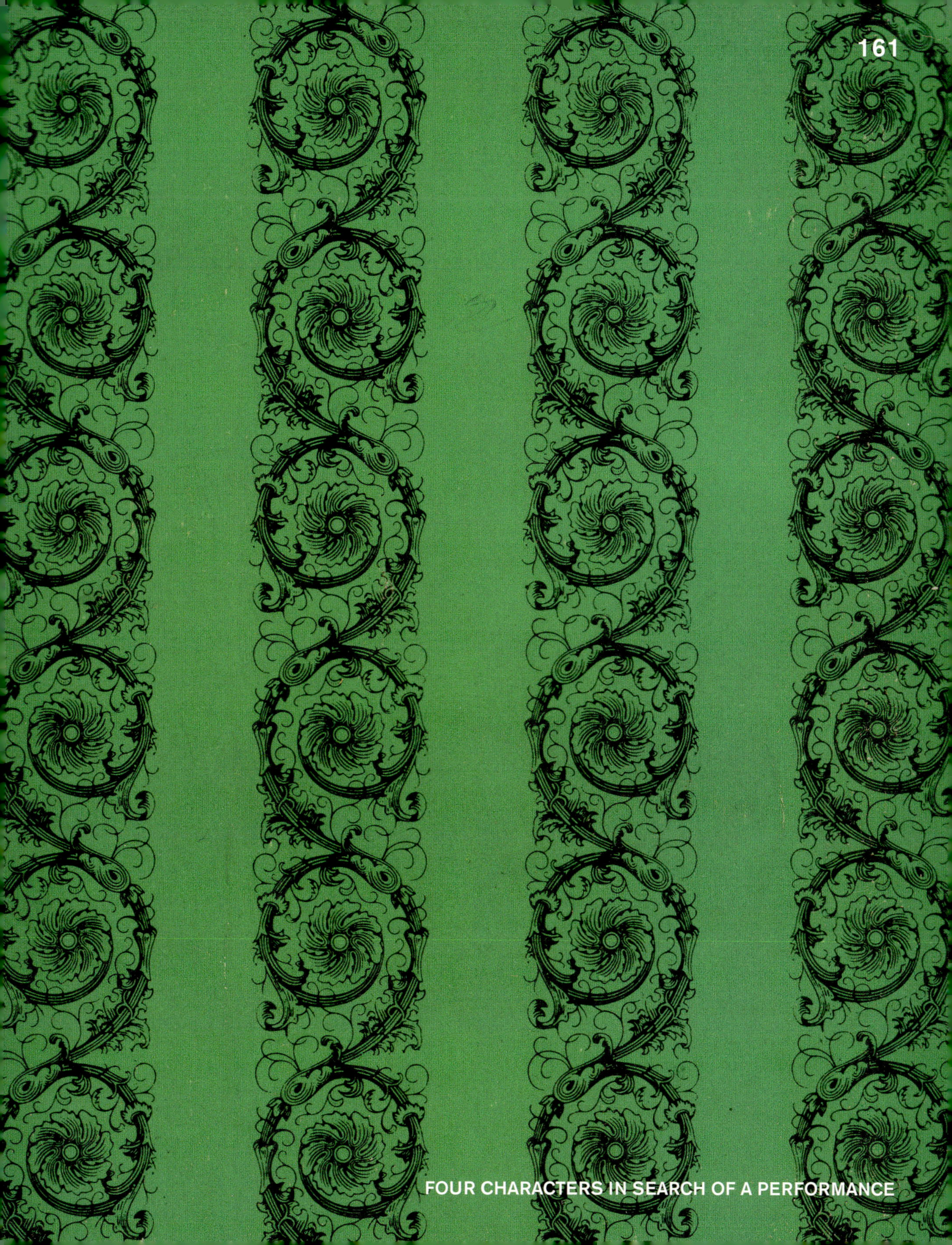

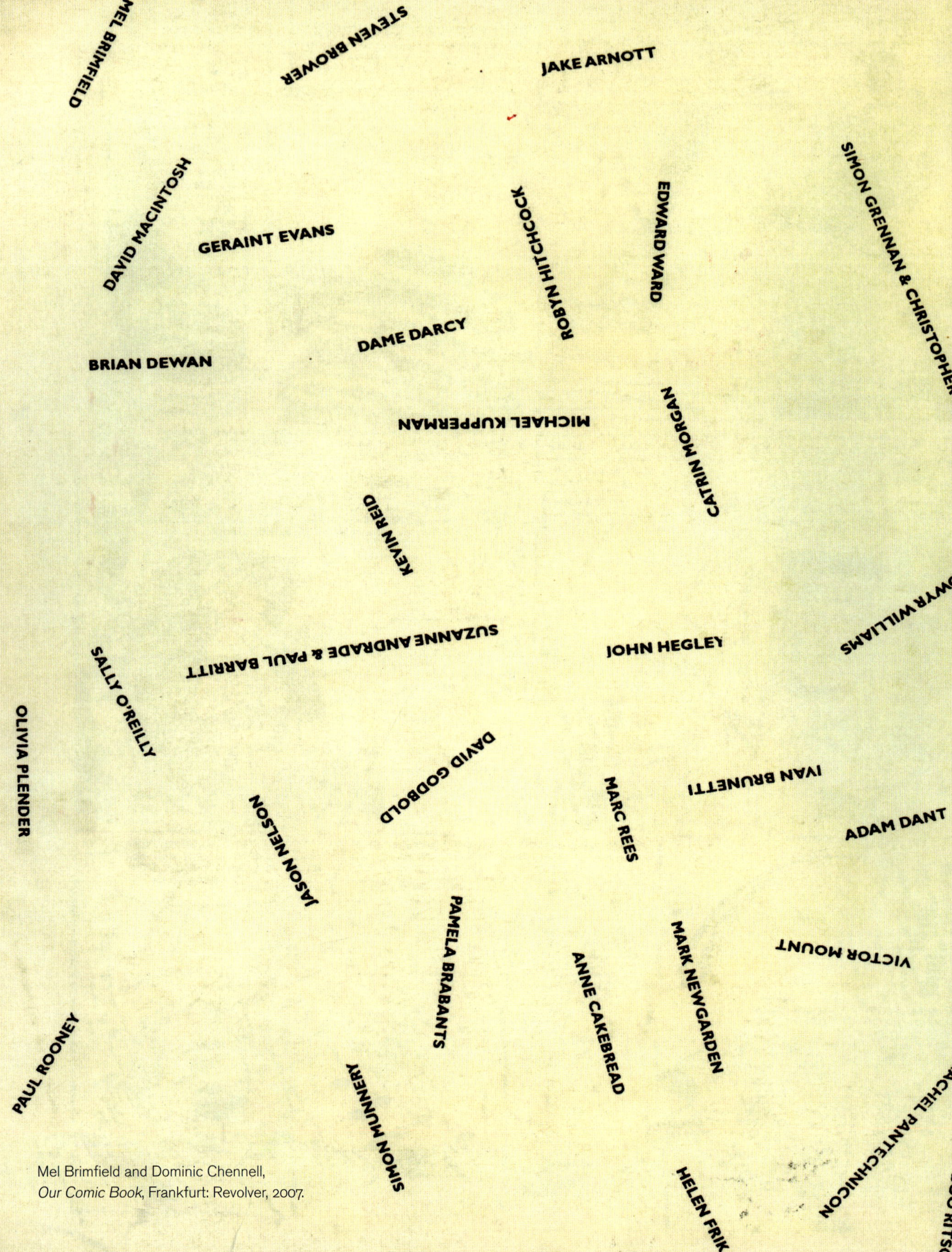

Mel Brimfield and Dominic Chennell,
Our Comic Book, Frankfurt: Revolver, 2007.

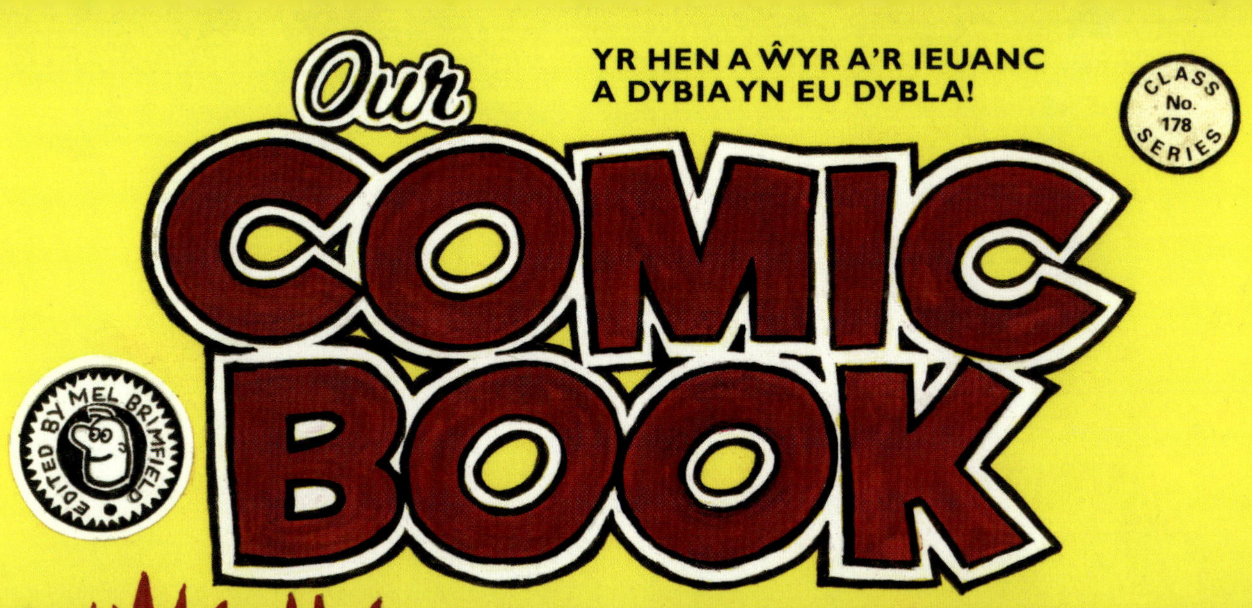
Our
COMIC BOOK
YR HEN A ŴYR A'R IEUANC
A DYBIA YN EU DYBLA!
CLASS No. 178 SERIES
EDITED BY MEL BRIMFIELD
Yes!
FREE GIFT!

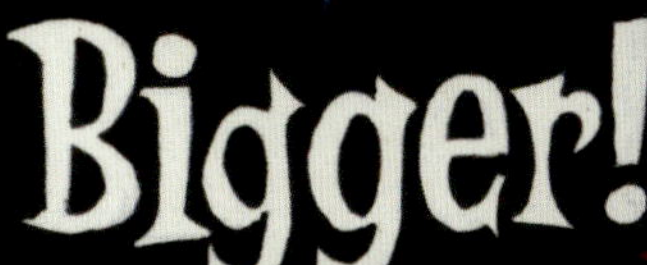
Bigger!

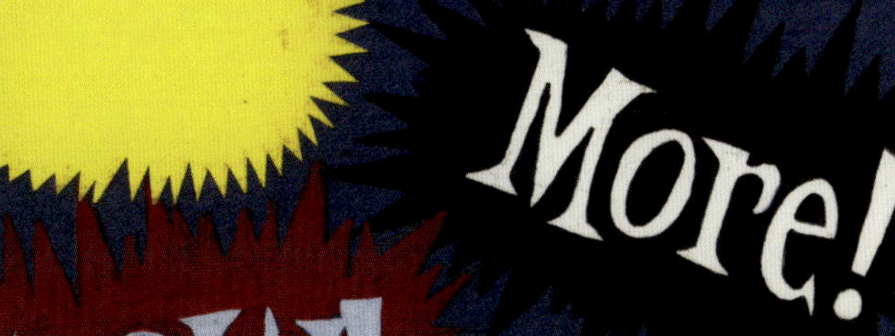
More!
WOW!
Better!
THICKER!
NEW!

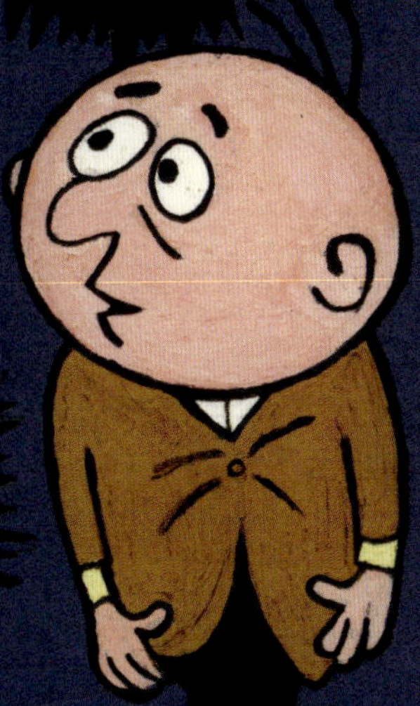

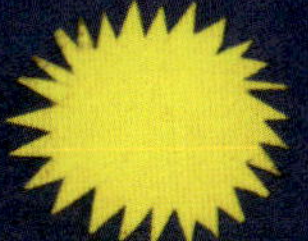

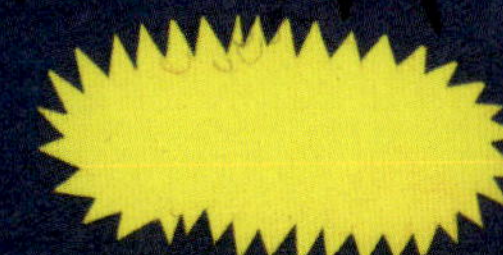

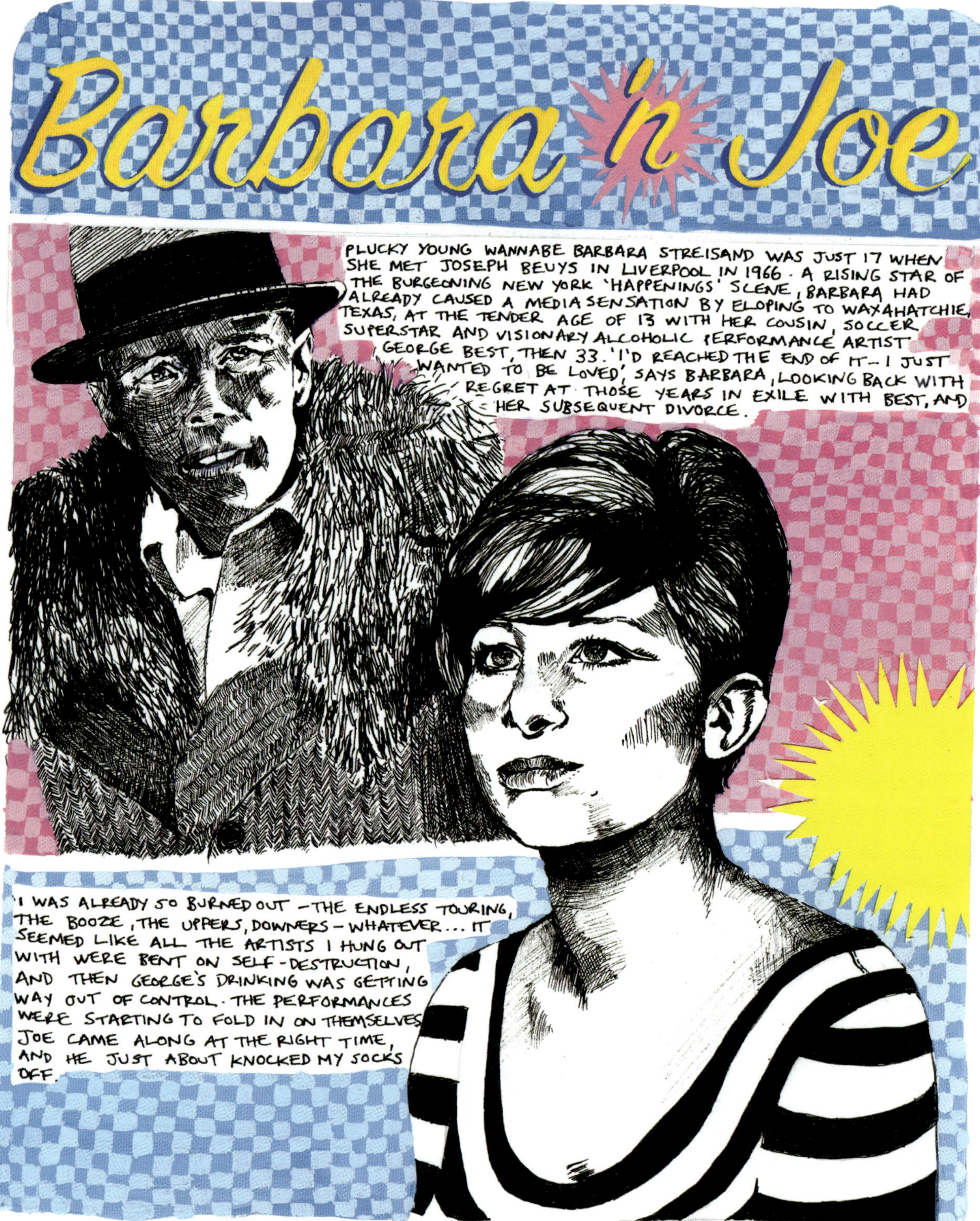

pp 164–171: *The Love Lives of the Artists–Barbara 'n' Joe*, 2010, each 11.4 x 15.4 in / 29 x 39 cm
Images courtesy the artist and Ceri Hand Gallery.

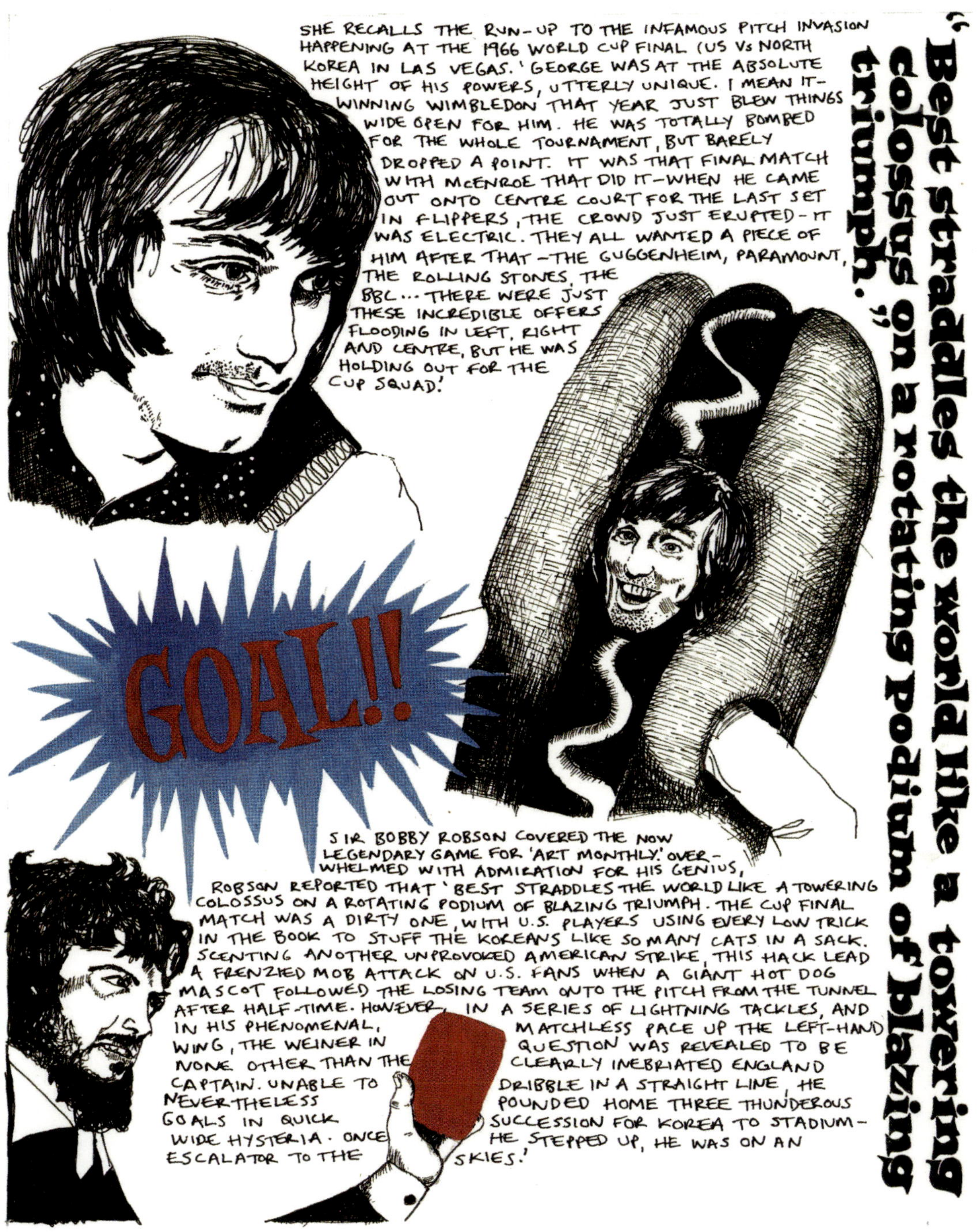
SHE RECALLS THE RUN-UP TO THE INFAMOUS PITCH INVASION HAPPENING AT THE 1966 WORLD CUP FINAL (US Vs NORTH KOREA IN LAS VEGAS. 'GEORGE WAS AT THE ABSOLUTE HEIGHT OF HIS POWERS, UTTERLY UNIQUE. I MEAN IT - WINNING WIMBLEDON THAT YEAR JUST BLEW THINGS WIDE OPEN FOR HIM. HE WAS TOTALLY BOMBED FOR THE WHOLE TOURNAMENT, BUT BARELY DROPPED A POINT. IT WAS THAT FINAL MATCH WITH McENROE THAT DID IT - WHEN HE CAME OUT ONTO CENTRE COURT FOR THE LAST SET IN FLIPPERS, THE CROWD JUST ERUPTED - IT WAS ELECTRIC. THEY ALL WANTED A PIECE OF HIM AFTER THAT - THE GUGGENHEIM, PARAMOUNT, THE ROLLING STONES, THE BBC... THERE WERE JUST THESE INCREDIBLE OFFERS FLOODING IN LEFT, RIGHT AND CENTRE, BUT HE WAS HOLDING OUT FOR THE CUP SQUAD.'
"Best straddles the world like a towering colossus on a rotating podium of blazing triumph."
GOAL!!
SIR BOBBY ROBSON COVERED THE NOW LEGENDARY GAME FOR 'ART MONTHLY.' OVER-WHELMED WITH ADMIRATION FOR HIS GENIUS, ROBSON REPORTED THAT 'BEST STRADDLES THE WORLD LIKE A TOWERING COLOSSUS ON A ROTATING PODIUM OF BLAZING TRIUMPH. THE CUP FINAL MATCH WAS A DIRTY ONE, WITH U.S. PLAYERS USING EVERY LOW TRICK IN THE BOOK TO STUFF THE KOREANS LIKE SO MANY CATS IN A SACK. SCENTING ANOTHER UNPROVOKED AMERICAN STRIKE, THIS HACK LEAD A FRENZIED MOB ATTACK ON U.S. FANS WHEN A GIANT HOT DOG MASCOT FOLLOWED THE LOSING TEAM ONTO THE PITCH FROM THE TUNNEL AFTER HALF-TIME. HOWEVER, IN A SERIES OF LIGHTNING TACKLES, AND IN HIS PHENOMENAL, MATCHLESS PACE UP THE LEFT-HAND WING, THE WEINER IN QUESTION WAS REVEALED TO BE NONE OTHER THAN THE CLEARLY INEBRIATED ENGLAND CAPTAIN. UNABLE TO DRIBBLE IN A STRAIGHT LINE, HE NEVERTHELESS POUNDED HOME THREE THUNDEROUS GOALS IN QUICK SUCCESSION FOR KOREA TO STADIUM-WIDE HYSTERIA. ONCE HE STEPPED UP, HE WAS ON AN ESCALATOR TO THE SKIES.'

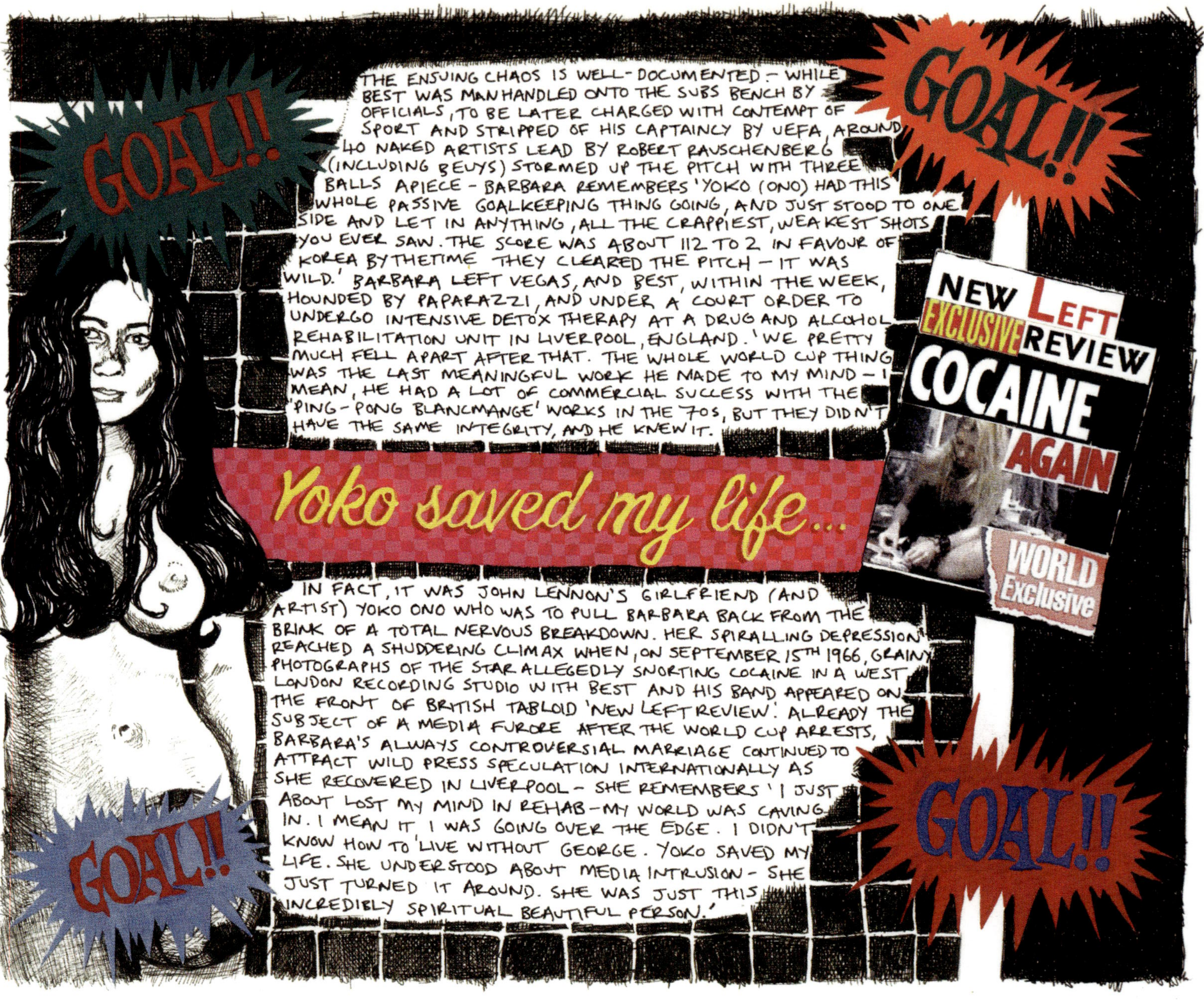
GOAL!!
GOAL!!
THE ENSUING CHAOS IS WELL-DOCUMENTED – WHILE BEST WAS MANHANDLED ONTO THE SUBS BENCH BY OFFICIALS, TO BE LATER CHARGED WITH CONTEMPT OF SPORT AND STRIPPED OF HIS CAPTAINCY BY UEFA, AROUND 40 NAKED ARTISTS LEAD BY ROBERT RAUSCHENBERG (INCLUDING BEUYS) STORMED UP THE PITCH WITH THREE BALLS APIECE – BARBARA REMEMBERS 'YOKO (ONO) HAD THIS WHOLE PASSIVE GOALKEEPING THING GOING, AND JUST STOOD TO ONE SIDE AND LET IN ANYTHING, ALL THE CRAPPIEST, WEAKEST SHOTS YOU EVER SAW. THE SCORE WAS ABOUT 112 TO 2 IN FAVOUR OF KOREA BY THE TIME THEY CLEARED THE PITCH – IT WAS WILD.' BARBARA LEFT VEGAS, AND BEST, WITHIN THE WEEK, HOUNDED BY PAPARAZZI, AND UNDER A COURT ORDER TO UNDERGO INTENSIVE DETOX THERAPY AT A DRUG AND ALCOHOL REHABILITATION UNIT IN LIVERPOOL, ENGLAND. 'WE PRETTY MUCH FELL APART AFTER THAT. THE WHOLE WORLD CUP THING WAS THE LAST MEANINGFUL WORK HE MADE TO MY MIND – I MEAN, HE HAD A LOT OF COMMERCIAL SUCCESS WITH THE 'PING-PONG BLANCMANGE' WORKS IN THE 70S, BUT THEY DIDN'T HAVE THE SAME INTEGRITY, AND HE KNEW IT.
NEW LEFT REVIEW
EXCLUSIVE
COCAINE
AGAIN
WORLD Exclusive
Yoko saved my life...
IN FACT, IT WAS JOHN LENNON'S GIRLFRIEND (AND ARTIST) YOKO ONO WHO WAS TO PULL BARBARA BACK FROM THE BRINK OF A TOTAL NERVOUS BREAKDOWN. HER SPIRALLING DEPRESSION REACHED A SHUDDERING CLIMAX WHEN, ON SEPTEMBER 15TH 1966, GRAINY PHOTOGRAPHS OF THE STAR ALLEGEDLY SNORTING COCAINE IN A WEST LONDON RECORDING STUDIO WITH BEST AND HIS BAND APPEARED ON THE FRONT OF BRITISH TABLOID 'NEW LEFT REVIEW'. ALREADY THE SUBJECT OF A MEDIA FURORE AFTER THE WORLD CUP ARRESTS, BARBARA'S ALWAYS CONTROVERSIAL MARRIAGE CONTINUED TO ATTRACT WILD PRESS SPECULATION INTERNATIONALLY AS SHE RECOVERED IN LIVERPOOL – SHE REMEMBERS 'I JUST ABOUT LOST MY MIND IN REHAB – MY WORLD WAS CAVING IN. I MEAN IT I WAS GOING OVER THE EDGE. I DIDN'T KNOW HOW TO LIVE WITHOUT GEORGE. YOKO SAVED MY LIFE. SHE UNDERSTOOD ABOUT MEDIA INTRUSION – SHE JUST TURNED IT AROUND. SHE WAS JUST THIS INCREDIBLY SPIRITUAL BEAUTIFUL PERSON.'
GOAL!!
GOAL!!

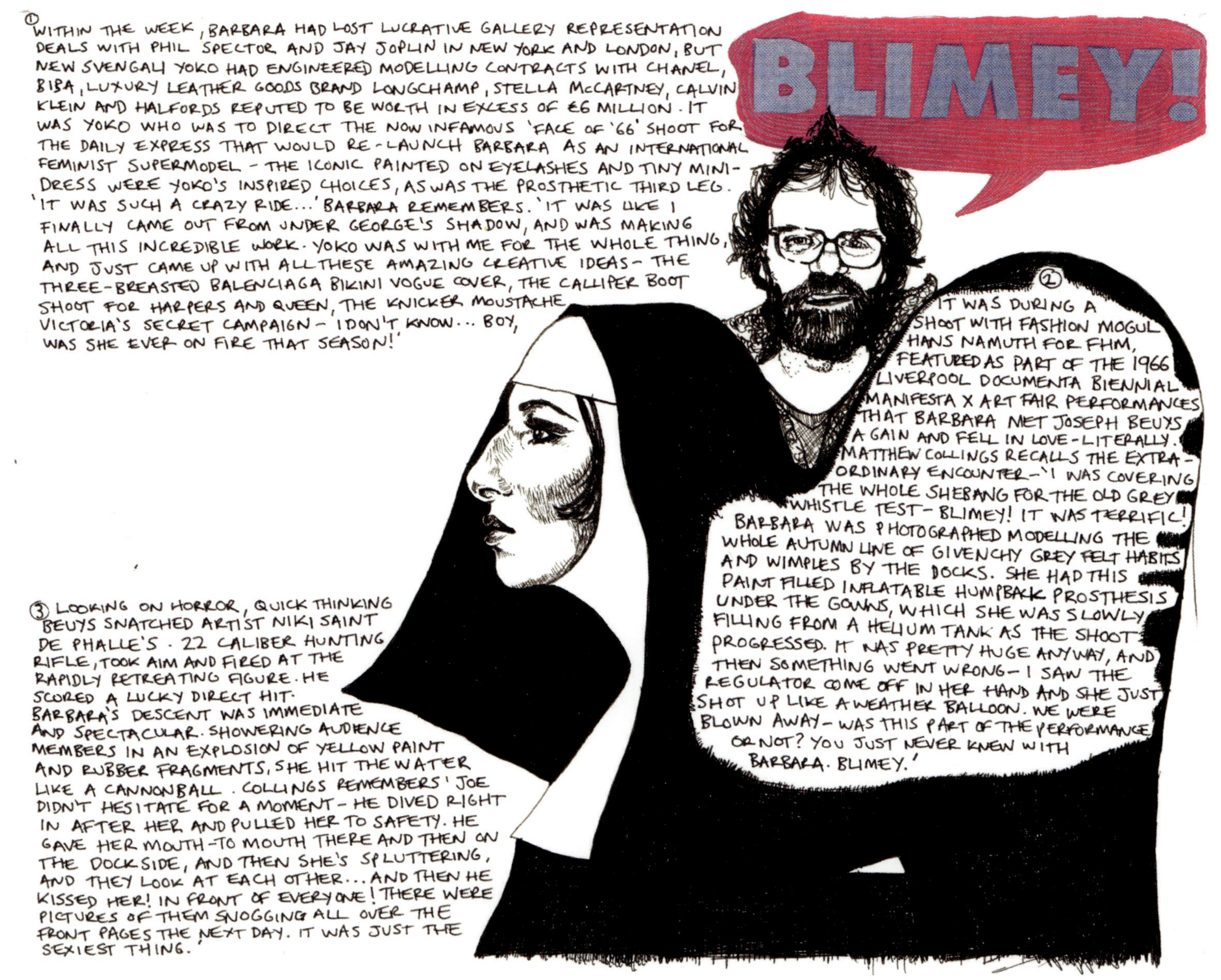

① WITHIN THE WEEK, BARBARA HAD LOST LUCRATIVE GALLERY REPRESENTATION DEALS WITH PHIL SPECTOR AND JAY JOPLIN IN NEW YORK AND LONDON, BUT NEW SVENGALI YOKO HAD ENGINEERED MODELLING CONTRACTS WITH CHANEL, BIBA, LUXURY LEATHER GOODS BRAND LONGCHAMP, STELLA McCARTNEY, CALVIN KLEIN AND HALFORDS REPUTED TO BE WORTH IN EXCESS OF €6 MILLION. IT WAS YOKO WHO WAS TO DIRECT THE NOW INFAMOUS 'FACE OF '66' SHOOT FOR THE DAILY EXPRESS THAT WOULD RE-LAUNCH BARBARA AS AN INTERNATIONAL FEMINIST SUPERMODEL – THE ICONIC PAINTED ON EYELASHES AND TINY MINI-DRESS WERE YOKO'S INSPIRED CHOICES, AS WAS THE PROSTHETIC THIRD LEG. 'IT WAS SUCH A CRAZY RIDE...' BARBARA REMEMBERS. 'IT WAS LIKE I FINALLY CAME OUT FROM UNDER GEORGE'S SHADOW, AND WAS MAKING ALL THIS INCREDIBLE WORK. YOKO WAS WITH ME FOR THE WHOLE THING, AND JUST CAME UP WITH ALL THESE AMAZING CREATIVE IDEAS – THE THREE-BREASTED BALENCIAGA BIKINI VOGUE COVER, THE CALLIPER BOOT SHOOT FOR HARPERS AND QUEEN, THE KNICKER MOUSTACHE VICTORIA'S SECRET CAMPAIGN – I DON'T KNOW... BOY, WAS SHE EVER ON FIRE THAT SEASON!'
BLIMEY!
② IT WAS DURING A SHOOT WITH FASHION MOGUL HANS NAMUTH FOR FHM, FEATURED AS PART OF THE 1966 LIVERPOOL DOCUMENTA BIENNIAL MANIFESTA X ART FAIR PERFORMANCES THAT BARBARA MET JOSEPH BEUYS AGAIN AND FELL IN LOVE – LITERALLY. MATTHEW COLLINGS RECALLS THE EXTRA-ORDINARY ENCOUNTER – 'I WAS COVERING THE WHOLE SHEBANG FOR THE OLD GREY WHISTLE TEST – BLIMEY! IT WAS TERRIFIC! BARBARA WAS PHOTOGRAPHED MODELLING THE WHOLE AUTUMN LINE OF GIVENCHY GREY FELT HABITS AND WIMPLES BY THE DOCKS. SHE HAD THIS PAINT FILLED INFLATABLE HUMPBACK PROSTHESIS UNDER THE GOWNS, WHICH SHE WAS SLOWLY FILLING FROM A HELIUM TANK AS THE SHOOT PROGRESSED. IT WAS PRETTY HUGE ANYWAY, AND THEN SOMETHING WENT WRONG – I SAW THE REGULATOR COME OFF IN HER HAND AND SHE JUST SHOT UP LIKE A WEATHER BALLOON. WE WERE BLOWN AWAY – WAS THIS PART OF THE PERFORMANCE OR NOT? YOU JUST NEVER KNEW WITH BARBARA. BLIMEY.'
③ LOOKING ON HORROR, QUICK THINKING BEUYS SNATCHED ARTIST NIKI SAINT DE PHALLE'S .22 CALIBER HUNTING RIFLE, TOOK AIM AND FIRED AT THE RAPIDLY RETREATING FIGURE. HE SCORED A LUCKY DIRECT HIT. BARBARA'S DESCENT WAS IMMEDIATE AND SPECTACULAR. SHOWERING AUDIENCE MEMBERS IN AN EXPLOSION OF YELLOW PAINT AND RUBBER FRAGMENTS, SHE HIT THE WATER LIKE A CANNONBALL. COLLINGS REMEMBERS 'JOE DIDN'T HESITATE FOR A MOMENT – HE DIVED RIGHT IN AFTER HER AND PULLED HER TO SAFETY. HE GAVE HER MOUTH-TO MOUTH THERE AND THEN ON THE DOCKSIDE, AND THEN SHE'S SPLUTTERING, AND THEY LOOK AT EACH OTHER... AND THEN HE KISSED HER! IN FRONT OF EVERYONE! THERE WERE PICTURES OF THEM SNOGGING ALL OVER THE FRONT PAGES THE NEXT DAY. IT WAS JUST THE SEXIEST THING.'

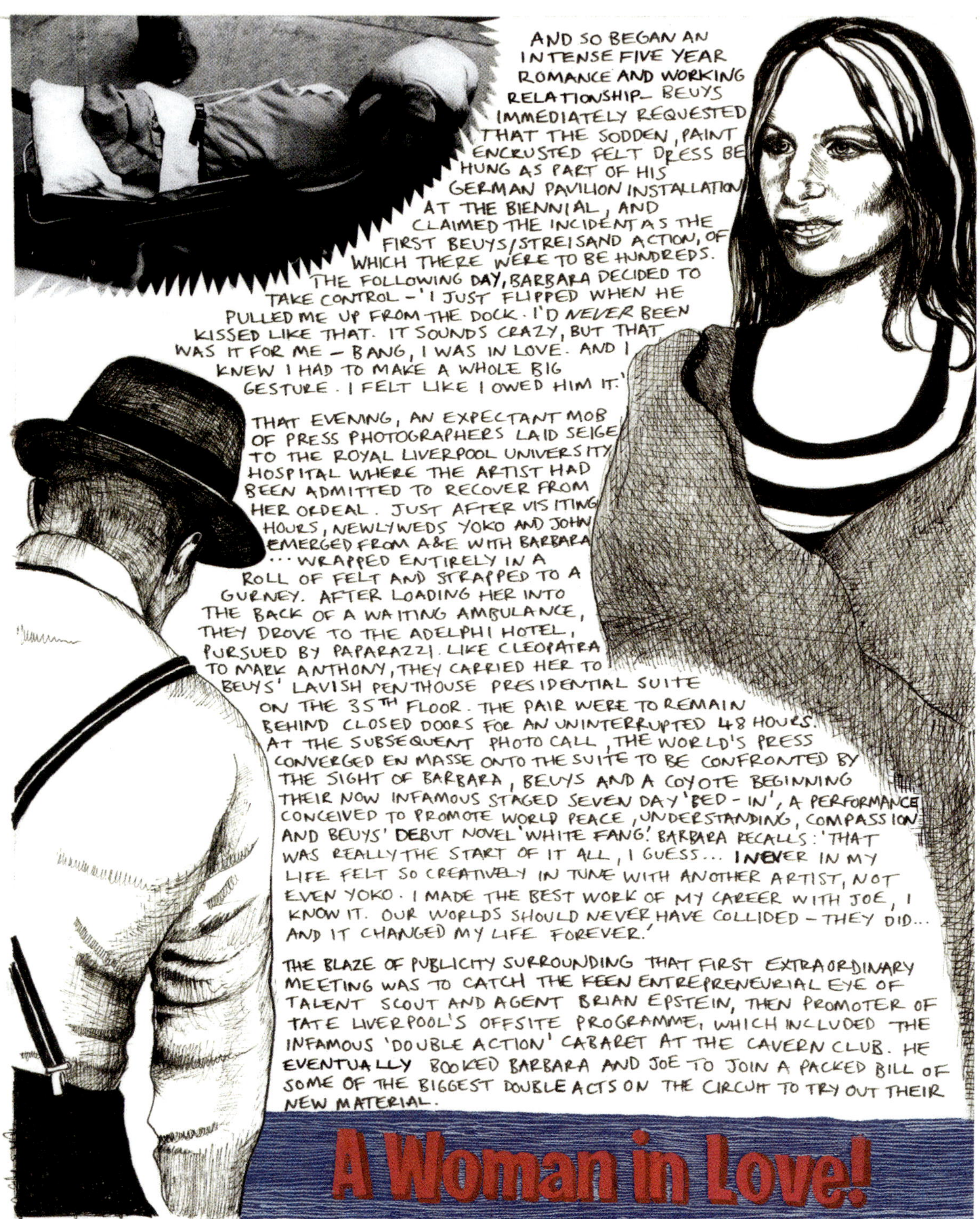
AND SO BEGAN AN INTENSE FIVE YEAR ROMANCE AND WORKING RELATIONSHIP. BEUYS IMMEDIATELY REQUESTED THAT THE SODDEN, PAINT ENCRUSTED FELT DRESS BE HUNG AS PART OF HIS GERMAN PAVILION INSTALLATION AT THE BIENNIAL, AND CLAIMED THE INCIDENT AS THE FIRST BEUYS/STREISAND ACTION, OF WHICH THERE WERE TO BE HUNDREDS. THE FOLLOWING DAY, BARBARA DECIDED TO TAKE CONTROL – 'I JUST FLIPPED WHEN HE PULLED ME UP FROM THE DOCK. I'D NEVER BEEN KISSED LIKE THAT. IT SOUNDS CRAZY, BUT THAT WAS IT FOR ME – BANG, I WAS IN LOVE. AND I KNEW I HAD TO MAKE A WHOLE BIG GESTURE. I FELT LIKE I OWED HIM IT.'
THAT EVENING, AN EXPECTANT MOB OF PRESS PHOTOGRAPHERS LAID SEIGE TO THE ROYAL LIVERPOOL UNIVERSITY HOSPITAL WHERE THE ARTIST HAD BEEN ADMITTED TO RECOVER FROM HER ORDEAL. JUST AFTER VISITING HOURS, NEWLYWEDS YOKO AND JOHN EMERGED FROM A&E WITH BARBARA … WRAPPED ENTIRELY IN A ROLL OF FELT AND STRAPPED TO A GURNEY. AFTER LOADING HER INTO THE BACK OF A WAITING AMBULANCE, THEY DROVE TO THE ADELPHI HOTEL, PURSUED BY PAPARAZZI. LIKE CLEOPATRA TO MARK ANTHONY, THEY CARRIED HER TO BEUYS' LAVISH PENTHOUSE PRESIDENTIAL SUITE ON THE 35TH FLOOR. THE PAIR WERE TO REMAIN BEHIND CLOSED DOORS FOR AN UNINTERRUPTED 48 HOURS. AT THE SUBSEQUENT PHOTO CALL, THE WORLD'S PRESS CONVERGED EN MASSE ONTO THE SUITE TO BE CONFRONTED BY THE SIGHT OF BARBARA, BEUYS AND A COYOTE BEGINNING THEIR NOW INFAMOUS STAGED SEVEN DAY 'BED-IN', A PERFORMANCE CONCEIVED TO PROMOTE WORLD PEACE, UNDERSTANDING, COMPASSION AND BEUYS' DEBUT NOVEL 'WHITE FANG'. BARBARA RECALLS: 'THAT WAS REALLY THE START OF IT ALL, I GUESS… I NEVER IN MY LIFE FELT SO CREATIVELY IN TUNE WITH ANOTHER ARTIST, NOT EVEN YOKO. I MADE THE BEST WORK OF MY CAREER WITH JOE, I KNOW IT. OUR WORLDS SHOULD NEVER HAVE COLLIDED – THEY DID… AND IT CHANGED MY LIFE FOREVER.'
THE BLAZE OF PUBLICITY SURROUNDING THAT FIRST EXTRAORDINARY MEETING WAS TO CATCH THE KEEN ENTREPRENEURIAL EYE OF TALENT SCOUT AND AGENT BRIAN EPSTEIN, THEN PROMOTER OF TATE LIVERPOOL'S OFFSITE PROGRAMME, WHICH INCLUDED THE INFAMOUS 'DOUBLE ACTION' CABARET AT THE CAVERN CLUB. HE EVENTUALLY BOOKED BARBARA AND JOE TO JOIN A PACKED BILL OF SOME OF THE BIGGEST DOUBLE ACTS ON THE CIRCUIT TO TRY OUT THEIR NEW MATERIAL.
A Woman in Love!

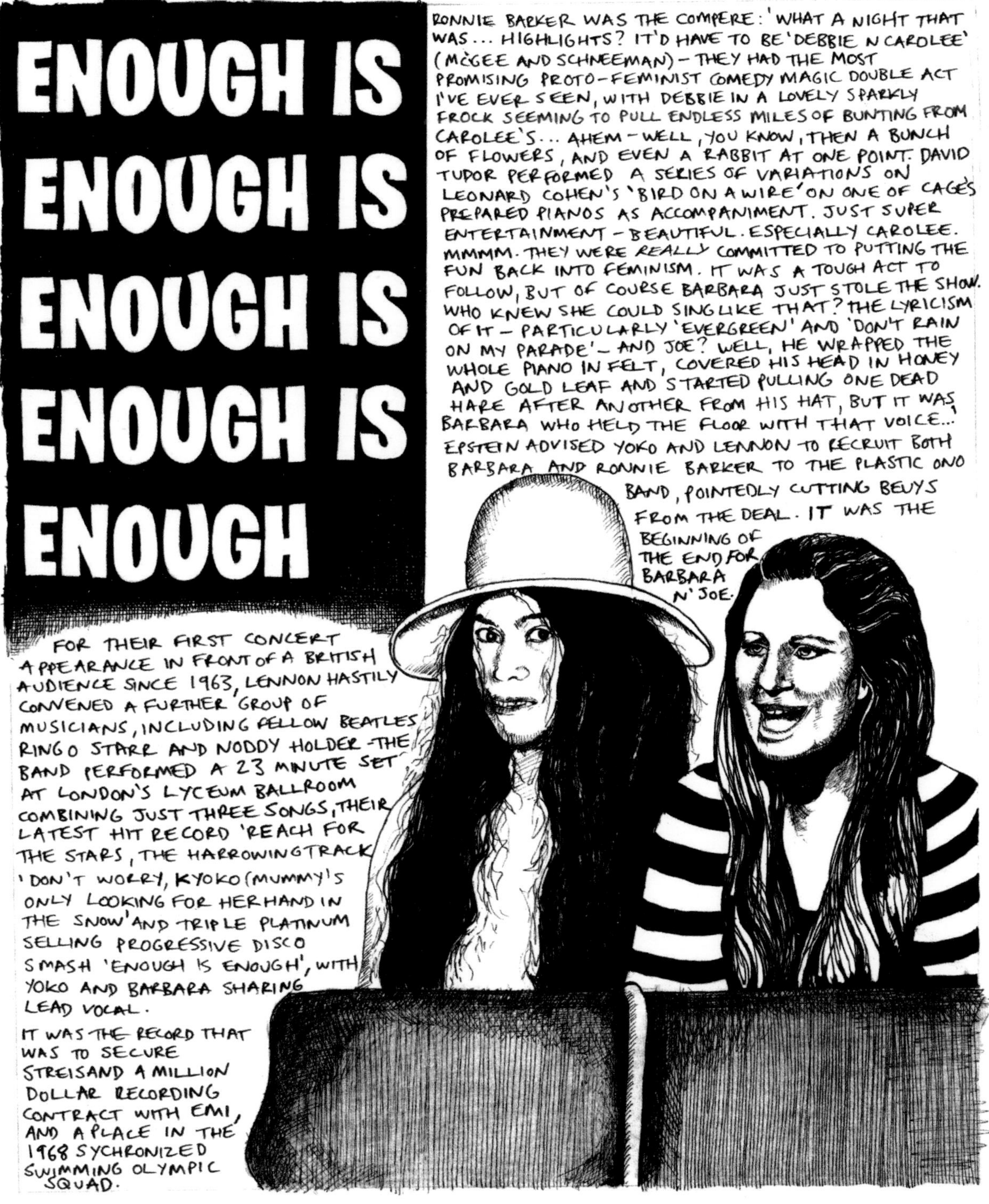
ENOUGH IS ENOUGH IS ENOUGH IS ENOUGH IS ENOUGH
RONNIE BARKER WAS THE COMPERE: 'WHAT A NIGHT THAT WAS... HIGHLIGHTS? IT'D HAVE TO BE 'DEBBIE N CAROLEE' (MCGEE AND SCHNEEMAN) – THEY HAD THE MOST PROMISING PROTO-FEMINIST COMEDY MAGIC DOUBLE ACT I'VE EVER SEEN, WITH DEBBIE IN A LOVELY SPARKLY FROCK SEEMING TO PULL ENDLESS MILES OF BUNTING FROM CAROLEE'S... AHEM – WELL, YOU KNOW, THEN A BUNCH OF FLOWERS, AND EVEN A RABBIT AT ONE POINT. DAVID TUDOR PERFORMED A SERIES OF VARIATIONS ON LEONARD COHEN'S 'BIRD ON A WIRE' ON ONE OF CAGE'S PREPARED PIANOS AS ACCOMPANIMENT. JUST SUPER ENTERTAINMENT – BEAUTIFUL. ESPECIALLY CAROLEE. MMMM. THEY WERE REALLY COMMITTED TO PUTTING THE FUN BACK INTO FEMINISM. IT WAS A TOUGH ACT TO FOLLOW, BUT OF COURSE BARBARA JUST STOLE THE SHOW. WHO KNEW SHE COULD SING LIKE THAT? THE LYRICISM OF IT – PARTICULARLY 'EVERGREEN' AND 'DON'T RAIN ON MY PARADE' – AND JOE? WELL, HE WRAPPED THE WHOLE PIANO IN FELT, COVERED HIS HEAD IN HONEY AND GOLD LEAF AND STARTED PULLING ONE DEAD HARE AFTER ANOTHER FROM HIS HAT, BUT IT WAS BARBARA WHO HELD THE FLOOR WITH THAT VOICE...'
EPSTEIN ADVISED YOKO AND LENNON TO RECRUIT BOTH BARBARA AND RONNIE BARKER TO THE PLASTIC ONO BAND, POINTEDLY CUTTING BEUYS FROM THE DEAL. IT WAS THE BEGINNING OF THE END FOR BARBARA 'N' JOE.
FOR THEIR FIRST CONCERT APPEARANCE IN FRONT OF A BRITISH AUDIENCE SINCE 1963, LENNON HASTILY CONVENED A FURTHER GROUP OF MUSICIANS, INCLUDING FELLOW BEATLES RINGO STARR AND NODDY HOLDER – THE BAND PERFORMED A 23 MINUTE SET AT LONDON'S LYCEUM BALLROOM COMBINING JUST THREE SONGS, THEIR LATEST HIT RECORD 'REACH FOR THE STARS', THE HARROWING TRACK 'DON'T WORRY, KYOKO (MUMMY'S ONLY LOOKING FOR HER HAND IN THE SNOW)' AND TRIPLE PLATINUM SELLING PROGRESSIVE DISCO SMASH 'ENOUGH IS ENOUGH', WITH YOKO AND BARBARA SHARING LEAD VOCAL.
IT WAS THE RECORD THAT WAS TO SECURE STREISAND A MILLION DOLLAR RECORDING CONTRACT WITH EMI, AND A PLACE IN THE 1968 SYCHRONIZED SWIMMING OLYMPIC SQUAD.

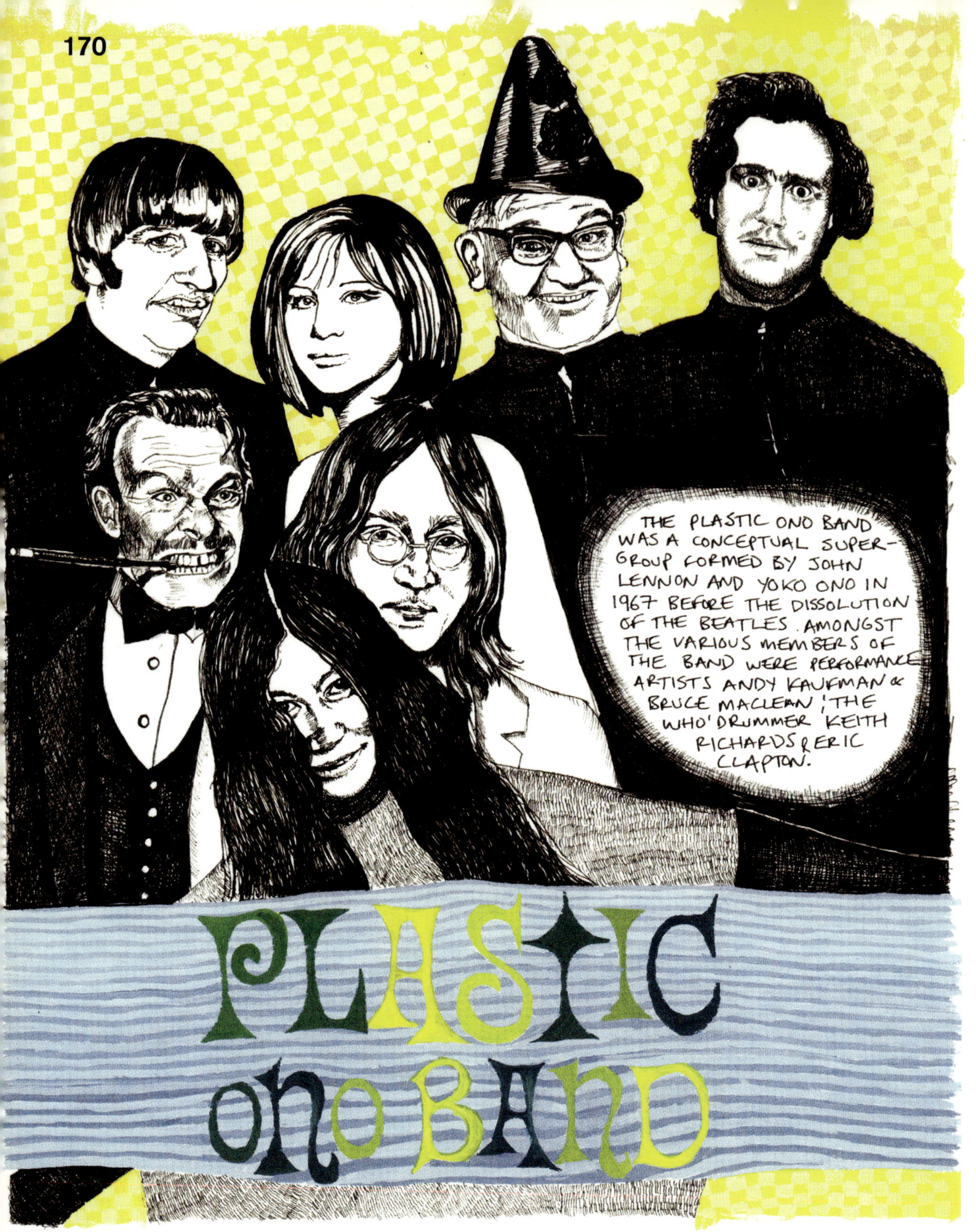
THE PLASTIC ONO BAND WAS A CONCEPTUAL SUPER-GROUP FORMED BY JOHN LENNON AND YOKO ONO IN 1967 BEFORE THE DISSOLUTION OF THE BEATLES. AMONGST THE VARIOUS MEMBERS OF THE BAND WERE PERFORMANCE ARTISTS ANDY KAUFMAN & BRUCE MACLEAN; THE WHO' DRUMMER KEITH RICHARDS & ERIC CLAPTON.
PLASTIC
ONO BAND

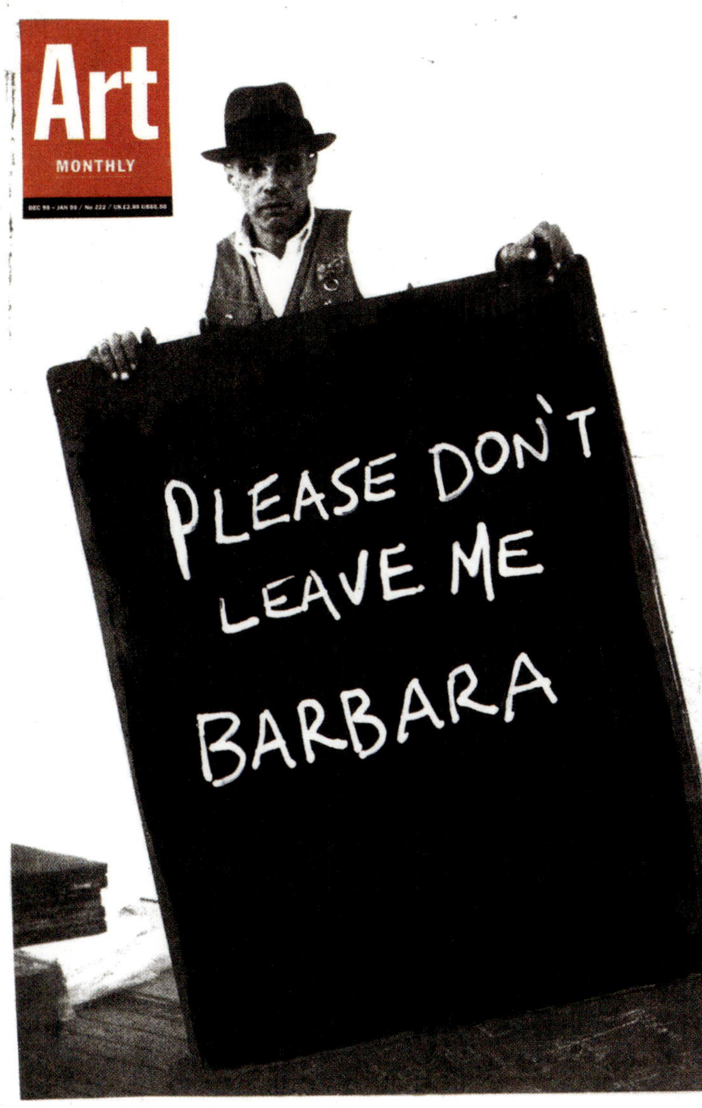

THIS WAS TO BE THE MOST PROLIFIC PERIOD OF STREISAND'S CAREER. SHE RECEIVED RAVE REVIEWS AND A LAURENCE OLIVIER AWARD FOR HER LEAD ROLE IN SMASH HIT BROADWAY MUSICAL 'SPRINGTIME FOR HITLER', AND HER HIGHLY PUBLICIZED 'COLOR ME BARBARA' SOLO EXHIBITION AT THE EVERSON MUSEUM IN SYRACUSE, NEW YORK WAS NEARLY CLOSED BY A FAN RIOT. IN THE NEXT THREE YEARS, SHE DIRECTED AND STARRED IN THREE FILMS, INCLUDING 'YENTL' FOR WHICH SHE WON TWO GOLDEN GLOBE AWARDS FOR BEST DIRECTOR AND BEST MOVIE AND ESTABLISHED HER STATUS AS AN INTERNATIONAL SEX SYMBOL. SHE ALSO RECORDED THREE ALBUMS, WON THE 1971 MIXED DOUBLES WIMBLEDON CHAMPIONSHIP WITH EX-HUSBAND GEORGE BEST, AND CORNERED THE EXERCISE TO MUSIC MARKET, GROSSING OVER $60 MILLION WITH HER 'BARBARA STREISAND WORKOUT.'

SHE RECALLS 'I GUESS REALLY BY THIS TIME I WAS STARTING TO OUTGROW JOE... YOU KNOW, I WAS BACK ON THE ROAD WITH THE BAND, AND JUST STARTING THIS SOLO CAREER, AND IT FELT LIKE HE WAS STIFLING ME WITH HIS CRAZY INTENSITY - I WAS STILL COMMITTED TO THE WHOLE 'BARBARA FELT FAT, JOSEPH FELT HAT' SERIES, BUT REALLY KEEN TO GET OUT AND EXPLORE OTHER AVENUES.' IN FACT, BARBARA HAD BEGUN A PASSIONATE CLANDESTINE AFFAIR WITH PLASTIC ONO BAND REGULAR ANDY KAUFMAN. 'WE WERE JUST THROWN TOGETHER ON TOUR. HE WAS IRRESISTABLE. HIS WHOLE APPROACH TO PERFORMANCE WAS JUST AMAZING. I NEVER SAW ANYTHING LIKE IT. AND WHEN HE ASKED ME TO WORK WITH HIM ON THE INTER-GENDER WRESTLING PROJECT, I JUMPED AT THE CHANCE. WHO WOULDN'T? AND JOE WAS BECOMING UNBEARABLE. HE COULDN'T TOLERATE MY SUCCESS. HE FILLED MY PIANO WITH RANCID FAT THE NIGHT BEFORE THE MADISON SQUARE GARDEN MUNCHAUSEN SYNDROME BENEFIT.... I GUESS IT WAS A NOD TO JOHN CAGE, BUT I WAS JUST FURIOUS - IT WAS THE LAST STRAW. I JUMPED ON A PLANE AND WENT TO ANDY IN MEMPHIS.

TO BE CONTINUED...
PART 2 -

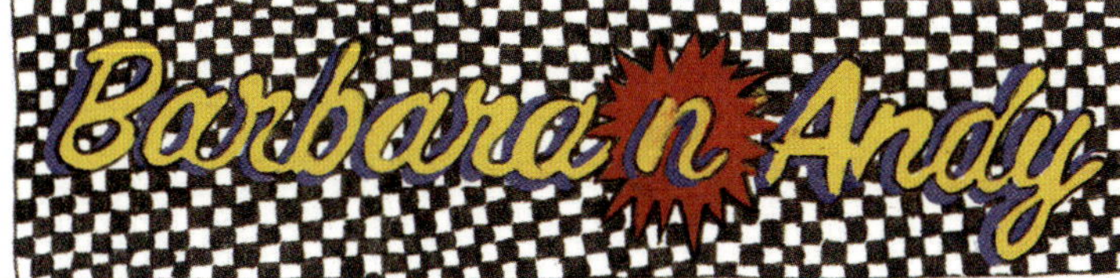

A LAST WORD FROM SIR FRANCIS SPALDING

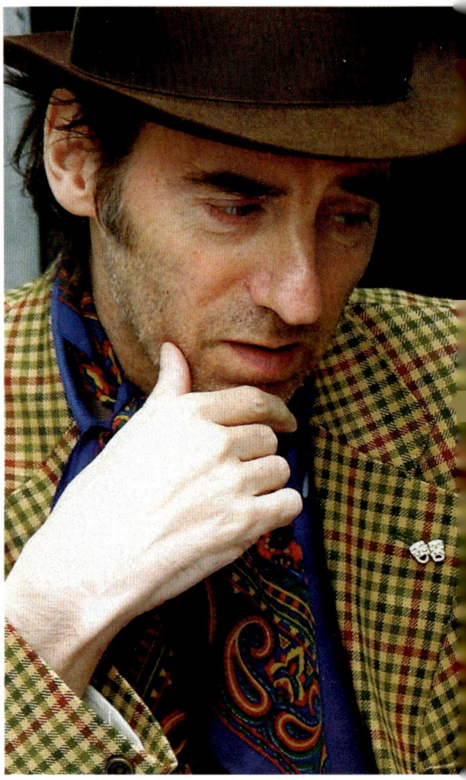

And so the first chapter of *This Is Performance Art* draws to a close. Mel Brimfield and I would like to take this opportunity to thank each and every one of the performers who have contributed their time and talent to the many different prongs of the project. That they continue to do so is testament to the enthusiasm and professionalism of the TIPA team, and to the watertight contracts issued in advance of the production process. In particular, the erstwhile Musical Director of the ongoing live series Paul Higgs deserves a special mention, as does photographer Edward Moore, the archivist of the majority of the collaborations in this book. The support given by Ceri Hand and her gallery is inestimable—Bravo! We would also like to thank the many and various institutions who have leant their financial and practical support to the complicated production methodologies we insist upon; in no particular order: Yorkshire Sculpture Park—Clare Lilley, Helen Pheby, Damon Waldock and Adrianne Neil, Camden Arts Centre—Ben Roberts and Jenni Lomax, Jerwood Visual Arts—Sarah Williams, Lancaster Institute for the Contemporary Arts—Matt Fenton and Richard Smith, and The Collective Gallery—Sarah Munro (Director until 2008).

At the time of publication, *This Is Performance Art—Part Two: Experimental Theatre and Cabaret* is set to launch as part of the Trashing Performance public programme in 2011. Trashing Performance is the second themed year of Performance Matters, a collaboration between the Department of Visual Cultures at Goldsmiths, University of London, the Department of Drama, Theatre and Performance at Roehampton University, and the Live Art Development Agency. Funded by the Arts and Humanities Research Council. www.thisisperformancematters.co.uk

AUTHORS' BIOGRAPHIES

Jon Wood is 'Research Curator' at the Henry Moore Institute, where he coordinates the research programme and curates exhibitions. He has written widely on twentieth century and contemporary sculpture. Publications include: *Articulate Objects: Sculpture, Voice and Performance*, 2009, (with Aura Satz); *Against Nature: the hybrid forms of modern sculpture*, 2008; *Modern Sculpture Reader*, 2007, (with Alex Potts and David Hulks); *Carl Plackman: Sculpture, Drawing, Writing*, 2007; *Freud's Sculpture*, 2006; *With Hidden Noise: Sculpture, Video and Ventriloquism*, 2004 and *Close Encounters: The Sculptor's Studio in the Age of the Camera*, 2001.

Matt Fenton is Director of Live at LICA (Lancaster Institute for the Contemporary Arts), the interdisciplinary arts organisation resulting from the merger of Nuffield Theatre Lancaster, the Peter Scott Gallery and Lancaster International Concerts. Previously Director of the Nuffield Theatre (2003–2009), Matt is a practising theatre-maker, and also teaches on the Lancaster University masters course in Professional Contemporary Arts Practice, a course he developed in response to the needs of early career artists.

Ceri Hand draws on 20 years in the art world, having previously acted as Director of Metal (Liverpool); Director of Exhibitions, FACT (Liverpool), where she was a contributing curator to Liverpool Biennial in 2004 and 2006; Deputy Director of Grizedale Arts, Cumbria and Director of Make, London. She established Liverpool's first contemporary commercial art gallery—The Ceri Hand Gallery—in 2008.

THANKS TO...

Paul and Jean Henry, Matt Fenton, Jon Wood and Ceri Hand, Duncan McCorquodale, Leonardo Collina and all at Black Dog Publishing, Edward Moore and all of the performers and artists involved in Mel Brimfield's project.

Black Dog Publishing Limited
10A Acton Street
London
WC1X 9NG

t. +44 (0)207 713 5097
f. +44 (0)207 713 8682
e. info@blackdogonline.com
www.blackdogonline.com

Designed by Leonardo Collina with the assistance of Rachel Pfleger at Black Dog Publishing.

British Library Cataloguing-in-Publication Data.
A CIP record for this book is available from the British Library.

ISBN 978 1 907317 35 4

Black Dog Publishing is an environmentally responsible company. *This is Performance Art: Mel Brimfield* is printed on FSC accredited paper.

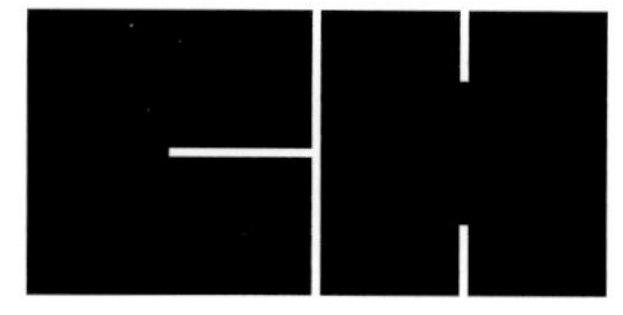

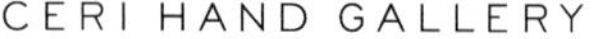

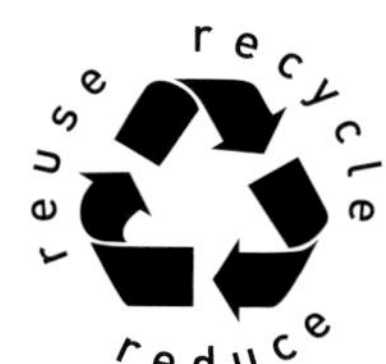

architecture art design
fashion history photography
theory and things

www.blackdogonline.com

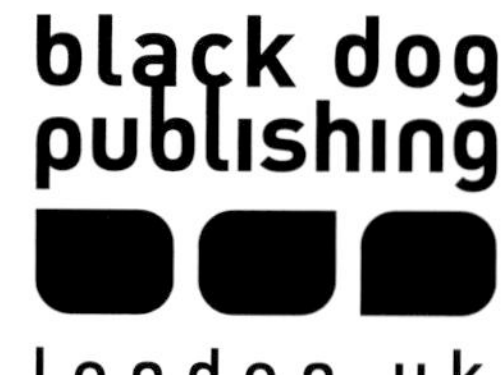

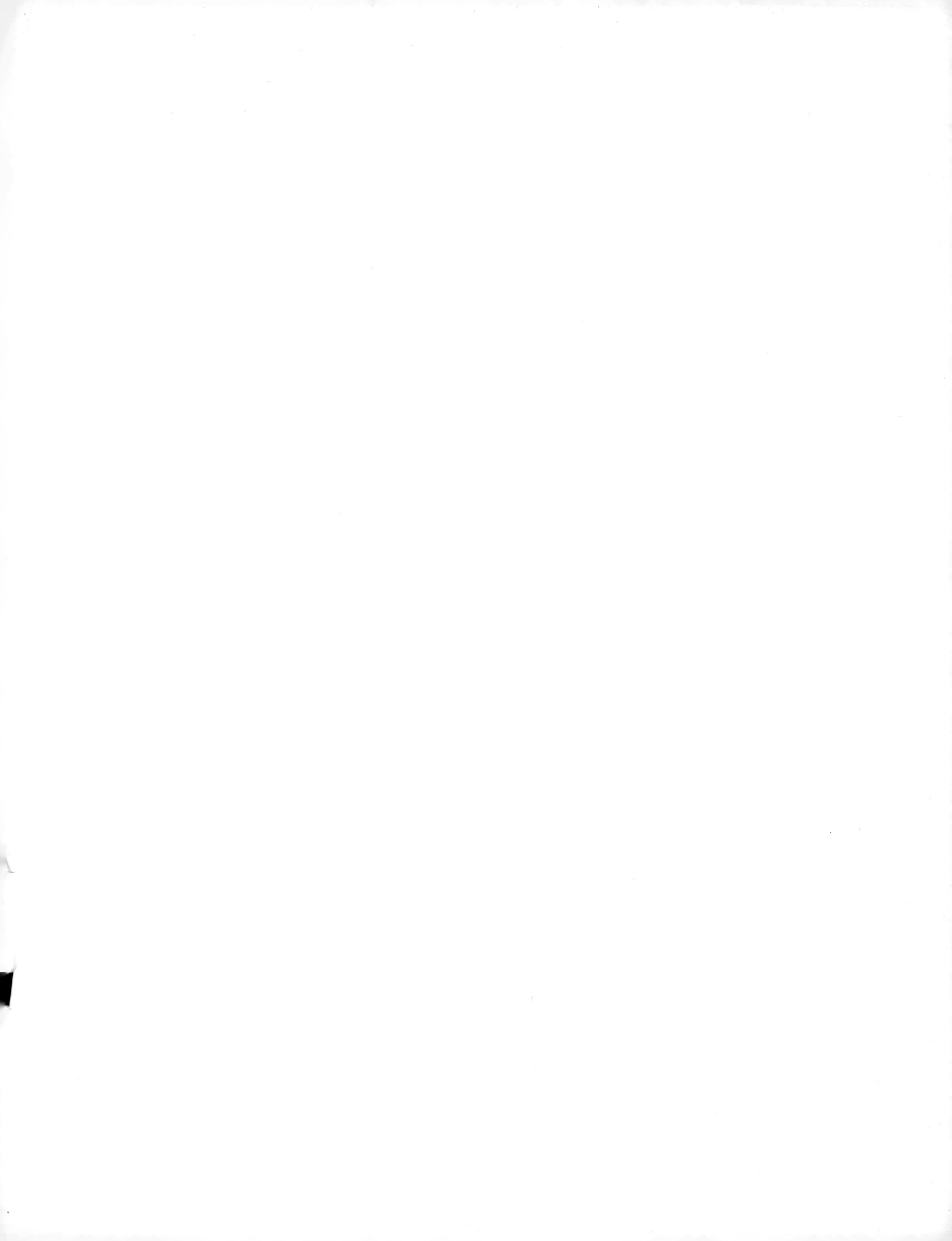